A Business History of In

In recent decades, private investment has led an economic resurgence in India. But this is not the first time the region has witnessed impressive business growth. There have been many similar stories over the past 300 years. India's economic history shows that capital was relatively expensive. How, then, did capitalism flourish in the region? How did companies and entrepreneurs deal with the shortage of key resources? Has there been a common pattern in responses to these issues over the centuries? Through detailed case studies of firms, entrepreneurs, and business commodities, Tirthankar Roy answers these questions. Roy bridges the approaches of business and economic history, illustrating the development of a distinctive regional capitalism. On each occasion of growth, connections with the global economy helped firms and entrepreneurs better manage risks. Making these deep connections between India's economic past and present shows why history matters in its remaking of capitalism today.

TIRTHANKAR ROY is Professor of Economic History at the London School of Economics and Political Science. He has published widely on South Asian history, global history, empires, and environmental history. His recent publications include *The Economy of South Asia: From 1950 to the Present* (2017) and *India in the World Economy from Antiquity to the Present* (2012).

A Business History of India

Enterprise and the Emergence of Capitalism from 1700

Tirthankar Roy

London School of Economics and Political Science

CAMBRIDGE
UNIVERSITY PRESS

University Printing House, Cambridge CB2 8BS, United Kingdom

One Liberty Plaza, 20th Floor, New York, NY 10006, USA

477 Williamstown Road, Port Melbourne, VIC 3207, Australia

314–321, 3rd Floor, Plot 3, Splendor Forum, Jasola District Centre,
New Delhi – 110025, India

79 Anson Road, #06–04/06, Singapore 079906

Cambridge University Press is part of the University of Cambridge.

It furthers the University's mission by disseminating knowledge in the pursuit of
education, learning, and research at the highest international levels of excellence.

www.cambridge.org
Information on this title: www.cambridge.org/9781107186927
DOI: 10.1017/9781316906903

First published 2018

Printed in the United Kingdom by TJ International Ltd. Padstow Cornwall

A catalogue record for this publication is available from the British Library.

Library of Congress Cataloging-in-Publication Data
Names: Roy, Tirthankar, author.
Title: A business history of India : enterprise and the emergence of capitalism
from 1700 / Tirthankar Roy, London School of Economics and Political Science.
Description: 1 Edition. | New York : Cambridge University Press, 2018. |
Includes bibliographical references and index.
Identifiers: LCCN 2017057287 | ISBN 9781107186927 (hardback) |
ISBN 9781316637487 (paperback)
Subjects: LCSH: India–Economic conditions. | India–Social conditions. |
Business–India–History. | Economic history.
Classification: LCC HC433 .R698 2018 | DDC 330.954–dc23
LC record available at https://lccn.loc.gov/2017057287

ISBN 978-1-107-18692-7 Hardback
ISBN 978-1-316-63748-7 Paperback

For
Asim Kumar Nanda

Contents

Figures

Maps

x

Tables

Boxes

Preface

When I started a career in economic history in the 1990s, interest in history was growing in the top economics schools of the world. The availability of cross-country historical income data, popularity of institutionalism, and new developments in the theory of growth rekindled interest in an old and half-forgotten question: Why do some countries grow rich and others remain poor? In the 2000s, historians criticised institutionalism. The exchange that followed became known as the divergence debate. In the last 20 years, the divergence debate formed the stem of the economic history field.

I joined this discussion from a base in Indian history, and with a vague feeling that the divergence debate did not serve India well. Over the years, that feeling developed into an argument. The argument has two parts. First, the theoretical models used to explain how the world became more unequal from the nineteenth century, failed to explain the recent emergence of India and China. Models that predicted divergence could not predict convergence in an easy way, and therefore, they were unreliable as theories about the past. Second, the debate encouraged the student of world history to ask the wrong question, that is, why India fell behind Europe and stayed poor. Capitalists in the region – where the volume of trade grew hundred-fold, and the fourth largest cotton mill industry of the world emerged in 1850–1950 – did not either fall behind or stay poor. By starting with the falling-behind question, divergence historians missed the central paradox of Indian economic history: the coexistence of robust capitalism and stagnant agriculture.

This book turns the narrative around. It is not about falling behind, nor about what went wrong with India. It is about capitalism, and what went right. As business history, it does what business historians do the world over, which is to study how firms, entrepreneurs, communities, and organisations adapt to the environment, or what happens to corporate governance when companies are run by families and small groups like the managing agents of the past. As economic history, it foregrounds what I believe is the biggest puzzle about India, indeed about emerging economies in general – how does capitalism grow in a region where capital is an expensive resource? The book is an attempt to answer this question.

The idea of the book emerged from my association with business historians of the Harvard Business School, especially Geoffrey Jones and Walter Friedman, who brought me in contact with other overview projects under way or recently finished. Franco Amatori and Andrea Colli contributed to the making of the book in a similar way. In gathering raw material, Prerna Agarwal, Bhanu Phani Krishna, and Harsha Tiwary provided invaluable help. On various occasions, I have discussed the subject or matters related to it with Michael Aldous, Hemant Bangur, Raj Brown, Rudra Chatterjee, Bishnupriya Gupta, Sunil Khilnani, Abhijit Pathak, Gita Piramal, Anand V. Swamy, Stefan Tetzlaff, Chinmay Tumbe, and Rusheed Wadia. I am grateful to all of them for the conversations. A detailed and helpful report from a Reader for the Press led to significant improvements on a draft.

I owe a special debt to Douglas Haynes and Ashok Desai. Haynes, who has made a major contribution to interpretations of Indian capitalism and is researching the frontiers of consumption and business history, advanced this project through comments, discussions, and encouragement. Desai, possibly the only economic historian to have served as a consultant to the Government of India, and a trenchant commentator on current economic affairs, read the manuscript with care, pointed out errors, suggested improvements, ruthlessly criticised when criticisms were due, and directed me to new readings. Their association with the project was a source of strength.

Before I conclude, a note on the use of sources is in order. Whereas Chapters 1–6 (ending at 1950) draw on scholarly research, including my own, Chapters 7–9 rely heavily on media reports drawn from *Business World* and *Business India* mainly, and online material available from newspaper websites (for one example, company history data from the stock market information page on specific companies available at http://economictimes.indiatimes.com/), as well as company websites. It is impossible to cite the hundreds of such resources I have used to construct narrative histories, and such citation would not necessarily add value to the bibliography. Therefore, I confine these citations to the minimum, and cite only when I quote from them.

1   Introduction

The Book

For almost a quarter of a century now, Indian economy has grown at an impressive pace. Private enterprise has led this growth. In the process, Indian companies have had to absorb new technologies and management ideas, reinvent or discard tradition, invite international partners, and become international themselves.

What Indians are now living through is only the latest in a series of episodes that reshaped capitalism in the region. In the 1950s and 1960s, businesses had to adapt to a socialist and protectionist environment. A hundred years before that, businesses responded to the opportunities and risks created by free trade in the British Empire. And before the British Raj came into being, businesses dealt with the collapse of the Mughal Empire in the north, and the rise of the East India Company on the southern coast. Each one of these episodes was organically linked with the others.

This is a business history of India in the last 300 years. The field is rich and well developed. But this book aims to be different in two ways. First, it offers a *connected* narrative, that is, it links different times, major episodes, Indian history with world history, and economic history with the experience of firms, families, and communities. While writing a connected story, the book also answers the question: Is there something distinctly *Indian* about Indian business history? Conventional answers to the question consider unique features of Indian society such as caste or India's subordinate position in the British colonial empire in the nineteenth century. Some may even deny the usefulness of the question. This book is different. It does have a leitmotif. And the leitmotif is neither caste nor colonial rule.

A business history is an interesting enterprise because it tells us how capitalists obtain the resources that are essential for capitalism to grow. These resources include capital, technology, trust, managers, organisation, and skills. For most of the years covered in the book, some of these resources were scarce in India. For example, compared with Europe, where financial and commercial capitalism modernised in parallel roughly from the 1600s, trade and industry expanded in nineteenth century India in the presence of limited financial development and high interest rates. Capitalism developed, anomalously, in a region where capital was in short supply. The aim of the book is to show how scarcities like these manifested, how they were dealt with, and who dealt with them.

Briefly, this book shows that transactions with the world economy eased these constraints in the long run, whereas locally, and in the short run, state policy and social conventions helped too. With the exception of a period of forty years in the mid-twentieth century (c. 1950–90), the region was characterised by considerable openness. It was open to trade, traded a great deal, and was also open to transactions in capital, know-how, and skills. From the nineteenth century, modern industry emerged in the region because trade created the capacity to obtain funds from and buy technology and skills from abroad. The state mattered mainly in sustaining openness. During 1950–90, the state intervened more deeply, curtailed openness, and controlled capital markets to push for industrialisation. The strategy raised investment, but proved unsustainable in the end, bringing back a modified type of openness. Both these pathways – led by openness or by the state – involved successes as well as failures, opportunities as well as risks.

In addition, this book has a secondary aim. The scholarship on Indian business history is usually narrative, biographical, and regional.[1] Students in management schools and economics courses are exposed to theories of entrepreneurship, of firm structure, and capital structure, which should have relevance for the history of entrepreneurs and firms in any region. The Indianist scholarship does not usually make connections between theory and history, leaving India's relevance to theory to be deduced. A business history should show how discourses about the origin of entrepreneurship, and ownership of firms, help thinking about the case in question. In that spirit, the next section will discuss history and theory in mutual relation. The discussion is selective and India-centred, in that it deals only with those topics where theories of

---

[1] The two aims of this book make it a distinct contribution to the field. However, excellent syntheses and surveys that attempt to render a coherence to the field have appeared recently. The interested reader should consult Dwijendra Tripathi, *The Oxford History of Indian Business*, New Delhi: Oxford University Press, 2004; Dwijendra Tripathi and Jyoti Jumani, *The Oxford History of Contemporary Indian Business*, New Delhi: Oxford University Press, 2013; and Medha M. Kudaisya, ed., *The Oxford India Anthology of Business History*, New Delhi: Oxford University Press, 2011. A new series in business history published by Penguin India since 2012, led by Gurcharan Das, has produced useful works on merchant communities and regions, but it is yet to address the colonial period fully. See also the entertaining and informative popular history books by Gita Piramal, especially *Business Legends*, New Delhi: Penguin, 1998. Finally, N. Benjamin and P. N. Rath's *Modern Indian Business History: A Bibliographic Survey*, Pune: Gokhale Institute of Politics and Economics, no date, is a useful reference on the older scholarship.

entrepreneurship and organisation have obvious relevance for the case study. For a more systematic introduction to the conceptual frameworks in use worldwide, readers will need to consult another work.[2]

This statement of aims suggests a map for the rest of the introduction. I will discuss, in that order, the field, the key question, links between theory and history, and plan of the book, in four sections that form the remainder of this chapter.

The Field

Business history scholarship in the last fifty odd years has developed around one main question, and a number of other subsidiary themes that bear an indirect relationship to it. The main question is this: What should be the unit of analysis, the society, the state, or the individual? The subsidiary questions relate to specific historical problems or episodes. For example, how we should read the coexistence of foreign and Indian capital in colonial India (c. 1858–1947), or what role big business played in shaping India's economic policy around 1950, or more recently, the difference between port cities and small towns in the pattern of capitalist development. These are some of the themes that have generated clusters of research and historiographical debates. These subsidiary topics will be discussed in appropriate contexts in later chapters. This section will deal with the main stem of the historiography: the unit of analysis problem.

If we exclude sponsored company histories and flowery biographies of a few stalwarts, serious scholarship on the subject began with a report written by the economist Dhananjay Ramchandra Gadgil in 1959, as an offshoot of an earlier work on industrialisation in India.[3] Gadgil's report made an emphatic claim that social collectives like caste and community should be the subject of business history. He had a point. Contemporary modernisation theory had suggested that entrepreneurship was an attribute of individuals who could see the future before others did. For India around 1700, entrepreneurship did not quite mean individuals like that. There are few biographies available to tell us which individuals were being prescient in sensing profit opportunities. More often, the successful capitalist was the member of an ethnic group, a community. Without the support of that group, enterprise would not succeed. The staple ingredient in Indian business history, therefore, is the business

---

[2] For example, Franco Amatori and Andrea Colli, *Business History: Complexities and Comparisons*, Abingdon and New York: Routledge, 2011.
[3] Dhananjay Ramchandra Gadgil, *Origins of the Modern Indian Business Class*, Poona: Gokhale Institute of Politics and Economics, mimeo, 1959.

community: the Parsis, Marwaris, Khatris, Bhatias, Jains, Bohras, Chettiars, Labbais, and many others.[4] The bias stems partly from the type of sources available to us, but we cannot say that it is entirely an illusion created by the sources.

In contemporary North American and Soviet scholarship on India, the idea that Indian entrepreneurship was embedded in society had already struck deep roots. Indian capitalists were seen through the lens of Max Weber and Karl Marx, as an undifferentiated type. The purpose was to show why India fell behind Europe since the eighteenth century in the potentials for capitalism, especially industrial capitalism, to develop. American theorists believed that 'entrepreneurship' was a scarce resource that a society needed crucially for 'take off to self-sustained growth' and suggested, after Weber, that the social organisation in India or China suppressed the entrepreneurial instinct.[5] In the 1940s, Soviet scholars characterised Indian capitalists as 'comprador', or agents of foreign capital, and incapable of industrialising on their own.[6] While the orthodox Marxist discussion about Indian capitalists was caught up in ideological debates along party lines, more independent Marxist works, such as Charles Bettelheim's, characterised the Indian big business as too mercantile, finance-oriented, and too inclined after quick profits to lead a deeper sort of capitalist transformation.[7]

---

[4] An American academic, Daniel H. Buchanan, wrote the first systematic work on 'capitalistic enterprise' in India. Buchanan too was fascinated by caste and religion, and believed these to be tools to understand Indian business. In his framework, the Hindu 'Baniya caste' was too mercantile to industrialise, the Muslims had not made much of an impact for reasons of their own, and the artisan castes were too poor and tradition-bound. This left the British, and the Parsis who did not share the traditionalism of the Hindus, with an open field. No doubt this analysis influenced American views about India for the next several decades. *The Development of Capitalistic Enterprise in India*, New York: Macmillan, 1934, cited text appears in p. 146.

[5] The precondition was 'the existence and freedom to operate of a new group of industrial entrepreneurs', Walt Rostow, 'The Stages of Economic Growth', *Economic History Review*, 12(1), 1959, 1–16. Many contemporary writers studied India to look for the presence of this condition and considered if it could be bypassed. In the 1950s, they encountered an India where a confident government led industrialisation. Bert F. Hoselitz predicted that a class of 'manager' entrepreneurs consisting of public officials would meet the condition in the initial stages of industrialisation, eventually yielding their place to the 'business' entrepreneur. See *Sociological Aspects of Economic Growth: An Adaptation*, Bombay: Vakils, Feffer, Simon, 1960, 59.

[6] The Marxist characterisation of the capitalists in India during the endgame of the British Empire was caught up in a battle between different factions of the left, particularly, a centre-left who saw Indian big business as a force of nationalism, and a harder left that saw the big business as a reactionary ally of the imperialists. Both agreed that they had played second fiddle to foreign capital during colonial rule. For discussion, see V. I. Pavlov, *The Indian Capitalist Class: A Historical Study*, Delhi: People's Publishing House, 1964; Suniti Kumar Ghosh, *The Indian Big Bourgeoisie*, Calcutta: Subarnarekha, 1985.

[7] Charles Bettelheim, *India Independent*, New York: Monthly Review Press, 1968, 73.

There were, and are, two types of reaction to these characterisations. Some scholars presented their research explicitly in opposition to these, emphasising individual agency or entrepreneurship more than the role of the society and social organisation like caste and community, and disputing the notion that Indian capitalism was deficient because it was constrained by society.[8] 'The available empirical data point to the fallacy of overemphasis on ... social organisation in the study of entrepreneurial development in India', writes Dwijendra Tripathi.[9] Others accept that there were deficiencies and problems of the situation in which capitalists operated, but see these deficiencies to be embedded in the state, or in politics. The hostile attitude of the British Raj, this scholarship suggests, posed an obstacle to rapid industrialisation in colonial India.[10] 'The development of Indian ... capitalism was ... stunted and severely limited' by the policies of the colonial state.[11] Still others believe the deficiencies to be embedded in structural conditions like shortage of capital, labour, technology, and demand, and then blame the British Indian state for not removing these obstacles.[12]

Anthropological studies of business communities to appear from the 1970s emphasised another dimension of social organisation. Far from making the Indian capitalists deficient in some sense, caste and community bonds helped them take risks and sense opportunities, as social ties fostered entrepreneurship rather than suppressing it. 'The joint family and strong particularistic caste loyalties', writes Thomas Timberg in *The Marwaris*, 'are the secret of success in Indian entrepreneurshi'.[13] And David Rudner explains the 'secret of success' of the Nattukottai Chettiar bankers in this

[8] Morris D. Morris, 'Values as an Obstacle to Economic Growth in South Asia: An Historical Survey', *Journal of Economic History*, 27(4), 1967, 588–607; Dwijendra Tripathi, 'Occupational Mobility and Industrial Entrepreneurship in India: A Historical Analysis', *Developing Economies*, 19(1), 1981, 52–68; Makrand Mehta, *Indian Merchants and Entrepreneurs in Historical Perspective*, New Delhi: Academic Foundation, 1991; Dwijendra Tripathi and Makrand Mehta, *Business Houses in Western India: A Study in Entrepreneurial Response, 1850–1956*, New Delhi: Manohar, 1990.

[9] 'Indian Entrepreneurship in Historical Perspective: A Re-Interpretation', *Economic and Political Weekly*, 6(22), 1971, M59–M66.

[10] Bipan Chandra, *The Rise and Growth of Economic Nationalism in India: Economic Policies of Indian National Leadership, 1880–1905*, Delhi: People's Publishing House, 1966. See also Aditya Mukherjee, *Imperialism, Nationalism and the Making of the Indian Capitalist Class, 1920–1947*, New Delhi, Thousand Oaks and London: Sage Publications, 2002.

[11] Bipan Chandra, Aditya Mukherjee, and Mridula Mukherjee, *India Since Independence*, New Delhi: Penguin, 2008, 18.

[12] Rajat K. Ray, *Industrialization in India: Growth and Conflict in the Private Corporate Sector, 1914–47*, Delhi: Oxford University Press, 1979; Amiya Kumar Bagchi, *Private Investment in India 1900–1939*, Cambridge: Cambridge University Press, 1972. Also on obstacles, Morris D. Morris, 'The Growth of Large-Scale Industry to 1947', in Dharma Kumar, ed., *The Cambridge Economic History of India, Vol. 2: 1757–1970*, Cambridge: Cambridge University Press, 1983, 551–676.

[13] Thomas Timberg, *The Marwaris*, Delhi: Vikas, 1973.

way: ' … varieties of financial instruments, patterns of inter-firm deposits, and even systems of accounting categories all revolved around the social organisation of their caste.'[14]

The attraction of 'caste' has a reason. India seems, to many scholars, to be a natural experiment for a beguilingly simple yet powerful theory of why culture matters to business performance. Business needs cooperation to succeed. Recent literature on 'business groups', institutional economic history, 'social capital', 'networks', and the origin of commercial law, stress this point in different ways.[15] In the past, cooperation was crucial to address four issues; specifically, poor information, missing markets, missing laws, and collective bargaining. In an environment where capital markets were missing and information scarce, social ties could act as channels for exchange of information and means of negotiation for cheap credit. Where commercial laws were undeveloped, social ties could be the means to enforce contract. Merchants also needed to negotiate with kings to obtain diplomatic immunity or the authority to follow their own civil law.

Cooperation in some of these senses may work better in the presence of strong social ties based on shared rituals, marriage rules, and commensality among members of a group. Ethnic combines like caste ensured that members followed rules by threatening to drive them out of society if they did not. The expectation that strong social ties did foster cooperation makes India, with its caste system, a field to test the idea. Nearly all usage of the idea with Indian examples have two features: common social identity of principal and agent, and the extended family or the community as the foundation of common identity.[16] The common identity ensured keeping of trust, or avoided agency costs that might appear in the presence of limited information, and performed a

---

[14] *Caste and Capitalism in Colonial India*, Berkeley and Los Angeles, 1994. Interestingly, both Timberg and Rudner deal with groups engaged in banking and moneylending, which suggests that bankers were indeed more reliant than others on markers of trust and loyalty, since they handled large sums of money.

[15] See, for a discussion, Tirthankar Roy, *Company of Kinsmen: Enterprise and Community in India 1600–1950*, New Delhi: Oxford University Press, 2018.

[16] On common identity, an example is Shoji Ito, 'A Note on the "Business Combine" in India', *The Developing Economies*, 4(3), 1966, 367–80. '[T]here existed between the family-firm and the trading community of which it was a member an informal relationship symbolized by a very strong sense of responsibility for the well-being of one's community fellows and an overt preference for dealing with them', Andrew F. Brimmer, 'The Setting of Entrepreneurship in India', *Quarterly Journal of Economics*, 69(4), 1955, 553–76, cited text appears in p. 557. This role of family or family-firm has also been stressed in Helen Lamb, 'The Indian Business Communities and the Evolution of an Industrialist Class', *Pacific Affairs*, 28(2), 1955, 101–16, and Morris D. Morris, 'Modern Business Organisation and Labour Administration: Specific Adaptations to Indian Conditions of Risk and Uncertainty, 1850–1947', *Economic and Political Weekly*, 14(40), 1979, 1680–7. See also, Tirthankar Roy, 'Capitalism and Community: A Study of the Madurai Sourashtras', *Indian Economic and Social History Review*, 34(4), 1997, 437–64.

variety of support functions such as supply of credit, easier travel, profit-sharing, and apprenticeship.[17]

This book does not discount the role of social ties in explaining business outcomes, and does not dispute that the concept or the idiom of caste carried a particularly strong moral force in India. Still, most historical evidence suggests that the use of caste or community as a principal business resource was prominent only in certain times and places. For example, in eighteenth century India, as the Mughal Empire collapsed and the axis of Indian capitalism shifted from overland trade to the ports, a massive migration and relocation of enterprise occurred. Most of the prominent business communities of the nineteenth century had changed the nature of their business during this political shift. Several groups, including the Marwaris, moved a long distance away from their original homes. They needed to reinvent cooperative bonds. Conditions were quite different in the port cities. The port city capitalist needed to develop links that cut across communities, not least because the scale of businesses had grown too much to rely on the resources supplied by friends and relations. If caste as a business resource is so historically specific, then we ought to employ the concept of the ethnic business community in a limited manner. Any attempt to claim more, and suggest that these notions could define Indian business in some essential ways, is likely to fail. There are two fundamental reasons why it would.

First, the theory would not fit the facts of history very well. Names of caste or community almost never fit perfectly with a core set of shared norms or values. The people that all North Indians used to call 'Marwari' around 1960 did not form a single caste, were very diverse and unequal among them, and did not conduct the same kind of business everywhere. The history of the Parsis shows as many instances of quarrel as of cooperation. Furthermore, when we do have biographical material on the pioneering industrialist, we should find many examples where their success happened despite resistance by the community. Community does not function in the way it did in the past any more. From the mid-twentieth century, if not much earlier, it started to become obsolete as a business resource, if not as a sentiment. We see this process in the 1920s when the leadership in collective negotiation passed on from sectarian bodies to national chambers of commerce. More recently, the maturity of capital and information markets made informal modes of exchanging information redundant. Globalisation changed communities from within. The Parsis started moving away from trade and industry as early as 1900, and gradually became a global set mainly engaged in the professions and the creative fields. A similar diversification has characterised all ethnic

---

[17] Thomas A. Timberg, 'Three Types of the Marwari Firm', in Rajat Ray, ed., *Entrepreneurship and Industry in India 1800–1947*, New Delhi: Oxford University Press, 1994, illustrates some of these services.

business groups of India, if at different speeds. The theory that caste or community is the definition of Indian business cannot easily explain why strong social ties become weak in these ways.

Second, if the strength of social ties is prone to be exaggerated, the importance of *weak* social ties is prone to be underestimated. In the nineteenth century port cities such as Bombay or Calcutta, which were home to many castes, religious groups, and languages, frequently partnerships formed between people who were not related by marriage, rituals, and commensality. These examples point at the 'the strength of weak ties'.[18] While caste members bound by strong ties may have secured cooperation within the group, groups that place too much value on loyalty to elders and conformity to norms are not very good at nurturing innovation and creativity. When many socially unrelated people have the chance to interact with each other, more novel ideas are exchanged among them. Another name for this situation is cosmopolitanism. Not surprisingly, factory industrialisation was a novel idea that succeeded in Bombay and Calcutta, and not in an interior business town such as Benares or Mathura, where many Indian banking families lived. Weak ties and not strong ones, cosmopolitanism, and not exclusive strategies by groups, allowed fuller play of entrepreneurship in the port city milieu.

Commenting on these themes in 1985, Rajnarayan Chandavarkar criticised the tendency of contemporary historians to explain new business formation in India either as a triumph of the entrepreneurial spirit or as a triumph of shared tradition.[19] Both approaches tend to overstate 'triumph', and understate failures. He showed how Indian businesses had to adapt to the persistently high cost of capital, even in a city like Bombay where the capital market was relatively developed. While this was the general situation, the few industrialists who did succeed in raising money easily, tended to take undue risks, make bad investments, and over-extend resources, often resulting in 'spectacular failures'.[20] The essay made a good case to look at the context of entrepreneurial decision more closely, suggesting that neither the entrepreneurial spirit nor social ties was a good enough resource to overcome the massive obstacles and scarcities capitalists often dealt with.

To sum up, we do need to understand the agency of the firms and entrepreneurs in context. This discussion should lead us to conclude that social constructs like caste or community as such do not supply a sufficient definition of the context. These things did play a role, but a contingent one, specific to some types of enterprise, and neither uniformly positive nor

---

[18] Mark Granovetter, 'The Strength of Weak Ties: A Network Theory Revisited', *Sociological Theory*, 1, 1983, 201–33.

[19] Rajnarayan Chandavarkar, 'Industrialization in India before 1947: Conventional Approaches and Alternative Perspectives', *Modern Asian Studies*, 19(3), 1985, 623–68.

[20] Ibid., cited text on p. 646.

uniformly negative a role. If society cannot define the context adequately, can state do that better?

An almost parallel argument can be made for that theory which attributes business failure by Indians too readily to British colonial repression, and business success of Indians readily to heroic struggles against British repression. Political environments matter, as we shall see, for various reasons and at all times. But the idea that it matters above all as repression, and in the guise of British imperial rule, begs in the assumption that the particular difficulties that Chandavarkar talks about did not exist before British rule, and disappeared after colonialism ended. This was far from the case. Merchants and industrialists struggled with the high cost of capital from before British rule and for long after the end of colonialism, as I will argue in a moment. The state does enter this story, mainly in two ways. First, the state was directly important as an investment agent for a relatively short time span in the mid-twentieth century. And second, in several indirect ways, especially as a legislating body, the state was also important in the colonial times.

While not losing sight of the state, this book focuses on the world economy, or markets and market integration more generally. The pervasive high cost of capital in the region supplies us with an ambitious pivotal question: how was this obstacle of a limited capital market overcome? And the answer revolves around the opportunities created by integration of the Indian economy with world markets in commodities and factors, and briefly in the twentieth century, around state intervention.

Why is the cost of 'capital' so crucial to the story?

The Question

From roughly 1700, private enterprise the world over needed to deal with challenges that were relatively new in origin. The emergence of large-scale transnational trading firms required raising big money. Industrialisation required even bigger amounts of money that would stay locked up in machines for a long time. From the financiers' point of view, this was a wholly new game from financing trade, where money circulated among known parties in a seasonal rhythm. Industrialisation required managing technology. Mass production of goods and services required managing a large and specialised workforce and reaching out to anonymous consumers. Railways and steam ships spread trade geographically, made firms mobile and multicentred, and demanded ways to manage distance. Successful adaptation to these challenges could enhance the capacity of the firms to make investments, raise productivity, offer higher wages, and create jobs, and in these ways lay the foundation for what Simon Kuznets called 'modern' economic growth.

Some of these problems were particularly challenging in India: trade costs were high (Chapter 2); capital was costlier; there were no indigenous industry-making machines; artisanal tools were simple in construction; artisanal skills were manual rather than mechanical in character; and labour was tied to land. With the financial and scientific revolution in Western Europe from the 1700s, a divergence in conditions would have emerged between Europe and India. This can be easily demonstrated with the example of cost of credit.

In the mid-1600s, 'good loans did not bring much over 6%' in England.[21] Rates for commercial loans in the Dutch Republic were not very different. From 1700, there was a sharp fall in interest rates from levels like these in the Dutch Republic, in England, France, and Italy. Interest rates in contemporary India were twice as high as in the major financial centres in Europe. Despite the emergence of big banking firms like the Jagatseths (see Chapter 4), there was no long-term tendency in interest rates between 1660 and 1760.[22] Shireen Moosvi shows that nominal interest rate fell somewhat (from 18 to 24 per cent modal rate to about 12) through the seventeenth century.[23] But 12 per cent for a trade loan was still high. Borrowing at such rates to trade, let alone to invest in industry, would very likely bankrupt most firms. When the British East India Company settled down to rule Bengal in the late eighteenth century, many of the clients of the bankers had been bankrupt military families. Their bankers charged them 30–40 per cent. Interest rates in the range of 10–12 per cent per year were common in 1772 among merchants (the East India Company took these rates as benchmark in debt disputes), 17–18 per cent common in 1857–8 (European businesses borrowed at such rates from Indian bankers), and 12–18 common in urban moneylending around 1910.[24] Provincial Banking Enquiry data show that in 1929, inland bankers of North India charged 9–12 per cent for loans to relatives, 18 per cent for loans to merchants, 24 per cent for loans to landlords, and 38 per cent for loans to peasants.

There was robust growth of corporate banking in India after 1860. Available data show that the share of private credit in GDP increased in India between 1870 and 1935. From the late 1700s, new banks formed, and banking laws

---

[21] Sidney Homer and Richard Sylla, *A History of Interest Rates*, New Jersey: John Wiley, 2005 (4th ed), 125, 139.

[22] K. N. Chaudhuri, cited in Irfan Habib, 'The Eighteenth Century Indian Economic History', in P. J. Marshall, ed., *The Eighteenth Century in Indian History*, Delhi: Oxford University Press, 2003, 100–22.

[23] Shireen Moosvi, ed., 'The Indian Economic Experience 1600–1900: A Quantitative Study', in Moosvi, *People, Taxation and Trade in Mughal India*, New Delhi: Oxford University Press, 2008, 1–34.

[24] Tirthankar Roy, 'Factor Markets and the Narrative of Economic Change in India, 1750–1950', *Continuity and Change*, 24(1), 2009, 137–67.

were reformed and remade in the same pattern as British company law. Bank deposits as a proportion of GDP increased from less than 1 per cent in 1870 to 12 per cent in 1935, and hovered around that percentage until the 1990s when it started rising again. There is little evidence (see interest rates just cited) that the cost of capital fell in response to these changes. After independence (1947), with the further growth of private corporate banks, the cost of short-term secured borrowing fell to 4–5 per cent (1950s). But long-term capital remained scarce. With the exception of a small number of top industrial firms, 'long-term credit ... was probably not available other than from the public market, ... or from the unorganized market in small amounts at very high rates'.[25] The situation did not improve after the nationalisation of the banks in 1969; the purpose of the move was explicitly to direct capital away from the larger businesses to make loans available for peasants and craftspeople.

Why was capital persistently costly in India? We can take three approaches to answering this question: institutional, political, and geographical-structural. To some extent, the Europe–India divergence since the 1600s in average cost of capital had been owed to exceptional tendencies in Europe itself. The emergence of joint-stock banking, a market in government securities, and wide use of negotiable instruments set the European pathway in financial development apart. One strand in the historical scholarship on Europe explains financial development by politics. Weber drew attention to the 'memorable alliance between the rising states and the sought-after and privileged capitalist powers that was a major factor in creating modern capitalism'.[26] Joseph Schumpeter explained financial development as a more autonomous process, one in which politics played a facilitating role. '[T]he rise' of capitalism, in this account, meant 'the development of the law and practice of negotiable paper and of "created" deposits', a process helped by state power to sanction commercial law as the law of the land, and in specific cases, the existence of central banks.[27] States burdened by large debt tended to swap debt for equity, which aided what development economists call 'financial deepening'. New institutional economic history suggests yet another manner of linking state formation and financial market

[25] George Rosen, 'The Structure of Interest Rates in India', *Economic Weekly*, 1960, 799–806.
[26] The example was the Bank of England that directly served the state and indirectly induced expansion in the capacity of the banking system. This sentence-segment from Weber's *Economy and Society* is a favourite of global historians, and is cited by, among others, Christopher Chase-Dunn, and Giovanni Arrighi. See Chase-Dunn, *Global Formation*, Lanham, MD: Rowman and Littlefield, 1998, 135; Arrighi, *The Long Twentieth Century*, London and New York: Verso, 1994, 12.
[27] Cited in Geoffrey Ingham, 'Schumpeter and Weber on the Institutions of Capitalism: Solving Swedberg's "Puzzle"', *Journal of Classic Sociology*, 3(3), 2003, 297–309.

formation.[28] States that are strong yet accountable should create conditions for financial development, mainly by guaranteeing its liabilities, which would also make the liabilities more tradeable.

There is nothing wrong with any of this, except that these arguments leave the experience of the non-European world open to inference. During the 1600s and 1700s, Indian states fought battles, were short of money, and would have benefited from a stronger financial system. That such an outcome did not occur is surely a puzzle. It is sometimes said that the East India Company in certain times pursued policies that may have reduced money supply in territories under its rule. No one knows the extent of the effect, however, and the problem of high cost of capital was not confined to limited periods of time or specific regions. The most plausible explanation for high cost of capital, I believe, is a geographical-structural one. Being a tropical monsoon region, Indian livelihoods display seasonal boom and slack in economic activity on a scale not visible in many other societies, and certainly not in the West. This condition made for large fluctuations in demand for money and interest rates within the year. The attraction of earning a windfall income in the short-term money market was so great that money was kept idle in the slack season rather than being lent long term.[29]

The great Indian paradox is this: no matter the scarcity of capital, capitalism flourished in India. The region was pivotal to the Indian Ocean trade in the seventeenth and eighteenth centuries. Indo-China trade in the early-1800s created enormous wealth in Bombay and Calcutta. The volume of long-distance trade in India grew from roughly 1 million tonnes in 1840 to 160 million in 1940.[30] With realistic estimates of national income growth, this extent of trade growth would mean a dramatic rise in the ratio of trade to income, possibly from 1 to 2 per cent in 1800 to more than 20 per cent in 1914. Between 1860 and 1940, employment in factories in India increased from near-zero to 2 million. The growth was comparable with that in the two other

---

[28] Douglass North and Barry Weingast, 'Constitutions and Commitment: The Evolution of Institutions Governing Public Choice in Seventeenth-Century Britain', *Journal of Economic History*, 49(4), 1989, 803–32; Nathan Sussman and Yishay Yafeh, 'Institutional Reforms, Financial Development and Sovereign Debt: Britain 1690–1790', *Journal of Economic History*, 66(4), 2006, 906–35.

[29] Tirthankar Roy, 'The Monsoon and the Market for Money in Late-colonial India', *Enterprise and Society*, 17(2), 2016, 324–57.

[30] This set of figures combines the volume of goods passing through the major ports around 1800 (Tirthankar Roy, *India in the World Economy from Antiquity to the Present*, Cambridge: Cambridge University Press, 2012) with the volume of goods carried by the railways and ports in 1940 (India, *Statistical Abstract for British India 1930–31 to 1939–40*, London: HMSO, 1942, 652–70, 712). The extent of the growth will be tempered by the quantity of trade lost – or gained – due to decline in overland trade and river-borne trade, because of the railways and ships. We do not know enough on these figures, nor on whether these systems were substitutes of or complementary to the railways and ships.

emerging economies of the time, Japan and Russia, but with few parallels in the tropical world. India – and Indians – led the contemporary developing world in the two main industries of the industrial revolution: cotton textiles and iron and steel. In 1928, 48 per cent of the cotton spindles installed outside Europe, North America, and Japan were in India.[31] In 1935, 50 per cent of the steel produced outside Europe, North America, and Japan was produced in India.[32] At the time of independence in 1947, the port cities in India were homes to some of the best schools, colleges, hospitals, universities, banks, insurance companies, and learned societies available outside the Western world. A big part of that infrastructure had been created by the Indian merchants and industrialists.

How do we explain this paradox? How did the capitalists overcome the scarcity of vital resources necessary for capitalism to develop? Economic historians recognise that a problem such as this one exists for more than half of the world that used to be called 'the periphery' of Western Europe. Inspired by Alexander Gerschenkron's writings, they coined the term 'late industrialisation', asked a similar question, mainly with reference to unified Germany, imperial Russia, Meiji Japan, and late-twentieth century South Korea, and answered the question with the proposition that activist states made the most significant difference, though the methods of state intervention differed.[33] I find the state-centric theories unconvincing and unhelpful to explain the main tendencies of Indian business history. Until 1950, India did not have a state that was either large or interventionist. A lot that happened in India before or after the rise of the West (c. 1850), happened because of actions by merchants and bankers, not governments. The state mattered much more after 1950, and what it did then entailed gains as well as costs for private enterprise, as we shall see.

During the times when the state was an indirect agent at best, the world economy played a more positive role. Cosmopolitanism and the strength of weak ties in the port cities and their satellites explain some of the risk-taking and offbeat decisions that did happen. In theory, resources in short supply can be obtained relatively easily if markets for capital, technology, and services are as open as the markets for goods. Free movement of capital and skilled labour can meet shortages to some extent. In the 1870s, the cotton mill owner of Bombay or Ahmedabad would hire foremen from Manchester; usually such

---

[31] Robert Dunn and Jack Hardy, Labor *and Textiles: A Study of Cotton and Wool Manufacturing*, New York: International Publishers, 1931, 25.

[32] BKS, 'The European Steel Industry: Production Trends and the World Market', *The World Today*, 6, 1950, 265–74.

[33] For statement and discussion, see Alice H. Amsden, 'Diffusion of Development: The Late-Industrializing Model and Greater East Asia', *American Economic Review*, 81(2), 1991, 82–6. Vivek Chibber, *Locked in Place: State-Building and Late Industrialization in India*, Princeton: Princeton University Press, 2003, contains a summary.

people came with the machines purchased there, and some of the pioneers teamed up with people with intimate knowledge of Manchester textiles. In the 2000s again, a lot of technology and skills came in along with foreign investment. Except for a few decades after 1950, factor markets were always relatively open in India.

The state was not unimportant. During the Mughal era and for a considerable time after the decline of the Empire, the revenue system served as a catalyst for a great deal of trading and banking enterprise. This effect was more muted in the seaboard, however. During British colonial rule, institutions and organisations also mitigated scarcity in some ways. Introduction of the joint-stock company helped entrepreneurs pool in public capital; and limited liability limited the owners' risks. The joint-stock principle came into India through European enterprise, but was consolidated via state intervention. The managing agency system, an Indo-British innovation, served a variety of roles in mitigating the shortages, one of these being conservation of managerial resources. Society also contributed to business formation. Caste, community, and family networks helped to mitigate the cost of credit to some extent, and helped in the supply of managers from within the family. But the world economy and the state created the framework for private enterprise to operate.

While markets and states explain the general patterns, biographies of entrepreneurs show how in specific instances specific tools were used to overcome shortage of key resources. Given the scarcity of biographies of some of the pioneers, we may never be able to write this story fully. Why, among hundreds of merchants and moneylenders doing routine business in Ahmedabad town in the 1850s, one gentleman decided to start a cotton mill at great odds and not with much help from fellow capitalists of the city, remains something of an enigma. A good biography does exist of this person. For most pioneers, the background to key decisions remains far more obscure.

Where sources are scarce, can theory shed some light?

Theory and History

The classic question for analytical business history is why some firms grow faster than others. Whereas economists interested in this issue focus on the structure of firms and markets, theories of entrepreneurship consider the individual behind the firm, and hold innovation and risk-taking to be the mark of entrepreneurship.

Older and newer theories of entrepreneurship share an interest in correct profiling of the innovative individual. Although interest in the individual has been revived recently via a desire to understand the tech firm prodigies, increasingly the mainstream scholarship does the profiling job in mundane ways, by making use of statistics, and seeking empirical regularity among small firms.[34] Systematic interest in the entrepreneur, however, has an impressive pedigree. It is tied to a curiosity about how capitalism works.

A central idea is that capitalism, unlike any other economic system known to humankind, is mainly made up of a set of people whose income is uncertain, and subject to risk. The Irish-French thinker Richard Cantillon, whose work is described as 'the springboard' for Adam Smith, saw virtually anyone who did not own land or work for wages to fit that description, though merchants fit it especially well.[35] Response to risk in an uncertain environment required such people to move capital between alternative uses, thus giving rise to a variety of dynamic outcomes, including the growth of towns and the creation of value in unexpected ways.

Although the entrepreneur as an agent of change became obscure when economic theory was remade in the twentieth century, the idea that allocation under uncertainty involved a kind of decision-making that economic theory did not capture well, lived on. Uncertainty, scarcity of information, and mistakes about information are so pervasive that they place economies perpetually off the demand-supply equilibrium, and drive some agents (call them entrepreneurs) to strive to improve their situation by reallocating capital. In Israel Kirzner's words, seeing how systematic this condition is would make economic theory 'a process-conscious market theory, which makes reference to entrepreneurship [as opposed to] an equilibrium market theory, which ignores entrepreneurship'.[36] Another name for 'process' is 'history'. Allocation of resources with full knowledge of alternatives is one thing, and allocation of resources while making guesses about correct knowledge is another thing. The latter is the normal condition of capitalism, and produces the type of individual whom Kirzner calls 'prescient'.

A parallel tradition in conceptualising capitalism as an intrinsically unstable and dynamic system derives from economic sociology, especially the economic history of Max Weber and Joseph Schumpeter. Weber recognised that capitalism in the form of a bundle of firms, markets, putting out contracts, banks, coded commercial law, and 'the privileged traditionalism of the guild',

---

[34] The state of the art is discussed in Paul Westhead and Mike Wright, *Entrepreneurship: A Very Short Introduction*, Oxford: Oxford University Press, 2013; Hans Landström and Franz Lohrke, eds., *Historical Foundations of Entrepreneurship Research*, Cheltenham: Edward Elgar, 2011; Mário Raposo, David Smallbone, Károly Balaton, and Lilla Hortoványi, eds., *Entrepreneurship, Growth, and Economic Development*, Cheltenham: Edward Edgar, 2011.

[35] Christopher Brown and Mark Thornton, 'How Entrepreneurship Theory Created Economics', *Quarterly Journal of Austrian Economics*, 16(4), 2013, 401–19.

[36] Israel M. Kirzner, 'Equilibrium versus Market Process', in Edwin G. Dolan, ed., *The Foundations of Modern Austrian Economics*, Kansas City: Sheed & Ward, 1976.

had been in existence in Europe from the late medieval age. Around 1600, 'this leisureliness was suddenly destroyed, and often entirely without any essential change in the form of organization, such as the transition to a unified factory, to mechanical weaving, etc'.[37] All that happened was that 'some young men from the putting out families' began to expand the scale of their business, changed the contracts and incentives, increased supervision, and *took control over production*. For Weber, 'the motive force' behind this transformation was not a change in the amount of capital employed, 'but, above all, of the development of the spirit of capitalism', which made control over the process that created economic value a new priority. Weber's conception of where that spirit came from in Europe and remained inchoate in India or China was not perfectly testable and yet drew an inordinate amount of attention. But the problem he posed remained and, consistent with his vision, it was a problem for global history. Did the motivational force behind capitalism appear at different times in different places, and if so, why?

Schumpeter, who would call such actions creating a 'new combination' out of existing resources, saw these actions as intrinsic to the modern history of capitalism, as Weber did. Unlike Weber, who left the historical origin of the propensity insufficiently explained, Schumpeter had a definite conception of the springboard of new combinations, which was growth of credit money by the banking system, and with it, new instruments like negotiable paper.[38] This historical condition from the 1600s made 'ruptures' more likely than before: 'And the agent of change is the path-breaking entrepreneur who, aided by the elasticity of the cash and credit system, is able at discontinuous intervals to wrest control of productive factors from their normal uses and reassemble them in novel combinations.'[39] Like Weber's 'spirit', credit money opens up a new question in global history: Does the growth of credit money and negotiable instruments occur at different times in different places, and if so, why?

Are these ideas useful in understanding capitalism in India? Yes and no. Because of source limitation, a great deal of entrepreneurship seems embedded in the behaviour of whole communities in India of the 1600s. It is difficult to see the agency of individuals, or even groups, in seeking control or creating

---

[37] Max Weber, *The Protestant Ethic and the Spirit of Capitalism* (Tr. Talcott Parsons, edited by Anthony Giddens), Abingdon and New York: Routledge, 2001, 30–1 (for this and subsequent citations in this paragraph). My reading of Weber is influenced by Richard Swedberg, 'The Economic Sociology of Capitalism: Weber and Schumpeter', *Journal of Classic Sociology*, 2(3), 2002, 227–55.

[38] Ingham, 'Schumpeter and Weber on the Institutions of Capitalism: Solving Swedberg's "Puzzle"'

[39] Lord Robbins, *The Theory of Economic Development in the History of Economic Thought*, London and Basingstoke: Macmillan, 1970, 16.

new combinations. And yet, there cannot be any doubt that something did change in this time. Indians had their own capitalism before the Europeans started trading in Asia in a big way. However, after 1600, the two traditions interacted ever more closely in the port cities, fusing into a new combination. Capitalism had been there before, but it was becoming a new thing thereafter, globally as well as in India.

The word 'capitalism' in the title of this book follows the Europeanist tradition of seeing a qualitative break around the 1600s, but does not follow Eurocentric definitions of what that break meant, which usually smuggle in preconceived notions of dominance and power. The manner in which markets and firms combined traditionally began to change in India too, roughly at the same time. Having said that, the precise contours of the change remain shadowy.

One thing is clear though. The joint-stock firms, corporate banks, negotiable credit instruments, coded commercial law, industrialisation, and a new imperial state that legislated after European precedent brought the two traditions nearer to one another; though irreducible differences remained between European enterprise in India and indigenous enterprise, as we shall see. This mention of firms, especially joint-stock firms, brings us to another important body of theory relevant for the historian.

Entrepreneurs create value. So do firms. A great deal of the theory of the firm builds around the idea of the limited liability joint-stock company. This was a revolutionary way to address many of the challenges that industrialisation posed; mainly, the problem of raising capital on a large scale, and to a more limited extent, professionalising management. For reasons that are not wholly clear, the joint-stock concept appeared earlier in Europe and was an importation into India in the 1800s with European expansion.

The joint-stock company concept solved some problems, but created a big new problem, one that did not exist in the purely family-run firms: that of corporate governance. The discourse on why the structure of ownership of a joint-stock company matters, starts from Adam Smith's conjecture that joint-stock firms can cause managers to misuse the owners' money. The conjecture led to the theory of agency in the 1970s, which highlights the role of 'monitoring' behind the value and performance of firms.[40] In a family firm, where managers are also the major owners, the cost of monitoring of managers by owners would be low. However, managers recruited from the family or those loyal to it will have less independence, which is not good for the firm. And majority shareholders from the family can short-change minority shareholders

---

[40] Michael C. Jensen and William H. Meckling, 'Theory of the Firm: Managerial Behavior, Agency Costs and Ownership Structure', *Journal of Financial Economicse*, 3(4), 1976, 305–60.

from the public.[41] For these reasons, diffused ownership combined with good monitoring systems may be ideal.[42] Good corporate governance can be defined as a bundle of practices that maximise shareholder value irrespective of the ownership structure.

Industrial firms with good corporate governance may still find themselves short of capital and opportunity for growth. The theory of the ideal capital structure of firms started by comparing debt and equity as two modes of funding firms' investment. Equity raised from the public is usually cheaper for the owners of the firm than raising debt. This definitely was the case in India which had a high-cost capital market, but raising more equity capital increases the threat of stock market takeover, and raises monitoring problems. Development of bank credit is safer for owners, but more costly. A large literature in financial economics makes the prediction that 'financial development' in the long run would make investment by firms, and therefore economic growth, more likely.[43] Financial development includes greater supply of money, changing the profile of the money suppliers, and improvement in regulatory law-making for better monitoring of corporate governance practices, all adding up to a fall in transaction costs in the credit market and in the direct cost of capital.

This overview of the literature on the firm leads us to make four propositions that clarify trends in business organisation in India since the nineteenth century, when the joint stock, limited liability, and the stock market became established concepts. First, there was a persistent, if slowly narrowing gap between two capital strategies. In starting new industrial or trading enterprises, Indian business firms usually resourced capital internally. Most Indian investors relied on their own money, or their friends' money. Those families who had been trading or banking for some generations, therefore, were likelier to make industrial investment, reinforcing community bonds. The link between own resources and new investment was close for the Europeans too, but Europeans tried using alternative ways to raise finance from an earlier point and to a greater extent than the Indians did. These alternative ways including selling shares in London, recruitment of non-family partners with money, and selling shares in India. And because they did, most European firms conformed more closely to the legal concept of the company or partnership than did the Indians.

[41] Michael J. Barclay and Clifford G. Holderness, 'Private Benefits from Control of Public Corporations', *Journal of Financial Economics*, 25(2), 1989, 371–95.

[42] Andrei Shleifer and Robert W. Vishny, 'Large Shareholders and Corporate Control', *Journal of Political Economy*, 94(3), 1986, 461–88.

[43] Raghuram Rajan and Luigi Zingales, 'Financial Dependence and Growth', *American Economic Review*, 88(3), 1998, 559–86; Ross Levine, 'Finance and Growth: Theory and Evidence', in Philippe Aghion and Steven Durlauf, eds., *Handbook of Economic Growth*, Vol. 1, Amsterdam: Elsevier, 2005, 865–934.

Second, both the Indian model and the Indo-European model involved own governance issues, as we shall see in Chapters 5 and 7 especially. Both types – the Indian-origin family firms and the Indo-European companies run by managing agencies – came to the stock market from the late nineteenth century. Managing agency contracts, in principle, weakened shareholder power, whereas management practices inside families were not transparent. The managing agency was eventually abolished in 1970 in recognition of its principal failing. Disciplining families was not easy, however. Indian companies generally resorted to the market more sparingly than did the foreign companies. This feature persisted until recent times. Company shares formed a small part of household savings and fresh investment until recently. Shareholding by owners and owner-affiliated companies and trusts in managed companies tended to be high. Bank loans were either expensive or limited. Other types of debt, such as debentures or long-term corporate bonds and fixed deposits, were expensive and used sparingly.

Third, both types needed to create a reputation for good corporate governance to improve their chance of raising money from the stock market. A reputation for good corporate governance was fixed on a family or on a managing agency. From this feature, a further effect followed: the emergence of the 'business group', a cluster of companies linked together either by a family name, like Tata, or by an agent's name, like Andrew Yule. Is reputation, attached to family name rather than company name, the reason why family firms survived in India for a very long time? The idea that reputation mattered to success in raising finance has generated an extensive literature.[44] Those who think reputation matters point at the persistence of the family-run businesses in India. Those who criticise the concept point at the difficulty in identifying a common pattern in family management, and the changing and evolving nature of involvement of the family.[45]

Fourth, in parallel with the difference in ownership of firms, there was a difference in management. Most Indo-European companies hired managers and recruited partners from a Britain-based pool, although some of them had wide experience of working in other parts of the empire before coming to India, or left India to join businesses in Southeast Asia or East Africa. If one advantage of a family firm was in arranging money from own sources or from

---

[44] Tarun Khanna and Yishay Yafeh, 'Business Groups in Emerging Markets: Paragons or Parasites', *Journal of Economic Literature*, 45(2), 2007, 331–72; Pankaj Ghemawat and Tarun Khanna, 'The Nature of Diversified Business Groups: A Research Design and Two Case Studies', *Journal of Industrial Economics*, 46(1), 1998, 35–61; Tarun Khanna and Krishna Palepu, 'Is Group Affiliation Profitable in Emerging Markets? An Analysis of Diversified Indian Business Groups', *Journal of Finance*, 55(2), 2000, 867–91.

[45] Surajit Mazumdar, 'The Indian Corporate Structure and the "Theory" of Emerging Market Business Groups', *History and Sociology of South Asia*, 6(2), 2012, 87–109.

social networks, another advantage was in resourcing management from within the family. Several of the largest business groups in the 1950s conformed to a classic model of a family firm, one that supplied *both* financial and managerial services from within the family. On average, the postcolonial generation of business magnates had many sons, which helped them do this without major problems. But increasingly, the scale of businesses grew too big for the demographic resources of families, and the supply of professional managers expanded. The material discussed in this book will suggest that in many conglomerates now, which are family-run in name, ownership and management have diverged. Owners usually engage actively in new ventures, but not in the running of existing enterprises. The family neither manages nor funds the companies, but functions as a loose kind of brand.

To conclude this discussion, how capitalists resourced capital, technology, and management skills, and with what consequence, lies at the heart of the book. Narrative history returns to this theme in almost every chapter. On every occasion, the state and world economy set the parameters, subject to which formal and informal institutions, and individual enterprise, make a difference. The balance between the ingredients varies, however. I distinguish five episodes during which these resources were obtained by different means.

Plan of the Book

The chapters that follow present a narrative history of enterprise, actors, and the political economic backdrop. Chapters 2 and 3 discuss firms and entrepreneurs against the backdrop of consolidation of the European companies on the coast, and the emergence of a new empire from maritime trade. I characterise India in 1700 as a world split between two halves: land-based trade and maritime trade. The two joined at times, but were mainly autonomous from one another. Capital was resourced by those who populated these spheres quite differently, with a significantly larger role for external finance in the maritime sphere. During the eighteenth century, the separation began to end as maritime traders captured state power, while the decline of state power in North India drove merchants and bankers towards the coast.

Chapters 4 and 5 study merchants and industrialists during the nineteenth-century globalisation, when new methods of sourcing capital, technology, and personnel came into existence. Corporate forms and corporate governance are big themes. A significant feature was the integrating role of agriculture. Trade was based on agricultural goods mainly; the main stem of banking was the finance of agricultural operations; and industrialisation was based on processing agricultural material. The integration made it possible for traders and bankers to move money from traditional activities (cotton trading) to non-traditional ones (cotton mill), and made for a certain balance in the external transactions. Agricultural export created the capacity to purchase the services of workers and managers from abroad, buy technology, and pay interest on foreign loans in this era.

The Great Depression upset the balance. Chapter 6 deals with the post-Depression reorientation and protectionist turn, when foreign trade lost its appeal, and industrialisation became the goal of state policy. After 1947, new instruments in addition to protectionism were employed in the pursuit of state-led industrialisation. Trade in general and traditional exports like agricultural goods and textiles fell in priority. With this shift, many firms and entrepreneurs nurtured in the earlier times disappeared. Chapter 7 explores how others got the chance to diversify and form conglomerates. Financing investment, however, had not been made any easier than before. Government regulation on private banking restrained the emergence of a capitalist financial system. Foreign capital had been restrained too. Taxpayers' money and scarce foreign exchange were spent on industries that did not create export capacity. Repeated shocks from the world economy (1967, 1973, 1979, and 1991) showed how badly the economy's capacity to finance investment had been compromised.

From the 1980s, industrialisation and protectionism lost their central role in driving business growth, and there was a gradual return to comparative advantage. This no longer involved agricultural export, but the export of labour-intensive industrial products, and skilled services. Completely new fields of entrepreneurship opened. Most old conglomerates and families retreated, relatively speaking. Chapters 8 and 9 show how the capacity to resource capital from the world vastly improved, enabling the import of technology. The domestic financial system, however, continued to be state-dominated and its capacity to support the ongoing transition was limited.

Whether we consider the 1600s or the 2000s, the two themes that bind the chapters together are state/politics, and the world economy or openness. These are the units of analysis here, in that interventions by the state, and input and ideas obtained from abroad created the environment, which families, communities, and individuals tried to make the best use of. Openness, which had always been a feature of the seaboard economies, began to play a different, more qualitative role from the 1600s with the entry of European joint-stock companies in Asian trade. The narrative starts from that theme, as we see in Chapter 2.

2   The Baseline at 1700

The Indian subcontinent is geographically diverse. A big part of it consists of the Indo-Gangetic Basin formed of the floodplains of two huge Himalayan river systems, the Ganges and the Indus (Map 2.1). The Basin has fertile land that in the past sustained cities, armies, trade, crafts, and states. Elsewhere, agricultural conditions were poorer. But the long coastline contained settlements of traders who conducted a lot of maritime trade around and near the Bay of Bengal, especially the Arabian Sea. Such settlements also occurred in the arid fringes of the western deserts, through which important overland trade routes passed. Around 1700, this composite land was ruled by the Mughal Empire (1526–c. 1720) in the Indo-Gangetic Basin, and by smaller states and semi-independent vassals of the Mughals nearer the coast. Although the Empire did possess ports, overall, it had weak penetration into the coastal areas and into the seas.

Therefore, two quite different types of capitalism functioned side by side, with limited interactions between them. One of these formed along the coasts, lived on maritime trade, and was sponsored by the coastal states. The other one formed in the interior, and served overland trade. The main geographical space for land trade was the Indo-Gangetic Basin. Relatively flat terrain, wheeled traffic, navigable rivers, and cities that were home to wealthy consumers, sustained land trade. Where river traffic ended, caravans began. Bullock caravans linked the Indo-Gangetic Basin with the Deccan Plateau where wheeled and river transport were less developed. Small pack animals crossed the Himalayas to link other parts of land-locked Asia with India. The Empire ruled from northern regions in the Indo-Gangetic Basin. The Empire possessed ports like Surat or Hooghly, but the coast was mainly ruled by smaller local states.

Although these two complexes intersected to some extent, they involved different groups of merchants, different goods, different clients, different sponsors, and possibly, different organisation. Land trade carried grain, silk, textiles, wool, horses, precious stones, and other luxury articles consumed by the military-political elite of the Mughal cities. Sea trade carried mainly cotton textiles. Land trade and the financing of land trade involved communities, such

Map 2.1 South Asia: Geographical features

as the Khatris and Marwaris, who did not have a significant presence in the ports. The sea trade involved communities, such as the Kachchhis, Tamil-speaking Muslim merchant groups like the Marakkayars and the Labbais, the Parsis after 1700, and several European trading firms and merchants, who had limited interest in the goods traded in the interior, and did not usually settle in the interior. The main clients of land trade were the residents of the towns of northern India. The main clients of sea trade were in West Asia, Africa, Southeast Asia, and increasingly in the 1700s, Europe. The fact that sea trade was more cosmopolitan and less state-dependent – that is, less tied to the revenue system – should make for fundamental differences in the nature of the firms and their institutional forms, but there is little information available on these differences.

The two business worlds had weak interaction between them. Several factors kept these complexes separate and parallel. One of these was high trade and transportation cost. Recent scholarship has established that trade costs were (relative to Europe) high in India before the railways started in the second half of the 1800s.[1] Another was politics. The Mughal state, by establishing peace over the vast Indo-Gangetic plains, integrated markets in this zone. Directly it gave many overland traders and town bankers the chance to make money from moving grain or converting grain into cash revenue. The sea was of marginal importance to the Mughals as a source of revenue. It gave them a convenient income and an access to silver, but it was not vital to their survival. The Mughal provinces with extensive sea trade, Bengal and Gujarat, were far enough away from the political centre in Delhi and Agra to maintain a partial autonomy.

This separation between land and sea trades began to end from the 1700s. European merchant firms like the British and the Dutch East India Companies arrived on the Indian coasts in the early 1600s; by the end of the 1600s, they were entrenched there, and in the next century, were joining politics in the interior world and trading in goods produced in the interior.

While the next chapter discusses the integration between the two worlds, this chapter describes the two worlds themselves.

Merchants and Bankers in Land Trade

In the relatively urban Indo-Gangetic Basin, merchant settlements were established in almost every town. Merchants owned boats and transported a variety of goods along the major rivers. Three big long-distance channels of trade involved movements of Bengal silk to North India, grains by bullock caravans from the Indo-Gangetic Basin to the coasts, and cotton from central and southern India to the textile-producing areas. Sushil Chaudhury suggests that the Asian merchants who organised overland trade in the Ganges-Jumna plains exported a lot of the artisanal goods from this region in the late 1700s.[2]

In the major cities of the Mughal Empire, large banking firms accepted deposits, and did business deals with the military and political elite.[3] Frustratingly little information is available on the names, business practices, and

---

[1] Roman Studer, *The Great Divergence Reconsidered. Europe, India, and the Rise to Global Economic Power*, Cambridge: Cambridge University Press, 2015.

[2] Sushil Chaudhury, *From Prosperity to Decline: Eighteenth Century Bengal*, New Delhi: Manohar, 1995.

[3] Karen Leonard, 'The "Great Firm" Theory of the Decline of the Mughal Empire', *Comparative Studies in Society and History*, 21(2), 1979, 151–67; Irfan Habib, 'Usury in Medieval India', *Comparative Studies in Society and History*, 6(4), 1964, 393–419.

histories of these firms. Mughal nobles 'themselves at times took a substantial interest in trade'.[4] Three Governors of Bengal, Mir Jumla, Shaista Khan, and Azimush-Shan, invested in trade, directly or through other merchants. The Europeans needed to negotiate with them commercial taxes and access to supplies.[5] Besides these exceptional warlord-merchants, there were of course many merchants and bankers. But we have little concrete information on the firms that they owned.

Instead of firms, we encounter Indian merchants as communities. The Punjabi Khatris were one such community. A steady migration of Khatri individuals into Bengal followed the Mughal invasion of the region (c. 1595). They resettled as court officers, military officers, and landholders under some of the larger estates, known as jagirs. The merchant-cum-banker Amirchand or Umichand, one of the East India Company's principal agents in the 1750s, was of Khatri origin.[6] In the mid-nineteenth century, Khatris were prominent in Calcutta as brokers and agents of European firms, though some of them were soon to be replaced by the Marwaris in that role.[7]

If the Khatri migration began from their position as partners of the Mughal Empire, Marwari migration followed a more commercial logic. Marwar stands for the Jodhpur region (a district and a former princely state of the same name, see Map 2.2) located in southwestern Rajasthan, western India. Marwari refers to a language spoken in Jodhpur and its neighbourhood, and in turn, the people who speak the language. Capitalists held important places in the courts of the princely states in this region. From this origin, the Oswal bankers, an endogamous commercial caste (jati) of this area, dispersed throughout northern India, being 'known under one denomination, Marwari'.[8] Outside the Marwar region, the term 'Marwari' included more than a dozen endogamous groups, the most prominent among them being Agarwal, Khandelwal, Srimali, Maheshwari, Jaiswal, and Oswal.

[4] Sanjay Subrahmanyam, 'The Mughal State – Structure or Process? Reflections on Recent Western Historiography', *Indian Economic Social History Review*, 29(3), 1992, 291–321.

[5] Farhat Hasan, 'Conflict and Cooperation in Anglo-Mughal Trade Relations during the Reign of Aurangzeb', *Journal of the Economic and Social History of the Orient*, 34(4), 1991, 351–60. See also on noblemen-traders of Golconda, Sanjay Subrahmanyam and C. A. Bayly, 'Portfolio Capitalists and the Political Economy of Early Modern India', *Indian Economic Social History Review*, 25(4), 1988, 401–24.

[6] John R. McLane, *Land and Local Kingship in Eighteenth-Century Bengal*, Cambridge: Cambridge University Press, 1993, 177.

[7] Thomas Timberg, 'Three Types of the Marwari Firm', *Indian Economic and Social History Review*, 10(1), 1973, 3–36.

[8] James Tod, *The Annals and Antiquities of Rajasthan*, Vol. 2 of 3, Madras: Higginbotham, 1926, 211.

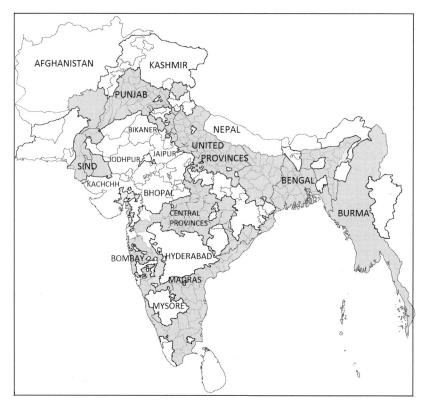

Map 2.2 British India (shaded) and princely states around 1900

Several of these merchant lineages were concentrated in the arid desert fringe. The region produced few goods of value to commerce, but was important to trade and banking. In the seventeenth century, when two powerful empires, the Mughal (1526–c. 1720) and the Safavid (1501–1722), ruled Southern Asia, Jodhpur town was at the intersection of two overland trade routes of great importance. These were the road between the Mughal capital Agra and Kandahar, a border town occupied by the Mughals and the Safavids at different times, and the road between Ahmedabad and Agra. These roads joined trade traffic along the river Indus and its tributaries. The economic rise of the trading communities from the desert fringe was connected to the prosperity of these territorial empires. In turn, individual Marwaris occasionally joined the Mughal court. One example was Todar Mal, the Emperor Akbar's minister and the supervisor of the first large-scale land survey. These courtier-merchants also owned landed estates, and a few even joined battles, but such cases were exceptional.

Marwaris were close to the regional Rajput states in the seventeenth century, most of which were vassals of the Mughals. Merchants and bankers were frequently recruited into high offices by the Rajput states, as the nineteenth-century European officers-cum-chroniclers James Tod and Alexander Forbes reported. In Phalodi, on the western border of Jodhpur, a seventeenth-century merchant had built a city state.[9] Outside Rajasthan, the major polities of northern India offered the traders legal autonomy and immunity, so they started to circulate over a large region. The Pax Mughaliana was an impetus to go further afield in search of such custom. Like the Khatris, a few Marwari firms followed Mughal territorial expansion eastward in around 1600 and resettled in eastern India. We do not know enough about the nature of their businesses, but silk textiles and banking were very likely included in the list, for Marwari firms were prominent in both these fields in the eighteenth century. There were, however, few known cases of Marwari relocation and resettlement outside northern India in these centuries.

The riparian highways linked seaports like Surat and Hooghly with the Punjab, where trans-Himalayan caravans descended in winter bringing goods from Central and West Asia for sale in fairs. Only small pack animals could negotiate the mountain passes, so the traders did not have high carrying capacity. It was also entirely seasonal. Typically, the traders carried low-bulk, high-value articles, such as silk and wool.[10] Trade in this setup was sometimes linked to sheep rearing. In such cases, the traders were formed of groups distinct from the merchants who operated in the plains.

In the Deccan Plateau, where roads were few and navigable rivers rare, the main mode of transportation of cargo was the bullock caravan. Unlike the trans-Himalayan caravans, bullock trains carried bulk goods like grain or cotton. But like the trans-Himalayan caravans, the caravan runners in the Deccan were not usually merchants. Among the merchants who owned ware-houses and establishments in the market towns, the caste names that repre-sented caravan runners were rare. The comparative advantage that the latter possessed lay elsewhere than in trade. It consisted of the knowledge of routes and of how to maintain livestock. Caravan routes started from market points located on the Ganges (like Mirzapur) and the Indus and went towards central, western, and southern India. The transporters known as Banjaras or Lambadas

---

[9] Thomas Timberg, *The Marwaris*, Delhi: Penguin, 2014.
[10] The trans-Himalayan trade with Central Asia has been studied by Scott C. Levi, *The Indian Diaspora in Central Asia and Its Trade, 1550–1900*, Leiden: Brill, 2002, 30–1, and Levi, 'India, Russia and the Eighteenth-century Transformation of the Central Asian Caravan Trade', *Journal of the Economic and Social History of the Orient*, 42(4), 1999, 519–48. Also on overland trade, Sushil Chaudhury and Michel Morineau, eds., *Merchants, Companies and Trade: Europe and Asia in the Early Modern Era*, Cambridge: Cambridge University Press, 1999.

managed these caravans. When the North Indian Sultanate spread its power southward in the fifteenth century, the caravans find mention. Especially during military campaigns in the Deccan, armies relied on caravans, and therefore sources on warfare tend to be informative on the organisation of the caravans.[11]

Towns in the Indo-Gangetic Basin contained many artisans. Some of the master artisans may have acted also as merchants, certainly as employers, but few details are available on this form of enterprise. Some of the most skilled forms of craft work took place in a type of unit called karkhana. The word karkhana, common to many Indian languages, derives from Persian. In its original Indianised meaning, karkhana was 'a place where business is done'.[12] More often, the place was a workshop or a warehouse. Any workshop would not qualify to be called a karkhana. The word would ordinarily mean a large-scale craft production workshop employing wage labour. In that respect, karkhana was the pre-modern factory.

Court officers and European travellers in the Mughal Empire described several large establishments like these in the cities. A common feature of these workshops was that they were owned or sponsored by the court officers. Since these officers formed a part of the consumer class, I would call this setup consumer-owned. In the nineteenth and twentieth century, we again encounter the term 'karkhana', in the Punjab carpet and shawl industries, for example. But now they were owned by merchants. In the mid-twentieth century, a cluster of textile-producing factories in the southern Maharashtra region (especially Sholapur) was also called karkhana. Most of them were owned by artisans. We cannot say how these three general types – consumer-owned, merchant-owned, and artisan-owned – were related, or whether they were related at all except by the generic name that attaches to all three.

The karkhana of the Mughal cities was mainly the consumer-owned type. Outside these units, there were surely households and workshops producing goods for the wider market, and surely these two worlds transacted between them. But we know little on that market-oriented artisanal sphere. The Mughal court officer in 1595, Abu'l-Fazl, said that town administration had a say in the appointment of guilds and guild masters.[13] These guilds worked together with the karkhana. The cities had a whole hierarchy of these, most of them owned by courtiers and individuals close to the court. At the very top, of course, was

---

[11] Bhangiya Bhukya, *Subjugated Nomads: The Lambadas under the Rule of the Nizams*, Hyderabad: Orient Blackswan, 2010.

[12] According to a later interpretation, Henry Yule, A. C. Burnell, *Hobson-Jobson: A Glossary of Colloquial Anglo-Indian Words and Phrases, and of Kindred Terms, Etymological, Historical, Geographical and Discursive*, London: Murray, 1903, 125.

[13] Abu'l-Fazl Allami, *Ain I Akbari* (tr. H. S. Jarrett), Calcutta: Baptist Mission Press, 1891, 42.

the imperial karkhana.[14] Any visitor to the Agra Fort today would marvel at the scale of the place. It was not merely a fort, but a fortified city. Being such, it needed stores and factories to locate inside the fort. This was the milieu where the royal karkhana operated.

Although Abu'l-Fazl mentioned 'guild', guilds in the north European sense – that is, associations bound by their own laws and independent of the state – were not common in this milieu. Most likely, they did not need to exist: the karkhana was powerful enough because its patron was a powerful individual. In one respect, however, the karkhana may indeed have resembled a guild. The goods made in the karkhana were rich in craftsmanship, and training was a very important matter. It is likely that guild-like rules existed to regulate the progression of ordinary artisans to master artisans. Again, little is known of the individuals who worked in these places for us to be more specific on how skills were formed and preserved.

Compared with the land sphere, the sea sphere was distinct in several ways, one of which was that it was more cosmopolitan.

Merchants in Sea Trade

The Arabian Sea has a special place in Indian business history. For centuries, the cities and settlements on the Arabian Sea littoral traded with each other, exchanging Indian textiles for horses, armaments, pearls, and ivory. In turn, some of the textiles were passed on to the Atlantic slave trade in Africa as a medium of exchange, or sent overland to European markets. Coastal merchants indigenous to the region bordering the Sea engaged in this business and developed sophisticated systems of banking and ship-building to support the mercantile enterprise. The Hindu and Muslim traders of Kachchh were examples of such people. In the seventeenth century, the Arabian Sea trade flourished thanks to the control that three powerful empires – the Ottoman in Turkey, the Safavid in Iran, and the Mughal in India – exercised on some of the key seaports. Transactions between these empires initiated a golden age of Arabian Sea trade. Much less systematic information exists on the Bay of Bengal trade (see next).

In 1498, a Portuguese mariner named Vasco da Gama reached Calicut, a seaport on the Malabar coast. He was the first European mariner to complete the journey from Europe to India via the Cape of Good Hope. By doing so, he demonstrated that it was possible for western European merchants to reach India without having to travel overland in West Asia. That route, being

---

[14] Tripta Verma, *Karkhanas under the Mughals, from Akbar to Aurangzeb: A Study in Economic Development*, Delhi: Pragati, 1994.

controlled by the Ottoman Empire and the Venetian and Genovese merchants, was not found safe enough by western Europeans. In the next one hundred years, first the Portuguese and later the English and the Dutch established trade links between Europe and Asia. In the late seventeenth century, other nations joined the contest for a share in Indian Ocean trade. The records left by these traders revealed a rich world of trade in the seaboard societies, including the chief port Surat.

An earlier scholarship saw this world as a kind of satellite to European trade.[15] That view has been revised in favour of one that sees it as a trading system in its own right, quite different from the one that existed in Agra or Delhi, and one that integrated India with West Asia, East Africa, Southeast Asia, and China.[16] Europeans came here because they were attracted by the goods already traded in Asia. Systematic knowledge of business enterprise remains biased towards those segments where European traders had direct or indirect interest. This is so because many European traders operated as employees of joint-stock companies, and these companies needed to keep more documents for the benefit of the head office than the Indian family firms who operated in these zones. Thus, the Arabian Sea trade and the Coromandel trade are better researched than the northern and eastern half of the Bay of Bengal, which joined the Bengal Delta with Burma, Indonesia, the Malaya, and further, with China, and where European traders did not usually go, but many Asians did. Equally less known is the trans-Himalayan overland trade that joined the Bay of Bengal trade with northeast India and East Asia. New books shed light on trade history in these zones, but the field still lacks information on the individuals and firms that conducted their trades here.[17]

---

[15] Immanuel Wallerstein, 'Incorporation of Indian Subcontinent into Capitalist World-Economy', *Economic and Political Weekly*, 21(4), 1986, PE28–PE39.

[16] The relevant scholarship is very large, a short list of representative works may include K. N. Chaudhuri, *Trade and Civilisation in the Indian Ocean: An Economic History from the Rise of Islam to 1750*, Cambridge: Cambridge University Press, 1985; Kenneth McPherson, *The Indian Ocean: A History of People and the Sea*, Delhi and Oxford: Oxford University Press, 1998; Om Prakash, *The New Cambridge History of India; Vol. II.5. European Commercial Enterprise in Pre-colonial India*, Cambridge: Cambridge University Press, 1998; Sanjay Subrahmanyam, *The Political Economy of Commerce: Southern India, 1500–1650*, Cambridge: Cambridge University Press, 1990; Lakshmi Subramanian, *Indigenous Capital and Imperial Expansion: Bombay, Surat and the West Coast*, Delhi and Oxford: Oxford University Press, 1996; Prasannan Parthasarathi, *The Transition to a Colonial Economy: Weavers, Merchants and Kings in South India, 1720–1800*, Cambridge: Cambridge University Press, 2001. For surveys and collections, Giorgio Riello and Tirthankar Roy, eds., *How India Clothed the World: The World of South Asian Textiles 1500–1850*, Leiden: Brill, 2009; and Tirthankar Roy, *India in the World Economy from Antiquity to the Present*, Cambridge: Cambridge University Press, 2012.

[17] A pioneering collection reflects the strengths and weaknesses of recent research on the Bay of Bengal region, see, Rila Mukherjee, ed. *Pelagic Passageways: The Northern Bay of Bengal before Colonialism*, Delhi: Primus Books, 2011.

Europeans who lived in Surat reported that there were substantial merchants in the town, who owned ships, carried valuable cargo, employed their own staff, and often received special treatment at the ports. A Bohra merchant Mulla Abdul Ghafur, and two Jain merchants, Virji Vora (c. 1585–1670) and Shantidas Jhaveri (c. 1580–1659) appear frequently in early English documentation from Surat. Their interests encompassed trade, shipping, and banking. These sources comment more about their political weight than about their business practices. Jhaveri became infamous for the hand he played in the religious politics of the sect, which prompted one historian to say that 'the Jain monks needed the businessmen as much as the businessmen needed them'.[18] European accounts show further that these firms gained from lending money to the Europeans, and occasionally forcing them to trade with them or trade in the Arabian Sea on their behalf.

Somewhat smaller in scale were the merchants who did not own ships and often worked as agents of the principal merchants. Below them were many small-scale merchants who carried generic cargo. Shipping was an important marker in this hierarchy. The conjunction of trade and shipping made the magnates at the top either partners or rivals of the European firms. One of the reasons for the vitality of Indian shipping was that it charged lower freight rates than the European ships in the routes that it was familiar with. However, there were not many merchant firms that owned ships, and shipping was not a popular field of investment. It was not, possibly because the ships were individually owned, and while insurance covered the goods, it did not cover the ships.

Compared with Surat, less attention has fallen on Kachchh further north, which conducted a lot of trade in the Arabian Sea. Kachchh is a region with unique qualities. Although poorly endowed with agricultural resources, it has a convenient situation on a navigable part of the eastern Arabian Sea. The ancient Mandvi port bears witness to this importance. Another factor was politics. The western coastal regions were ruled by small states that depended heavily on income from trade. This dependence was owing to the poor agricultural conditions in the region, or more directly, to the fact that marine transport costs were much lower than land transport costs. In turn, these states, though nominally vassals of the Mughals, could exercise a great deal of independence in policy. They used their freedom to create a model of rule where merchants and bankers had a prominent place in local politics, not only during warfare, the all-too-common palace intrigues, or natural disasters, but also in normal times. Merchants and bankers helped the business of governance. They collected taxes, did revenue farming, made loans, and took part in

---

[18] Makrand Mehta, *Indian Merchants and Entrepreneurs in Historical Perspective*, Delhi: Academic Foundation, 1991, 18.

administration, whereas the states helped them by offering lucrative contracts and implicitly recognising their internal laws and practices.

The merchant groups in question established diaspora networks in port cities around the Arabian Sea. They conducted complicated financial operations including bills of exchange (hundis) and insurance, and their bills were accepted in the distant trading points thanks to the diaspora network. Vaishnavite temples and monasteries effectively became banks, clearing houses, and guarantors of reputation. Community law had great force. The merchants had considerable interest in ship-building, which in turn encouraged the timber trade. In banking, trading, ship-building, and navigation, master–apprentice hierarchies were highly developed, showing how much skills were valued and how skills formed.[19]

European entry into this world occurred in sporadic ways in the 1500s. By 1650, Europeans were important actors in the coastal world. And they represented a different type of firm from the Indian ones.

European Merchants

Soon after da Gama discovered the sea route to southern India, other Portuguese mariners reached the Indian Ocean with the intention of taking control over the Indonesian spice trade. The move led to several well-defended settlements to appear on the coasts of Konkan, Persia, the Arab peninsula, East Africa, and Malacca in the Malay Peninsula. Portuguese efforts to license or collect protection money from shipping on the long routes was a partial success at best, though it did lead to a lot of local conflicts. Gujarati shipping on the west coast and Javanese shipping on the east gained from these conflicts, at the expense of Arab shippers.

The English East India Company was established as a trading firm in 1600, with a licensed monopoly to trade in the Indian Ocean. The Dutch Company followed a year later. The English and the Dutch East India Companies entered the Indian Ocean around 1600 with the same aim, but different means from the Portuguese. The shared aim was to take control over spice supplies from Indonesia. The shareholders of these companies were merchants, and preferred diplomacy rather than muscling their way into Asian trade. Diplomacy would mean different things in different parts of Asia, but generally involved obtaining a license to trade against payments to the court.

Conflict with the Portuguese was inevitable as this process unfolded, because all Europeans shared similar trading interests. But in the early seventeenth century, the Portuguese enterprise had dispersed too much to maintain

---

[19] Chhaya Goswami, *Globalization before Its Time: The Gujarati Merchants from Kachchh*, New Delhi: Penguin, 2016.

hegemonic ambitions, and after a series of decisive battles, the English were entrenched in the Indian seaports. The Dutch also consolidated their position in Southeast Asia and the southeastern coast of India. Spices were initially the most coveted Asian good, but since Indian cloth was easily accepted in exchange of Indonesian spices, a hold over both trades, as the Dutch had, helped.

As the seventeenth century progressed, Indian textiles emerged as an article of trade in their own right, thanks to interest from Europe. Whereas cotton cloth entering Asian trade was often plain, cloth that went to Europe tended to be printed, dyed, embroidered, or painted; and therefore, in those areas in India where these decorative technologies were highly developed or the dyes were available from local material, trade flourished. The colour factor favoured the southeastern or Coromandel coast particularly, and to a smaller extent, Gujarat. Indian cloth was famous in European markets for sophisticated use of colour and design, as well as the particular shades that locally available organic dyes, such as indigo, imparted on the cloth. Another kind of distinctiveness of some Indian cotton cloth was fineness, which derived from the availability of long-staple cotton locally, and the ability of the spinners and weavers to make good use of these. The production of such cloth, muslin, had made certain areas of lower Bengal known to international trade from much before the Europeans came.

The Europeans were more secure from local states in the Coromandel, large swathes of which were ruled by small independent states that valued their association with the European traders. But in Bengal, they had to negotiate trading rights with the rulers of a major province of the Mughal Empire. Diplomacy and bribery were the best policy here, though these tools failed at times in the presence of competition between Europeans, and in the British case, competition between the East India Company that held a monopoly charter and numerous private traders who disregarded the charter.

Because trade entailed conflicts, the Dutch and the English created their own fortified settlements on the coast when they could. They feared one another, needed to possess some policing power against competitors, and occasionally ran into disputes with the Mughal court or the governor. Their construction project was politically more feasible in the Konkan and Coromandel coasts. Elsewhere, it attracted suspicion from the Mughals, and resistance from shareholders of the English company, who viewed this as an extravagance. In this backdrop, the fact that the English (later British) Company ended up with three fortified settlements in Bombay (1661), Calcutta (1690), and Madras (1632) was a matter more of fortuitous circumstances than careful planning. Madras was purchased from the tiny kingdom of Chandragiri, Bombay was a gift (technically a dowry) from the Portuguese in a gesture of reconciliation, and Calcutta was leased from a vassal of the provincial ruler.

Although these sites helped the Company consolidate its limited naval power, and involved the Royal Navy after it was established in 1660, they were not protected well enough from attacks by European rivals or local powers. That these settlements did not suffer outright attack by the Mughals and the rising Maratha forces was partly sheer luck, though they came close to such disaster. Governing them was not an easy matter either. The Company had to set up institutions for governing these territories, but they could not claim to be sovereign rulers here. Who, then, was the ruler? The English Civil War (1641), the Glorious Revolution (1688), and more generally the uneasy relationship between the Crown and the Parliament caused troubles to the Company in England and in India, and made it difficult for all parties concerned to answer the sovereignty question. Its business privilege was a monopoly charter to trade in the 'East Indies' granted by the Crown. This monopoly was under attack not only from the private traders, but even from the Company's own employees trading on the side, who lobbied the Parliament seeking to have the charter withdrawn. There were many European privateers and pirates in the Arabian Sea, whom the Company officers secretly helped. Angry about such patronage, the emperor Aurangzeb almost ended English trade in Surat and Bombay.[20] Private trade survived the years of monopoly charter by sometimes defying and sometimes befriending the local officers of the Company.

Almost all European firms operating in India worked through an Indian agent or broker. Sometimes, the broker belonged in a commercial group. Several of them used the relationship as a springboard for entry into trade. The broker was more than an intermediary, but a figure with considerable managerial responsibilities. The broker was responsible for enforcement of contracts between the trading firm and the hundreds of artisans residing in villages and working from homes. The Company officers', as much as the private traders', daily duties included discussing matters concerning contracts, disputes, and deal-making. These issues occupied pages of the 'consultation books' of the British East India Company. As the scale of the business and the scale of contractual transactions increased, the importance of the agent or contractor in the commercial machine increased too. As far as we know, these contracts did not have any indigenous precedent, and Indian law did not protect these. Legally, the companies could do little when the contracts were disregarded, which is why the broker was so important to the trade.

Current historical scholarship acknowledges that the contracting situation was unstable and the risk of breach of contract was high. The instability is read to mean that the artisan producers of textiles had a lot of bargaining

---

[20] Tirthankar Roy, *The East India Company: The World's Most Powerful Corporation*, New Delhi: Allen Lane, 2012.

power.[21] By implication, they were deprived of this power when the Company became the ruler of Bengal.[22] These hypotheses overlook the fact that the Company's own position was not very strong at any time because of the absence of adequate commercial law. Indo-European trade suffered from pervasive contract enforcement problems.[23] If by taking over power, contracts became easier to manage, then by implication any merchant would want power (see also Chapter 3). Brokers and agents were a means to bypass these problems and reduce the costs. But they were an imperfect solution, because the brokers could cheat the firm, and the firm was aware of this. The relationship between the agent and the firm, therefore, was fraught with mutual distrust as well as dependence.

In the early 1600s, the chief agents of Coromandel were local warlords and chieftains. By the end of the 1600s, the profile of the brokers changed. The ability to obtain money more than the ability to command soldiers started to matter more as the scale of the business grew. Usually, the new generation of brokers were merchants with considerable financial resources, as well as easy access to the textile artisans. For example, in Calcutta, the agents were recruited from the families of the Seths and Basaks, textile merchants, and in the capital of Bengal, Murshidabad, they were North Indian merchants in the mid-1700s. In Madras, the agents were Telugu merchants. The chief agents in Surat were an exceptional group, Parsis, who were engaged in diverse professions and took to trade readily.

The work the agents did was quite diverse, ranging from secretarial or managerial to contractual and the enforcement of contracts. In the second role, the agent was a type of head merchant with whom the Company contracted in the first instance for the supply of goods. This was the proper meaning of the term 'broker'. The South Indian term 'dubash' (literally meaning interpreter) connoted a more managerial role. Choosing any one individual above others of similar qualifications to be the head broker was fraught with the risk of a disruptive quarrel among Indian merchants, which the documents of trade referred to frequently.

Ananda Ranga Pillai was probably the most famous of all such agents, because he kept a diary that was translated and published more than a hundred years ago. Pillai managed a great deal of the French East India Company's

---

[21] Prasannan Parthasarathi, *Why Europe Grew Rich and Asia Did Not: Global Economic Divergence, 1600–1850*, Cambridge: Cambridge University Press, 2011.

[22] Om Prakash, 'From Negotiation to Coercion: Textile Manufacturing in India in the Eighteenth Century', *Modern Asian Studies*, 41(5), 2007, 1331–68.

[23] Rachel E. Kranton and Anand V. Swamy, 'Contracts, Hold-up, and Exports: Textiles and Opium in Colonial India', *American Economic Review*, 98(5), 2008, 967–89. See also Roy, *India in the World Economy*, and Roy, *East India Company: The World's Most Powerful Corporation*.

trade in the 1740s, and occasionally managed the private trade of some of the officers. In doing so he had to maintain an army of subcontractors, and supervise shippers, transporters, bankers, and artisans spread over a coastline a thousand miles long. He had immense influence. As the head of the French Company Joseph François Dupleix pointed out to Pillai, 'from Cape Comorin [to] Bengal, ... Golconda, and ... Mysore, there is not one who is not [his] friend, and there is none who will not honour [his] drafts and bonds'.[24] But Pillai himself often complained about his situation. His expenses were heavy and the profits relatively small.

Recent scholarship has shed much light on several other brokers, and their rivals. Indranarayan Chaudhuri of Bengal, who worked for the French in the early eighteenth century, Narasu of Pondicherry and his rival Sunku Rama, and Rustam Manock or Manek of Surat are some of these examples.[25] The accounts show that the brokers were usually exceptionally capable and exceptionally lucky people at the same time. All, or most of them, made a great deal of money, while often taking great political and professional risks to do so. But these accounts do not yet add up to a substantial picture of the mercantile world in these areas.

While the agents were sometimes unhappy about their situation, the Companies were almost always wary of the agents' influence. Agency was not hereditary, but the debts of a deceased agent to the Company passed on to the next generation who did not always want to honour them. Under Indian customary law, such liability was limited, whereas under European law, the liability was unlimited. More seriously, the agents were sometimes powerful figures locally, and were suspected of double crossing. If the Company had a dispute with the king, the agent's conflict of interest came out in the open. In 1678–9, the dubash of Masulipatnam, Kola Venkadri, secretly negotiated with the King of Golconda, and was imprisoned by the English as punishment. Kasi Viranna, the chief dubash or 'sole merchant' of Coromandel between 1660 and 1690, was deeply distrusted by the Company management for reasons that are not altogether clear. In 1670, Khem Chand Shah, the chief merchant of Balasore, whom the British with their characteristic regard for Indian names called Chimchamshaw, was caught between the Mughal governor and the Company establishment and harassed by both. Further, agents in different communities turned agency into a battle between communities. In Surat, the

[24] H. Dodwell et al (tr), *The Diary of Ananda Ranga Pillai*, Vols. 1–12, Madras: Government Press, 1904–28, cited text in vol. 2, p. 156.
[25] See, for example, S. Jeyaseela Stephen, 'Revealing and Concealing: The Business World of Middlemen and Merchants in the French Commercial Enterprise in Pondicherry (1674–1741)', 99–112, and Aniruddha Ray, 'Two Indian Brokers of the French East India Company in Eastern India during the first half of the Eighteenth Century', in C. Palit and P. K. Bhattacharya, eds., *Business History of India*, Delhi: Kalpaz Publications, 2006, 113–36.

Parsi and Hindu merchants tried to play the Company against one another in the 1730s. The bitter disputes between Rustam Manock and the Hindu Jagannath Laldas on the one hand, and between Manock's sons and the Company on the other, were quite typical.

Bengal, Coromandel, and Gujarat were the main textile supply regions for the European traders. Of the three, Gujarat was accessed first, Coromandel next, and Bengal dominated the eighteenth century trade in that order. Most systematic studies of European companies have concentrated mainly on Bengal and Coromandel.[26] The Gujarat scholarship has grown more recently.[27] In all three regions, textiles for export were produced in large villages easily accessible from the port city, like Surat, Masulipatnam (Fig. 2.1), or Calcutta. The Company officers did not travel to the interior often, and provided incentives to weavers to locate near the warehouses. Around 1700, such settlements of artisans were growing in the periphery of Calcutta and Madras. Cotton weaving centres, for export or otherwise, attracted spinners, and encouraged long-distance trade in cotton towards these areas.

Headmen in these exporting villages would then contract with the agents and brokers of the Companies to supply a certain quantity and quality by a certain date. When European companies competed in the same place, the power of the headmen rose, and some may have taken on a fully fledged mercantile role. Their power was exercised in negotiations as well as breach of contract on delivery time, or quality of cloth delivered. Equally, the headmen could use their power to bully or exploit the weavers. P. Swarnalatha's research on the Coromandel textile manufacturers suggests that the weavers tended to accept a headman's authority more readily when the latter was seen as a caste-fellow, and contested the authority when he was from outside the community and an imposition from above.[28]

---

[26] Om Prakash, *The Dutch East India Company and the Economy of Bengal, 1630–1720*, Princeton, NJ: Princeton University Press, 1985; Tapan Raychaudhuri, *Jan Company in Coromandel, 1605–1690*, The Hague: Martinus Nijhoff, 1962; S. Arasaratnam 'Weavers, Merchants and Company: The Handloom Industry in Southeastern India 1750–1790', *Indian Economic and Social History Review*, 17(3), 1980, 257–81; Subrahmanyam, *Political Economy of Commerce*; Parthasarathi, *Transition to a Colonial Economy*; Chaudhury, *From Prosperity to Decline: Eighteenth Century Bengal*; Hameeda Hossain, *The Company Weavers of Bengal: The East India Company and the Organization of Textile Production in Bengal, 1750–1813*, Delhi: Oxford University Press, 1988.

[27] Ghulam Nadri, *Eighteenth-Century Gujarat: The Dynamics of Its Political Economy, 1750–1800*, Leiden: Brill, 2009; Pedro Machado, 'A Regional Market in a Globalised Economy: East Central and South Eastern Africans, Gujarati Merchants and the Indian Textile Industry in the Eighteenth and Nineteenth Centuries', in Giorgio Riello and Tirthankar Roy, eds., *How India Clothed the World: The World of South Asian Textiles 1500–1850*, Leiden: Brill, 53–84.

[28] Potukuchi Swarnalatha, 'Revolt, Testimony, Petition: Artisanal Protests in Colonial Andhra', *International Review of Social History*, 46(1), 2001, 107–29.

Fig. 2.1 View of Masulipatnam, 1676
Source: Chronicle/Alamy Stock Photo. After an illustration in Philip Baldaeus, 'A True and Exact Description of the most Celebrated East-India Coasts of Malabar and Coromandel'

Conclusion

As this rather uneven account has shown, traditional business communities ruled trading and banking in the interior. We encounter them as communities rather than as firms or individuals. We do better on the maritime world, where traders, agents, and bankers often appear by name.

There were crossovers between these two segments of the land and the sea. Mughal nobles wanted to earn money from maritime trade, they valued their access to Surat and Hooghly, and occasionally Dutch and English traders tried to procure indigo from markets near Agra. Textiles and horses straddled both maritime and overland trades. Still, examples where maritime merchants settled inland or interior merchants participated in maritime trade were exceptional and infrequent.

The state mattered crucially to the functioning of the inland world. Equally, foreign trade was crucial to the survival of the seaboard. But the seaboard capitalists suffered from political anxieties too. A persistent worry for the Europeans, for example, was to make contracts work, where there was neither a legal notion of contract nor an agency to enforce these. Negotiations with local kings broke down often due to mutual distrust.

It is plausible that officers of the Companies wished for a political settlement of these problems. In 1700, acting on that impulse would have been dangerous. But it was not so dangerous a course of action in 1750. The balance between the land and the sea was changing, initially because the Mughal Empire was in decline, and also because none of the successor states commanded economic and political capital comparable to what the Empire had at its peak. We will find out in Chapter 3 what happened next.

3   The Indian Ocean Sphere: 1700–1850

Chapter 2 described the land trade and the sea trade. This chapter will describe how their separation began to end. Early in the 1700s, the Mughal Empire disintegrated, and merchants and bankers started to leave their former settlements on overland trading routes, for the safety of the capital cities of new states like Awadh, Bengal, Hyderabad, Maratha domains in central India, and Gujarat. In the late 1700s, warfare and conflict would cause the decline of many of these states as well. The cities with a secure future at this time were Calcutta, Bombay, and Madras, three settlements under the British East India Company. Merchants and bankers now went to these cities or developed strong connections there. At the turn of the next century, these towns had transformed from the Company's garrison and fort to Indian business cities.

During the 150 years covered in this chapter, state power changed in India. In the last quarter of the eighteenth century, the Company was changing from being a business firm to a political entity. Between 1757 and 1765, the British East India Company emerged as the effective ruler of Bengal, one of the richer independent states of post-Mughal India. It was also a strong military force in Bombay and Madras. In 1813, the monopoly charter was withdrawn, and trade became formally free. The effect was dramatic as not only European private merchants, but also artisans, planters, skilled professionals, and fortune-hunters, migrated from Britain to the port cities.

While trading and diaspora links between Britain and India were thus developing, the Industrial Revolution unfolded in Britain. India changed from being a textile exporter to a textile importer, and at the same time, started exporting agricultural goods, like opium, indigo, cotton, and tea to Britain and to the Company's sphere of influence in China. In the early 1800s, Indo-European firms based in Bombay, Calcutta, and Madras exported agricultural goods that came from the interior. Sea trade and land trade began to converge.

What did this twofold change mean for business firms? Migrant merchant families relied on their own traditional contacts and organisation. At the same time, in the port cities, new types of hybrid enterprises emerged. These businesses adopted British law to some extent, and because they did, we begin to see the 'firm' in a more legalistic sense towards the end of the period. Companies formed, stock markets developed, and public money was invested in industry and banking. Trade profits accumulated during this time would finance an industrialisation drive in the second half of the nineteenth century (Chapter 4).

This chapter describes the experience of firms and communities during these years. It covers the migration of capitalists from one world to the other, and the beginning of agricultural export trades on a large scale. This chapter shows how a new economic system, one founded on a closer integration of trade, banking, and industry, was beginning to emerge closer to the seaboard. The rise of European power in these coastal regions was the agent of this change.

Indian Ocean-Going Merchants

Indian merchants, shippers, and bankers who formerly served intra-Asian trade needed to adapt to the rise of European dominance in the Indian Ocean and the decline of the Mughal, Ottoman, and Safavid power over the Arabian Sea. This adaptation is a major theme in the business history of the eighteenth century. Two contending stories exist on the transition. First, the Indians lost ground to the Europeans while their patrons lost political power. And second, the Indian traders turned into middlemen, or 'comprador' as the Marxists disapprovingly called such people. Both stories overstate the Europeans' commercial prowess and understate the Indians' capacity to shape the course of history.

Some support for the decline story comes from Surat, especially the experience of the 'ship-owning merchants'.[1] Some of the ship-owners did not survive the simultaneous decline of the Persian, Ottoman, and Mughal empires. According to Ashin Das Gupta, the decline of the Indian merchant marine began when the local rulers increased pressures on them to fund wars. Those who 'faced extinction at the hand of Indian administrators exchanged that dangerous position for a constricted existence'.[2] Surat finally became the Company's territory in 1759.

A study of the Kachchhi traders, who operated in the Arabian Sea's market before the advent of the British, tells a somewhat different story.[3] The Kachchhi merchants gained from European trade, and withstood well the decline of empires. They could do so thanks to their own resources, which included well-developed institutions of commerce and banking, knowledge of

---

[1] Ashin Dasgupta, 'The Maritime Merchant and Indian History', *South Asia*, 7(1), 1984, 27–33; Om Prakash, 'The Indian Maritime Merchant, 1500–1800', *Journal of the Economic and Social History of the Orient*, 47(3), 2004, 435–57.

[2] Ashin Das Gupta, *The World of the Indian Ocean Merchant 1500–1800*, New Delhi: Oxford University Press, 169.

[3] Chhaya Goswami, *The Call of the Sea: Kachchhi Traders in Muscat and Zanzibar, c. 1800–1880*, Hyderabad: Orient Black Swan, 2011.

the seas, shipping, and ship-building, history of collaborating with political actors, and access to both maritime and overland trade routes. In short, they were simply too good as merchants to be driven to a 'constricted existence'.

From both the Gujarat littoral and the Coromandel, we find examples of merchants and shippers who continued in coastal trade without too many problems. Pedro Machado shows evidence of significant persistence of Indian shipping in the Arabian Sea, to the extent that 'decline' seems like an 'exaggeration'.[4] After all, the Company's own ships did not transport materials and supplies, such as grain or timber, along the Indian coast. They did not even shuttle between the three Company ports often. But the growth of these ports and their strategic value in the warfare that ensued encouraged coastal trade. While the great ship-owning merchants of Surat in the 1600s did go under, Indian coastal groups overall benefited from the rise of British power in the Arabian Sea. They went further afield and formed diaspora. Gujarati merchants in Mozambique, Muscat, and East Africa signify dominance of Indians over the Arabian Sea. Because of western Indian advance in coastal shipping, merchants from Bombay and Surat retained control over the Arabian Sea.

On the Konkan coast and Malabar, communities of Muslim merchants and shipwrights carried on coastal trading. These communities – the Marakkayars of Coromandel, whose name derived from the name of a local model of boat, and the Mapillahs of Malabar –were formed of converts to Islam and of settlements of Arab merchants who once carried on spice and horse trades. Although these groups owed allegiance to the local kings, the kingdoms themselves being small, the merchants played a limited political part compared with their counterparts in the states that ruled over the Indo-Gangetic basin.[5] Therefore, they were both vulnerable to targeted attacks, such as those the Portuguese subjected the Arabs to after Vasco da Gama, and more resilient to the passage of empires in the long run. In the 1800s, these groups were not necessarily mercantile. They were also engaged in service and agriculture.

Ship-owning merchants were fewer and of more limited capability in the Bay of Bengal, especially in Bengal itself. This was so, partly because navigation in the Bengal delta presented more difficult conditions for ocean-going ships. A study of Akrur Datta, a Bengali freight contractor of late eighteenth-century Calcutta, shows that several individuals owned and arranged to construct small vessels that distributed cargo from ocean-going ships along the unpredictable rivers of the Bengal Delta.[6] But the business did

---

[4] Pedro Machado, *Ocean of Trade: South Asian Merchants, Africa and the Indian Ocean, c.1750–1850*, Cambridge: Cambridge University Press, 2014, 76.

[5] Frank S. Franselow, 'Muslim Society in Tamil Nadu (India): An Historical Perspective', *Journal of the Institute of Muslim Minority Affairs*, 10(1), 1989, 264–289.

[6] Shubhra Chakrabarti, 'The English East India Company and the Indigenous Sloop Merchants of Bengal: Akrur Dutta and His Family, 1757–1857', *Studies in History*, 20(1), 2004, 131–157.

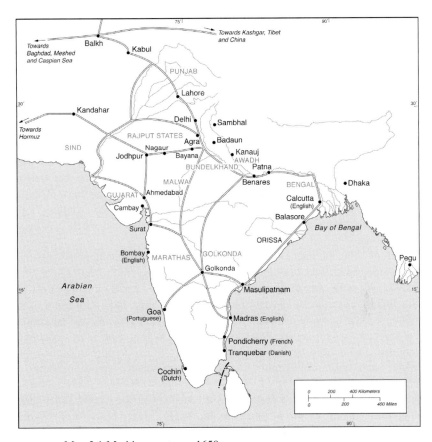

Map 3.1 Maritime routes c. 1650

not survive because the main client, the Company, ceased to trade and because the boats were not sturdy enough. Datta's family turned into merchants and agents of American trading firms in Calcutta. Bengali regional historiography sometimes frets over the fact that the Bengali merchants did not do as well in Calcutta as their counterparts in Bombay, and blames their risk aversion or preference for landlordism for this.[7] In fact, if the European element is taken out, the northern part of Bay of Bengal had never been as large a trading zone as the northern Konkan was. The Arabian Sea trade connected powerful and wealthy empires; the Bay of Bengal trade did not.

---

[7] For a discussion and critique of these views, see Chittabrata Palit, 'Bengali Business Enterprise and the BNCCI', in Chittabrata Palit and P. K. Bhattacharya, eds., *Business History of India*, Delhi: Kalpaz, 2006, 251–8.

The group that adapted best to the rise of Company power on the west coast was the Parsis.

Parsis of Bombay

The Parsis were remnants of the Zoroastrian population of Iran who did not convert to Islam after the fall of the Sassanian Empire. They escaped conversion, it is said, by migrating, first to Hormuz and Khorassan in the seventh century, and then to the coast of Gujarat in the eighth century. Towns on the Gujarat coast became their main homes. Although many owned orchards and gardens in more recent times, traditionally the group was engaged in a variety of professions, including artisanal ones. Nineteenth-century writers of Parsi history noted that the Parsis had no destitute citizens, few soldiers, few farmers, and above average living standards. They also had social insurance institutions.

Before 1700, the Parsis were not mainly a seafaring population. Yet, several Parsi individuals were prominent in Indian Ocean trade in the mid-1700s. The move to business was an outcome of new opportunities of trading that arose in the Indian Ocean with the consolidation of the East India Company as a political force in western India. Parsi solidarity, egalitarianism, and education helped them make use of these opportunities. At the same time, economic mobility also created tensions within the group, to the point that keeping the social and cultural identity of the group intact would become a challenging task.

Several Parsis migrated from Surat to Bombay in the 1700s. After they acquired Bombay, the British took the shipwright Lowjee Nusserwanji Wadia from Surat to set up a ship-building yard for them. Some of the Parsis were originally carpenters by profession, and took over ship-repair and ship-building in partnership with the Company, while some took a controlling position in the important coastal trade in Malabar teak. Others moved into coastal shipping, and eventually joined the Indo-Chinese trade in Malwa opium. A system of apprenticeship helped the master builder to pass down skills along the family lines. The shipwrights reinforced skill formation by also sending sons and nephews to England to undertake training. For example, in 1838, the shipwright of Surat, Nowrojee Jamsetji, sent his son and nephew to learn the craft of building steam ships. When the Company began its withdrawal from India trade (after 1813), and then from China trade (1833), the Parsi shippers bought up some of the ships and refitted these for coastal and China trade. Wars with China (1839–42) and Burma (1824–6) saw these ships being heavily used for supplies. When Indian opium emerged as the main export to China, and the proceeds from opium funded tea imports from China, the Parsi ship-owning merchants played a part in the trade between Bombay and Canton.[8]

Other than the shipwrights, the first commercial Parsi residents of Bombay were probably grocers for the town, also engaged in the very useful side business of procuring safe and good quality liquor for the city. In the eighteenth century, one set of families, the Wadia, developed shipping while three others, engaged in commerce, reached Burma, China, Mauritius, and Aden. They set out a pattern that was to become the hallmark of Parsi enterprise in the nineteenth century. The names were Banaji, Modi, and Readymoney. Between 1813, the end of the Company's charter, and the Opium War of 1839, several firms had entrenched themselves in India-China trade, and connected Bombay with Mauritius, Aden, and Canton in a network of exchange of goods, money, and manpower. The transformation of the wealthy members of the community from artisan-shipwright-broker of the Gujarat littoral to export merchants in Asian and African ports had been completed. Money made in overseas trade flowed into a variety of local enterprises, from real estate in Bombay to coffee plantations in Malabar. Among the leading Parsi merchants of the nineteenth century, Jamsetjee Jeejeebhoy started his career as an assistant in several Parsi firms selling opium in China (Fig. 3.1). The industrialist Jamsetji Tata also had his apprenticeship in China.

Parsi shippers made the transition to steamships quite well. One such example was Ardaseer Cursetjee, the head of the dockyard in Bombay in 1852, the 'chief engineer and inspector of machinery', that is, in charge of repair and maintenance of ships in the government marine under the Company.[9] Cursetjee was born c. 1808. He was apprenticed to the master builder of the Bombay dockyard at the age of 14. When he was a senior assistant, the conversion of sailing ships to steam began in earnest. On recommendations from the master, he took training in constructing and maintaining steam engines in England, and was appointed to be the head of Bombay dockyard in 1848. Shortly thereafter, his son arrived in England to receive training as a shipwright. When the son took over, the works produced boilers, small engines on the principle of marine engines, 'cut and lengthened' iron ships, but did not

[8] More details on Parsi enterprise before the Opium War can be found in Ashok V. Desai, 'The Origins of Parsi Enterprise', *Indian Economic and Social History Review*, 5(4), 1968, 307–18; Asiya Siddiqui, 'The Business World of Jamsetjee Jeejeebhoy', *Indian Economic and Social History Review*, 19(3–4), 1982, 301–24; Amalendu Guha, 'The Comprador Role of Parsi Seths 1750–1850', *Economic and Political Weekly*, 5(48), 1970, 1933–6; and Amalendu Guha, 'More about Parsi Seths – Their Roots, Entrepreneurship and Comprador Role, 1650–1918', *Economic and Political Weekly*, 19(3), 1984, 117–32.
[9] British Parliamentary Papers, cited in Tirthankar Roy, *India in the World Economy from Antiquity to the Present*, Cambridge: Cambridge University Press, 2012.

Fig. 3.1 Jamsetjee Jejeebhoy, c. 1857
Source: Chronicle/Alamy Stock Photo

build complete iron ships. He employed European engineers of ships docked in the port as foremen of the different departments.

Did 'community' matter to the Parsis' business success? In ritual terms, the Parsis maintained distinctiveness and exclusiveness in comparison with other religious groups. Community courts carefully preserved rituals, and were often embroiled in fierce quarrels over the correctness of these rituals. Did the ritual community coincide with a business community? It is not clear at all that their social practices contributed to their business success. Like many other communities, the Parsis recruited top managers and partners in their firms from other Parsi families. But there were many exceptions to the rule. Jejeebhoy, when established in the trade, formed partnership with a Gujarati Hindu and a Muslim merchant. The inter-ethnic enterprise did not work too well because of mutual suspicion, but a trend had been established. The mill owner Dinshaw Manockjee Petit was first an assistant and later partner to a European, and his father was broker of a European firm. Collaboration with Europeans was especially common in shipping as we have seen.

Continued participation in Arabian Sea trade also led to collaborations with big European partners. An example is the Parsi firm Adenwalla, of which the most famous member was Hormusji Dinshaw. The firm had maintained, through their shipping, close contact with the Arab peninsula and East Africa: 'The firm deals in exports and imports besides being bankers, naval agents, ship-owners, managing agents for mills and steamship companies such as the Bombay Persia Steam Navigation Co., British India Steam Navigation Co., and other British Italian Dutch and Norwegian Shipping Companies.'[10]

Such was the world on the coast. What about the interior and overland trade?

Inland Merchants

It is impossible to say with the data that are available if Indian merchants and bankers operating on overland routes experienced a rise or a fall in wealth with the decline of the Mughal Empire (c. 1720). It is certain that political upheavals increased risks and encouraged many of them to migrate. Warfare and insecurity in the north at first drove many merchant firms towards the capital cities of the successor states. The Rajput states were caught up in a series of debilitating succession disputes in the 1700s, suffered repeated incursion of the Maratha forces of central India, and the trade routes under their protection were in disarray. This chaos mattered to the Marwaris especially.

Still, Indian bankers operating from these states gained something from the eighteenth-century turmoil. They funded states driven to bankruptcy by wars. Along the coast, the bullion for payment of Indian goods was imported in the shape of Spanish silver coins. The inland bankers arranged to have them re-

---

[10] Ambelal Naranji Joshi, *Life and Times of Sir Hormusjee C. Dinshaw*, Bombay: Taraporevala, 1939, 71.

coined for a fee, or simply exchanged the peso for Indian money. The Company needed the bankers to borrow money when bullion ran out, and convert the currency of one kingdom into that of another. In the eighteenth century, profits and revenues earned in Company-ruled Bengal were sent to the other branches by means of bankers' drafts, or hundi. The major operators in the hundi market were the Indian bankers.

Increasingly, these businesses were gravitating towards the coastal regions. Marwaris are a particularly good illustration of this further mobility in the eighteenth century. Some of the earliest streams of Marwari migration went to the princely states. Two central Indian states that rose from the ashes of the Empire, Indore and Hyderabad, received Marwari firms in the eighteenth century. But the successor states themselves were too weak to protect trade and trade routes. Their guarantee of security was not enough, and the business opportunities seemed to dry up by 1800. At around the turn of the nineteenth century, merchant and banking communities went more often to the British territories or formed links with these. In Indore, Marwari merchants, who were involved in the inland trade in central Indian opium, formed a link between the Company port of Bombay, one of the points of transit, and central India.[11]

For Marwari history, the transformation of the Company into a political power (see next) marked an important moment of change. From middle Bengal, the axis of their operation moved towards Calcutta. Marwaris remained rare in the description of trading communities of contemporary Calcutta, but they were present in substantial numbers in Cossimbazar, or Kasimbazar, the prominent trading town in the interior of Bengal where the Company's operation concentrated in the seventeenth century. In this part of Bengal, several Jain temples and shrines bear witness to the sponsorship of Marwari merchants from the late-Mughal era.

In this part of Bengal, an Oswal house known as the Jagat Seth were the principal licensed money-changer in Bengal under the rule of the Nawabs who succeeded Mughal rule. Their immense importance as a financial firm was owed to the importance of Bengal as a trading area in the mid-eighteenth century, and in turn, to European presence in Bengal. The European traders could not get anywhere in business without the service of the firm that converted imported silver into local money. That service, and associated banking services in a usually cash-strapped state, made the Jagat Seth a crucial player. Their political influence was demonstrated during the coup that saw the East India Company officers take over power in Bengal. The Jagat Seth was a secret ally of the Company.

---

[11] The description draws on Jogendranath Bhattacharya, *Hindu Castes and Sects*, Calcutta: Thacker Spink, 1896; R. V. Russell, *The Tribes and Castes of the Central Provinces of India*, London: Macmillan, 1916; Thomas Timberg, *The Marwaris*, New Delhi: Allen Lane, 2014.

Important as they were in their own time, the Jagat Seth was an exception rather than the rule. We cannot read from these examples anything about the condition of banking in general. The Jagat Seth was so visible in the European records because the firm was a monopoly and close to the state. Soon after the Company assumed political power and tried to unify the monetary system, the house of the Jagat Seths lost relevance and declined quickly. In any case, by 1820, Cossimbazar was as good as abandoned. Some of the prominent Oswal firms of the town had by then become moneylenders and landholders, and shifted base to other towns in central Bengal.[12] From early in the nineteenth century, Marwari entry into Calcutta became larger in scale and diversified in business interest. In Bombay, there were few Marwari houses, and they shared economic space with the more prominent Parsis and Gujarati Jain merchants. In Calcutta, their position was stronger.

After the end of the Company's charter in 1813, some indigenous traders joined the trading firms that the Europeans formed in the port cities. A few were partners, but many more served them as bankers and subcontractors. Unlike the local Bengalis, Marwaris rarely joined Indo-European firms as partners or agents. But they carried on banking, and money was in high demand in the cities. The beginning of large-scale import of machine-made textiles from Manchester from the 1820s attracted indigenous merchants in even greater numbers to Calcutta. Some of the Marwari families that became prominent in trade and banking in the nineteenth century, including the founders of what Thomas Timberg calls 'great firms', migrated from Rajasthan towards eastern India before 1850.[13] From the middle of the 1800s, Marwari entry into Calcutta became bigger in scale and diversified in business interest. They took hold over the trade in raw jute and share broking in the late 1800s, and retained hold over banking throughout.

If the Parsis had a ritual identity after all, it was never easy to define a Marwari merchant with reference to ritual identity. And yet, outside Rajasthan 'Marwari' began to acquire a precise meaning in the mid-nineteenth century. This was so because by 1850, in nearly every business town of northern India, a Marwari settlement had appeared. The members spoke a different language from that of their clients, were relatively wealthy, transacted with the town population in a variety of ways, and thus formed a visible minority. The drive to assimilate with the local society was also quite strong, especially in the small towns. The history of the Marwaris in the nineteenth century would display these two opposite pulls.[14]

---

[12] Bhattacharya, *Hindu Castes and Sects.*   [13] Timberg, *The Marwaris.*
[14] Anne Hardgrove, *Community and Public Culture: The Marwaris in Calcutta, 1897–1997*, New York, NY: Columbia University Press, 2001, contains useful discussion on the emergence of a Marwari identity.

If the Marwari and Khatri migration (see Chapter 2) was mainly an Indo-Gangetic Basin affair, the caravan runners were active in the Deccan Plateau. In the eighteenth century, two distinct factors stimulated caravan operations. One of these was the demand for raw cotton in the coastal weaving villages on Coromandel and Bengal making textiles for Europe trade. The trade was so well organised that the British East India Company tried and failed to divert it to get enough raw cotton for export, possibly to China. They succeeded somewhat, but only in the nineteenth century when the decline of hand-spinning made more cotton available for export.

The second factor was the supply of grain to mobile armies. The service of the caravans mattered crucially to battlefield success and the ability to sustain wars in the interior of the Deccan Plateau, because moving grain from the ports to the interior was not an easy job, and none of the major powers of the time, Hyderabad, Mysore, and the Marathas, had significant access to the sea. Knowing the value of their service, the kings offered the Banjaras immunity and protection. The East India Company had much better access to the sea, but still needed these groups when fighting wars in the interior.[15]

As conflicts increased in frequency, the Banjaras could not stay out of politics. Incentives were offered to induce them to stay loyal to the Company – possibly other powers too followed the same tactics – and breach of contract was punished. In the process, the Company collected a great deal of data on the scale and organisation of the Banjaras around 1790. They found that the Banjaras were formed of two main camps, Rathor and Bartia, together in charge of 170,000 animals, or a combined capacity to carry 10–12,000 tonnes.[16] The figure represents a tiny percentage (possibly just one per cent) of plausible scale of grain production and consumption of the Deccan region. By contrast, the cargo carried by the railway companies operating in the Plateau in 1900 was eight million tonnes. Not surprisingly, the enterprise of the Banjaras declined rapidly after the railways opened up and as a group their

---

[15] Captain John Briggs (Persian interpreter in the Hyderabad court), 'Account of the Origin, History, and Manners of the Race of Men called Bunjaras', *Transactions of the Literary Society of Bombay*, Vol. I, London: John Murray, 1819, 170–97. See also Robert Gabriel Varady, 'North Indian Banjaras: Their Evolution as Transporters', *South Asia*, 2(1), 1979, 1–18; and Joseph Brennig, 'Textile Producers and Production in Late Seventeenth Century Coromandel', *Indian Economic and Social History Review*, 23(4), 1986, 333–55. On the nineteenth century, useful references to the Banjaras can be found in Ravi Ahuja, '"Opening up the Country"? Patterns of Circulation and Politics of Communication in Early Colonial Orissa', *Studies in History*, 20(1), 2004, 73–130; and N. Benjamin, 'The Trade of the Central Provinces of India (1861–1880)', *Indian Economic and Social History Review*, 15(4), 1978, 505–14. On 'crimin-alization', see Bhangiya Bhukya, '"Delinquent Subjects": Dacoity and the Creation of a Surveillance Society in Hyderabad State', *Indian Economic and Social History Review*, 44 (2), 2007, 179–212.

[16] Briggs, 'Account of the Origin'. See also Henry Thomas Colebrooke, *Remarks on the Hus-bandry and Internal Commerce of Bengal*, Calcutta, 1804, 163.

livelihood disappeared. That, however, does not diminish the crucial role they played in feeding armies during a turbulent period in the history of the Deccan.

In the late eighteenth century, cities in the heart of the Mughal Empire were losing people, which would mean that the artisans producing luxury goods lost sponsorship and jobs, and probably had to relocate like the merchants.[17] This sphere of manufacture did not disappear completely from northern India, as we shall see in the next chapter. In some of the princely states, the consumer-owned karkhana (Chapter 2) persisted. In the princely states, the urban artisan industries organised in workshops did exist, with a more explicit role of the merchants in owning them or trading in their wares.[18]

From about 1810, the artisan industries would suffer another shock, increasing import of British textiles into India. The import caused a decline in artisanal production, especially in hand-spun cotton yarn and iron.

Decline of Textile Crafts

A major negative effect of the integration of regions in India with overseas trade was the decline of the artisanal textile industry. From about 1820, a growing quantity of cotton yarn and cloth was being imported from Manchester into India. From three million pounds in 1820, the volume of yarn import reached 31 million in 1860 and stabilised there. Cotton cloth import increased from zero in 1820 to 825 million yards in 1860, about 40 per cent of total cloth consumption.[19] There is little dispute among historians that the importation of textiles of such order caused loss of livelihoods. It is, however, difficult to estimate its scale and implications for the economy at large. There are some indirect estimates of employment loss, but the methods adopted are not perfect, and the presence of part-time household workers in the spinning industry makes employment hard to define.[20]

A measure of cloth and yarn production (1795–1940) based on cotton production and trade produces three interesting results. First, the production of hand-spun yarn fell steadily in the nineteenth century to near zero by 1900. Second, the production of hand-woven cloth displayed a clear U-shape; a fall until the mid-nineteenth century, and a rise thereafter. And third, the peak

---

[17] On data on town size, see Tirthankar Roy, *An Economic History of Early Modern India*, Abingdon and New York: Routledge, 2013.

[18] Nandita Prasad Sahai, *Politics of Patronage and Protest: The State, Society, and Artisans in Early Modern Rajasthan*. Delhi: Oxford University Press, 2006.

[19] Tirthankar Roy, 'Consumption of Cotton Cloth in India, 1795–1940', *Australian Economic History Review*, 52(1), 2012, 61–84.

[20] For a discussion of these measures and the evidence, see Tirthankar Roy, *Rethinking Economic Change in India: Labour and Livelihood*, Abingdon and New York, NY: Routledge, 2005.

period of the fall in both spinning and weaving occurred in 1860–80, which suggests that it was not the British Industrial Revolution as such, nor overseas trade, but railway expansion that caused the most damage to these livelihoods.

Speculating economic impact is difficult because we do not have *any* sources that directly capture the disruption to artisan livelihoods, none at least to do justice to the magnitude of the disruption, and little concrete information on compensatory livelihoods, alternative options, and the real choices made by the suffering artisans. In part, the silence of the sources may reflect the fact that many sufferers (from the fall of hand-spinning) were women working part-time, and the sources available did not think it important to record their distress. A study of craft industries in Bengal shows, furthermore, that industry conditions differed so much that one single story to fit all industries cannot be told.[21] Further, during the peak period of the fall (1860–80), trade in general was rising, as was cotton cultivation, and uncultivated land was still available, all of which make it necessary to know something more definite about available choices than the sources permit.

If the artisan experience is shadowy, can we better interpret the impact of this fall – known in current scholarship as 'deindustrialisation' – upon merchants? Cloth and yarn imports of increasing magnitude came as a profitable opportunity for many British trading firms operating in the ports and their Indian associates. Chapter 4 discusses many examples of British trading firms that went into the textile import business from the 1820s or 1830s. It must surely have caused a huge disruption among businesses formerly engaged in the distribution of handmade yarn and cloth. We know woefully little about this loss, except some impressionistic evidence. For example, Bengali weaver merchants (Seths and Basaks) formed a section among the wealthy citizens of Calcutta in the late eighteenth century. Names of some of the oldest markets and settlements of the city bear witness to their influence. By 1850, the wealthy business elite of the city no longer included this type of merchant. But, then, stories of outsight bankruptcy among textile trading firms are conspicuously rare.

The fall in textile crafts due to the loss of rich customers and mass market affected the economy of the inland cities adversely. Anand Yang's study of Patna shows that a late eighteenth-century boom based on revenue-farming, banking, and manufacturing came to an end around the middle decades of the nineteenth century with the decay of artisanal production. But after that shock, trade and finance revived again in the city, now based on agricultural trade and finance. Patna was a major centre of the new face of trade and banking in the

---

[21] Indrajit Ray, *Bengal Industries and the British Industrial Revolution, 1757–1857*, New York, NY and Abingdon: Routledge, 2011.

late 1800s, and a representative case.[22] This style of trade will be discussed fully in Chapter 4.

Overall, it may be safe to conclude that the merchants coped with the transition better than the artisans did, which would obviously mean that moving money to newer ventures was not as difficult a challenge in the rising cities as moving skills would be. That still leaves us with the interesting finding that handloom cloth production displayed a revival after 1880, a subject to which I will return in Chapter 4.

Rise of a New State

The Company's territorial acquisitions happened in stages between 1765 and 1818. By 1856, when Awadh and Punjab had come into British possession, the balance of political power had shifted in India completely. From long before, capital tended to gravitate towards areas under Company control. The fall of the Mughal Empire led to a shift of enterprise from Hooghly and Surat towards Calcutta and Bombay. The threat of attacks by the Maratha mercenaries based in central India forced many rich Bengalis to migrate from the western districts of Bengal to Calcutta in the 1740s. Madras drew trade away from Masulipatnam, the chief port on the Coromandel belonging to the declining Golconda state. The Parsis left Surat for Bombay, Marwaris from western India went to Calcutta, Telugu merchants from Coromandel to Madras, and Bengalis from western Bengal to Calcutta. The backdrop to these moves was the rising power of the Company.

The British East India Company in 1750 was the largest European trading firm in India, and for some time, its business had been shifting towards Bengal. Several factors were at work behind the shift. Bengal, especially western Bengal, had a good transport system thanks to its numerous rivers. Bengal was well cultivated, and food here was cheaper than elsewhere. The French East India Company threatened the British in Madras, and forced them out of the city in 1746. In Bengal, the British were the stronger force. Bengal also allowed the Company to diversify its export basket from plain or printed cotton, to include muslins, indigo, saltpetre, and opium. The Company was increasingly interested in Chinese tea, and a part of the silver bullion that it imported to pay for Asian trade was diverted into the East Asia trade. Calcutta was a convenient port of transit between Europe and China, especially from the turn of the nineteenth century when Bihar opium began to be used to balance the Europe-China trade.

---

[22] Anand A. Yang, *Bazaar India: Markets, Society and the Colonial State in Bihar*, Berkeley, CA: University of California Press, 1998, Ch. 5.

No wonder then that the origin of British rule in India occurred in Bengal. There was no outright conquest; rather, the formation of the new state happened via four distinct processes of change that were organically linked to trade. One of these was warfare, including Anglo-French military competition in the wake of the War of Austrian Succession (1740–8), and the Seven Years War (1756–63). These conflicts spilled over into battles in India between the two merchant firms. Competition in trade was inextricably linked to military rivalry. The major theatres of the Anglo-French wars were the Carnatic and Bengal regions, and on a minor scale, Mysore and Mauritius during the Napoleonic wars. The British emerged victorious in the most important battles. Long before the last of these engagements, the Treaty of Paris in 1763 had all but destroyed French ambitions in India.

The second process was conflict between the Company and the local state in Bengal, in which the prominent merchants and bankers of Bengal secretly allied with the Company, ensuring the king's downfall. The conflict was partly a trade dispute, though it was complicated by two things. The dispute involved the private merchants' right to conduct tax-free trade in Bengal. Technically, these merchants were rivals of the Company. But the Company officers often took their sides because they worked secretly as trading partners. The second element was the secret support of Indian capitalists. Indian merchants saw their future interests as being better protected by the foreign merchants than by the feudal warlords. The historian Chris Bayly suggested that the emergence of the British Empire was based on an uneasy interdependence between 'Indian forms of capitalism and forces generated by the European world economy'.[23] The intrigues in Bengal were an example of this.

The third process was the reaction in Britain to the Company's acquisitions. Conquest was never a popular idea among the Company's shareholders in London, who resented the expense. The Company did not make a success of its governance either. For a few years, it used taxes in Bengal to fund trade, which caused a scandal. A terrible famine in Bengal (1770) showed how ineffectual the Company was as a state. In reaction to these scandals, the Parliament started playing an active role in the governance of Bengal from 1772. Its first significant move was to appoint an old India hand as the Governor, Warren Hastings, who would initiate administrative, institutional, and military reforms that left a long-term legacy. Between 1772 and 1784, Parliamentary acts enabled the legislature to have oversight of Indian governance, creating the framework of a British-Indian governmental system that would remain in place until the interwar period.

The fourth and final change occurred in the identity of the Company, which transformed itself from a trading firm to a facilitator of trade. When its

---

[23] C. A. Bayly, *Indian Society and the Making of the British Empire*, Cambridge: Cambridge University Press, 1990, 204.

monopoly ended, the textile export trade was already in decline, and the export of indigo and cotton was on the rise. The Company tried to revive its trading fortunes briefly by trying to export cotton, but discovered that it did not have the capacity to organise inland trade, and left these trades to Indian and European merchants. A lucrative export trade did emerge after 1813, in cotton, indigo, and opium, and the Company helped these trades by taking special measures, as we shall examine.

The transformation of the East India Company from a merchant firm into a political power raises the question of how much like a business the Company really was during this time or at any other. Some experts suggest that in its internal management, that is, in the transactions between its directors and employees, the Company resembled the modern multinational company, in that it pursued strategies that enabled the managers to economise on transaction cost and reduce opportunism by agents.[24] This reading does not easily explain the Company's propensity to join politics against the wishes of the directors. Others suggest that the Company's transformation into a state power reveals that the agents or branches enjoyed a great deal of autonomy.[25] As they engaged with local states in a condition of general conflict, the branches armed themselves, and made common cause with private traders who violated the Company's monopoly charter, defying the shareholders and the directors in doing so.

The puzzle about the Company does not end there. When it acquired power in Bengal (1757–65), it was still militarily weak in relation to the biggest forces of the times, the Marathas, the Afghans, Awadh, Hyderabad, and a little later, Mysore. The British did not fight with all of them, they did not need to. More often, alliances between the Company and some Indian powers fought others. The Company had a few major reverses, but in the end prevailed in the most consequential battles. And they did despite a broad uniformity in military technology and strategy between the major contenders. Why they won these battles is a puzzle. One recent study offers a solution by suggesting that the backing of the English Parliament made the Company's promises more credible to most Indian allies than those made by the other Indian states.[26] Another attributes the success to the Company's efforts to raise a standing army, funded by a more efficient fiscal system that took shape after reforms in landed

---

[24] Ann M. Carlos and Stephen Nicholas, '"Giants of an Earlier Capitalism": The Chartered Trading Companies as Modern Multinationals', *Business History Review*, 62(3), 1988, 398–419. See also Santhi Hejeebu, 'Contract Enforcement in the English East India Company', *Journal of Economic History*, 65(4), 2005, 496–523.

[25] Holden Furber, 'Review of A. Mervyn Davies, *Clive of Plassey: A Biography*', New York: Charles Scribner's Sons, 1939, *American Historical Review*, 45(3), 1940, 635–7.

[26] M. Oak, and A. V. Swamy, 'Myopia or Strategic Behavior? Indian Regimes and the East India Company in Late Eighteenth Century India', *Explorations in Economic History*, 49(3), 2012, 352–66.

property right in the late eighteenth-century Bengal, whereas its rivals used unreliable mercenaries or went bankrupt in the process of fighting wars.[27]

What did the political change mean to business in this time? As long as the Company continued to trade, its mutation into a political power may have helped enforcement of contracts with weavers, sometimes by the use of coercion.[28] But the Company soon reduced trading, and after 1800, its main contribution was to nurture private trade passing through Bombay, Calcutta, and Madras.

How did the business of the ports change after British ascendance?

The Business of the Ports

Expatriate enterprise was concentrated in the ports. There were small settlements of Europeans in the interior towns too. From long before the Great Indian Mutiny (1857–8) took the lives of many expatriate merchants in the interior, and the indigo mutiny (1859–60) ended the career of the expatriate indigo planter in the Bengal countryside (see next), business directories and guides discouraged the European from venturing too deep into the countryside. The risk of losing money advanced to local producers and sellers was a serious problem. The boatmen 'abscond soon after the receipt of the money in advance'; or 'the villainy' of the peasant 'may occasion a total loss to the manufacturer'. There was more. 'One of the most embarrassing circumstances to commerce in the upper provinces is the want of a common standard of Weights and Measures.'[29] The chaos continued long into the ascendance of official metrology.

Documents of the Company courts working in the three ports in the mid-to-late eighteenth century hint at another potential problem of doing business in the country. These courts were crucial in overseeing succession and inheritance of mercantile property, because many mercantile disputes concerned succession. It is easy to imagine that a business in the interior would not receive a similar quality of legal redress because the courts and the scope of English law were restricted to the ports.[30] Long after British rule had extended into North India, an inconclusive debate occurred in the Law Commission

---

[27] Roy, *Economic History of Early Modern India.*

[28] Prasannan Parthasarathi, *The Transition to a Colonial Economy: Weavers, Merchants, and Kings in South India, 1720–1800*, Cambridge: Cambridge University Press, 2001; and Om Prakash, 'From Negotiation to Coercion: Textile Manufacturing in India in the Eighteenth Century', *Modern Asian Studies*, 41(5), 2007, 1331–68.

[29] James Purves, *The East India Merchant; or, a Guide to the Commerce and Manufactures of Bengal and the Upper Provinces*, Calcutta, 1819, 4, 17, 21.

[30] Madras Presidency, *Mayor's Court Minutes, 1745–46*, Madras, 1937, 102, 124, 227. Also, Tirthankar Roy and Anand V. Swamy, *Law and the Economy in Colonial India*, Chicago, IL: University of Chicago Press, 2016.

(c. 1840) over whether commercial disputes in the interior should be settled with reference to the 'Law Merchant', which would demand of Indian judges a thorough training in English common law, or of local custom, which was neither coded nor known to anybody in the judicial system.[31] In effect, there were no commercial *lex loci* outside the port city. The message was clear: leave inland trade to Indians. The fear of inland trade began to weaken from the late nineteenth century, when the expansion of the railways and local administration made it easier to penetrate 'up-county', as we shall see in the next section, but Europeans avoided being there physically.

The most lucrative traded goods were opium, indigo, tea, and cotton. Indigo was the main blue dye used in the textile industry. As the cotton spinning industry took off in Britain, the demand for indigo rose too. The Caribbean islands were at first the main sources of supply (around 1790), but the Napoleonic wars made supplies from the Atlantic uncertain. Three regions in India – Bengal, northern India, and Gujarat – were long famous for production and trade in high-quality indigo. The scale of Indian production, however, was small in relation to the new demand.

European investment – mainly British but not exclusively so – in production and processing of indigo in Bengal provided a solution. The investors, misleadingly called 'planters', processed leaves in a factory whereas the leaves were purchased from peasants. The business grew rapidly between 1813 and 1846.[32] Towards the end of the period some of them also owned land, which they were not allowed to do in 1813. Firms in Calcutta financed the operation and marketed the goods. They were trading enterprises, with a banking arm to manage repatriation of profits and do some deposit and lending businesses as well. The six main firms were Palmer, Fergusson, Alexander, Colvin, Macintosh, and Cruttenden. The overlap between indigo trade and banking was a source of risk, as fluctuations in indigo prices invariably caused bad debts to build up. Two such episodes, in 1833 and 1846, finished off many of these hybrid firms.[33]

The trading firms of Calcutta, and a few of Bombay as well, were formed of Indian and European partnership. Private European trading firms in Calcutta started with the 'agency houses'.[34] They either occupied spaces vacated by the Company or engaged in businesses sponsored by it. Some of them were

---

[31] Indian Law Commission, *Copies of the Special Reports of the Indian Law Commissioners*, London: HMSO, 1847, 702, 662. Law merchant was the body of commercial law practised by merchants in medieval Europe.

[32] Ghulam A. Nadri, *The Political Economy of Indigo in India, 1580–1930: A Global Perspective*, Leiden: Brill, 2017.

[33] The history of these hybrid partnerships is now well-researched. See, for example, Anthony Webster, *The Twilight of the East India Company: The Evolution of Anglo-Asian Commerce and Politics, 1790–1860*, Rochester: Boydell and Brewer, 2009.

[34] Amales Tripathi, *Trade and Finance in the Bengal Presidency, 1793–1833*, Calcutta: Oxford University Press, 1979, 2nd ed.

branches or representatives of trading firms established in Britain, and some were set up by former Company employees who had completed indenture. From this pool, which drew in Scottish, Welsh, English, German, and French capitalists, some traders moved inland and set up indigo-processing factories. Others remained in Calcutta and conducted the three major functions connected with indigo: shipping, financing, and insurance. Most of these merchants and their offshoots went out of business during the indigo speculations of the 1830s and the 1840s. A famous case of boom and bust was Paxton, Cockerell, Trail – later Palmer and Co. The son of William Palmer, a Company officer and a contemporary of Hastings, established the firm. Palmer and Co. was a partnership between the brothers George and John Horsley Palmer, and their main business was indigo trade.[35] Fig. 3.2 displays a contemporary drawing of a business area of the city.

There were several Indo-European firms as well. Three significant partnerships were Carr Tagore, Oswald Seal, and Rustomji Turner. Others such as Ramdulal Dey acquired wealth as a broker, in this case of American merchants. The commercial crises of the 1830s and 1840s either ended these firms or made them irrelevant. Possibly the only example of an indigenous trading firm from the indigo-opium phase which survived into the twentieth century was Prawnkissen Law.

The failure of the agency houses of Calcutta occurred in two episodes, 1829–33, and 1846–7. Both episodes were triggered by indigo price fluctuations. However, they affected a somewhat different set of actors. The 1829–33 crash ended the career of a generation of mainly European agency houses, like Palmer. Some of the same actors joined new ones to float a new set of trading houses. In the process, their interests diversified from indigo to coal, sugar, silk, inland shipping, tea, and the import of British goods. The most prominent firm of the time, Carr, Tagore, also started a bank: the Union Bank. Dwarkanath Tagore (1794–1847), who led the firm, started his early life as a landlord, reportedly an efficient but ruthless one, and invested profits from land in a variety of businesses. He did this so successfully that Carr, Tagore acquired a brand image for management, and was invited to manage ventures floated by other people. Thus, Carr, Tagore, Blair Kling suggests, set a pattern that was to evolve into the managing agency system in later years (see Chapter 5).[36] Tagore died in England in 1847, when the second crash was in full swing. Carr, Tagore might have survived had he lived in Calcutta then, but

---

[35] Anthony Webster, 'An Early Global Business in a Colonial Context: The Strategies, Management, and Failure of John Palmer and Company, 1780–1830', *Enterprise & Society*, 6, no. 1 (2005), 98–133.

[36] Blair Kling, 'The Origin of the Managing Agency System in India', *Journal of Asian Studies*, 26(1), 1966, 37–47.

Fig. 3.2 Burrabazar, Calcutta

Burra Bazaar, Calcutta. The Burra Bazaar, or 'great market'. 'On the right, sitting under an awning, are two money-changers; on the left is a fakeer begging alms, and selling charms. Two merchants, a Jew and a Mogul, occupy the middle of the foreground; and a Durwan, or doorkeeper, sits on a rattan stool on the left' (original description from Capt. R. Jump, *Views in Calcutta*, 1837). Compared with this description, a hundred years later, Burrabazar was predominantly a Marwari cluster containing residences, offices, shops, and warehouses.
© British Library

the other partners of the firm had poorer credit and adverse reputation. The failure of the Union Bank sealed its fate, and the firm closed its doors in 1848. The surviving partners regrouped and floated new enterprises, which had an undistinguished history. More significant survivals were some of the ventures supported by Carr, Tagore itself, the Assam Company in tea, for example.

Opium again was an old and familiar article of trade in India, which grew thanks to a new market for Indian opium in China. After 1813, the Company still held a monopoly in China trade, and was interested in buying Chinese tea in Canton. At first paid for with silver, the tea began to be financed with the sale proceeds of opium. In India, the trade and almost all of the shipping were done by private traders, Europeans and Indians in Calcutta, and Indians in Bombay. In Calcutta, the processed opium came from Bihar districts, whereas in Bombay, opium came from the princely states in central India. Marwari merchants, as we have seen, played a role in the inland trade. So did the Parsis.

As for indigo, profits from opium stimulated shipping, banking, insurance, remittance, trading companies, and auction houses, and were in turn invested in coal mining, ship-building, tea estates, construction, and some of the pioneering factories of Bombay and Calcutta. The three ports also exported a great deal of raw cotton first to China and then to Britain, and started to import cotton yarn and piece-goods in large quantities from 1810. The effect of these businesses upon trade volumes was not very large until 1831, but shipping tonnage rose from less than 300,000 tonnes of cargo from the three leading ports in 1831 to over three million in 1858.

One of the Bombay merchants engaged in all this, Charles Forbes, began his career in China trade and shipping and developed a wide range of partnerships with Parsi shippers and merchants. Forbes also contributed to a singular development of lending money to the government. The first major loan made out by Forbes and Co. and Bruce, Fawcett and Co. in 1813 is believed to have started a public debt market in western India. The East India Company had taken loans before from Indian bankers, the Trawadi Arjunji Nathji of Surat being famous among the Company's creditors. Arjunji Nathji financed the Arabian Sea trade in the late eighteenth century when he shrewdly switched to be the Company's banker.[37] In a period of warfare, such moves had political implications. By contrast, the loans made out by a group of merchants were less political in intent.

Similar firms in Madras had a slightly different set of trading interests. The Welshman Thomas Parry arrived in Madras in 1788 and formed a partnership with a Madras merchant, whose main business was banking and insurance.[38] At the end of the century, Parry was on his own, doing marine insurance, and

---

[37] Lakshmi Subramanian, *Three Merchants of Bombay*, New Delhi: Penguin, 2016.
[38] G. H. Hodgson, *Thomas Parry: Free Merchant, Madras, 1768–1824*, Madras: Higginbothams, 1938.

suffered some losses during the Napoleonic wars. After 1801, he entered the first of many industrial ventures, a tannery, and in 1806, entered the indigo trade. None of these new avenues made him much money. At the same time, Parry became involved in what was known as the Carnatic debt scandal (1809). It was believed that some of the bonds issued by the late Nawab of Carnatic to his creditors were forged. Parry held Carnatic bonds, and suspecting that some of the holders of the forged bonds would push for redemption first, raised an alarm. Parry already had an uneasy relationship with the Madras authorities, and the scandal forced him to leave the city. In 1818, William Dare joined the firm, Parry, Dare, and put the house in better shape. When Thomas Parry died in 1823, the firm was established on a firmer footing. Between 1823 and 1842, the business of the company diversified from being a banking and shipping agency to managing coffee estates in Mysore and cotton export trades. Parry, Dare was one of the creditors of a pioneering iron manufactory at Porto Novo (see next), and lost money on it.

The Scottish firm James Finlay began in 1765 as a cotton mill owner and textile trader in Scotland and continental Europe. In the 1830s, it started buying cotton from India and in 1862, opened a branch in Bombay. Finlay later expanded into South Indian tea plantations, and also owned cotton mills in Bombay and jute mills in Calcutta.

At the end of the eighteenth century, John Binny was a private merchant, who changed occupation from medicine to trading in Madras. His firm maintained the maritime connection. Later in the nineteenth century, that connection took the form of a handling agency on behalf of the British India Steam Navigation and the Madras Port Trust. Binny and Co. owned boats and barges, took part in coast-to-coast trade, and expanded into caravan trade, as the Calcutta firm Bird did in north Bihar (Chapter 5). In the late nineteenth century, Binny (like Parry and Finlay) started manufacturing, and owned the Buckingham Mill, one of the largest cotton textile mills in South India.

The Company government was heavily involved in the new commerce. Opium was cultivated under government licence in Bihar (the licensing system came in place between 1772 and 1786). In Bihar, the government collected a tax on the profits; in central India, it collected a transit tax. In China, the Company's power was of crucial help to shelter foreign traders from the Chinese state, which did not like the trade. In turn, the opium revenues were an important item of government income until the 1870s. The government policy with respect to cotton was to encourage large-scale cotton plantations in the American pattern, but these efforts did not become profitable for the entrepreneurs. The government was less involved in the indigo trade, but did get drawn into legislation on contracts in the light of disputes that occurred in indigo sales. From the 1840s, Calcutta emerged as a transit port for shipment of indentured labour to tropical colonies, a flow that was to grow into one of the biggest migrations of free (that is, post-slavery) labour in history.[39] Again, the government was involved both as a facilitator and as a regulator.

These trades left a colourful legacy. From today's perspective, they also raised serious moral issues. But using the present-day perspective to judge the past is always unreliable, and can give us a biased and distorted view of nineteenth-century trade. Opium was a prohibited substance in China, and the trade carried on thanks to the enterprise of the coastal Chinese merchants and the muscle power of the Company combined. It may seem that the Company was pushing drugs. Substance abuse, however, was not yet a global concern, and opium was extensively and legally consumed within India. Indigo trade likewise involved moral issues because the planters and their Bengali executives often employed coercion to enforce contracts. The level of acceptability of coercion and violence in trade was greater in 1850 than it is today, not necessarily because the Europeans were everywhere bullying the peaceful Asians, but violence was routinely used to enforce compliance within local societies as well. The European planter did not do anything the Bengali landlord or zamindar would not do to a peasant whose rent was in default, which was to beat him up in a special room made for the purpose.

Returning to the subject of the cities where these trades were concentrated, the trades left different sorts of legacy. They transformed some firms from traders to industrialists. Tata or Sassoon made money in commodity trade and invested in textiles. There was nothing similar between opium and cloth, except the people who moved money from one to the other over a generation. The new wealth changed the cultural life of the port cities. The Company state from the late 1700s sponsored classical Indian learning because it saw Sanskrit and Persian legal texts as a possible foundation for a system of Indian law. Some European merchants, scholars, and officers took to this enterprise, and produced painstaking works in the process. The rich Indian merchants did not care much for Indian classics, but wanted an English education as well as scientific and technical education in Calcutta and Bombay. Thus, the philanthropist and publicist Jagannath Sankarsett, himself from a business family, was instrumental in the establishment of the Elphinstone College in Bombay (c. 1840). Meanwhile, Cowasjee Jehangir and Dwarkanath Tagore of Carr, Tagore and Matilal Seal of Oswald Seal donated money and land to the Calcutta Medical College; Jamsetjee Jejeebhoy donated money to the Grant Medical College in Bombay; and Cowasji Jehangir of the Readymoney family

---

[39] On indigo, opium, and cotton trades of the early nineteenth century, see Tirthankar Roy, *India in the World Economy from Antiquity to the Present*, Cambridge: Cambridge University Press, 2012. On the contractual disputes in these trades, read R. E. Kranton and A. V. Swamy, 'Contracts, Hold-up, and Exports: Textiles and Opium in Colonial India', *American Economic Review*, 98(5), 2008, 967–89, and Roy and Swamy, *Law and the Economy in Colonial India*.

Fig. 3.3 Premchand Roychand, merchant of Bombay, in the nineteenth
century (see text)
© Premchand Family Archives

and Premchand Roychand (see Fig. 3.3) donated to the University of Bombay.
These efforts enhanced the cosmopolitan profile of the cities, and the cosmopolitan outlook of groups like the Parsis or the urban Bengali.

Alongside trading firms, banking firms emerged too, but they had quite an
unstable career.

Strong Trade, Weak Banking

Corporate banking began in India in the early 1800s in two ways. The trading firms of Calcutta, known as the agency houses, did banking on the side. At the same time, joint stock banks were started too. The main clients of both types of firms were traders in the port cities, government servants, and expatriate military personnel. Remittance of money between India and Britain on account of trade and income transfers were the main businesses conducted by the agency houses, and in this business, the bills issued by the East India Company were their competitor. With banking founded on such a narrow and shaky basis, it was not surprising that one bad trading season could potentially cause a contagious crisis. The banking licence or charter limited the liability of the corporate banks, but not all corporate banks operated with charters. In any case, when a crisis happened, the Europeans could take recourse to insolvency law and escape personal ruin, but their Indian associates could not do so.[40] By the 1840s, a new style of banks, exchange banks, emerged to finance trade especially between India, China, Ceylon, Mauritius, Southeast Asia, and Australia. Three of these – the Oriental Bank (1845), the Chartered Bank of India, Australia and China (1857), and the Chartered Mercantile Bank of India London and China (1858) – were either registered in London or started in India and shifted base to London. In the 1890s, the *Economist* magazine called this set the Eastern Banks.[41]

Although the Company gave banking licences reluctantly, joint stock banks did develop because the traders needed them. A small subset of these banks, formed of the Bank of Bengal, Bank of Bombay, and Bank of Madras, was part-owned by the government and did the government's own transactions, from credit to discounting to note issue. This custom gave them some stability. But most private banks suffered high mortality.[42] The reason for this was the interdependence between banking and trading, and in turn, reliance of trade on one or two agricultural goods that did not have a stable market. When the export basket diversified after 1860, joint stock banking, still tied to agricultural exports, became a steadier business. Indigo was always risky because the price fluctuated a lot. But that was not the main reason behind the financial crises that occurred in Calcutta. What with money being scarce in general, banking suffered from a propensity towards insider lending. In 1833,

---

[40] Amiya Kumar Bagchi, 'Transition from Indian to British Indian Systems of Money and Banking 1800–1850', *Modern Asian Studies*, 19(3), 1985, 501–19.

[41] John McGuire, 'The Rise and Fall of the Oriental Bank in the Nineteenth Century: A Product of the Transformations That Occurred in the World Economy or the Result of Its Own Mismanagement', paper presented at the 15th Biennial Conference of the Asian Studies Association of Australia, Canberra, 2004.

[42] Bagchi, 'Transition from Indian to British Indian Systems of Money and Banking 1800–1850'.

a loss of its financial business brought down Palmer. In 1846 the failure of the Union Bank (1829–47), an Indo-European partnership, was especially damaging.[43]

In Bombay, stockbroking was a new pursuit and one indirectly linked to trade, in that money moved between commodity and share trading. The stock exchange started in 1855. The cotton exchange was set up in 1844. A shortage of American cotton in Britain during the American Civil War, and consequent rush for Indian cotton, raised prices many times. When this happened, merchant profits were used to buy shares in newly floated companies, in banking and in real estate. In 1860, there were sixty share-brokers in the city, and their leader was a thirty-year-old Gujarati Jain named Premchand Roychand. At the peak of the cotton famine, there were two hundred individuals recognised as brokers, and Roychand ruled the financial market like a king.

Before the boom, Roychand was a cotton shipper, with interests in opium and gold, and partner of Ritchie Steuart and Co. His role as a broker to the Liverpool merchant Steuart meant that he was to 'guarantee the firm against any losses which it may incur in its advances on cotton and other shipments to a variety of dealers'. And this he could do because of his intimate knowledge of 'the financial position of almost all the large wealthy traders in cotton and opium'.[44] At the height of the cotton famine, Roychand started to procure advance information on Liverpool prices. He sent out small boats into the coastal waters when a Liverpool ship was due in the harbour. The British partner would often supply privileged information to the ship captain that would, via the boat people, reach the warehouse of the cotton-trading firm a day before it reached everyone else.[45] A word from Roychand was a guarantee of quality in any new enterprise.

When the price of cotton started falling at the end of the boom (1865–66), the financial and real estate crash led the trading world of Bombay to bankruptcy. The crash brought many new companies down along with the share-brokers. The bounce back in Bombay, however, was quite quick. It was evident that the financial system had acquired certain strengths despite the speculation. When the business picked up again, the brokers had a new instrument to transact in: shares in cotton textile mills.

The cosmopolitan character of the cities attracted artisans and adventurers. The first significant moves to set up factory industry arose from these pools of migrants, and occurred in iron, a material found in plenty in India.

---

[43] Blair B. Kling, *Partner in Empire: Dwarkanath Tagore and the Age of Enterprise in Eastern India*, Berkeley and Los Angeles, CA: University of California Press, 1981.

[44] D. E. Wacha, *Premchund Roychund: His Early Life and Career*, Bombay: Times of India Press, 1913, 41.

[45] Ibid., 44–5.

Industrial Firms

In the eighteenth century, iron was imported in growing volumes from Britain into India. Some of it was consumed by the Company itself as cannons, gun parts, or construction material. The Company's informants told the Indian officers that iron ore and charcoal were available in the near vicinity of Calcutta and Madras, and that an extensive household industry in iron smelting existed in the rural areas. But, typically, these areas were hilly and forested and the administration had limited reach. Extensive iron smelting carried on in these areas, almost always in tiny tribal hamlets by small teams. Adventurous individuals, including people who had been iron masters in England and wished to seek fortunes in Asia, offered to start large-scale charcoal smelting factories in these regions. The Company was willing to offer them forest lease and a captive market.

Andrew Duncan in Birbhum, one Davis and a Drummond in the Kumaon hills, and perhaps most famously, Josiah Marshall Heath of the Porto Novo works near Madras, were the best-known iron masters who came to India between 1812 (Duncan) and 1825 (Porto Novo). The Calcutta partnership firm George, Jessop started a foundry a little before Porto Novo, which did not have an iron smelting unit tied to it, and possibly for that reason, survived into the twentieth century.

Smelting shops, on the other hand, faced particularly high trade costs. Almost all the pioneering factories in iron smelting failed; some, like the Porto Novo firm, failed after decades of struggle. They failed not because the government was indifferent. If anything, the relationship between the Company and these firms was especially close. Both parties underestimated the huge difficulties involved in making a success of an iron factory in the British model. Costs of transporting wood for charcoal or iron ore was large in the Deccan Plateau which did not have big rivers. The factories could not easily attract and retain European foremen. If smelting was conceived on a large scale, mining happened on old methods, and capital in India was expensive unless one belonged in established banking communities. The existence of the Indo-European trading-cum-banking firms of Calcutta, one of which (Alexander) financed Porto Novo, did not do much to cheapen capital for industrial enterprise, because their main business, indigo, was highly unstable.

Towards the end of the time span covered in this chapter, a new industry of great promise was beginning to grow in India: tea plantations. Tea drinking became a national habit in Britain in the eighteenth century, and tea became one of the main articles of trade between Britain and China. Substitution of Chinese tea with tea grown in India had been an ambition of individuals associated with the Company for nearly fifty years, before experiments in Assam showed this to be a feasible commercial proposition. Encouraged by these experiments, the first Company-sponsored tea estate came up in 1839. The biggest growth of private enterprise in tea, however, was to occur later (Chapter 4).

Conclusion

What had changed between 1750 and 1850 in the business environment of India? In the political sphere, the most obvious change was that a new and powerful state had emerged from the eighteenth-century turmoil. The new state emerged from maritime trade. That fact alone would not explain why it was keen to sponsor maritime trade. After all, its own business interests had declined. It was keen to do so because Britain wanted Indian indigo and tea; opium emerged as a bridge between Europe and Asian trades; trades generated revenue; Parsi and Indo-European firms demonstrated the profitability of the India-China-Britain business exchanges; and India offered fields of investment and employment for British resources. In different ways these new forces, it was thought, would sustain the economy of a mainly maritime state. Politics and globalisation, in other words, reinforced one another.

The port cities in these years saw a new style of firms emerge. They formed of clusters of migrants, were experimental and opportunistic rather than tradition-bound, and were interested in trading agricultural goods (indigo, opium, tea) rather than craft goods. Some of them functioned as partnerships in the British style, some as family firms in the Indian style, while others were still built around the entrepreneurship of single individuals. Weak financial systems plagued this set throughout. The conditions did not rule out enterprise and investment, but added a great deal of risk. These years, therefore, were not yet ripe for structural change. Trade volumes, and possibly average incomes, changed little.[46] Industrial entrepreneurship was a story of one failure after another.

The end of the agency houses appeared to remove the type of Indo-European ventures that had dominated Calcutta in the early nineteenth century, and defined the emergence of modern enterprise in the city. Did their decline signify a failure of entrepreneurship, especially Bengali entrepreneurship? Did this retreat somehow owe to the consolidation of colonial power? These readings can be questioned. Increasingly, the nineteenth-century globalisation demanded a more capital-intensive and multinational type of trading firms (like Volkart or Ralli, see Chapter 4) to operate in international commerce, a

---

[46] Stephen Broadberry, Johann Custodis, and Bishnupriya Gupta, 'India and the Great Divergence: An Anglo-Indian Comparison of GDP per Capita, 1600–1871', *Explorations in Economic History*, 56(1), 2015, 58–75.

demand these India-bound entities were too small and too undercapitalised to meet. In this environment, indigenous firms often retreated to local trade supplying the highways of overseas trade, and Bengalis continued to be engaged in that sphere. Overseas trade at the same time was reorganised under big and adequately capitalised companies. It was the cost of capital, not entrepreneurial deficiency or colonialism, that ended the Indo-European partnership firms that had once dominated commodity trades like indigo.

Still, these years and the new enterprises that formed in the cities initiated two deeper processes that would make a big difference in the late 1800s. First, business organisation was being established on a firmer footing partly in response to the risks. Towards the end of this period, we see commercial law, partnership, even joint stock companies, and managing agency, being used more extensively than before. Second, the most important livelihood of the region, agriculture, was beginning to join maritime trade. This unprecedented integration of the two spheres of business – the land and the sea, agriculture and foreign trade – was a revolution in the making. The process was limited and patchy to begin with, and involved a few special goods. It would not succeed without government intervention. Still, these trades of the port cities were starting to reshape the interior business world. There were Indian and European trading firms who sold cotton, indigo, and opium, Marwari and Gujarati bankers and share-brokers who took part in the speculative bubbles, and numerous Indian importers of cotton textiles from Britain to India.

With the opening of the railways and the joining of the grain trade in the export market, the integration of land and sea and the crossovers of people between agricultural and maritime trades reached another level, as we learn in Chapter 4.

4 Capital and Empire (1850–1930): Trade and Finance

After the British Crown took over administration of the Company's territories in India (1858) the integration of agricultural production with overseas trade was built on a stronger foundation than before, based on modern transport and communication infrastructure, administrative and military integration of the interior with the coast, and a legal framework. The imperial state intervened in the economy mainly by legislating on property and contract. Whereas the aim of property law was to ensure revenue, the aim of the latter was to integrate the Indian economy with the Britain-centred world economy.[1] Standardisation of law was a vital matter for the British Empire, which functioned as a giant customs union with few formal barriers to the movement of goods, capital, and labour between its parts. Standardisation of commercial law was a condition for this setup to work.

Trade volume grew manifold. Businesses specialised into segments. Three nineteenth-century technologies – railways, steamships, and the telegraph – greatly reduced trade costs.[2] Laws helped joint-stock and limited liability to be used more widely.[3] Companies formed in manufacturing, in trading, and in banking. What did these companies do? Most firms, corporate or family run, Indian or European, either traded directly or had an interest tied to trade.

Historians observe that trade was free in this time within the imperial sphere. In fact, free factor movement was a more significant thing than free trade. From about 1860, British capital inflow into India increased,

---

[1] Tirthankar Roy and Anand V. Swamy, *Law and the Economy in Colonial India*, Chicago, IL: University of Chicago Press, 2016.

[2] John Hurd II, 'Railways and the Expansion of Markets in India 1861–1921', *Explorations in Economic History*, 12(4), 1975, 263–288; John Hurd II, 'Railways', in Dharma Kumar, ed., *Cambridge Economic History of India*. Vol. 2: 1757–1970, Cambridge: Cambridge University Press, 1983. For a recent survey of research on trade costs, Dan Bogart and Latika Chaudhary, 'Railways in Colonial India: An Economic Achievement?' in Latika Chaudhary, Bishnupriya Gupta, Tirthankar Roy, and Anand V. Swamy, *A New Economic History of Colonial India*, Abingdon and New York, NY: Routledge, 2015, 140–60.

[3] On the legal foundations of corporate growth, see Radheshyam Rungta, *The Rise of Business Corporations in India 1851–1900*, Cambridge: Cambridge University Press, 1970.

69

along with migration. It was easy for a company based in India to hire managers and technicians from abroad and sometimes to borrow abroad. The balance of payments bears witness to the fact that businesses were doing this on a large scale. Trade was ordinarily in surplus, and the surplus balanced a net payment for services purchased abroad, both by the government and private enterprise, and transfers made by the British working in India.

As the financial system expanded to be able to fund trade, agricultural business boomed. While corporate banks and big indigenous banking firms financed mainly merchants, some of the money they invested every season filtered through the hands of medium- and small-scale moneylending firms down to the peasant cultivators. A part of the trading and banking profits earned in agricultural trade were re-invested in industry. The main industries, cotton and jute textiles, processed agricultural raw materials. An experience in trading these goods made the move to industry more likely.

The singular feature of capitalism in this time, therefore, was interdependence between trade, finance, and industry. The glue holding these three parts together was agricultural trade. Money made in one activity helped the others develop, and this interdependence imparted a certain stability on the balance of payments. Without the export of agricultural commodities, such as grain and cotton, the cost of purchases such as overseas capital and labour could not be paid for.

These benefits of an integrated economic system were confined to the port cities, and towns closely linked to the major ports. Railway networks did not penetrate deep enough, and roads feeding into the railways were often seasonal, of poor quality, or non-existent. The difficulties of doing business in India did not discourage modern corporate enterprise, but confined it to the cities where there was a concentration of big merchants and bankers, where institutions worked better, and more new ideas passed by.

Chapter 4 describes the evolution of modern business firms in the backdrop of the emergence of an integrated economic system based on agricultural trade. Trade itself is a good point to begin from.

Commercialisation

Table 4.1 and Figs. 4.1–4.4 process data available from national income research and official trade statistics. Of the two series, the national income one is constructed by multiplying employment with an estimated average income. The average income figure tends to underestimate capitalist incomes, because it is hard to estimate profits in trade. Therefore, we now live with the absurdity that whereas

Table 4.1 *Measures of growth (annual percentage change) in agriculture, trade, and modern industry: 1872–1947*

	Agriculture	Trade		Manufacturing	GDP	Population
		Volume	Income			
1872–99	0.7[a]	7.5[b]	NA[a]	10.2[a]	0.9[a]	0.4[d]
1900–47	0.3[d]	2.4[b]	1.6[c]	3.8[d]	1.1[d]	0.7

All growth rates are exponential based on the series.

a. Alan Heston, 'National Income', in Dharma Kumar, ed., *Cambridge Economic History of India*, Vol. 2, Cambridge: Cambridge University Press, 1983. Heston does not report trade separately from services for this period. Growth rate of all services was 0.6 per cent.

b. Tonnage of cargo handled in Indian ports and all railways, India, *Statistical Abstracts of British India*, Calcutta: various years.

c. S. Sivasubramonian, *National Income of India in the Twentieth Century*, New Delhi: Oxford University Press, 2000. National income at 1938–39 prices, for agriculture, 'commerce and other transport' and manufacturing, respectively.

d. Kingsley Davis's estimate, cited in Leela Visaria and Pravin Visaria, 'Population', in Dharma Kumar, ed., *Cambridge Economic History of India*, Vol. 2, Cambridge: Cambridge University Press, 1983.

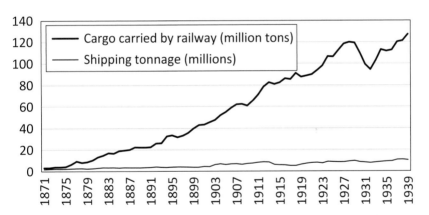

Fig. 4.1 Goods handled by ports and railways: 1871–1937 (m tonnes)
Source: India, *Statistical Abstracts of British India*, Calcutta or Delhi: Government Press, various years

real income generated in trade increased about three or four times between 1800 and 1940, volume of trade increased more than a hundred times. Trade figures possibly include some double-counting, but these are still a more realistic measure of commercialisation than national income data.

No matter, both data sets establish that the capitalist sectors – trade and manufacturing – did extremely well in colonial India. Since trade was much larger of the two in the volume of income created, overall growth was driven more by commerce than industry. Agriculture did not do well, and agricultural incomes even dragged down overall growth. The statement would not hold equally well for all regions, but overall, and relative to trade and manufacturing, agriculture moved slowly. Capitalists gained more than the peasants. This finding can be explained in two alternative ways; that capitalists exploited the peasants, possibly aided by colonial law or imperial power, or that productivity of land was low due to geographical reasons, so that the return to cultivation was depressed even as the return to capital was high. Marxist historians favour the former story. I do not think they are right, because the explanation would not easily account for regional variations in peasant fortunes. It would not hold, for example, in Punjab canal colonies as well as the arid Deccan Plateau. A productivity account, on the other hand, can explain the stagnation in peasant income on average, without forcing us to believe that all regions took part in commercialisation in the same way.

The numbers behind the growth of trade are impressive, from 1 million tonnes in 1840 to 160 million in 1940 (see Chapter 1). The major part of the growth occurred in goods carried by the railways. Certainly, the railways drew some business away from boats, carts, and caravans. But the difference in efficiency between the railways and these other systems was so large that it is safe to assume that the new system enabled a lot more trade than before, and increased profitability of trade. Railway studies confirm the conjecture. This conclusion applies with particular relevance in the Deccan Plateau where pre-railway bulk transportation system consisted of the extremely slow and labour-intensive bullock caravans. Although the ports show up in Fig. 4.1 as a minor carrier of goods, this is an illusion. The railways carried raw agricultural produce like grain and cotton, while the ports carried high-valued textiles or tea, in addition to grain or cotton.

What did this commercial boom mean for the economy? To answer this question, I return to national income data and combine a set of indirect estimates available for the early nineteenth century with the data set available for the early twentieth century. Economists conventionally analyse national income through the threefold division, primary, secondary, and tertiary sectors. The division is not necessarily useful for business history, since the tertiary sector combines two very dissimilar entities, public administration and private trade, and the practice overstates the difference between manufacturing and trade. If what is said before about the interdependence between these activities is true, we should club these together instead. Therefore, I follow a different division. Agriculture remains a class by itself. But the rest of the economy is divided into governmental and private.

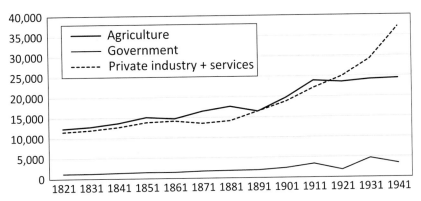

Fig. 4.2 Real net output (Rs. m) in 1946–7 prices
Sources:
1821–1871: Stephen Broadberry, Johann Custodis, and Bishnupriya Gupta, 'India and the Great Divergence: An Anglo-Indian Comparison of GDP per Capita, 1600–1871', *Explorations in Economic History*, 56(1), 2015, 58–75, Table 11 (Indian Real Output 1600–1871) used to convert 1871 Net Product figures from Alan Heston's 'National Income', in Dharma Kumar, ed., *The Cambridge Economic History of India*, Vol. 2, Cambridge: Cambridge University Press, 1983
1871–1901: Heston's 'National Income'.
1901–1941: S. Sivasubramonian's series of Real Net Output (1938–39 prices) converted into Alan Heston's 1901 levels, *National Income of India in the Twentieth Century*, New Delhi: Oxford University Press, 2000

Fig. 4.2 shows an acceleration in private enterprise around 1870. Agricultural growth was significant until about 1920. Thereafter agricultural growth decelerated, and growth in private capitalistic enterprise continued. This long-term divergence between peasant agriculture and capitalistic enterprise is fundamental to understanding what was going right and what was wrong with Indian economic growth during the time of the British Raj. Capitalism went right. Peasant production went wrong. Underlying the divergence between peasants and capitalists was a divergence in productivity of the two activities. This is shown with 1900–47 data in Fig. 4.3. There was 'modern' economic growth driven by productivity gains in trade and manufacturing, and absence of modern economic growth in agriculture (Fig. 4.3). The divergence in per capita incomes had also been owed to population growth, which was slow in the nineteenth century and rapid in the twentieth (Fig. 4.4).

The weakness of agriculture is not of concern in this book, but the robustness of capitalism is. These activities had three main parts: trade, finance, and industry. It is useful to discuss how business conditions and organisations changed in these three activities in mutual interaction.

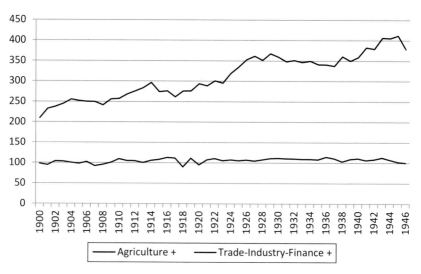

Fig. 4.3 Net output per person (Rs. in 1938–9 prices)
Source: S. Sivasubramonian, *National Income of India in the Twentieth Century*, New Delhi: Oxford University Press, 2000

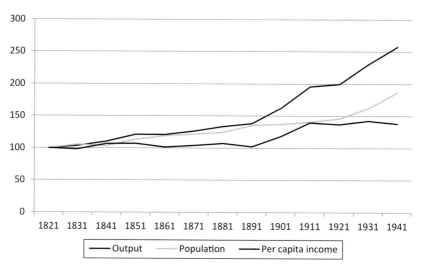

Fig. 4.4. Real net output (1821 = 100) and population 1821–1941
Source: See under Fig. 4.2

The Meaning of Trade

Interpretations of trading in colonial India have long been overburdened by a Marxist-nationalist preoccupation with power, the question being – how did Indian traders manage to function in a world where the colonial state must have favoured European merchants? The question is not particularly useful because the working of colonial power in the field of business cannot be clearly defined or observed. Unlike in the New World and parts of Africa, where the European settler population manipulated law to grab land and impose labour servitude, the British Empire did not create institutions that favoured the settlers.[4] Informally, expatriate officers and managers dined and clubbed together, but beyond the occasional anecdote, how those social ties translated into business advantage, nobody knows.[5]

The Marxists assumed that Indian traders played second fiddle, were compradors or agents of the foreigners.[6] Alternative views have developed mainly in reaction to this presumption. The historian Rajat Ray, for example, accepts that the expatriates were the 'ascendant' and dominant forces.[7] But the Indian traders, Ray suggests, possessed unique advantages in an expatriate-dominated commercial system. Calling them 'bazaar firms', Ray shows that the bazaar formed an important link between the European firms and the Indian peasants. Claude Markovits, in the same spirit, accepts the position that the Europeans dominated the highways of trade, but stresses 'the ability of South Asian merchants to maintain significant areas of independent international operations throughout the period of European economic and political domination'.[8] The word independence here presumes a significant dependence to begin with.

---

[4] Tirthankar Roy, 'The British Empire and the Economic Development of India 1858–1947', *Revista de Historia Economica – Journal of Iberian and Latin American Economic History*, 34 (2), 2016, 209–36.

[5] A well-known application of the idea is that the large British-owned corporate banks discriminated against Indian borrowers; see Amiya Kumar Bagchi, *The Evolution of the State Bank of India, Vol. 2, The Era of the Presidency Banks 1876–1920*, New Delhi: State Bank of India and Sage Publications, 1997, 48. The theory of racial discrimination in the credit market can be seen as a special case of the theory of business group formation, which posits a distinction between an insider and an outsider credit markets; except that racial discrimination is not a necessary explanation for such dual markets to exist. Information asymmetry between lenders and borrowers can explain it better, because *every* banker, whether Indian or European, practised discrimination with respect to potential clients.

[6] For example, Amalendu Guha, 'The Comprador Role of Parsi Seths 1750–1850', *Economic and Political Weekly*, 5(48), 1970 1933–6.

[7] Rajat Ray, ed., *Entrepreneurship and Industry in India, 1800–1947*, Delhi: Oxford University Press, 1992, 13–30; also G. Balachandran, ed., *India in the World Economy 1850–1950*, Delhi: Oxford University Press, 10, 35.

[8] 'Structure and Agency in the World of Asian Commerce during the Era of European Colonial Domination (c. 1750–1950)', *Journal of the Economic and Social History of the Orient*, 502/3), 2007, 106–23; *The Global World of Indian Merchants, 1750–1947: Traders of Sind from Bukhara to Panama*, Cambridge: Cambridge University Press, 2008.

I do not find much value in the language of dependence and independence. The implied hierarchy between a dirty bazaar where betel-chewing Indians felt at home, and the air-conditioned office of the multinational company, is an orientalist fiction. In a different context, Morris David Morris urged the business historian to understand co-existence of ethnicities in terms of comparative advantages. 'Where knowledge is imperfect and is distributed differently among groups,' Morris wrote, 'the reactions to any economic situation will be varied.'[9] This, I find, is a more acceptable approach than the hierarchical one.

Europeans concentrated in overseas trades. Indian firms controlled overland trades feeding into the seaports. Indians also dominated banking, especially that part of it which financed agricultural operations and post-harvest trade. Indians alone could conduct the kind of financial transactions needed to fund peasant production. Land trade and sea trade imposed different kinds of demand upon credit transactions, in turn leading to hard, but not fixed, segmentation between the two spheres of trade. Indians knew the countryside better and the Europeans knew the intercontinental trade and potential partners in London or Liverpool better, and many were afraid of the countryside. One side could not function without the other, thanks to the integration between the land and sea trades. The ethnic divide derived from the need to specialise in different parts of the system by using different resources. Further, although Indians were more dominant in land trade whereas most sea trade firms were Europeans, there were significant exceptions to this rule.

Indian traders in the early 1800s understood this interdependence well enough, and defended Company's rule. That sentiment served the Raj especially well during the great Indian Mutiny in 1857–8, when the crucial supply zones that started from the port cities functioned smoothly, and numerous merchants in these cities and in the besieged ones in the interior expressed support for the Empire. Without the support of Indian businesses of the time, the British would have lost their Indian rule in 1858. Again, from a presentist perspective, we can dismiss this support as comprador sentiment of loyalty to a superior foreign power. More likely, the Indian merchant saw the Raj to be a force working for the kind of capitalism in which they had built a stake, a better bet than the remnants of Mughal feudal warlords who led the other side.[10]

That sentiment apparently persisted into the late nineteenth century. British India had little to offer by way of a well-articulated 'economic policy' except

[9] Morris David Morris, 'South Asian Entrepreneurship and the Rashomon Effect, 1800–1947', *Explorations in Economic History*, 164, 1979, 341–61. For another version of the view, see Bishnupriya Gupta, 'Discrimination or Social Networks? Industrial Investment in Colonial India', Competitive Advantage in the Global Economy (CAGE) Working Paper No. 110, 2013.

[10] Tirthankar Roy, 'The Mutiny and the Merchants', *The Historical Journal*, 59(2), 2016, 393–416.

an imposition of free trade on dependent territories including the colonies.[11] Since Britain itself stuck to a low-tariff trade regime after 1850, it did not think it necessary to justify or defend a low-tariff regime in the Empire. The policy faced a resistance from Bombay's cotton mill owners, who demanded and were denied protection from Manchester until 1927. But merchants were not known to complain about free trade. Surely, they profited from the connections forged by the Empire. Bombay's merchants exported cotton to Liverpool, sold opium and cotton yarn in Hong Kong, and imported textile machines and foremen from Manchester. Calcutta's Marwari merchants were dependent on the custom of the European managing agency houses (Fig. 4.5). The Khojas of western India expanded their presence in Kenya, Uganda, and Zanzibar thanks to the expansion of British authority in these places (Fig. 4.6).

A serious criticism of this globalisation took shape around 1900. The leading critic of the British Indian economic system, the Parsi merchant-publicist-politician Dadabhai Naoroji (1825–1917), targeted what he called the 'drain' of wealth from India to Britain. Drain was an expansive term that included types of transfer between India and Britain that could be legitimately attacked, and types of transfer like repatriation of profits that obviously created value for India. Naoroji wrote his book in anger, and did not make a clear distinction. At times, his language befitted a mid-twentieth-century Marxist revolutionary more than a nineteenth-century Parsi merchant, '[f]oreign capital does nearly all the work, and carries away all the profit. Foreign capitalists ... make profits from the resources of British India, and take away those profits to their own countries'.[12] Still, there were legitimate targets in his critique. He pointed out, for example, that the British Indian state paid a large sum of money to Britain on account of the pensions and salaries of expatriate officers. The army was often deployed in imperialist battles that had nothing to do with the defence of Indian borders.

Although Naoroji's book *Poverty and Un-British Rule* became a canon for the nationalist discourse, which was shaped by lawyers more than capitalists, it is not clear that his views were shared by the capitalists. It is unlikely that Indian merchants, whose businesses traversed Natal, Aden, Bombay, and Hong Kong, would want Indian defence to protect only a land border around India. Another Parsi parliamentarian, Mancherjee Bhownagree (1851–1933), stoutly defended the Empire and became deeply unpopular in India for that

---

[11] On free trade, see Peter Cain, 'British Free Trade, 1850–1914: Economics and Policy', ReFresh (Economic History Society), www.ehs.org.uk/dotAsset/11cabff5-3f6a-4d69-bba0-1086d69be6c7 .pdf (accessed 1 August 2017).

[12] Dadabhai Naoroji, *Poverty and Un-British Rule in India*, London: Swan Sonnenschein, 1901, 265.

Fig. 4.5 Marwarree brokers (see also Fig. 4.3)
Source: DeGolyer Library, Southern Methodist University, William Johnson
Photographs of Western India

reason. Bhownagree shared with Naoroji the criticism of British Indian military expenditure, but not Naoroji's sentiment about foreign business. For someone who campaigned hard to encourage and protect Indian business in South Africa, Bhownagree could not possibly rail against 'foreign' business in

Fig. 4.6 Kojahs
The Khojas (derived from Khwaja, or pious) were a Muslim trading community
that dispersed from Gujarat and Sind to East Africa, possibly from as early as the
twelfth century, and globalized further in the late twentieth century. Their presence
was valued by the colonial states in Africa. After 1947, a few Khoja business houses
in Pakistan established industries and banks (for example, Habib Bank). The most
famous member of the community in India is Azim Premji, an engineer who
converted the family edible oil business into one of the world's largest information
technology firms (see Chapter 8 on IT). This is a nineteenth century photograph,
one of a series in the collection of Henry Bartle Frere, Governor of Bombay, and
which includes the previous image on the Marwaris.
Source: DeGolyer Library, Southern Methodist University, William Johnson
Photographs of Western India

India, as Naoroji did.[13] In short, Naoroji's anti-globalisation rhetoric came from a certain perspective more than a real injustice done to India. A contradiction was unfolding between globalisation and nationalism. Some believed that the Empire-sponsored globalisation was bad for India, and found in Naoroji's book a powerful endorsement of that belief. But merchants, by their silence or disinterest in the issue, appeared to hold that globalisation was not a bad thing. With little research done on the subject, merchant attitudes remain a matter of speculation.

So who were the merchants?

Global Trading Firms

The global trading firms were British in origin or, like the Sassoons who came from Iraq or the Ralli from Greece, developed strong links with Britain. However, their nerve centre was in India. Without exception, they retained connections with London, Liverpool, and in some cases Odessa, Shanghai, Canton, and Nagasaki. The London connection took the shape of steady deals between the Indian firm and a London counterpart, which arranged to auction goods brought there, procure goods in Britain for trade in Asia, and occasionally, provide capital, managers, and partners. Although sometimes the long-distance links were managed by a single family, this was rare. Partners were more frequently recruited from the associate firms. Given these broad parameters, the origin and operation of the firms differed.

One subset of global firms originated in the early nineteenth-century trade in India. For an important example from Bombay, the merchant firm started by Charles Forbes c. 1800 was a long survivor (Chapter 3). So were Thomas Parry, Binny, and Finlay of South India. Since some of these companies turned industrial after 1850, we will meet them again in Chapter 5.

A second subset arrived in India mid-century. James Greaves came to India around 1850 as a trader in cotton and textile machinery. He formed a partnership with George Cotton in the next decade. Both individuals were then working as technicians and managers of cotton mills of Bombay for some time. The partnership Greaves Cotton moved more firmly into textile mill agency after James' son John Greaves joined the firm in 1874. The family of David Sassoon were Turkish Jews and bankers to the Pasha of Baghdad. David's father visited Bombay in 1832 and liked the city so much as to decide

---

[13] On Bhownagree's views on military expenditure, Jamsetjee Ardaseer Wadia, *The Artificial Currency and the Commerce of India*, Bombay: Jamsetjee Nusserwanji Petit Parsi Orphanage, 1902, 106. See also the biographical sketches of Naoroji and Bhownagree in Natesan & Co., *Famous Parsis*, Madras: Natesan, 1930.

to move there permanently. David Sassoon inherited his father's trading firm, which continued trade in Persian and Indian products, and Lancashire textiles. Around 1860, the firm exported yarn to China and Japan, and established strong links there. In the 1870s, the Sassoon family moved into textile manufacturing and real estate development. The second son of David Sassoon, Elias David or E. D. Sassoon, set up an independent trading-manufacturing group, again with bases in Bombay and China.

In Cochin in Kerala, Robert H. Peirce and Patrick Leslie formed Peirce, Leslie and Co. in 1862. The firm conducted trade in Malabar spices and acted as agents for the British India Steam Navigation Co. From the end of the 1800s, the company started producing coffee in estates managed by it, as well as trading in coffee. It didn't give up its links with trade until the mid-twentieth century. In the 1840s, the Wallace family entered the India trade in Burma. Their Bombay Burmah Trading Corporation supplied Burma teak to the Indian railways.[14] Lewis Alexander and George Wallace were London merchants who took over a trading firm in Bombay to conduct trade in indigo, pepper, spices, among other products.

In Calcutta, the indigo crisis of 1846 killed at once two models of expatriate enterprise that had gained acceptability in the 1830s and 1840s. In one model, the trader had a partner, who was the European owner of a factory located deep in the countryside and processed an agricultural commodity for export. The model became acceptable partly because it simplified contractual issues between the trader and the producer, and partly because it was believed to be an answer to the poor quality and uncertain supplies of prepared indigo that came from inland. The rural manufacturer was not necessarily a planter in the American style, but was expected to contract with peasants who had established property rights on the land. The indigo mutiny, which was essentially a widespread failure of contracts between the planters and the peasants (1859–60) revealed that the manufacturer did not have adequate legal means to enforce these contracts, whereas their use of coercion to do so embarrassed the state.[15] The second model that died with the end of indigo was the merchant-owned bank with an undiversified base (Chapter 3). Nearly all the large trading firms of Calcutta that survived the 1846 crisis entered manufacturing, or more accurately, managed trading firms started by others. Banking was left to the banks. This set, therefore, will be discussed in more detail in the next chapter.

A third subset of global firms was engaged in grain trade, and came to India after railways opened the interior to the ports. From the last quarter of the

---

[14] A. C. Pointon, *The Bombay Burmah Trading Corp. Ltd., 1863–1963*, Southampton: Wallace Brothers, 1964.

[15] Tirthankar Roy, 'Indigo and Law in Colonial India', *Economic History Review*, 64(1), 2011, 60–75.

nineteenth century and until the Great Depression, exports from India consisted of primary commodities (wheat, rice, cotton, jute, wool, oilseeds, semi-processed hides and skins) and the largest import was cotton textiles. In both cases, European firms dominated the overseas operations. The Europeans, however, did not dominate the channels that brought these goods from the interior to the ports, despite having branches in the interior of India.

Salomon Volkart (1816–93), who hailed from a business family in Zurich, was established in Italy as a commodity trader when the partnership with his younger brother started simultaneously in Winterthur and Bombay in 1851. In the same year, Pantia Ralli (1793–1865) set up an operation in Calcutta. Volkart cited turbulent times of the Italian Risorgimento as the reason for a move to India. But he also understood that Indian cotton was a promising line to enter, just as Ralli seemed to shift the axis of his wheat trade away from Odessa and the Mediterranean towards India. Rallis were already established as a trading house in London when the move to India happened. In India, the Rallis had a diversified trading operation. The export goods included grain, cotton, and hides, and later Ralli also moved into shipping, insurance, and managing mills. Both companies established branches in Bombay, Calcutta, Karachi, and Madras. Ralli also had a branch in Pondicherry. Through buying agencies, cotton presses, and gins established in cotton-growing districts, Volkart and Ralli established business empires in India.[16] In 1951, business in India still formed over two-thirds of Ralli's operations, but already the Partition had divided up their South Asia interests, and damaged their prospects as traders.

A late but significant addition to this set of global firms was the Japanese merchant. The first Japanese trading firms, like the Mitsui-affiliated cotton trader Toyo Menka, entered in the 1890s. Recent scholarship on Japanese trade in South Asia has underscored several factors behind the very rapid growth in its scale in the next thirty years.[17] These were competitive shipping, efficient information exchange between Bombay and Osaka, partnership with Indian businesses (Tata in Bombay and Andrew Yule in Calcutta were among the partners), and the role of Indian merchants in Kobe, Singapore, and Hong Kong in conducting the import trade from Japan.[18] From around 1900, a

---

[16] George Reinhart, *Volkart Brothers: In Commemoration of the Seventy-Fifth Anniversary of the Foundation*, Winterthur: G. Binkert, 1926; Christof Dejung, 'Bridges to the East: European Merchants and Business Practices in India and China', in Robert Lee, ed., *Commerce and Culture: Nineteenth-Century Business Elites*, Farnham: Ashgate, 2011, 93–116.

[17] Between 1883 and 1928, total trade of India with Asia increased much faster than trade of India with the West. See Kaoru Sugihara, 'Japan as an Engine of the Asian International Economy, c. 1880–1936', *Japan Forum*, 2(1), 1990, 127–45.

[18] Naoto Kagotani, 'Up-country Purchase Activities of Indian Raw Cotton by Toyo Menka's Bombay Branch, 1896–1935', in S. Sugiyama and Linda Grove, eds., *Commercial Networks in Modern Asia*, Richmond: Curzon Press, 2001; William D. Wray, 'Nodes in the Global Webs of

number of Parsi cotton merchants were starting to form agency with Japanese trading firms. A. B. Paymaster, Pheroze Sethna, and Nusserwanji Guzdar were linked with first Mitsui Bussan Kaisha, later Toyo Menka Kaisha. Paymaster was in cotton selection and broking business since the 1880s, initially supplying to Britain and local mills.

In the interwar period, partnership between the Japanese Sogo Sosha and Indian merchants extended further. The former set was keen to buy Indian cotton and experienced success in selling textiles in India. This was the first time that a non-Empire country provided both British and Indian trade competition. That fact, and the suspicion that the Japanese export effort was supported by an undervalued currency, led to a series of government interventions regulating the trade. But already, it had created a large network of collaboration between the Japanese and the Indians.

In the 1920s, Paymaster had formed a partnership with a Marwari trader, Anandiram Podar. Podar purchased a moribund mill called Hope, renamed it Diamond, and sold it to a syndicate formed of Toyo Menka and Podar. The mill was further renamed Toyo Podar and stood as the most important example of Japanese foreign investment in Bombay before World War II. Another spillover of the collaborations between trading firms was a cluster of match manufacturing factories.[19] The India-Japan trading networks were sufficiently large and yet sufficiently distant from the Europe-India ones to confirm the hypothesis that they represented an emergent Asian economic alignment.[20] In any case, it was plagued by rising nationalism in both countries. After 1929, Indo-Japanese trade relations were in difficulties from which they did not recover. Japan's iron and steel industry asked for protection from Indian pig iron, in retaliation of India's textile industry's demand for protection from Japan's textile imports (Chapter 6). The desire for military security strengthened protectionist sentiment in Japan.[21]

A fifth subset of global trading firms with their major centre of operation in India consisted of the produce brokers. The produce brokers were rather more akin to the commission agents in grain trade, who sold goods on behalf of merchants but were not employees of these merchants, except that the brokers also advised the buyer and the seller on the quality of the goods sold. The term

Japanese Shipping', *Business History*, 47(1), 2005, 1–22; Hiroshi Shimizu, 'The Indian Merchants of Kobe and Japan's Trade Expansion into Southeast Asia before the Asian-Pacific War', *Japan Forum*, 17(1), 2010, 25–48.

[19] Takashi Oishi, 'Indo-Japan Cooperative Ventures in Match Manufacturing in India: Muslim Merchant Networks in and beyond the Bengal Bay Region, 1900–1930', *International Journal of Asian Studies*, 1(1), 2004, 49–85.

[20] Sugihara, 'Japan as an Engine'.

[21] John Sharkey, 'Attitudes of the Japanese Iron and Steel Industry to Indian Pig Iron Imports, 1919–1929', *Japan Review*, 7, 1996, 159–84.

'broker' in Indian business history has been used in two distinct meanings: as an agent of trading or manufacturing firm (Chapter 3) and as an auction coordinator. The tea broker, who survives to the present day, was an auctioneer, as well as a quality adviser; that is, a tea taster. Without their judgement on quality, the auctioneer would not know what price to start the auction from and what price to expect in the end.

Within a few years after the Company's China monopoly ended (1833), tea auctions began in London and Liverpool. London's Mincing Lane was the main site of the auctions and housed several brokerage firms. These firms procured tea from the plantation companies as well as counterpart broker firms in Calcutta. For example, Thomas Cumberledge and Moss, later Thomas Cumberledge and Inskipp, a London broker, appears in the historical accounts of two Indian firms, J. Thomas, the premier broker of Calcutta, and Warren, a tea planter group from Assam. J. Thomas was a long survivor. Robert Thomas, a Welshman, born c. 1808, came to Calcutta in 1833.[22] He formed a series of 'produce broking partnerships' with other European traders. His major interest was indigo, but he also did business in sugar, saltpetre, Manchester cloth, silk, coal, and bullion. Thomas almost certainly suffered in the indigo crisis, but seemed to reorganise in the 1860s and 1870s. By general agreement between planters and traders, two broking firms subsequently came to control the indigo trade; Thomas and Co. was one, and William Moran and Co., later Carritt-Moran, was another.

Chapter 3 mentioned that the Europeans avoided settling down or operating as merchants in the interior of the country after the Indian Mutiny. This sentiment was weaker in the 1930s. There were merchants in the interior, usually small firms, trading in craft goods and local produce. This is the sixth subset of global trading firms. In South India, a string of smaller ports exported rice, along with a large variety of minor exportable goods like cashew, coir, tea, carpets, and special textiles such as Madras handkerchiefs. Gordon Woodroff was a big player in this milieu. In the 1920s two European firms, Beardsell and Brunschweiler, dominated the Madras handkerchiefs export trade from the southeastern coast to West Africa. In North India, several European firms had carpets made on contract by master artisans. C. M. Hadow, founded in 1888, operated from Srinagar in Kashmir. German Otto Weylandt, possibly the biggest buyer of carpet in Agra, was a multinational firm that owned factories in Punjab and West Asia around 1900.[23] On the Coromandel coast, the famous Madras export firm Arbuthnot made Eluru carpets on contract.

---

[22] The following description of the firm is based on Dipak Roy, *A Hundred and Twenty-Five Years: The Story of J. Thomas and Company* Calcutta, c. 1976.
[23] India, *Royal Commission on Labour in India*, Vol. 2, pt. 2 London, 1931: HMSO, 89–90.

In Mirzapur, a town near Benares, the European capitalist heritage (like the tea broker of Calcutta) is part of a living memory. Prior to the nineteenth century villagers in this area had woven carpets, probably of cotton rather than woollen pile. Mirzapur's location – near a big market (Benares), a centre of wool production (Kanpur), and on the main east-west trunk road – made it suitable for trade. It is not known exactly when the European traders moved in; the pioneer was reportedly an indigo factor of the area. Around 1880, there were two firms based here, E. Hill and Tellery. Both firms invested money in loom-sheds, arranged to hire expert designers and dyers from Kashmir and Punjab, and invited master artisans to execute contracts in the factory. The work had shifted to woollen-knotted carpet, which is what the foreign market wanted. They set up factories in one account because 'the weavers are not sufficiently reliable to be trusted to weave in their own houses'. In turn, the master artisans liked the arrangement because 'the European firms can pay better wages, and give greater continuity of work'.[24] In 1932, partnerships between F. H. Oakley, F. H. Bowden, and a Taylor, already engaged in buying carpets for export, merged to set up the third European firm, Obeetee Private Limited. Obeetee exists today as a subsidiary of a dynamic Indian business group, whose main interest is in tea. The Obeetee records show that the three firms resorted to both loom shed and contract purchases, that there was keen competition between them for good-quality work, occasional poaching of skilled artisans, constant anxiety over quality control, and growing fear of artisan-entrepreneurs.

A seventh subset of global traders should include agents and subsidiaries of importers of chemicals, metals, and machines. Several leading British multinationals that were prominent in India in the late twentieth century had their origin as an importing office around 1920. The import of machines and intermediate goods were done differently between industries. In cotton and jute textiles, the agents or branches of machine manufacturers in Britain usually conducted sales. The system was entrenched because a part of their duty was to ensure after-sale service via foremen sent by the parent firm. Platt Brothers were the largest suppliers of cotton mill machinery until the advent of ring spindles. Other machinery firms included John Hetherington and Sons, Dobson and Barlow, Asa Lees and Co. and Taylor, Lang and Co. The supplier profile changed after the advent of ring spinning. Howard and Bullough of Accrington supplied spinning machines for the first shop floor that used only ring spindles (Greaves Cotton). The Manchester firm Benjamin Goodfellow fitted the steam engines, and Messrs Tinker Shenton installed the boiler for this mill.

---

[24] Ibid., 89.

In several types of metals and engineering goods, the main consumer was the government, which procured these articles from Britain because the India Office was authorised to issue tenders. These Britain-centric systems were under pressure from the late nineteenth century because of campaign and competition from independent trading firms. One of the campaigners was Richardson and Cruddas, a Bombay-based trading firm dealing in steel for public works, which worked hard to change the system of government procurement.

By 1920, there were a string of British engineering firms, which exported goods to India but also at the same time were looking to expand trading agencies in India. One example was the Calcutta firm Alfred Herbert dealing in machine tools. Alfred Herbert was the branch of a Coventry machine toolmaker, and as such obtained goods from the parent firm. They also manufactured in India on a small scale. Other examples of firms in a similar situation would include Marshall, Sons (agricultural machinery and traction engine-maker and trader, based in Lincolnshire), Stewarts and Lloyds (Birmingham firm making iron and steel tubes), Westinghouse Electric (London firm with presence in South America and Asia, dealing in electrical installations), Thornycroft (shipbuilders), George Cradock (wire rope manufacturers of Wakefield), Campbell Gas Engine (oil engine manufacturers and traders of Halifax), General Electric (formed of a merger between Thomas Edison's company and Thomson-Houston, both electric light equipment manufacturers and traders), Saxby and Farmer (railway equipment manufacturer, of Kilburn and later Chippenham), British Thomson-Houston (branch of an American company), and Mather and Platt (Manchester engineering firm).

In the twentieth century, the range of consumer goods imported from Britain expanded to include such new articles as cosmetics, sewing machines, processed food, bicycles, and cars. Trading agencies of foreign manufacturers were started to create a loyal consumer base for these products. The Indian subsidiary of the food processing firm Unilever was an example. The household chemicals firm Reckitt and Colman started a trading unit in India in the 1920s. Imperial Tobacco Company in India started as a subsidiary of the British American Tobacco in 1910.

Selling these goods to Indians was a challenge, for few Indian buyers were brand-sensitive. The printed newspaper was the major advertising channel, and in a society with low literacy rate that did not count for much. Selling branded consumer goods would mean creating a whole new type of retail trading network. In meeting that need, the Indian agent and wholesaler played a vital role and an innovative one. The local agent was sometimes recruited from the established Indian mercantile groups, but the agent performed a more entrepreneurial, more advertising-oriented, service than in the other trades.

The fascinating story of the great dealer of Singer sewing machine, N. M. Patell, is a case in point.[25] Patell was influential in shifting the target of marketing from the expatriate and Indo-European population towards the Indian tailor and middle-class Indian women. In doing so, he faced the displeasure of European bosses who believed the strategy would fail and wanted more European staff to be employed in India. Patell persisted with great success. A somewhat similar story of entrepreneurship in marketing can be told in other successful durable goods of the time, like bicycles and typewriters. Both tools were used mainly by the males for a long time. But in the big cities, where women worked in offices in increasing numbers from the 1940s, many new typing schools catered to women. The potential for these goods did not escape the notice of Indian business groups (like Godrej), who started making typewriters, bicycles, and sewing machines.

Agency of this kind sustained Indian traders. And as these examples show, agency was a field of entrepreneurship in marketing. Most Indian trading firms, however, joined the huge field of grain trade, even dominating it.

Indian Traders

The simultaneous decline of the Asian empires had hurt the Arabian Sea trade and finished off some ship-owning merchants. Chapter 3 has shown that shipping carried on, with a significant stimulus from the Sino-Indian trade. The Parsis, who did well in Indo-China trade, had always been a coastal group, and did not have much penetration inland. While China trade declined from the late nineteenth century, prominent Parsi businesses moved to manufacturing, import trade, real estate, and to other professions. They also held shares of big companies of the time, like the Great Indian Peninsular Railway.

By far the biggest field of investment of Indian groups was the grain and cotton trade. The prominence of the Gujarati merchants and bankers in Bombay owed a lot to the cotton export trade carried on all along the Gujarat coast, which interlinked Bombay, Broach, and Ahmedabad in networks of exchange of goods, money, and capitalists. Grain trade was spread out even more, and penetrated most villages in India.

Unlike Ralli or Volkart, big firms did not dominate the overland trade in grains. Small firms and their local financiers did. Little information on inland trading systems is available before the end of the 1920s. Better description is available from the 1920s, which also occasionally reflected on the history of

---

[25] David Arnold, 'Global Goods and Local Usages: The Small World of the Indian Sewing Machine, 1875–1952', *Journal of Global History*, 6(3), 2011, 407–29. Also, Andrew Godley, 'Selling the Sewing Machine around the World', *Enterprise and Society,* 7(3) 2006, 266–314.

the trade. I will use these descriptions to reconstruct the history of the trade. No matter which place we look, there were two major players in local grain trade – the commission agent and the buyer's agent – and a third minor player, the local landlord-cum-moneylender. The commission agent rented a space in a market or a warehouse and sold in bulk to the buyer. The buyer's agent or the company agent went into the village to directly contract purchases with the farmer. At the third level, landlords, shopkeepers, and professional retail bankers lent money to cultivators and accepted repayment in grain that they sold to the other two actors. In the remote cotton areas of Khandesh or western Deccan, for example, neither the big commission agency nor the buyer agency had much penetration, and both actors waited for the crop to come to the more accessible bazaars, brought there by local traders.[26]

The first two groups operated from towns that had railway stations and banks. Almost certainly, the scale of this operation expanded with the infrastructure. These assets made it possible for merchants to transport grain by rail, to use the railway receipt or invoice to draw bills of exchange known as *hundi* from an indigenous banker based in Bombay, Calcutta, or Madras, and to cash that bill in the bank.[27] The merchants and their agents owned carts, grain pits, and warehouses, and sometimes successfully persuaded the bank to open cash credit accounts for them on the security of the crop. Europeans were completely absent from these local transactions, but they did occasionally figure in the railway town, both as company agents and as commission agents. Several examples could be found in Punjab and the Krishna-Godavari delta, where long-distance grain trade had grown very large, and in the jute markets of the Bengal delta.[28]

The main centre of grain cultivation for export was the Indus-Gangetic plains, and the main ports carrying grain for export were Bombay, Karachi, Calcutta, and Madras. There were also concentrations of trade inland, for example, in Punjab. The construction of canal colonies in the late nineteenth century made the Punjab plains central to long-distance trade, and stimulated an agriculture-based urbanisation. The emergence of Lyallpur or Faisalabad, now Pakistan's leading industrial town, had owed to its location in a

---

[26] M. L. Dantwala, *Marketing of Raw Cotton in India*, Bombay and New York: Longmans Green, 1937, 31–2.

[27] For a history of negotiable instruments and especially attempts to legalize and regulate it, see Marina Martin, 'An Economic History of the Hundi 1858–1978', PhD Dissertation of the Department of Economic History, London School of Economics and Political Science, 2012.

[28] For example, Owen Roberts of Lahore, interview in Punjab Provincial Banking Enquiry Committee, *Report of the Punjab Provincial Banking Enquiry Committee, 1929–30*, Vol. 2, Calcutta: Government Press, 1930, 994–6; and Innes and Co. of Kakinada, a partnership between an Indian and a European, started c. 1870 as exporter of jute, rice, oilseeds, and jaggery. The firm also owned rice mills. Indian Industrial Commission, *Minutes of Evidence Taken before the Indian Industrial Commission, 1916–18*, Vol. 3, London: HMSO, 1918, 88.

prosperous agricultural zone that developed trade and banking. Although not in the canal zones, Lahore and Multan gained from this prosperity and contributed to it by supplying trading and financial services. From the 1860s, Karachi grew in importance as one of the main ports to receive cargo sent from Punjab and Sind down the Indus. In this way, a new urban pattern emerged in the territory that became West Pakistan after 1947.

The railways were crucial to the grain trade not only because they reduced costs of trade, but they also carried price information. Until independence in 1947, there was little evidence of forward trade in grain in the smaller towns, though Bombay Commodity Exchange – earlier known as Bombay Cotton Trade Association – was doing forward trades from 1875 onwards. A merchant settled in the country had limited access to export price information. Although the post office network had spread, many villages did not have a telegraph office in the vicinity as late as the interwar period. Trade publications were of no use to the local growers who did not read English. Therefore, commission agency or an auction type of sale prevailed, as it had done for a long time before European ascendancy in the export business. The difference was that much of the bulk business now took place near the railway station, which suggests how critical a role the railway played not only in reducing transportation cost, but also enabling the local actors gain access to capital as well as to information.[29]

Three institutional features of the inland commodity trade were important for a business history. First, we know of traders in the interior by their community names rather than the names of firms. The Marwaris dominated the jute trade, Muslim and Eurasian merchants the leather trade, and other Hindu and Jain communities the grain trade, even though commission agencies with major European firms sometimes enabled a few individuals or families to acquire a reputation distinct from that attached to the community. Some of the future Marwari industrialists of Calcutta had acquired such a reputation in the late nineteenth century.[30] Birlas were a well-known example from jute trade. Second, a study of local trade cannot separate itself from a study of local credit. In fact, in the exceptional cases where a local merchant firm was mentioned by name, the mention happened because it was a banker as well, and issued hundi bearing the name.

Third, the agent of foreign companies, despite being sponsored by wealthy European firms, did not carry much weight in the countryside. The buying agencies of firms like Ralli, Volkart, or Toyo Menka had the backing of

---

[29] William Roberts and O. T. Faulkner, *A Textbook of Punjab Agriculture*, Lahore: Civil and Military Gazette Press, 1921.
[30] Thomas A. Timberg, 'Three Types of the Marwari Firm', *Indian Economic Social History Review* 10(1), 1973, 3–36.

foreign firms and joint-stock banks. But their agents could not go very far without the help of the commission agents. In the nineteenth century, the Ralli Brothers tried to buy wheat and oilseeds direct from cultivators and bullock caravan runners in the western Gangetic plains, but switched to commission agents in the interwar period.[31] Their limited access to the production site reflected two advantages the local commodity traders possessed over them. One was transportation. The latter owned carts or knew where to hire them. But more than that, they were better tuned to the credit needs of farmers.

Thanks to links with the port city, a reverse flow of investment occurred inward. Tired of dealing with 'frauds' or the poor quality of cotton sent from the interior to the coasts, some Bombay and Ahmedabad firms set up cotton gins in the countryside. Another bigger field was joint-stock banking, which experienced a boom in the interior towns where a lot of the action was. In the evidence just cited, one Marwari mercantile firm, Debi Prashad (started in banking 1840), was a fully fledged banker in 1920. The business drew in deposit accounts from the rich Indian residents, and the European community of northern Bihar. It still retained its separate identity from the European banks, being financed mainly out of the capital of the joint family.[32] In the western Gangetic plain, local merchant-bankers contributed capital to newly set-up indigenous joint-stock banks.[33] These bottom-up banks more readily accepted the mortgage of produce, which partly replaced the business of unsecured loans, also known as 'the hand-note system' of moneylending.[34]

Tanned hides were a semi-processed natural resource, the trading of which had some similarities with the grain trade. In tanned hides, a similar flow of capital from outside to the interior, as previously mentioned, took place. Leather export was a major field for Muslim merchants of the time. By contrast with the other commodities, hides and skins were necessarily processed in the locality, and therefore entailed strong ties between the local merchants and the tannery owner. Indeed, the two classes were often indistinct. From the last quarter of the nineteenth century, hides and skins emerged as a major exportable commodities. At the peak of the trade, just before World War I, 100,000 tonnes of hides and skins left India. Thereafter, the trade was redirected to the domestic market.

Tanned and cured hides formed a rather curious product. Like grain, it came from the countryside. But unlike grain, Indian or naturalised Indian firms dominated the export trade. The managing agencies of Calcutta had marginal interest in the trade, possibly because hides were re-exported and not destined

---

[31] United Provinces Provincial Banking Enquiry Committee, *Report of the United Provinces Provincial Banking Enquiry Committee, 1929–30*. Vol. 2, *Evidence*, Calcutta: Government Press, 1930, 3.

[32] Ibid., 158.

[33] *Report of the United Provinces Provincial Banking Enquiry Committee, 1929–30*, 83.

[34] Sinha, *Early European Banking*, London: Macmillan, 1927, 244.

for the British market alone. Apparently, the Hindu trader also had an aversion to hides. Muslims, Parsis, Eurasians, and the Chinese, therefore, came to dominate the tanning trade. Many German trading firms (Schroeder Smidt, Schmidt Cohen and Fuchs, Wuttow Guttman) were prominent in the trade through Calcutta. The exit of the Germans during World War I led the Muslim merchants to consolidate their hold on trade and enter manufacture. In Bombay in the late nineteenth century, Bohras and Memons, the Muslim trading castes, owned tanneries and controlled a considerable part of the export trade.

The deep link between trading and banking has been mentioned on several occasions already. It deserves more attention because of the peculiar features of grain trade.

Banking

The Value of Cash

Liquidity was the key to agricultural trade. Most debtors could not read documents. Besides, the conduct of agriculture under tropical monsoon conditions was marked by high risk and extreme seasonal fluctuations. Therefore, loans needed to be advanced to a vast army of local merchants suddenly, and for short periods among clients who were too far away from banks and discounting facilities, and who were not usually literate. Negotiable instruments would not work in this system, only money would.

Of course, a great deal of trading in the interior did involve negotiable instruments issued by bankers elsewhere. Through the hundi, money did circulate between the interior and the port cities. Patna and Calcutta, Bombay and Sholapur, and Madras and Coimbatore were networked in this fashion. But the transactions in these bills, at least the ones issued by the most reputed firms, were confined to the big banking firms and did not penetrate much locally.[35] In the big city financial market, corporate banks and big Indian banking firms participated on equal footing. In their deals with small-town bankers and traders, indigenous bankers needed to lend on personal security. Here, branches of corporate banks and European banks could not operate easily, for the Indians had a deeper and more extended network of personally known clients than did the agents of European or corporate banks. In this exchange of information on who was trustworthy and who was not, social networks mattered.

Because cash was so important, banking and bullion became connected businesses. Gold ornaments were often mortgaged in large consumption loan

---

[35] Tirthankar Roy, 'Monsoon and the Market for Money in Late Colonial India', *Enterprise and Society*, 17(2), 2016, 324–57.

deals. Gold was the next best thing to cash in the finance of agricultural trades. Bankers needed to be experts on the purity of the metal, an expertise that made some of them successful players in the bullion exchange. If the Parsis, Gujaratis, or Europeans dominated the port-city markets, the Marwaris supplied liquidity 'upcountry'. A clearer picture of Marwari entrepreneurship begins to emerge when we turn to banking and gold (see next).

Corporate Banks

Traders understood the need for joint-stock banks, and from time to time, invested money to start one. Corporate banking started as an adjunct to the agency houses, which were mainly trading houses, in the early 1800s as we have seen in Chapter 3. The joining of the two activities increased the scope for insider lending and passed on trade risks to the banking business. After 1858, joint-stock banking re-emerged on a different foundation. Company law strengthened the legal standing of banking firms. Government business helped a few of these, which later merged to form the Imperial Bank. The business provided by the princely states likewise favoured a few Indian banks (the Bank of Baroda, for example). Elsewhere, such as Punjab or South India, agricultural trade gave local banks good business. Corporate banks, however, financed long-distance trade. Financing local merchants, warehouse owners, transporters, and ultimately, peasants, was not a business the corporate banks could undertake easily, as we have seen.

Even when the biggest bank of the 1920s, the Imperial Bank, had a branch operating in the town, the big merchants did not borrow from the bank. In Bhagalpur town in north-eastern Bihar, they did not do so because they did not like secured credit. The Bank's practice of advancing against produce '[gave] too much publicity' to the transaction; the security of grain stocks did not satisfy the banks either for 'in bulk storage there [was] great danger of fraud as regards quantity and quality'.[36] There were no licensed warehouses. The Bank would not accept the handwritten notes offered in evidence of grain stock available as collateral, nor would they lend in the absence of audited balance sheets. The information asymmetry in this case led the banks to introduce a tiered structure of trade credit (first class, second class, and so on), but this system did not work too well outside Calcutta. It was impossible for the manager transferred from Calcutta to be sure who was second class and who was first class in a bazaar in Bihar.

---

[36] Provincial Banking Enquiry evidence, merchant-banker cited in Roy, 'Monsoon'. The practice of bank advances against grain stores varied between regions.

Corporate banking, therefore, stayed confined to financing other bankers, and long-distance traders.

Indian Family Firms in Banking

The bankers usually belonged in specific castes and communities, the prominent among these being the Multani and the Marwari, the Bengali Saha, Nattukottai Chettiar, Kallidaikurichi Brahmins in South India, the Gujaratis in Bombay, and occasionally Rohilla Afghans, though the main business of the last-mentioned was consumption credit. The small group of income tax-payers in 1920s India consisted of a few of these bankers. In South India, the town banking business was dominated by the Nattukkottai Chettiars, the Multanis, the Marwaris, and the Kallidaikurichi Brahmans. The Chettiar community business was in Burma and Malaya until 1930, but considerable transaction was done in Madras as well.[37] In 1930, their involvement with agricultural trade or financing cultivation was minimal; much of the Madras firms' business concentrated on remittance of money through hundis issued by them between Malaya, Burma, and Madras. By contrast, the small community of Multani bankers was sometimes engaged in financing agricultural trade by acting as the intermediary between the merchant and the joint-stock bank.[38] They did not, however, lend directly to the peasants or on stock in trade. In busy season, they borrowed from their principals in Shikarpur, and from the Imperial Bank.

As they appeared in sources from the 1920s, these bankers never financed peasants, but financed each other, and bigger clients such as landlords, warehouse owners, merchants with personal reputation, agents of outstation trading firms, tea estates, and traders buying jute, tobacco, and chilli crops where these cash crops were grown.[39] They discounted trade bills and issued remittance instruments when they were branches of Bombay or Calcutta firms, or had close links with the latter. They financed merchant-transporters who could furnish bills of lading from the railway company. Some of these firms were of a size comparable with that of the corporate banks. About six big indigenous banking firms in Calcutta together did as much business as the state-run Imperial Bank.[40]

---

[37] Madras, *The Madras Provincial Banking Enquiry Committee*, Vols. 1–4, Madras: Government Press, 1930, Vol. 3; and David Rudner, *Caste and Capitalism in Colonial India – The Nattukottai Chettiars*, Berkeley and Los Angeles, CA: University of California Press, 1994; Raman Mahadevan, 'Pattern of Enterprise of Immigrant Entrepreneurs – A Study of Chettiars in Malaya, 1880–1930', *Economic and Political Weekly*, 13(4–5), 1978.

[38] Madras, *The Madras Provincial Banking Enquiry*, Vol. 1, 191.

[39] Bengal, *Bengal Provincial Banking Enquiry Committee 1929–30*, Vols. 1–3, Calcutta: Government Press, 1930, Vol. 1, 188.

[40] Ibid., 186–7.

These big firms did not exist in isolation of the small firms. The mainstay of the banking business was to finance agricultural trade and production, and this business crucially depended on the city firms' ability to fund those smaller firms that operated from the market towns in the interior, and these latter's ability to fund the rural moneylender who gave unsecured loans to the peasant cultivator.

Unlike in the ports, the inland order conducted a business that was highly seasonal in nature. During the sowing and harvest seasons of the main crop, interest rates rose to very high levels. In the slack season, there was money to spare. There were no big firms in the interior and very few bank branches. The inland grain merchant, therefore, was also a banker.[41] Research done during the Provincial Banking Enquiry Committee (1929–30) yielded hundreds of references to the link between grain trade and moneylending.

The banking side of the business ran on an intricate network of personal connections. The big merchants did not lend to the peasants directly. Instead they supplied money to a group of commission agents who travelled between the countryside and the town. These merchants in turn gave money to traders settled in the cultivating area. They, in turn, lent to the peasants. These concentric circles of credit relations reduced the risks of lending for the big merchant, for while no one lent on security, no one lent without intimate knowledge of the client.[42] Informal credit ruled this world not because formal credit was scarce, or the Europeans short-changed the Indians. Rather, information problems restrained both the supply and the demand for bank credit for commodity trade.

In the cotton trade in western India, the first buyers of the crop were travelling merchants or commission agents rather than salaried agents of the mills or the exporting firms. Bombay agents picked up this cotton assembled in the larger market connected by rail. In jute trade too, we see the same features: European exporters and mills had local agents, but these agents or brokers bought goods from local trading firms rather than from the cultivators. Banks did not lend to the business directly, because they were unable or unwilling to accept raw jute for hypothecation.[43]

When we get closer to the small town or village where the produce came from, practically anyone with cash to spare in the busy season went into lending money. Still, some communities did significantly more business than

---

[41] 'Very many [trading] firms add banking to their main business, mainly for employing their funds in the slack season.' Sinha, *Early European Banking*, 244.

[42] Messrs. Khialiram Kedarnath, grain and oil merchants, Lachman Sahu Gopal Sahu, grain dealers, Gopi Sahu Munshi Sahu, grain merchant, and Seth Jhunjhunwala, banker, grain merchant and cloth dealer, Bihar and Orissa Provincial Banking Enquiry Committee, *Report of the Bihar and Orissa Provincial Banking Enquiry Committee, 1929–30*, Vol. 1, Patna: Government Press, 1930, 21.

[43] Indian Central Jute Committee, *Report on the Marketing and Transport of Jute in India*, Calcutta: Government Press, 1940, 117.

others, because they formed parts of a network of city banker, town banker, and local merchants. Perhaps no other community displays this network effect better than the Marwaris.

Marwari Banking

The Marwaris were mainly bankers. Their hold on banking and practices of intra-community lending meant that the Marwaris collectively had easier access to liquid wealth, cash for short. Preference for cash would have acted against putting money in long-gestation projects such as factories. Numerous other groups also engaged in agriculture and moneylending as the Marwaris did. Not surprisingly, few of them took to large-scale industry, which remained a preserve of the city capitalist. The former actors valued liquidity more than the prospect of a low long-term return, because they worked in a high risk geographical and economic environment. The historiography of the Marwari has generally underestimated their involvement in credit.

Two representatives of the Marwari Trades Association of Calcutta confirmed in 1922 that banking was indeed 'the chief business of the Marwari community'.[44] That general statement was largely true. And yet, banking came in a wide variety of forms, dividing the community into many professionally distinct fragments. At one end was the neighbourhood moneylender and shopkeeper rolled into one, located in an agricultural village. At another end was the jute trader, textile importer, stock broker, bullion dealer, and banker located in Calcutta and Bombay. Both these images are stylised, for there were small moneylenders in the metropolitan cities, and there were big players in the commodity trading interior zone.

Among the big players around 1900, we might include the Khandelwal banking houses of Mathura, the Oswal bankers of middle Bengal, the Srimali and Porwal bankers in Ahmedabad, the Maheshwari bankers in Jubbulpore, and the Debi Prashad of north Bihar – not to mention the warehouse owners in market towns, transporters, jute balers, and cotton ginners. Several of these firms in the 1920s operated more or less like any commercial bank would. In fact, many town bankers interviewed by a large-scale survey of banking around 1929 were Marwaris.[45]

It is useful to think about Marwari engagement in the money market in terms of two spheres, one rural and one metropolitan. The rural credit market was

[44] Cited in Roy, 'Monsoon'.
[45] The firm of Debi Prashad, dating from 1840, was an example; see United Provinces, *Report of the United Provinces Provincial Banking Enquiry Committee 1929–30*, Vol. II, Evidence, Calcutta: Government Press.

stimulated partly by the colonial property right reform in land, which saw strong forms of ownership right emerge around 1840, supported by adequate documentation, legislation, judiciary, and police. Much rural lending continued to be unsecured; still, a greater proportion than before used land as mortgage. It is likely that demand for loans also increased because land mortgage had become easier. In any case, it was well-known that the level of debt varied with ownership rights rather than with poverty. Agricultural commercialisation involved greater circulation of cash in the countryside than before.

The rural lending business by the Marwaris caused a minor political scandal in 1875. In the Bombay-Deccan region, the proprietors of land were the peasant cultivators under an arrangement known as 'ryotwari'. Ryotwari was a contract between the state and the peasant-proprietor of land, stating that the latter would pay taxes to the state at agreed rates and in return enjoy property right on the land. Among other effects, the contract made land a more suitable mortgage than before and increased loans taken on land mortgage. Between 1840 and 1865, parts of this region experienced a large expansion of cotton production for export. In the summer of 1875, in Poona and Ahmednagar districts of the Deccan, indebted peasants attacked moneylender property and burnt account books. The administrators reacted quickly with legislation restricting transfer of mortgaged land, fearing that the riots had happened because the moneylenders were taking possession of land.

The Deccan Riots Commission that followed these disturbances, and subsequent reports and enquiries, referred to the moneylender simply as the 'Marwari' and sometimes as the 'rapacious Marwari', even though the Marwaris were not the only capitalists in the countryside.[46] The anti-Marwari and anti-outsider sentiment had been building up for at least three decades prior to the riots. A book published by a professor of Poona College in 1852 delivered the first of many diatribes against the 'race of foreign moneylenders – the Marwarries'.[47] The date of this work suggests that the migration of Marwari bankers in the cotton cultivation regions increased from the 1840s, though we cannot be sure of that.

The administrative view was biased by an anxiety about possible peasant unrest, and specifically the fear that British rule had empowered the banker and transformed him into an exploitative character. 'The introduction of the English law of contract and transfer of property, and the increase in the habit of litigation', it was alleged, had caused indebted peasants to lose their land to 'foreign' capitalists.[48] The Marwaris were said to encourage over-borrowing

---

[46] India, *Royal Commission on Indian Currency and Finance*, Vol. 4 of 4, London: HMSO, 1896, 98.

[47] H. Green, *The Deccan Ryots*, Bombay: Bombay Gazette, 1852, 7.

[48] R. V. Russell, *The Tribes and Castes of the Central Provinces of India*, London: Macmillan, 1916, 131.

against land titles, and on several occasions obtained decrees to possess land, even though they rarely started cultivating land. The Riots Commission described the 'Marwaris as aliens and indifferent to public opinion; as landlords, they follow the instincts of the usurer, and make the hardest terms possible with the tenant'.[49]

The impression the colonial officers created of the Marwaris as exploitative and opportunistic players ready to take advantage of their peasant-clients was a lasting one. Although one officer expressed the plausible fear that the anti-Marwari rhetoric 'dealt a blow at the capital of the thrifty shopkeeper', the general policy remained biased in favour of the borrower.[50] The rural lender became a villain of the countryside. The Marwari had to bear a large part of the opprobrium heaped upon the moneylender by generations of government officers. Later, left-leaning economists reinforced the bias, as the anti-lender ideology became an article of faith in independent India. In fact, the fear of mortgaged land being transferred was exaggerated. The trouble would not have been worthwhile for most small-scale lenders. What proportion of the loans was backed up by security is not clear either. The unsecured creditors carried enormous risk of default given the unstable agricultural conditions in the Deccan.

Whatever the effect of the Deccan Riots on the peasants, more big bankers seemed to shift to the city and to trade thereafter. Almost certainly, a series of provincial legislation restraining the bankers, and the increasing prevalence of landlords and rich peasants making loans, pushed the professional bankers to play a more indirect role in agriculture. These developments added to the push to shift to the safety of Calcutta or Bombay.

By 1900, there was not one substantial town outside of South India that did not have a settlement of Marwari bankers and traders in it. Still, a definite geographical pattern did emerge. Marwari migration to eastern India was larger than all other flows, slowly giving rise to 'a zone of Marwari dominance' in Bengal, Assam, Orissa, and Bihar.[51] The rate of Marwari migration into Calcutta was probably higher than the population growth rate between 1881 and 1931.[52] Most of the prominent Marwari houses of the city around

---

[49] India, *Index to the Report of the Commission Appointed to Inquire into the Working of the Deccan Agriculturists Relief Act*, Calcutta: Government Press, 1894, 70.

[50] India, *Papers Relating to the Deccan Agriculturists' Relief Act during The Years 1875–94*, Calcutta: Government Press, 1897, 462.

[51] Claude Markovits, 'Merchant Circulation in South Asia (Eighteenth to Twentieth Centuries): The Rise of Pan-Indian Merchant Networks', in Claude Markovits, Jacques Pouchepadass, Sanjay Subrahmanyam, eds., *Society and Circulation: Mobile People and Itinerant Cultures in South Asia 1750–1950*, London: Anthem, 2003, 150.

[52] Thomas Timberg, *The Marwaris, from Traders to Industrialists*, New Delhi: Vikas, 1978, 88.

1900 had migrated to Calcutta during the last quarter of the nineteenth century. The history of such houses, including Baldeodas Birla, Badridas Goenka, Bansidhar Jalan, H. P. Poddar, Ramkrishna Dalmia, Babulal Rajgarhia, and others, suggest that their main interests in 1900 were in jute baling, mining, land-holding, and import agency. By the end of the interwar period, these firms had entered the jute industry. On a smaller scale they entered sugar, paper, cement, construction, and share-broking.

In Calcutta, the Marwaris were engaged in the raw jute trade. They owned a number of jute presses and baling units in the jute growing regions of Bengal. They exported jute to a limited extent, and supplied raw material to the several dozen jute mills around Calcutta operating under mainly Scottish ownership and management. Before World War I, the Marwaris entered the gunny export business. They did not do so as regular export firms, but as speculative sellers. That is, they would buy small lots from the mills and hold stocks or sell forward to the shippers. The significant feature of the business was their willingness 'to furnish ample cash security for any business contracted; consequently, the mills had no hesitation in dealing with them'.[53] Liquidity, again, was the key resource.

The jute trading business might have remained an opportunistic one but for World War I, when huge profits were to be had from the existing stocks. The rise of forward market rates encouraged some export firms to join in the forward trade, and fears arose among non-Marwari firms that the Marwari firms would corner the entire jute trade. Although the trade stabilised after the War, the balance of financial power did shift. During the Depression, one or two jute mills were started with Marwari capital, and European mills borrowed money from Marwari merchant-bankers. The relationship opened doors of jute mill management to Marwari merchants.[54] This was a significant concession, for the Marwaris resented the often-rude treatment they received from the European mill managers.[55] Nevertheless, the move did not signify a fundamental change in the character of the urban Marwari enterprise. Most firms remained tied to trading and banking. Among the few who set up factories, or the elite, there was considerable difference and randomness in the way they did so.[56]

---

[53] India, *Report on the Marketing and Transport of Jute*, New Delhi: Government Press, 1940, 89.

[54] Omkar Goswami, 'Then Came the Marwaris: Some Aspects of the Changes in the Pattern of Industrial Control in Eastern India', *Indian Economic and Social History Review*, 22(2), 1985, 225–49.

[55] Maria Misra, *Business, Race, and Politics in British India c. 1850–1960*, Oxford: Oxford University Press, 1999, 132–6.

[56] Gijsbert Oonk, 'The Emergence of Indigenous Industrialists in Calcutta, Bombay and Ahmedabad, 1850–1947', *Business History Review*, 88(1), 2014, 43–71.

Conclusion

The late 1800s were witness to a revolution in business. Earlier in the nine-teenth century, trade was composed of a few goods procured from regions within easy access from the port city: Malwa opium, Khandesh cotton, Bihar opium, or Bengal indigo. The interests of the big firms of this era were tied to one of these commodities. By contrast, in the second stage, the range of commodities had diversified, and commodities such as wheat or cotton were procured from greater distances. The big merchant firms of this era dealt in a more diversified basket of goods, and formed a part, perhaps a small part, of the enormous network of trading and banking, the mainstay of which were small local firms.

This world was segmented by ethnicity, caste, and community, because these identities were correlated with distinct sets of known clients. That knowledge was crucial in local banking especially. Differences also emerged in business organisation. Indians relied more on family ties in obtaining managers and money than did the Europeans, who tended to recruit non-family partners and tried to get money from London. Expatriate firms used the legal form of a partnership more often than did Indian firms. The expatri-ates were short of personnel with whom they could communicate and whom they could trust; therefore, they needed, more than the Indians did, to make unorthodox choices about managers. The prevalence of family or community among the Indians was not just a survival of tradition. Community ties were a conduit for exchange of information about clients. And these ties were at times reinvented.

The network built on agricultural trade was large and spread everywhere, but its capacity to invest money in industry was concentrated in a few cities. In port cities, the money market was well developed in the twentieth century. There were joint-stock banks, and the banks and prospective shareholders required their clients to be firms of a standard legal type rather than being kinship groups or the legal fiction created by British Indian law of the 'Hindu family'. Joining the money market, therefore, required the trading firm to acquire a degree of formal identity. Information flowed through more public channels. In overland trade, by contrast, there were very few banks, and those that did exist would not lend to the peasants. In this world, merchants and bankers preferred to deal with people they knew personally. Here family and community networks were especially useful.[57]

---

[57] Dejung, 'Bridges to the East', explains the reliance on agents with reference to costs of credit operations in an analysis of Volkart's operations in China.

Differences between the port cities were there too. For example, indigenous merchants in Bombay tended to be bigger firms than their counterparts in Calcutta. The difference stemmed partly from the trajectory that Parsi entrepreneurs had charted in the former city. The key to their success was shipping. A great deal of the cotton trade was also centred in western India, where Gujaratis ruled. By contrast, Bengal did not produce a major export grain, and did not have comparable growth of local trading-financing networks as in Gujarat. Tea trading was in the hands of expatriates because it was produced by expatriate planters and went abroad.

Trade profits would not automatically be converted into industrial investment, however. Industry was a totally different type of enterprise from trade, as we shall see in Chapter 5.

5 Capital and Empire (1850–1930): Industry

The trading world that joined the land (agriculture) and the sea (foreign trade) enabled industrialisation in an important, if indirect way. Marketing agents, managers, machines, and engineers needed for a factory to succeed were in short supply in 1850. Agricultural export created the capacity to pay for skilled services and machinery purchased from abroad. Merely the capacity to import machines or hire abroad would not be enough to explain factories. Industry required a great deal more money than did trade, and kept capital locked in for longer. Money was difficult in India. Leveraging would be suicidal for industries in this world, unless the process was carefully planned.

Here, organisation mattered. These resources were procured by different groups by different means. Indians usually operated in the home market, recruited managers from within the extended family, raised investment money from existing businesses, friends, and family. Those people already in long-distance trade had better chance of doing this – another way that agricultural trade helped industrial investment. The Europeans relied more on knowledge of foreign markets and agency networks in these markets. They recruited managers and partners from abroad. Most raised money from London, though increasingly they floated shares in India (mainly Calcutta). Because of these differences, the Europeans were more likely to use the corporate form for their firms, whereas Indians used a hybrid between a family and corporate, adapting the mix depending on their access to capital markets. Both sets of actors relied equally on the recruitment of technical people from abroad.

Because stock markets were undeveloped in India, the London money market did not value Indian investment highly until the railway companies began operation. Banks financed trade and not industrial investment. Industrial firms needed to tap into trading profits. This was true both of Europeans and Indians. But after the Indian Mutiny ended and Crown rule began (1858), a different type of foreign firm entered India. These came to India from an industrial base in Britain, or were fortune hunters with some money who joined industry after a short career in trade. I call them born-industrial, though the term should not be read literally. The British Empire spawned these enterprises in a sense. Faster transportation links, uniform legal framework, and the use of one official language within the Empire encouraged capitalists to become mobile. The Empire also increased the scope of public–private partnership and indirectly led to greater associational activity.

The emergence of modern industry was offset to some extent by a decline in traditional industry in the 1870s. However, based on the experience of the cotton handloom industry, we now know that the decline of the handicrafts was arrested from the 1870s, and reversed from around 1900.[1] More on this topic later.

This chapter describes the profile of some of the leading families and firms who invested in industry. Let us first consider the European investors.

European Industrialists

South India

Some of the European industrial firms of the twentieth century had trading origin.[2] The early history of Finlay was discussed in Chapter 3. In the 1870s, James Finlay started jute mills in Calcutta, and in the next decade, began selling Indian tea. By 1900, they owned the major part of the tea trade market in the Anaimalai and the Nilgiris, which were consolidated under four companies listed in London. Their other ventures included a cotton mill in Bombay and a sugar refinery in United Provinces. In the 1830s, ownership had passed on to a former partner, John Muir, and the firm stayed as family-controlled until 1924. Their core business by then was selling tea worldwide, in which business the London partner companies played an important role.[3]

Another South Indian enterprise, Harrisons and Crosfield, began as a Liverpool tea trader in 1844, and ventured into tea estates in Ceylon and South India in only about 1900. By then their distribution network was spread over a large area in Asia and the Pacific, and the firm was beginning to produce rubber in

---

[1] Tirthankar Roy, 'Consumption of Cotton Cloth in India, 1795–1940', *Australian Economic History Review*, 52(1), 2012, 61–84.

[2] In writing this section I have relied on a number of sources. Besides works cited in specific contexts, the sources include the *Oxford Dictionary of National Biography* (Ernest Cable, Edward Benthall, James Lyle Mackay, John Muir, Henry Neville Gladstone, Yule family); Somerset Playne, *Bengal and Assam, Behar and Orissa: Their History, People, Commerce, and Industrial Resources*, London: Foreign and Colonial Compiling and Publishing, 1917; Stephanie Jones, *Merchants of the Raj*, Basingstoke: Macmillan, 1992; Barry Barker, *Investment in India*, Bombay: Bombay Chamber of Commerce and Industry, 1961; and Lionel Carter, *Chronicles of British Business in Asia 1850–1960: A Bibliography of Printed Company Histories with Short Accounts of the Concerns*, Delhi: Manohar, 2002.

[3] See Geoffrey Jones and Judith Wale, 'Merchants as Business Groups: British Trading Companies in Asia before 1945', *Business History Review*, 72(3), 1998, 367–408, for a study of James Finlay.

Malaya. It abandoned partnership quite late, in 1908. Long after the founder of Parry, Thomas Parry, had died (1824, see Chapter 3 on Thomas Parry), his firm acquired sugar factories on the south-eastern coast, and by 1855, added more sugar plants. With these acquisitions, Parry changed from being a trading to a manufacturing firm. In the third quarter of the nineteenth century, Parry joined an emigration agency and began gold mining. Its sugar interests by then had emerged as the core of the business, with the addition of a distillery. In the 1890s, the firm merged with the East India Distilleries (EID) registered in London, to form EID Parry. In the early twentieth century, EID Parry briefly diversified into engineering, but its core business remained focused on sugar and insurance. In 1948, the company shifted its registration to India. McDowell, a former servant of the East India Company, on completing his indenture, set up a wine-merchant business in Madras in 1825. Later partners moved into blending spirits, then to blending tobacco, and processing and manufacturing these two products. McDowell is now the most famous brand among indigenous whiskies in India.

The biggest site of European investment in industry was Eastern India, as we shall learn next.

Eastern India

If we look only at legally registered firms, Calcutta was a European city. An approximate measure of the relative share of the Indian and European communities in the formal businesses of Calcutta would be the shareholding in the Bank of Bengal. In 1904, the proportions were 84 and 16 per cent between Europeans and Indians, respectively.[4] Of course, this is only an indicative measure.

There were many born-industrial European enterprises in this region. Jute and tea furnish the most examples. Jute is a natural fibre grown mainly in southern West Bengal and Bangladesh. It is used as a raw material for sacking cloth. The demand for sacks increased in the nineteenth century in keeping with the volume of international commodity trade. Until about 1850, Bengal raw jute was processed by a handicraft industry, and by mills outside India, mainly in Dundee in Britain, and somewhat later in Germany.[5] But already, mechanised jute spinning and weaving had started near Calcutta. George

---

[4] G. P. Symes Scutt, *The History of the Bank of Bengal: An Epitome of a Hundred Years of Banking in India*, Calcutta: A. J. Tobias, 1904, 104.
[5] The handicraft industry is studied by Indrajit Ray, 'Struggling against Dundee: Bengal Jute Industry during the Nineteenth Century', *Indian Economic and Social History Review*, 49(1), 2012, 105–46.

Acland's mill of 1855 was the pioneer. In a short time, the Indian industry grew to become a virtual monopoly in the world. Between 1869 and 1913, the number of mills increased from 5 to 64, and employment from 5–10,000 to 215,000. Until World War I, the industry was entirely owned and managed by Europeans.

A second field of European enterprise was tea. When the Company lost its monopoly of China trade (1833), it turned to India for supplies of tea. Assam, which had become part of British India in 1825, had the ideal climate and topography for tea plantations. Efforts to develop plantations in Assam began. The first Indian tea was made in a government experimental farm and arrived in England in 1838. Encouraged by the reception, the Assam Company was formed the following year taking over the government's farms. Also in 1838, the government set up rules for leasing out land to plantation companies. The terms were liberal, and in some cases liberalised further over time.

From the late nineteenth century, and especially after railway links between the Calcutta port and the Assam gardens had improved, there was a massive expansion of tea cultivation in Assam. Companies registered in London were the investors. The area under tea gardens grew from 154,000 acres in 1880 to 337,000 acres in 1900. Meanwhile, the number of workers increased from 184,000 to 665,000. Gardens sprang up in the Darjeeling hills and the Dooars region in north Bengal, and in the Surma valley in Eastern Bengal. Nearly 75 per cent of tea farming land, however, was in Assam. The share of Indian tea in Britain's market increased from 7 per cent in 1868 to 54 per cent in 1896. Unlike Assam, in Dooars and Surma Valley local capitalists owned some of the smaller gardens.

Who were the pioneers in the born-industrial set? Andrew Yule (1834–1902), merchant and industrialist, started and managed jute, coal, and tea companies in Calcutta. The group's London associates were George Yule and later Yule, Catto, main shareholders of Morgan Grenfell. Gillanders Arbuthnot was founded in Calcutta in 1833 by John Gladstone, trading in textiles and indigo. In 1843, Gladstone, Wyllie (after James Wyllie) and later Gladstone, Lyall were among the leading Calcutta trading and insurance firms of the nineteenth century, known as Gillanders Arbuthnot. John's grandson Henry Gladstone led diversification into jute around 1880. Before 1947, Gillanders owned Indian Copper, which produced practically the entire output of copper in India.

Jardine Skinner formed in Bombay in 1825, and reconstituted in Calcutta in 1844. It had common ancestry with the east Asian conglomerate Jardine Matheson, founded by the China traders William Jardine and James Matheson. Jardine Skinner started in jute with Kamarhatty Company in 1877 and Kanknarra Company in 1882, and later diversified to tea. George Henderson was a Calcutta merchant who founded the Baranagar Jute Factory in 1857, one of the earliest jute mills in the neighbourhood of Calcutta. McLeod was a partnership engaged in jute agency with Dundee before they established a string of jute mills (1907–12). The group's founder Charles McLeod was first a jute trader (1880s) and later the manager-owner of the McLeod group of jute mills, of which Soorah, Kelvin, and Empire were the most important.

Indigo agency was the source of prosperity for a Calcutta concern that turned industrial, Kilburn. C. E. Schoene, Calcutta merchant in indigo, founded the firm in 1842. E. D. Kilburn, with family history in silk trading, joined him in 1847 as partner. Its survival through the worst years of indigo probably owed to an early diversification into cloth, rice, and jute. Cloth came from Liverpool, rice was sent to Australia, and jute went from Bengal to Dundee. The firm later diversified into shipping, engineering, and tea, and managed the oldest tea company in India, Assam Company, from 1867. By 1900, Kilburn was a managing agent for several tea estates. Kilburn's greatest legacy was an electricity generation and distribution firm called Calcutta Electric Supply Corporation, set up in 1897 with a contract to supply electricity to users in Calcutta. The firm exists today as one of the better-managed utility companies in a generally inefficient industry dominated by government companies, and is owned by the R. P. Goenka group of Calcutta.

Shaw Wallace imported Manchester piece goods, cement, metals, and paper and exported hides and skins and raw cotton. Walter Duncan, who started the partnership that was to become Duncan Brothers, a name in tea plantation and jute mills, was originally a tea and jute exporter (after a short stint as an employee of the Bank of Bengal). Anderson Wright started as a merchant house in Calcutta, and owned or managed jute mills (including Kharda Jute), coal mining company, insurance, trading, and shipping line to Natal. Its London counterpart was Clarke, Wilson and Co.

Offbeat cases of traders turning industrial include T. A. Martin of Messrs. Walsh, Lovett & Co., a Birmingham firm that dealt in metals and construction material in South America and opened a branch in Calcutta (1874). Later in the nineteenth century, Martin formed a partnership with a Bengali, R. N. Mukherjee, to set up the largest engineering firm in Eastern India, Martin Burn. From 1918, the firm managed Indian Iron and Steel Co or IISCO, which, along with Tata Steel, was an indigenous integrated steel factory.

In the 1830s, Robert Mackenzie, partner of William Mackinnon after 1847, was a piece-goods trader in Ghazipur (Bihar). Between 1847 and 1856, the partnership (Mackenzie died in a shipwreck in 1852) was still engaged in merchandising, when Mackinnon started the British India Steam Navigation (Fig. 5.1).[6] The shipping company gained from a mail contract with the

---

[6] J. Forbes Munro, *Maritime Enterprise and Empire: Sir William Mackinnon and His Business Network, 1823–1893*, Woodbridge: Boydell and Brewer, 2003.

Fig. 5.1 The British India Steam Navigation Company's mail steamers
alongside Latter Street Wharf (Rangoon), 1920s
© British Library

government. One of the companies connected with the group, Mackinnon-
Mackenzie, invested in tea estates and jute manufacturing, and was one of the
leading managing agencies in Calcutta between 1860 and 1900. James
Mackay, Earl of Inchcape, joined in 1874 and was in charge around 1900,
when the company invested heavily in jute, including India Jute Mill. Closely
allied with this group was another, Macneill Barry. General merchants Duncan
Macneill and John Mackinnon established Macneill and Co in 1876, which
joined the Inchcape group in 1914. They owned and managed tea, jute, inland
navigation, and Ganges Rope Co. They later merged with Kilburn.

The early history of the big Calcutta group called the Bird Brothers again
illustrates (like Kilburn and Mackinnon-Mackenzie) how important doing
business with the government was to some of the trading firms of the Empire
era. Samuel Bird supplied indentured labour to government construction
projects.[7] Among early side businesses of the firm were railway contracts for
loading and unloading goods between boats and trains; a government

---

[7] Godfrey Harrison, *Bird and Company of Calcutta*, Calcutta: Anna Art Press, 1964.

contract to unload grain from ships in Calcutta; and a bullock caravan train between Darjeeling, a European settlement, and Sahibganj, a railway junction. Some of its original businesses, such as the labour contract, the railway contract, and the bullock caravans were in decline in the 1870s, and the firm of Bird needed to reinvent itself. In two major steps taken in 1874 and 1875, the Birds acquired Oriental Jute Company's assets, took over the McAllister managing agency, and also took over a coal mine, coincidentally from the same McAllister.

The entry of Bird in India had happened when banking was still limited, capital market non-existent, and laws not clearly set out. They were not the only firm that made the move from commerce to industry by taking over the assets of a defunct business. But even that did not save them from financial trouble. Though a great deal of the background to these moves remains unknown, the Birds were helped in these projects by their few friends in Calcutta, which included the family of Ernest Cable, later head of the firm, and the Dignams of Orr, Dignam, the leading business solicitors of Calcutta. In a little over ten years, Bird had changed from a trading firm to a manufacturing firm, but the changeover was not complete. Their contract labour business continued, and many large government construction projects came their way. Ernest Cable (1859–1927) became a partner of the firm in 1886. Thereafter, Bird diversified into jute and coal. In 1917 Bird acquired F. W Heilgers, a German managing agency with interests in paper, jute, and coal. Major Heilgers's companies were Kinnison Jute and Naihati Jute. Around 1947, Bird and Heilgers was headed by Cable's son-in-law and partner Edward Benthall (1893–1961).

The Scotsman Thomas Duff came to Calcutta after a stint with the Borneo Company in the 1870s, and founded two jute companies, Samnuggur Jute Factory (1873), and Titaghur Jute Factory (1883). Thomas Duff and Co. took on the agency of the Victoria Jute Factory Co. in 1888 and that of the Angus Company in 1933. It was registered in London until 1949, when it registered in India. The holding company was based in Dundee. Turner Morrison was a shipping firm established by Alfred Turner (c. 1860) as an extension of the Liverpool trading house Turner and Co. They managed the Asiatic Steam Navigation Co. Alexander Lawrie and Stephen Balmer set up Balmer Lawrie in the 1860s, which first went into tea, and then developed in engineering and coal. Octaviaus Steel was mainly engaged in tea, coal, railways, and limestone.

Last but certainly not the least, was Williamson Magor, the largest tea producer in the world today and a company owned by B. M. Khaitan of Calcutta. Two individuals of Calcutta, J. H. Williamson, whose brother had an association with the Assam Co, the first tea company of India, and R. B. Magor, an employee of the Great Eastern Hotel in Calcutta, started Williamson Magor in 1869 with a main interest in tea.

Kanpur and Bombay

Mirzapur, as we have seen, was mainly a trading town. By contrast, nearby Kanpur had developed from a trading town to a manufacturing one, led by both European and Indian capital. The most famous Indian industrial family of Kanpur, Juggilal Kamlapat, came from a Marwari trading firm, Ramnath Baijnath. But this was a later development.

Kanpur was probably the largest settlement of European traders in northern India before the Indian Mutiny of 1857. Several families here were established as indigo planters and tobacco traders. Several of these settlers lost their lives during the Mutiny, including one Christie who was the co-founder of what was to become the largest firm of Kanpur, Begg Sutherland. But Kanpur's advantageous location and its subsequent emergence as a large garrison helped European and Indo-European enterprise revive soon after.

Begg Dunlop was founded c. 1850 by David Begg, indigo trader and planter, in Calcutta. The firm diversified in jute during the headship of George Sutherland around 1900. Sutherland's involvement led to the formation of Begg Sutherland, which managed six Kanpur cotton mills. The principal company Alliance was a multi-unit jute mill of Calcutta. The largest European company of Kanpur, the British India Corporation, was the product of a collaboration between five Kanpur merchants, George Allen, W. E. Cooper, Bevan Petman, J. Condon and Gavin Jones, who, between 1876 and 1894, started woollen mills, cotton mills, and leather factories in the city.

The other prominent Kanpur entrepreneur, who set up a large leather manufacturing firm, was William Cooper of Cooper Allen. Cooper came from a landholding family in England and was in his early career a commodity trader and indigo planter. His partner George Allen had a similar profile in business. Many other British individuals who became prominent in the industrial world of Kanpur had been artisans or managers of estates in their early years. In a pattern reminiscent of jute, in Kanpur, Europeans owned big saddle and harness factories, whereas Muslim traders supplied them with hides.[8] A. H. Creet, an Armenian born in Persia, set up one of the best-known and early private tanneries in the city. Creet, who migrated to India in 1874, was first a jeweller in Lucknow, then a dealer in leather, and finally proprietor of the Cawnpore Tannery in 1896. A decade later, a partnership between William Stork and two Muslim hide merchants of Delhi and Kanpur, bought the factory.

Bombay had fewer European enterprises. In the second half of the nineteenth century, the three largest European firms – Greaves, Brady, and

---

[8] Somerset Playne, *The Bombay Presidency, the United Provinces, the Punjab, etc.: Their History, People, Commerce and Natural Resources*, London: Foreign and Colonial Compiling and Publishing Co, 1917–20.

Killick – did not originate in trade or industry, but in the enterprise of skilled mechanics. They were more akin to the Martins of Calcutta. Around 1880, an American trading firm, Stearns Hobart & Co., entered Bombay's history as the first company to propose a mass urban-transit system (horse-drawn tram). This proposal was the foundation of the Bombay Electric Supply and Transport Company, which now runs Bombay's buses.[9]

The connection between trade and manufacture was much closer with the Indians. In fact, there were very few born-industrial ventures among them.

Indian Industrialists

British industrialisation had established cotton as a major export article from India and export merchants began to build contacts with British ports and manufacturing centres. The Parsis, who were already familiar with apprenticeship in Britain relating to ship-repair, took to this road without much difficulty. The 1860s crash in Bombay led to widespread bankruptcy among the contemporary trading firms, and the Parsi firms took a very big hit. The small group of wealthy individuals who survived the crash had already spread risks by investing in industry.[10]

Dinshaw Petit (1823–1901) was the most famous personality to have done so. Although a pioneering cotton mill set up by Cowasji Davar had appeared ten years before the crash, the decade after the crash saw the transformation of Bombay from a trading to a manufacturing city. Petit's apprenticeship had happened in a European trading firm with operations in China and opium. Petit survived the cotton famine crash to establish more mills, and his success in turn attracted others to invest in mills. His agent Nowrosjee Wadia (1849–99) started Bombay Dyeing in 1875. The move by Jamsetji Tata (1839–1901) from China and Africa trades to the Alexandra Mill was another instance of this pattern. In Tata's case, this move was followed by the Empress Mills (1874–7) of Nagpur. Already, Jamsetji was developing an interest in the prospect of steel (see next). Nine out of the thirteen mills set up in the 1870s belonged to Parsi owners.[11] In 1914, there were 95 cotton textile mills in India; 34 had been started by Parsi entrepreneurs.

---

[9] On the subsequent history of the firm, see William J. Hausman, Peter Hertner, Mira Wilkins, *Global Electrification: Multinational Enterprise and International Finance in the History of Light and Power, 1878–2007*, Cambridge: Cambridge University Press, 2008, 108.

[10] Ashok V. Desai, 'The Origins of Parsi Enterprise', *Indian Economic and Social History Review*, 5(4), 1968, 307–18.

[11] Rajnarayan Chandavarkar, *The Origins of Industrial Capitalism in India*, Cambridge: Cambridge University Press, 1994.

The interdependence between trade, industry, and finance played a very important role in sustaining industrialisation. The combination of cotton textiles and cotton trade was an advantage. Cotton mills procured machines and foremen from Lancashire, to which market Bombay's merchants sold cotton. The export market for raw cotton, which boomed during the American Civil War, reduced in importance somewhat, but Lancashire remained a steady and a major buyer of cotton. The Indian mills sold a large part of their output of yarn to ports in China where again Bombay's merchants had sold cotton. The joining of trade with finance was also an advantage. Trade in cotton mill stock expanded in response to mill construction and growth of public shareholding. The Parsis had set up banks and loan societies in the 1840s and the 1850s. Cowasji Davar's energy mainly went into banking rather than industry. After the cotton market speculation, and in Bombay's subsequent growth as a financial market, Gujarati stockbrokers and bankers took the lead. In the 1870s more than three hundred share brokers met almost daily under a banyan tree, where the stock exchange stands now.[12] Capital moved from trade into mills more easily thanks to the mediation of stockbrokers.

Among other communities who invested in cotton mills were the Khojas, the Bhatias, the Gujarati traders and bankers with their base in Ahmedabad, and the Bombay-based Baghdadi Jews. Several of them had some history of collaboration with Europeans. Some had withdrawn from more active maritime trade as European firms based in London took control of the maritime trade. Others had expanded their commercial operations further afield into overland trade, a legacy of the pre-European pattern of regional integration. The owners of the first cotton mills came from these communities, and partly from European trading houses dealing in cotton.

The pioneering names among cotton mill owners included Petit, Wadia and Tata (Parsis), Currimbhoys (Khoja), Sassoons (Jews), Khatau Makanji, Morarji Goculdas, Thakersey (Bhatias from Kutchch), and Greaves Cotton, W. H. Brady, and Killick Nixon (European houses). The origin of Ahmedabad's mill industry was more rooted in Hindu and Jain business. Among the prominent names, Sarabhais and Lalbhais, were Jain traders already prominent as pedhis. Pedhi would usually mean a company, establishment, or a business house; it could also mean charitable trust, such as the Anandji Kalyanji Pedhi active today looking after the religious and cultural well-being of the Shwetambar Jain community.[13] Many pedhis were bankers. A few industrial groups originated in Asian trade. The Khoja firm of

---

[12] Bombay, *Report of the Bombay Stock Exchange Enquiry Committee*, Bombay: Government Press, 1924, 3.
[13] See www.anandjikalyanjipedhi.org/ (accessed 5 August 2017).

Currimbhoy Ebrahim had started as cotton yarn exporters to China. The Sassoons (see Chapter 4) also conformed to this pattern.

The relative scale of Parsi big business was shrinking from the end of the nineteenth century. Other than Tata, Wadia, and Petit, one major industrial group emerged, Ardeshir Godrej (1868–1936), in the early twentieth century. Godrej was an offbeat figure in this set. A trained lawyer practising in Zanzibar in his early life, he returned to Bombay and developed an interest in lock-making. He took a patent on a new design, and on that foundation built a factory making locks and deposit boxes. This was the start of a diversified business group with interest in furniture, soaps, and real estate.

Running a cotton mill was a very risky business. Community network was of little help in meeting the most important challenges. The absence of an organised capital market was a constant source of instability. Longevity of mills tended to be short, and profits fluctuating. The business only survived because there were many trading firms available to buy up liquidating property. Between 1885 and 1925, out of the 100 odd mills in Bombay, 45 mills were taken into liquidation and reconstructed under other names; 12 were burnt down or closed and dismantled; 16 transferred to agencies; and 24 were working under the same agencies. Of these 24, only 5 belonged to five pioneering and long-surviving groups: Maneckji Petit, Morarji Goculdas, Hindustan under Thakersey Moolji, Khatau Makanji, and Sassoon. Several of Bombay's mills changed hands many times. Coorla Mills, for example, was one of the earliest ventures set up in 1860 by Bomanji Wadia, and changed hands twice (first Cossimbhoy Dharamsey and later Merwanji Framji Panday) before the company running it was liquidated in 1886 and Jamsetji Tata purchased the premises and started the Swadeshi Mills. A similar example was Albert and Victoria. In the case of Alexandra, the owner was convicted for mismanagement of funds. Also tainted by a corruption scandal was Dwarkadas Dharamsey, who managed three mills that changed hands. Greaves Cotton took over premises started by Manchester firms in Bombay, and the Sassoons took over a cluster of small and unprofitable mills. K. M. Hiramanick, a Parsi merchant, managed a number of mills, some of which eventually ended up with the Currimbhoy group. The City of Bombay Mill, started by Mancherji Banaji, was taken over by the managing agent W. H. Brady. Indeed, in many cases of changeover, the agent took over both ownership and operation of the mill.[14]

After Bombay, Ahmedabad was the second major centre for the development of the textile industry. Although Ahmedabad was not a port city, British acquisition in 1818 'brought about significant changes in the climate of

---

[14] S. M. Rutnagur, *Bombay Industries: The Cotton Mills*, Bombay: The Indian Textile Journal Limited, 1927.

enterprise' in the city.[15] Business firms of Ahmedabad, for example, started making routine use of British Indian commercial law, which, among other effects, activated the real estate market and real estate development in the city. Prominent bankers, therefore, welcomed the integration of the city in British India. In 1863, Bombay and Ahmedabad were connected by a direct train line. Thereafter, while artisanal enterprise may have suffered somewhat, the bankers and traders of Ahmedabad could think of operating in a wider geographical zone that included the cotton-growing Bombay port Khandesh to the east, and cotton-growing Broach to the south. Khandesh itself was connected by rail with Ahmedabad via Surat in 1900.

In the eighteenth century, Ahmedabad bankers did considerable business with the numerous princely states that ruled western India. In the 1810s, they financed the opium traffic between central India and Bombay. Shortly thereafter, the government of the East India Company devised several schemes to promote export of raw cotton from the western coast. Individuals connected with the trade tried to start spinning mills themselves. In these businesses, again, Ahmedabad bankers occasionally made some investment. In this way, capitalists of the city had developed considerable familiarity with cotton textile trade and manufacture when mill construction started in Bombay city. By 1850, both Bombay and Ahmedabad belonged in the huge complex of cotton trade and financing of cotton trade then emerging in western India.

The biography of the pioneer industrialist of Ahmedabad, Ranchhodlal Chhotalal (1823–98), shows that this prehistory of trade and banking did not naturally lead to the emergence of an industrial entrepreneur. What he had inherited from his family or learnt from observing the cotton traders apparently played a small part in his evolution into an industrialist. Chhotalal came from a Nagar Brahmin family. Nagar Brahmins were often appointed as court officers in the princely states of western India, and in that capacity, acquired proficiency in languages, including Persian, Marathi, and English. Chhotalal travelled a lot too, and through these travels, he acquired the two most important features of his curriculum vitae: exposure to Europeans and experience of living in different parts of India.[16]

Chhotalal worked as an officer of the Company agent in several states, and though he lost this job owing to his alleged and unproven role in the Lunavada state succession dispute, he was proficient in English and had among his closest associates two British individuals: one an army officer known as Fuljames, and the other one a ginning mill owner of Broach known as Landon.

[15] Dwijendra Tripathi and Makrand Mehta, 'The Genesis of the Cotton Textile Industry in Ahmedabad', IIMA Case Study No, IIMA/ECO0115, Ahmedabad, 1970.
[16] S. M. Edwardes, A Memoir of Rao Bahadur Ranchhodlal Chhotalal, Exeter: William Pollard, 1920.

When the plan for a mill was first drawn up (and later abandoned), Fuljames had supplied information on the textile industry in Britain, and Landon offered to fund half the cost of a textile mill. Three Baroda bankers, two princes, and Chhotalal himself would contribute the other half. Bankers of Ahmedabad refused to subscribe any money. The project was revived again around 1858. Already Landon had started a spinning mill in Broach, and Davar's and Maneckji Petit's had been working for a few years in Bombay.

The machines for the mill were purchased in England through the agency of the merchant, later Parliamentarian and public intellectual Dadabhai Naoroji (1825–1917). One set of machines never arrived. The second set took many months to reach Ahmedabad because of poor transport links with the port of Cambay. Installation of the factory was delayed by repeated misfortune with British engineers. Still, by 1863 it was up and running and by 1870 had grown about four times the original scale and added weaving, thanks to the efforts of Edington and Whittle, two engineers. As these companies made profits and offered large dividends, nine per cent in some years, some of the original shareholders sold their stake. In this way, there emerged a secondary market for mill shares.

Chhotalal was one of the first industrialists to take up a leadership role in city administration. As in the business ventures, in his political ones he also faced resistance from other merchants of the city. He was trying to push through water supply and underground drainage schemes by the Ahmedabad municipality. The move was opposed by the wealthy residents of the city who feared more taxes on them. The mainly European and Parsi engineer corps was divided in their view of the merits of these schemes. In the worst phase of the dispute, Chhotalal faced violent physical assault in a public meeting. His extensive political connection, personal wealth, and goodwill with the British administration eventually saw these schemes through.

Despite a violent beginning, the joining of business with public adminis-tration was to become a model for the future. Industrialists were big city residents almost without exception. They joined the administration of city municipalities, where the principle of self-government was first tried. Their exposure to organised institutionalised politics was from the start greater than that for merchants and bankers in the interior of the country. This exposure made them politically central, both to the imperial administration and to their own community of capitalists. Both these factors were active especially in the port cities. The second-generation owners of long-surviving textile mills all tended to be prominent public figures, working not only for community-bound charity or educational projects as many Parsis did, but also in the municipality, port management, famine relief, and general and women's education. For some examples, Gordhandas Khatau, son of Khatau Makanji, was an elected member of the Bombay Corporation; Lalbhai Dalpatbhai, the Ahmedabad mill owner, was an elected member of the Ahmedabad District Board; Sylas Moses, a senior manager of the Sassoon group, was a member of the Bombay Port Trust; George Sutherland, partner of Begg Dunlop, was a Sheriff of Calcutta and an elected member of the Bengal legislature. Similar, if fewer, examples can be found also among artisan-entrepreneurs of these times (see next).

Ranchhodlal was an early example of the entrepreneurs who made their views about politics and economic policy known in public. He was neither a free trader nor a protectionist, but advocated free trade with those countries which offered free trade to Indian goods and protection for others. In this view, Britain was an equal trade partner of India's, and no specific worries were expressed about British competition in the textile market itself. Later, such public presentation of opinions about economic policy became institutionalised in associations, and after World War I, the activity was becoming politicised as well.

Most Indian industrialists emerged from cotton and textile trade, and as industrialists, retained their ties with textiles. Ardeshir Godrej was an exception to this pattern. Another figure broke with the pattern in a more decisive way. The emergence of the largest and most diversified conglomerate in postcolonial India was owed to this break.

J. N. Tata and Tata Steel

Jamsetji Tata, hailing from a family of priests, joined his father's trading firm in the 1850s. While engaged in trades between India, China, and Britain, he travelled to and lived in Hong Kong and Shanghai. In the 1860s, trading interests also took him to England, where he had the chance to develop a good understanding of cotton textile manufacturing. During the American Civil War, Tata made considerable profits, but lost a lot of his assets in the subsequent crash. When a commissariat contract helped rebuild his firm somewhat, Tata decided to put his experience gained in England to effect. In 1869, he bought an oil mill in Bombay and turned it into a cotton mill (Alexandra Mill). In 1877, a second mill followed in Nagpur (Empress Mill), an offbeat location for a large factory at the time, but in terms of costs for accessing material, an advantageous one. This factory was the first Indian mill to introduce ring spindles, ventilation, and dehumidification. In 1886, the third of the three main textile factories was set up (Swadeshi) in Bombay.

Tata's central Indian enterprise brought him in contact with geological reports that informed him of large coal and iron deposits in the British Central Provinces. In 1900, he obtained prospecting licences in the areas that were considered the most promising, and left for the United States of America to meet steel manufacturers. Following this visit, the geologist C. M. Weld came to India to prospect in these regions. The results were disappointing, but Weld was asked and agreed to stay on for more enquiries. In 1903 and 1904, a series of discoveries were made of iron and coal deposits within reasonable proximity, one major find being located inside the princely state of Mayurbhanj. The team then included Weld, P. N. Bose, and the American Charles Perin.

Jamsetji died in 1904, but in the knowledge that an integrated steel factory would be possible. The plan was far from being materialised. His sons Dorabji and Ratanji Tata, along with other members of the inner circle of Tata firms, tried to raise the enormous sum of money that would be needed to realise the plan. Their effort to persuade British investors met with little success. Unless a share of control was offered, foreign investors did not want to join the enterprise. Mainly with money invested by Indian capitalists and princely states, and the engineering consultancy provided by the American firm Kennedy, Sahlin and Co, Tata Steel started operation in 1908.

The early history of the company depicts a struggle to survive many challenges with limited financial means. The major user of steel then, the railways, imported its stock. The need to hire an expensive foreign engineering corps, repeated problems with machinery and quality of material, and achieving coordination between the divisions, were some of the other problems. World War I offered unusual opportunities to the firm because steel was in worldwide shortage. After the war, government policy turned somewhat sympathetic towards domestic firms, and Tata Steel was promised both tariff protection and a railway contract, provided it could become internationally competitive within the near future. Thus began the Greater Extension Programme of the late 1920s. The programme ran into rough weather because worldwide steel was then in excess supply. Tariffs needed to be raised, and the government raised it (Chapter 6). However, the continuing problems also revealed that the firm needed to change its management model, that is, retrain workers, reduce the number of workers, raise productivity, and shed its dependence on highly paid foreign engineers. By 1935, the programme was completed successfully, that is, while raising the scale of the plant, the firm managed to greatly reduce employment. This was, however, achieved at the cost of industrial relations in the main plant.

Other Industries

If we exclude textiles and steel, the other industries where factories and mechanised or semi-mechanised operations ruled were formed of a few isolated firms. In the interwar period, protection encouraged the sugar industry (more on this in Chapter 6). Kanpur and Madras were the main centres of leather manufacture. Some of the Kanpur tanneries, and especially the

European and Eurasian ones, were started to meet the demand for leather from large local users, such as the army, the mill, or the transport industry. A young man in his twenties, G. A. Chambers, was an assistant in one of the Madras tanneries, when in 1903 he began trading on his own account. Shortly after, he rented a tannery at Pallavaram to start chrome tanning. The largest Madras firm, the Chrome Leather Co., evolved from this venture, its growth owing to a partnership with the great Madras house and coachmakers Simpsons, who needed chrome leather for upholstery. As in Bombay, the firm also supplied cotton-mill spare parts.[17]

As mentioned before (Chapter 4), Hindu trading groups did not take to leather, probably for religious reasons, leaving the field open to Muslim and Eurasian merchants. Some of the most successful Muslim tanners in Kanpur – including the firms of H. M. Halim, Abdul Gafoor, M. A. Wasay, and H. Nabi Baksh – accumulated capital through the agency of the European tanneries, or as agents of German trading firms. The exit of the Germans during World War I (Chapter 4) invited Indian capital into the industry. In Bombay in the late nineteenth century, Bohras and Memons, the Muslim trading castes, owned tanneries and controlled a considerable part of the export trade. The trading group called Khojas financed leather trade. In the 1890s, the Khoja or Muslim merchant was 'to the Mochi [leather-worker] what the Bania [rural merchant-moneylender in this case] [was] to the agriculturist'.[18] That is, they were mainly financiers. Sometimes they lent money to tanneries. When debts were left unpaid, the Khoja trader took up a bankrupt factory and ran it.

Trade and production of craft goods, by contrast with the examples just discussed, were much less capital-intensive. But a capitalist consolidation of sorts was underway in this field too.

The Transformation of the Crafts

Chapter 3 mentions the surprising finding of a U-shaped trend in the production of cotton cloth in the handloom weaving industry between 1795 and 1940, the inflexion occurring around 1880. This is surprising because labour productivity continued to diverge between mechanised and handmade weaving systems. And yet, the fact of a revival in artisanal production of textiles is indisputable. The largest craft in colonial India, cotton handloom weaving,

---

[17] Based on Somerset Playne, *Southern India: Its History, People, Commerce, and Industrial Resources*, London: Foreign and Colonial Compiling and Pub. Co, 1914–5, 145–6, 213, 688, 701–3; and *Indian Leather Trades and Industries Year-Book*, Madras, 1967.

[18] A 1906 government report cited in Tirthankar Roy, *Traditional Industry in the Economy of Colonial India*, Cambridge: Cambridge University Press, 1999, where a fuller range of source citations on the leather merchant can be found.

engaged about a third of the industrial workforce of 13 million in 1901. Handlooms increased their output of cotton cloth from 677 million yards in 1880 to 1945 million yards in 1940. This was a general pattern. In iron-making, in woollen and silk textiles, and several other industries, the production of manufactured raw material (like yarn) was quickly taken over by mechanised imports. But artisans held steady in the production of consumer goods and finished goods for the final market. Between 1870 and 1931, employment in the handicrafts fell at the rate of 2–3 per cent per year.[19] But even as employment fell, income arising in the handicrafts increased, or labour productivity increased. This is confirmed by the fact that most types of skilled artisan wages rose between 1900 and 1935.[20]

What has this finding to do with business history? It suggests three important conclusions about the nature of capitalist transformation in small-scale industry in these years. First the concept of 'deindustrialisation', commonly employed as a description of what happened to the crafts as a whole (see Chapter 3), should be discarded. Second, craftsmen rather than merchants were beginning to play a more entrepreneurial role in this time. And third, a process of capital accumulation was underway in artisan clusters that formed in the small towns, which we may miss noticing if we stay too focused on the port cities and their satellites. How do we know any of this?

Until the 1980s, the most accepted position on the question – what happened to the crafts – was that the Industrial Revolution and free trade led to a great decline in traditional industry. The implication was that the surviving artisans survived by accepting lower wages and greater poverty. The process was known as 'deindustrialisation', as a deliberate contrast with the word 'industrialisation'. While not disputing that artisanal livelihoods did suffer decline in the nineteenth century, some scholars in the 1980s suggested that 'deindustrialisation' had too much of a finality. It does not do a good job of explaining the link between crafts in the past and modern industry in the present. Since so much of modern industry used craft skills in various forms, there must be a connection between the two worlds. Another story was needed.

This story, which builds largely on the link between the handloom weaving and modern textile industry, has two components. First, consumption patterns of textiles and many other consumer goods were diverse enough to demand both handmade and machine-made goods. Their products were not always substitutes, and the handmade technology imparted certain qualities in the product that the buyers recognised as distinct and which they valued. Thus,

---

[19] The relevant data sets come from the censuses of India, various years. The range of growth indicates problems of definitional nature.

[20] Tirthankar Roy, 'Globalization, Factor Prices, and Poverty in Colonial India', *Australian Economic History Review*, (1), 2007, 73–94.

in the standard women's apparel, sari, where border designs were a marker of distinctiveness, tradition, and beauty, handloom weaving held on its own; whereas in plain working wear used by men, machine-made cloth was more commonly used. The revival of handloom weaving (and a few other similar crafts), therefore, had owed to a uniquely artisanal resource, skills, more than money capital.[21] In general, small-scale industries, especially those that demanded craft skills, showed remarkable persistence in the early twentieth century, despite lack of access to capital, and poor infrastructure in the small towns where they clustered.

Secondly, far from suffering loss of custom due to free trade, those artisans who carried on *gained from free trade*, for trade brought to their reach cheap machine-made inputs (cotton yarn, metal looms and parts, and chemicals like dyes), and increased their tradability. In these industries, inequality increased, as merchants made money whereas wages did not change much. Some of these merchants employed the poorer artisans in wage-based workshops (see also discussion on 'karkhana' in Chapter 2). This last tendency was present especially in western India in the interwar period.[22] Skilled artisans were especially prone to migration, in search of better business, and they were often welcomed by town authorities. Handloom weavers of western India relocated when possible near cloth and yarn markets, met new types of consumer demand, invested in new tools and processes, and defined the professional character of several industrial towns in western India.

The evolution in handloom weaving gave rise to weaving factories sometimes called 'power looms'. The first power-loom factories appeared in the textile towns of western India (like Sholapur, Malegaon, Ahmednagar, and Ichalkaranji) at the turn of the century. Their number grew in the interwar period, but until 1940 they did not attract much attention in contemporary reports.[23] When they did get noticed, it was found that migrant handloom weavers established these power-loom factories. Why did handloom weavers switch to power-driven looms? The difference in the cost of acquiring a power loom against a handloom was small, especially after local fabrication of looms began. And the handloom was too slow a machine when markets enlarged in scale. Above all, the handloom weavers switched because they could, they understood the loom mechanism too well to miss the chance. The connection between craft skills and modern industry was also visible in parts of the leather

---

[21] The comparable cases of textiles and iron manufactures is discussed in Tirthankar Roy, 'Knowledge and Divergence from the Perspective of Early Modern India', *Journal of Global History*, 3(4), 2008, 361–87.

[22] Tirthankar Roy, *Artisans and Industrialization: Indian Weaving in the Twentieth Century*, Delhi: Oxford University Press, 1993; Roy, *Traditional Industry*.

[23] India, *Fact-Finding Committee (Handlooms and Mills)*, Calcutta: Government Press, 1942.

industry, gems and jewellery, carpets, printed textiles – all large export articles from the early twentieth century.

What has any of this to do with business history? The historian Douglas Haynes develops an argument about capitalism based on a study of the small-scale textile industry in western India. Arguing that the belief in the inevitability of the decline of the crafts stems from an understanding of industrialisation derived from European history, or the experience of the port cities, his book 'centres an understanding of industrial capitalism squarely in the history of the broader structures of the regional economy rather than in Europe or the colonial ports of India'.[24] The key sites were small towns, and the key actors the skilled migrant handloom weavers who formed settlements here. These towns were 'small' in comparison with the centres of factory industry, such as Ahmedabad or Bombay, but they grew rapidly in the late twentieth century, partly upon a livelihood base laid by artisan production. The 'small town' in the book, in other words, represents a distinct form of regional capitalism.

Haynes' work offers a particularly useful description of the 'weaver-capitalist', an emerging body of relatively wealthy employers who led the transition to power loom. Although technically factory owners, the factories they operated were quite different from the factories of Bombay and Calcutta. They hired fellow community members, made use of paternalistic relations, and used the idioms of caste and community to create a family-like atmosphere in the work site. And yet, by the very logic of capitalist development, inequality increased, living standards of migrant workers fell behind those of employers and traders, and all of that inevitably encouraged labour mobilisation.

In silk textiles, especially the traditional artisanal settlements like Kanchipuram in South India or Murshidabad in Bengal, descriptions available from around 1900 mention individuals who rose through the ranks to become shop owners in big city markets, wholesale suppliers of raw materials, campaigners of new tools and processes, community leaders, and 'master weavers' who put out work to neighbours.[25] In the 1880s, Joykrishna Mandal was one of the richer weavers of Mirzapur in central Bengal. He was the master-weaver for forty to fifty local families. They executed his contracts under supervision of Joykrishna himself, who was responsible for the quality of work done in his 'firm'. He executed large orders from Calcutta or Bombay and had 'great influence with their fellow caste-men'. Mrityunjoy Sarkar was one of Joykrishna's men in 1887, who was, by 1900, the most important master-weaver

[24] Douglas E. Haynes, *Small Town Capitalism in Western India: Artisans, Merchants, and the Making of the Informal Economy, 1870–1960*, Cambridge: Cambridge University Press, 2012, 6.
[25] I draw on Tirthankar Roy, 'Out of Tradition: Master Artisans and Economic Change in Colonial India', *Journal of Asian Studies*, 66(4), 2007, 963–91.

of the same area. He died a wealthy man in 1903, and had been influential behind the adoption of many improvements in designed fabrics. Nalli Chinnasamy Chetti of Kanchipuram, a weaver of the Padmasali handloom weaving community, established in 1928 a sari shop in Madras, which became the nucleus for one of India's largest silk sari retailers today, Nalli Silks.

Again confined to Bengal, but now from the metal product industry, Prem Chand Mistry of Kanchannagar had started as a generic toolmaker in the 1890s, but ended (c. 1905) with a large workshop using oil engines to drive lathes. L. V. Tikekar, a weaver-capitalist of Sholapur in western India, set up one of the first and the largest handloom factories of that town (1899), pioneered the power loom, and set up a factory to manufacture looms and equipment in Sholapur. Tulasi Ram of Madura, member of the Sourashtra weaving community of the town, was a dyeing technologist who revolutionised yarn-dyeing in Madura, and stimulated the handloom weaving enterprise of the entire Sourashtra community. Sir Pitti Theagaraya Chetty, a weaver-capitalist, was instrumental in the spread of the fly-shuttle pit loom in Madras Presidency. Mohammad Yaar Khan, a merchant-manufacturer of the metal product industry in Moradabad, introduced standardisation and quality control in the engraved brassware export trade.

In some of these cases, master artisans became public figures by drawing upon community and political resources. Tulasi Ram was known as a social reformer among the Sourashtra community. A member of the National Congress until the early 1910s, Theagaraya Chetty later played a role in the non-Brahmin movement and formation of the Justice Party. He was also the President of the Madras Corporation.

Returning to corporate business, the evolution of business organisation during these years deserves a separate section because of the new laws that came into existence to protect the joint-stock company.

Business Organisation

Company

Until 1850, partnership was the general form of ownership and management, which made raising finance and hiring managers difficult at times. Still, legal recognition of partnership brought British law, courts of law in India, and Indian practice, into alignment. Limited liability was formally recognised in the first Companies Act of 1850. It was not until the 1860s that its coverage became comprehensive. The period 1860–65 saw a boom in company formation and share markets. The crash that followed exposed the organisational weakness of the companies so hastily formed. The 1870s saw a revival of company formation, but now new and reformed company laws increased stability. The Bombay stock exchange was organised in 1875.

Until very recent times, professional managers played a minor role in managing Indian businesses, and company directors were drawn from family and friends. Whether a company had public shareholding or not, if it was Indian owned it was family managed, and usually in the main owned by the family. Both Europeans and Indians used family ties to run businesses in the nineteenth century. Europeans used non-family managers more whereas the Indians the family more. But then, in India, the notion of the family was an expansive one, and merged with the notion of the community formed of caste and religious ties. This was, of course, inevitable in the presence of strong ritual communities, which maintained commensality and marriage rules quite strictly. In that case, the family included members related to each other by marriage, and marriage took place according to certain inclusion-exclusion rules. On top of this, law recognised succession rules among Hindus that empowered the joint family, and weakened testamentary rights. Law, effectively, defined the 'Hindu Undivided Family' as a partnership in which partners were joined by birth right. And none could easily exit the partnership or turn out others from it.[26]

If the Indian family firms recruited managers from within their family, extended family, and community networks, Europeans did so to a more limited extent. They used the legal contract of managing agency more often.

Managing Agency

The agency contract involved one firm, usually a partnership, to manage a set of companies, usually publicly held. In some cases, the promoter started a company and wrote a management contract between the company and itself. The idea of a management contract had originated in the insurance business in the early-nineteenth century. It survived the 1840s depression that destroyed many of the firms that had used this system. By the 1870s it changed form to some extent and became established in large-scale industry, mining, and plantations. Despite its importance, many practices associated with the operation of the system remained outside legislation until 1956.

The system had significant advantages. First, the promoter and the manager were often identical firms or families. But with the agency contract, the owners ensured two types of earning for themselves, dividend and commission, thus reducing the exposure of their income to market shocks. Further, commission

---

[26] Tirthankar Roy and Anand V. Swamy, *Law and the Economy in Colonial India*, Chicago, IL: University of Chicago Press, 2016.

was a cost and written off against profit. Therefore, it was not subject to income tax. Dividends were part of profit and taxed. Second, by having reputation fixed on an established management firm, the promoters ensured interest from the wider public in start-ups. This second effect can be read as conservation of managerial resources, since the reputation of one manager was shared by old and new firms alike. Third, the reputation effect allowed the managed company to raise money from the share market, without fear of losing control, because the managing agency contract ensured continued control of the original owner.

Although the concept was widely used, it was never an easy matter to read the implications of managing agency for corporate governance, mainly because in the case of the joint-stock company, the managing agency contract was practised in two different ways. If the agent was a majority shareholder in the managed company, it could potentially write the contract in such a way that minority shareholders had little chance to monitor or influence managers. If the agent was a minority shareholder in the managed company, by sheer force of numbers the owners had a better chance to observe and influence their behaviour. Both types, of course, used the company law to access equity and debt.

In the colonial times, most Indian-owned companies belonged in the first set and most European-owned companies belonged in the second set. If a managing agent promises low monitoring cost, shareholders would reward new enterprises floated and managed by it by investing money. The European companies commanded greater trust of public shareholders. The result was that the European managing agents evolved into 'conglomerates' around one agency firm, that is, one agency firm managed many companies often in unrelated fields among themselves. In all cases, the agency firm had only a small holding in the managed companies, sometimes none at all. They were recognised as mass managers, and managed firms whose equity was sold mainly to British expatriates and their family. Indian managing agents managed a small number of firms, and effectively owned them, generally by keeping equity small and owning most of it.

Indian companies were not badly governed due to this difference. The point rather is that the same law served different ends for them. Managing agency was a device for the family to retain control. Even when the standard legal partnership was used by everyone, among 'the old-established merchants in India, partnership has been strictly limited to members of the same family'.[27] Indian firms did not usually recruit top managers from outside the family, whereas Europeans recruited partners from related businesses, who were not

---

[27] Playne, *Southern India*, 661.

necessarily family members. They relied far more on what may be called an early form of the managerial market, which circulated people between London, Calcutta, Bombay, East Africa, and Southeast Asia.

Management

Most histories of European firms in India are histories of managers rather than families. In the late eighteenth and early nineteenth century, these managers were of a different kind from the ones today. Among the top managers, purely professional managers were rare. They were sometimes traders heading one firm, who teamed up with others to form a partnership, or they were salaried employees who moved up to become partners. This history of management is inseparable from the history of partnership as convention and as law. The partners were recruited from a social pool, but not necessarily. Evidence does not suggest that in the actual recruitment process, ethnic identity mattered more than the experience and capital of the people being recruited to head a firm. Ethnic identity may have mattered somewhat in the recruitment of junior workers.

This kind of firm is the subject of a rich literature. Sponsored histories of large Indo-British conglomerates like the Bird, Andrew Yule, Parrys, the Assam and Jorehat (Jorhat) companies, J. Thomas, and Williamson Magor, supply excellent descriptive accounts of the companies, and biographies of the managers who headed them.[28] They provide colourful accounts of their lives in India, and a useful if somewhat stylised view of India itself. They do not always suggest a notion of the firm, that is, the rules by which investment decisions were made. Academic histories of European enterprise in India address this issue of the nature of the firm, as well as the nature of the business

[28] Anon., *Andrew Yule & Co., Ltd, 1863–1963*, Edinburgh: privately printed, 1963; Godfrey Harrison, *Bird & Company of Calcutta, 1864–1964*, London: privately printed, 1964; Hilton Brown, *Parry's of Madras: A Story of British Enterprise in India*, Madras: privately printed, 1955; H. A. Antrobus, *A History of the Assam Company, 1839–1953*, London: privately printed, 1957; H. A. Antrobus, *A History of the Jorehaut Tea Company*, London: Tea and Rubber Mail, 1947; Peter Pugh, *Williamson Magor Stuck to Tea*, Cambridge: Cambridge Business Publishing, 1991; Colm Brogan, *James Finlay and Co. Ltd: Manufacturers and East India Merchants, 1750–1950*, Glasgow: Jackson, 1951; Anon, *A Century of Progress (Greaves Cotton & Company)*, Bombay: Greaves Cotton, 1960; John S. Gladstone, *History of Gillanders Arbuthnot and Co., and Ogilvy Gillanders and Co.*, London: privately printed, 1910; W. K. M. Langley, ed., *Century in Malabar: The History of Peirce Leslie & Co. Ltd. 1862–1962*, Madras: Madras Advertising Co, 1962; R. H. Macaulay, *History of Bombay Burmah Trading Corporation Ltd.*, London: privately printed, 1934; Dipak Roy, *A Hundred and Twenty-Five Years: The Story of J. Thomas and Company*, Calcutta: privately printed, c. 1976; Champaka Basu, *Challenge and Change: The ITC Story: 1910–1985*, Calcutta: Orient Longman, 1988.

environment in India with more analysis and insight. This is still a small literature, but it has seen significant contributions in the recent times, especially in relation to the early-to-mid nineteenth-century trading firms.[29]

Conclusion

The foundation of business growth in the Raj era was interdependence between commodity trade, banking, and industry. Traders and bankers started factories. The textile-based factories used agricultural raw material. Tea was an agricultural product. Banks financed grain trade, directly or indirectly. Mass transportation was a tool to aid agricultural trade.

This was a powerful machine because its parts were interrelated. By allowing money made in one part to move to the others, the system reduced risks and fostered entrepreneurship. The industrialising cities illustrate this potential. The big puzzle of Indian industrialisation, that a modern capital-intensive industry appeared in a capital-scarce region, is solved when we note this feature.

But another puzzle remains. Not everyone trading went in unconventional directions. Few did. What factors made conventional traders enter unconventional fields? Did community make entrepreneurship more likely? The pioneer industrialists are often introduced in biographies as representative members of a caste or community. But community and industrial entrepreneurship were not as closely correlated as we may think. First, few among the trading and banking communities entered industry; the majority did not. Second, biographies reveal how atypical some of the pioneers were in respect of their social origin. To Cowasji Davar, who started the first cotton mill in Bombay, community was no big help and the mill was wound up soon after anyway. For Ranchhodlal Chhotalal, community was either irrelevant or an obstacle. Tata Steel cannot be explained by its Parsi origin. Setting up a large integrated cotton textile mill was an offbeat decision for any Indian merchant in 1850, and evidence suggests that the fellow merchants at best stayed aloof, and at worst tried to stop the pioneers from doing new things. Community networking was not totally irrelevant. Community mattered once an idea had been shown to be profitable. When the pioneering industrialist of Bombay and Ahmedabad started a second factory, there was more positive response to the call to finance it. When the shareholders of the old mill sold their stake, the shares were eagerly purchased by professional traders and bankers.

---

[29] Anthony Webster, *The Life and Business of John Palmer of Calcutta, 1767–1836*, London: Longmans, 1993; Michael Aldous, 'Avoiding "Negligence and Profusion": Ownership and Organization in Anglo Indian Trading Firms, 1813–1870', PhD dissertation, London School of Economics and Political Science, 2015.

More than communal sentiment, cosmopolitanism played a positive role behind start-ups, meaning exposure of Indian business to foreign merchants, foreign markets, British technologies, British engineers, and artisans. The few who could manage the challenge of a move from trade to industry were based in the port cities and their satellites. The cities had deeper capital markets, were destinations for immigrants, had courts and legal professionals, and were sites for circulation of knowledge on technology and organisation. Of the major trading-banking communities, there were several that were active and highly mobile along overland trade routes. They were also prominent in financing agriculture, but did not industrialise on the same scale as the Parsis, the Gujaratis, and the European trading firms did. Marwaris are good examples of this. They did not because they were not cosmopolitan in the sense described. Whereas among the pioneering firms of Bombay and Calcutta there were many that formed of partnerships between Europeans and Indians, there are few notable examples of partnership between Europeans and indigenous bankers and overland traders like the Marwaris.

The main 'takeaway' from this story is that trade, and not the financial market, funded industrialisation, at least initially. The deep integration of trade and industry suffered a shock during the Great Depression of 1929, and then from the growing nationalist movement, which frowned upon foreign trade. A new era was taking shape in the 1930s and beyond, as we see in Chapter 6.

6   State and Industrialisation: 1930–1950

The temporary collapse of exports during the Great Depression reduced the capacity of firms to hire, borrow, or buy machines abroad. Industrialisation did not stall, for protectionist tariffs were made available from the mid-1920s. Protection was selective, and did not amount to discarding the old trading order. But protectionism established industrialisation as a priority for the state.

The average tariff rate in India had been going up from before the Great Depression (Fig. 6.1). Historians of Indian industrialisation explain the trend in relation to India's changed position within the Empire after World War I.[1] The rulers saw the contribution of Indian industry to the war effort as sufficiently valuable to consider this concession. The move would not hurt British interests too much, for protectionism could be modified to protect the customs union. Imperial goods would still enter India at low tariffs whereas goods from other emerging economies, especially Japan, would face barriers.

State aid was not confined to protection. In fact, in the aftermath of the depression, all types of business had to appeal to the state for help. The formation of elected legislature in the provinces under two constitutional reforms (1919 and 1935) empowered politicians and campaigners to intervene in favour of indigenous capitalists. But although the state was more ready to step in, state aid beyond a moderate level of protection and these isolated interventions, was negligible.

[1] Amiya Kumar Bagchi, *Private Investment in India*, Cambridge: Cambridge University Press, 1972, 43–7; Rajat K. Ray, *Industrialization in India: Growth and Conflict in the Private Corporate Sector, 1914–1947*, Delhi: Oxford University Press, 1979; M. D. Morris, 'The Growth of Large-Scale Industry to 1947', in Dharma Kumar, ed., *The Cambridge Economic History of India Vol. 2. c. 1757–c. 1970*, Cambridge: Cambridge University Press, 1983, 553–676; B. Chatterji, *Trade, Tariffs* and *Empire: Lancashire and British Policy in India 1919–1939*, Cambridge: Cambridge University Press, 1992; Aditya Mukherjee, *Imperialism, Nationalism and the Making of the Indian Capitalist Class, 1920–1947*, New Delhi, Thousand Oaks, CA, and London: Sage Publications, 2002; David Lockwood, *The Indian Bourgeoisie: A Political History of the Indian Capitalist Class in the Early Twentieth Century*, New York, NY: I. B. Tauris, 2012.

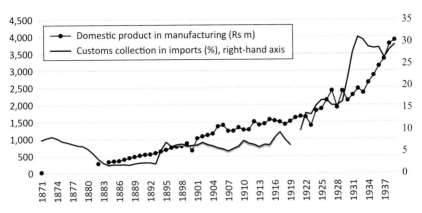

Fig. 6.1 Industrialisation and customs collection 1871–1939
Source: India, *Statistical Abstracts of British India*, various years

The real significance of state aid during these twenty years does not lie in how much was done. It derives instead from the fact that, for the first time in the history of the Empire, industrialisation and not trade became the cause the state should espouse. Besides, whereas trade and finance were served by small firms, industry was in the hands of large firms with political voice. It was the voice of the big industrialist, and not the traders, moneylenders, and artisans that would prevail in the negotiations that unfolded in these twenty years over the future shape of economic policy in India.

This chapter discusses the origins of protectionism and how it changed capitalism in interwar India.

The Origins of Protection for Industry

Import substituting industrialisation or ISI started in the 1920s due to shifts in British colonial policy.[2] The realisation that Indian resources had contributed to the allied war effort led to three commissions of enquiry. The Indian Industrial Commission (1916–18) had a mainly fact-finding mission. But the other two – the Fiscal Commission (1922), and Stores Purchase Committee (1920) – had immediate effects on policy. One of these commissions recommended protection to selected industries of domestic origin, and another recommended that the government should buy manufactured articles for its own use from Indian sources as far as possible.

---

[2] The discussion on protection in this and other sections of the chapter draws on Tirthankar Roy, 'The Origins of Import Substituting Industrialization in India', *Economic History of Developing Regions*, 32(1), 2017, 71–95.

With government expenditure at 3–5 per cent of GDP in 1900, and the import value of stores not exceeding 2 per cent of GDP and 10 per cent of total import, it may seem that the decision by the government to procure manufactured articles from India rather than Britain would make little difference to industrialisation. But, in fact, the government accounted for nearly half of net capital formation and a third of gross capital formation in 1900. The difference is not fully explained, but probably meant that government-owned assets lasted longer. In short, the government was the principal buyer of metals, machines, chemicals, railway material, and construction material. Any change in the policy of purchase, therefore, would have significant implications for industrial diversification in India.

Before 1920, the Stores Department of the India Office in London bought goods on behalf of the Government of India. This was a highly bureaucratic process, in which the parties with a direct interest in the transaction, that is the departments in India and manufacturing firms in Britain, had little say. The transactions, therefore, took much longer than was necessary and cost more money as well. Further, the system compromised on the quality of after-sales service. Large construction projects and railway projects required sustained service contracts between the supplier and the consumer, which the system could not ensure since the India Office stood between the two.

Both buyers and sellers resented London's meddling, and favoured private contracts drawn in India. British and Indian trading firms importing these goods formed a lobby to induce the government to change its policy. They included the trading offices in India of British engineering firms (see Chapter 4). Their British counterpart could bid for tenders invited by the London office, but with their eyes on expansion in India, they sided with the move for an India-based and decentralised purchase system. A relaxed stores purchase policy would enable them to deal equally with the government and the growing private sector clients in India. Furthermore, 'the establishment of such branches is the first step towards the actual manufacture of the goods in India and doubtless in time will lead to it'.[3] Late in the nineteenth century, an engineering trading firm Richardson and Cruddas started the campaign. After the war, others joined the battle, including the cluster of British engineering firms trying to expand their Indian operations, large Indian-origin manufacturing firms like Tata Steel and Martin Burn, and some Indian trading firms as well. For example, the Marwari Chamber of Commerce, and the United Provinces Chamber of Commerce, both composed of Indian traders with only a marginal interest in metals or machinery trades, expressed strong support for Indian procurement.

Whereas the British engineering firms had an interest in a reformed stores purchase, Indian businesses had a stake in tariff protection. Protection was

---

[3] India, *Report of the Stores Purchase Committee*, Vol. I (Report), Simla: Government Press, 1920, 143.

made available after 1925, both for revenue reasons and as an industrial promotion measure. The practical rule for its application was called 'discriminating' protection. This would mean that an applicant for protection needed to establish a case for it. The case was deliberated on by a committee. The ideology behind discrimination was that open markets rendered significant advantages to the Indian economy, which protectionism should preserve and not give up. For example, open markets ensured easy access to machinery and intermediate goods, resources that were expensive in India.

There was an established opinion, shared by Indian and British observers of industry alike, that labour productivity tended to be relatively low in India across the board, and especially low in modern industrial sectors such as machines and metals. Trade was one way to mitigate that disadvantage. While protection was inevitable, protection entailed a trade-off between domestic production and efficiency of production, and needed to limit the scope of the policy to those cases where the efficiency costs of domestic production would be modest and transitory. Economists endorsed that approach. For example, C. N. Vakil of what was known as the Bombay school of economics wrote that 'hope is held out that, the supervision of the Tariff Board, which the Commission recommends, will mitigate the effects of [the] disadvantages' of protection.[4]

Contemporary discussion recognised that there were two other ways of nurturing a domestic industrialisation utilising, rather than curtailing, international economic relations. One of these was foreign investment, and the other one, setting up domestic industry with skilled labour from abroad. Indeed, in most modern factories such as steel, engineering, cement, sugar, and paper, the posts of managers, chemists, and technical supervisors were filled by Europeans and later by Americans. The proportion varied. In a highly material-intensive industry like cement, neither equipment nor labour were a significant problem. But Tata Steel relied heavily on foreign engineers working in all departments of the factory. In steel rolling, glass making, wires and cables, and tinplate, specific tasks required foreign workers. In European-owned firms, managerial and technical positions were usually filled in with Europeans.

The idea that Indian productivity was low and therefore protection should be selective, came under sharp attack. After the formation of Congress governments in the provinces in 1935, Congress politicians, intellectuals, and businesses close to the party made public statements about tariff policy, which rejected the discrimination element of protectionist policy. 'The conditions for the grant of protection ... are difficult of fulfilment', the All India Congress Committee declared in a report on tariff policy.[5] When Japanese competition in the Indian textile market peaked, a report prepared by the Indian

---

[4] C. N. Vakil, *Our Fiscal Policy*, Bombay: Taraporevala. 1922, 125.
[5] All India Congress Committee (AICC), *Indian Tariff Policy*, Allahabad: AICC, 1935, 33.

National Congress attributed Japanese efficiency to 'inferior conditions of labour' in Japan, rather than the notoriously sloppy housekeeping of cotton mills in Bombay and Ahmedabad.[6] A small number of Indian industrialists who were vocal and politicised in this time joined them in the 1940s. They argued that the charge of inefficiency attached to Indian producers and therefore, a clause on efficiency harmed the Indian industrial class. They claimed that protectionism should be used more as a tool to nurture *indigenous* capital. Protection of consumer interest was at worst an imperial ploy, and at best an overrated virtue.

Two things had hardened political opinion: the push for Imperial Preference in the early 1920s, and the rising voice of aspiring industrialists in nationalist politics. The Imperial Preference treaty protected British industry in India while protecting Indian industry against non-British competition. A section of Indian business, and especially the group that closely allied with Mahātmā Gandhi's leadership, contended that the imperial government was trying to protect British trading interest in India. In practical terms, the industrialists sided with the treaty, but they did so reluctantly. Homi Mody, representative of Bombay's mill owners and signatory to the treaty, was said to agree to it with the hope of securing the support of Lancashire for stronger protection against Japan, and became very unpopular among his peers in the process.[7] Interestingly, this vocal group did not include the biggest single-firm beneficiary of discriminating protection, Tata. Tata's agreement to preferential tariffs was a controversial move, taken at the risk of isolation, and provoked a strong reaction from the leading nationalist, Ghanshyam Das Birla.

World War II disrupted these discussions, but when it ended, the Tariff Board was virtually dead and there was no serious dispute over the view already articulated by the Congress that tariff policy needed to be simplified and generalised if tariffs were to act as 'an effective instrument of a properly worked out national economic policy'.[8]

Before World War II, thirteen industries received protective tariffs. These thirteen were: cotton textiles, iron and steel, paper, matches, sugar, gold thread, magnesium chloride, artificial silk, salt, heavy chemicals, plywood and tea chests, wheat and rice. In the first eleven cases, the Indian Tariff Board considered the case for protection and set the level, periodically revising it. In the last two cases, the government imposed tariffs without reference to the Tariff Board. Protection reshaped Indian industry in quite different ways, not only because it was discriminating, but also

---

[6] AICC, *Indian Tariff Policy,* 13.
[7] Claude Markovits, *Indian Business and Nationalist Politics: The Indigenous Capitalist Class and the Rise of the Congress Party 1931–39,* Cambridge: Cambridge University Press, 1985, 88–9.
[8] AICC, *Indian Tariff Policy,* 32.

because the conditions of the industries differed. The contrasting examples of steel and textiles illustrates the difference well.

The Success and Failure of Discriminating Protection: Steel and Textiles

Steel

When World War I ended, there were four large steel producers: Tata Iron and Steel; the Indian Iron and Steel; the Mysore Iron Works; and the Bengal Iron Company. Only Tata produced finished steel on a large scale. Indian Iron and Steel did not produce finished steel, and the Bengal Iron had stopped doing so before the war. Mysore Iron Works produced alloy and special steels on a small scale, and made charcoal pig iron.

Tata had a naturally sheltered market during the war because of disruptions to the supplies of continental steel. When the war ended, the factory was left with a large underemployed workforce, including overpaid foreign workers and engineers. The whole industry suffered from worldwide overproduction. Japan, formerly a buyer of Indian pig iron, started to procure from Manchuria and Chosen (Korea).

Going by its own stated rules, the Tariff Board could easily have let Tata perish in the crisis, or forced it to specialise in pig iron instead of finished steel. But this did not happen. The logic of discrimination took over, and Tata negotiated its case with the Tariff Board. In 1924, Tata made the case that it deserved the chance to finish an ongoing expansion plan. Politically, the fact that Tata had accepted preferential treatment of British goods in the Indian markets may have helped its own case. The firm had to come back for more protection in the next two years, each time it was granted higher tariffs or a bounty. The government also induced the railways to buy the entire requirement of rails from Tata.

While Tata negotiated with the Board, critics of the firm (including a former employee turned trade union leader, Maneck Homi) made a strong case that Tata needed much better housekeeping. Their furnaces consumed too much coal and produced too little output. Too many people were employed. Of all Indian industrial firms, Tata relied on foreign technicians most heavily and persistently. This was an understandable decision in an integrated steel factory in India, but cost the firm a lot of money. Although these criticisms embarrassed the firm, Tata did not lose government support. For, Tata Steel was already following the remedy implied in the attacks on it. Between 1925 and 1932, it reduced workforce from 32,500 to 25,000, installed more modern machinery, relieved many highly paid foreigners,

Fig. 6.2 Tata Steel Factory in Jamshedpur, 1940s
© Dinodia Photos/Alamy Stock Photo

and achieved greater efficiency of the Indian workmen. By 1935, the firm had delivered on its promise, and could foresee that by 1940 it would not need protection any more (Fig. 6.2).

The moral of the story is that the conditionality and negotiability element of the policy – the very idea of discrimination – pushed the firm to become a competitive producer of steel. Cotton textiles were a completely different story. Protection allowed the industry to stay as inefficient as it was before, probably more than before.

Cotton Mills

Labour productivity in the Indian cotton mills had always been low. In 1931, one weaver in Osaka handled six looms, in Bombay, one weaver handled two. In 1940, 450,000 workers in the cotton mills in India processed three-to-five million bales of cotton. In Japan, the same quantity of cotton was processed by 190,000 workers in the same year. A similar difference existed between India and North America or England. Chinese practices in the 1930s were not as good as Japan, though most Chinese mills were owned by the Japanese, but they were about one-third more efficient than mills in Bombay and Ahmedabad, based on spindle-worker and loom-worker ratios.

The productivity divergence has inspired several contributions from scholars, including those who think, mistakenly in my view, that this divergence can supply a clue to why standards of living in all of India fell behind that in the West and Japan. The explanations for the productivity divergence run as follows. Managerial decisions regarding choice of technology are emphasised in one set of works.[9] This line of reasoning is more applicable to spinning than weaving. Another argument, advanced by Gregory Clark in particular, emphasises the level of effort supplied by the average worker, and leaves the effort level to be explained by cultural factors.[10] Taking the efficiency argument further, Susan Wolcott attributes the divergent effort level to union resistance to rationalisation.[11] Bishnupriya Gupta argues that the managers failed to see the existence of a virtuous circle between wage and efficiency.[12]

---

[9] Keijiro Otsuka, Gustav Ranis, and Gary Saxonhouse, *Comparative Technology-Choice in Development: The Indian and Japanese Cotton Textile Industries*, London: Macmillan, 1988; and Yukuhiko Kiyokawa, 'Technical Adaptations and Managerial Resources in India: A Study of the Experience of the Cotton Textile Industry from a Comparative Viewpoint', *Developing Economies*, 21(2), 1983, 97–133.

[10] Gregory Clark, 'Why Is Not the Whole World Developed? Lessons from the Cotton Mills', *Journal of Economic History*, 47(2), 1987, 141–73; Gregory Clark and Robert C. Feenstra, 'Technology in the Great Divergence', in Michael D. Bordo, Alan M. Taylor, Jeffery G. Williamson, eds., *Globalisation in Historical Perspective*, Chicago, IL and London: University of Chicago Press, 2001.

[11] Susan Wolcott, 'Perils of Lifetime Employment Systems: Productivity Advance in the Indian and Japanese Textile Industries, 1920–1938', *Journal of Economic History*, 54(2), 1994, 307–24.

[12] Bishnupriya Gupta, 'Work and Efficiency in Cotton Mills: Did the Indian Entrepreneur Fail?', University of Warwick Working Paper, 2003.

I hold labour institutions responsible.[13] Most nineteenth-century employers of wage labour did not hire and manage workers themselves, but hired them through contractors who were also in charge of training and personnel management. Millowners specialised in managing money, and took little interest in technology or in personnel matters. This system entailed a conflict of interest. The contractors would not incentivise training for the fear that the most skilled workers would emerge as their rivals. The system of indirect employment, in short, had a built-in bias against skill formation. Besides, the contractors were influential people but not necessarily the most skilled people themselves.

In the 1890s, Bombay faced its first major failure, when it lost the Chinese market for yarn quickly to Japanese producers. In the interwar period, Japan brought the competition closer home, and started to undermine Indian mills in Indian markets. During World War I, the cotton mills of Bombay and Ahmedabad improved the quality of the cloth they produced. But the labour–equipment ratio was still much higher in Bombay than its competitors elsewhere in the world. The difference did not matter very much if competition was confined to Europe and North America where wages were higher. But wages were similar between Japan and India. An overvalued Indian currency in the 1920s made matters worse. The root of the problem, however, was the inefficiency of the Indian mills.

Cotton mills of Bombay, therefore, wanted protection, first from Manchester (1927), and then from Japan (1932). The first Tariff Board enquiry on textiles in 1927 urged the mills to rationalise and improve efficiency. Some Bombay firms responded to the call and there was an improvement in operational efficiency in some cases. But unlike steel, on this occasion, the Board was dealing with an industry of 200-odd firms of very different conditions. No sensible industry-wide plan on modernisation was possible. In Bombay, an industry-wide rationalisation was blocked by militant trade unions. In the second enquiry conducted in 1932, therefore, modernisation was no longer a significant issue. Instead, the mills made their case for tariff protection by saying that the success of the Japanese mills was owed to the overexploitation of female workers, a line that the communist trade unions endorsed, even though it weakened their case by implying that Indian mills were models of welfare in comparison with Japan. India being a cotton exporter to Japan, the two countries had a stake in continuing to trade, and a market share agreement was reached. The agreement condition was that protection would stay.

The moral of the cotton mill protection story is that discriminating protection failed to improve things when structural inefficiencies were too deep-rooted, industry too diverse, and labour too resistant to change. One might add

---

[13] Tirthankar Roy, 'The Role of Labour Institutions in Industrialization: Japan and the Crisis of the Cotton Mills in Interwar Mumbai', *Economic and Political Weekly*, 43(1), 2008, 37–45.

that after the cotton mill interests joined the nationalist campaign by the 1930s, the political compulsions were too strong for the Tariff Board to ignore.

Business in the Interwar Years

World War I and the protection created unprecedented opportunities for some Indian capitalists. The war had left with them a great deal of cash, which was invested in industry. Protection offered a chance to diversify quickly away from cotton textiles and into fields like sugar or paper. Several Indian groups responded to this opportunity in the interwar years, leading to the emergence of business groups or conglomerates in these years, usually from an original foundation of cotton textile production. The most important conglomerate to emerge in these times was the Marwari family, Birla.

Birla

The Birla family's journey into big business can be said to have begun with a cotton trading firm set up by Shiv Narain (1840–1909), a merchant from Pilani in Rajasthan. His adopted son Baldeodas Birla expanded the business, shifted to Calcutta, and it was Baldeodas' sons who entered industry in the interwar period. The eldest son Jugal Kishore (1883–1967) inherited the trading firm, with interests in cotton, jute, and opium trades. The third son Ghanshyam Das or G. D. Birla (1894–1983) and the fourth son Braj Mohan (1905–1982) were the pioneering industrialists. The second son Rameshwar Das (1892–1973) was based in Ahmedabad and acquired several textile mills, including Century Mills of Bombay, originally established by Nowrosjee Wadia.

The managing agency firm was Birla Brothers. Ghanshyam Das was the key figure in running the firm between the wars (Fig. 6.3). In 1919, Birla Brothers started the Birla Jute Manufacturing Company Ltd., an Indian-owned firm in a mainly European-dominated industry. The modern Birla industrial empire began with the jute mill. Ghanshyam Das then diversified into cotton textiles, setting up Jiyajorao Cotton Mill in Gwalior in 1923, and taking over the ailing Kesoram Cotton in Calcutta in 1919.

Until the early 1930s, Birla's progression was textile-oriented, and as such, resembled that of other Indian groups in this time. Thereafter, there was a spate of diversification and vertical integration that set the group apart and placed it in a uniquely strong position to lead private investment after independence. Protection was clearly the impetus behind some of these ventures. From cotton and jute, the group diversified into machinery and machine parts for cotton and jute textiles, in the form of two companies Texmaco and Cimmco. Just before independence, the group enterprises included paper (Orient Paper Mill, Brajarajnagar, 1939), sugar

Fig. 6.3 Ghanshyam Das Birla with the Congress politician Vallabhbhai
Patel, c. 1940
Source: Photographer Margaret Bourke-White, LIFE Picture Collection, Getty Images

(Upper Ganges, 1932, and others), cotton (Kesoram, Calcutta, 1919; Jiyajirao,
Gwalior, 1923; Century Mills, Bombay), jute (Birla Jute and other firms, Calcutta),
engineering (Texmaco, Calcutta, textile machinery and foundry, 1939), shipping,

tea (Jayshree Tea, Assam, 1945), silk and synthetic fibres (Gwalior Rayon, 1948), banking, insurance, coal mining, newspapers, automobiles (Hindustan Motors, near Calcutta, 1942), and a large number of trading firms.

Shri Ram

In 1889, a North Indian merchant Gopal Roy established the Delhi Cloth and General Mills Company (DCM) in Delhi, along with two Agarwal bankers. Gopal Roy was the employee in one of these firms, and an Agarwal himself. He held a small quantity of the shares, but officiated as the Secretary of the company, effectively the managing director. The majority shareholders in the company were the two bankers, a few landlords, and other businesses of the town. Around 1900, Shri Ram (1884–1963), Gopal Roy's nephew, joined the business, and took charge of the company in 1909. During the World War I, contracts for the army and for the civilians in the new capital Delhi, enabled the company to make large profits, and Shri Ram to increase his shareholding.[14]

In the 1930s, DCM had a rough time from Japanese competition in cotton textiles in the Indian market. When Indian cotton and sugar received protection, Shri Ram established the Lyallpur Cotton Mill (in Pakistan as it is now), and a sugar mill in Daurala near Delhi. In the same decade, he took over Bengal Potteries (started in 1895), and acquired Jay Engineering Works, a Calcutta firm making light engineering goods. During World War II, DCM and Lyallpur made large profits by selling tent and garments for the army, whereas both Bengal Potteries and Jay Engineering manufactured war materials. The Lyallpur mill was lost during the Partition, many employees of the mill migrated to Delhi and into the Swatantra Bharat Mill started in 1948. The migrants included Jagannath Ganju, who played a key role in reorganising the textile marketing operation after 1948.

Walchand Hirachand

After the advent of steam, Indian shipping and ship-building, it is often said, suffered a decline. No hard evidence exists to support the claim, and it is inconsistent with the huge growth of river-borne and coastal trade that occurred after 1859. It would be more accurate to say that a much bigger growth in intercontinental trade was carried entirely in British-owned and British-made ships. The business was capital-intensive, like airline operations

---

[14] Khushwant Singh and Arun Joshi, *Shri Ram: A Biography*, Bombay: Asia Publishing House, 1968.

now, and offered positive returns to scale. A wide global network allowed the firms to spread risks, and made them able to take low profits and offer low rates in new lines or potentially competitive lines. Few Indians could match such scale of investment.

The market for both cargo and passenger traffic between India and Europe was dominated by one player, Mackinnon-Mackenzie. The firm had its beginnings in Glasgow, where William Mackinnon (1823–93) had started his career as an employee in an East India trading firm. In 1847, Mackinnon and his friend Robert Mackenzie went to Bombay to trade (Chapter 4). About ten years later, the firm set up a steam navigation company to ply the route between Calcutta and Rangoon, and in a few years, evolved into one of the largest shipping companies in the nineteenth century world, the British India Steam Navigation Company.[15] In 1913–14, under Inchcape management, the company merged with the other big player in the Indian Ocean, Peninsular and Oriental or P&O, though the two firms retained their distinct identity until 1972.

With a rapid growth of trade in the backdrop, shipping offered opportunities. Not surprisingly, between 1860 and 1925, over one hundred companies were registered in India with Indian capital. Their capital base was small, operations confined mainly to the coastal trade, and even here it was hard for them to resist price competition by the big firms. Many, therefore, remained small and local. The failures included a company started by Jamsetji Tata in 1894, Bengal Steamship Co, and the Swadeshi Lines. There were at the same time a few survivals, which continued to operate in niche areas.

In 1919, Walchand Hirachand (1882–1952), a merchant and banker based mainly in Sholapur, bought a hospital ship that had done service during the war, and belonged to the Scindia of Gwalior. The ship, S. S. Loyalty, was docked in Bombay and waiting for a buyer, until a chance encounter with an Englishman during a train journey enlightened Hirachand. He was determined to develop a shipping line with this acquisition, and persuaded three other Bombay entrepreneurs to join him: Kilachand Devchand, Narottam Morarjee, and Lalubhai Samaldas. From this collaboration emerged the Scindia Steam Navigation Co, and the most formidable challenge that Mackinnon-Mackenzie was to face in the interwar period.[16]

Walchand hired experienced consultants and understood the importance of increasing scale. But Scindia Steam Navigation ran into trouble while trying to

[15] J. Forbes Munro, 'From Regional Trade to Global Shipping: Mackinnon Mackenzie & Co. within the Mackinnon Enterprise Network, in Geoffrey Jones, ed., *The Multinational Traders*, London and New York, NY: Routledge, 1998, 48–65; J. Forbes Munro, *Maritime Enterprise and Empire: Sir William Mackinnon and His Business Network, 1823–93*, Woodbridge: Boydell and Brewer, 2003.
[16] A good account can be found in Dwijendra Tripathi and Makrand Mehta, *Business Houses in Western India: A Study in Entrepreneurial Response, 1850–1956*, New Delhi: Manohar, 1990.

break into P&O's traditional monopolies, like India-Burma trade in rice and timber. The rival reduced prices, offered concessions to traders, and pushed Scindia to the brink of bankruptcy. Hirachand's best hope was to make a case for protection in the legislature that had come into being after the 1919 constitutional reforms. The legislature was not yet ready to listen to the plea, but these moves turned the episode political and invited the government as a third party in future negotiations.

On several occasions in 1921–2, Inchcape offered to buy Scindia, exploiting what seemed increasing dissension within the board of the company between members who wanted to sell and those who wanted to fight on. In 1923, a compromise was reached, wherein Scindia would give up any ambition to enter the Bombay-UK lines, restrict capacity expansion, and refrain from passenger service. The agreement was ratified in 1933, again with government participation. In 1937, Scindia expanded into passenger service for the Hajj traffic with a new company called Mogul Lines. If this was a profitable move, the coming World War II made normal business impossible.

Scindia's fortunes turned dramatically after 1947. Within months after independence, the government of India announced strong and unrestricted protection of coastal shipping for Indian liners. Scindia dominated this market with almost no foreign competition after 1952. Its moves to expand into intercontinental shipping, with the aid of discounted ships acquired after the war, ran into price competition with European and American rivals, which it could not withstand.

This whole episode of Scindia's struggle has been read by Indian historians in a nationalistic light. In his own words, Hirachand was 'fired by ... patriotic desire', whereas his rivals were playing an imperialist game of crushing nationalist opposition. On one occasion, he explained to Inchcape that he had every right to supply shipping for 'the motherland', to which Inchcape drily replied that 'motherland' had nothing to do with competition in business. That Scindia was fighting a nationalist war is a sentimental narrative. Scindia's woes had nothing to do with politics. Hirachand had ventured into a highly capital-intensive business, and could not possibly gather the money to create a company that operated on competitive scale. In the end, it was the government's intervention that saved the firm through market sharing.

Ramkrishna Dalmia

In 1933, a sugar factory on the western bank of the Son river in eastern India became the nucleus of the conglomerate later known as the Dalmia-Jain or Sahu-Jain group. Since 1907, the factory site had been connected to the Delhi-Calcutta railway line through a light railway link called Dehri-Rohtas railway, managed by a Calcutta firm called Octavius Steel. The name Rohtas derived from the ancient Rohtasgarh Fort located about 30 miles south of the factory site. By 1950, the factory site had grown into an industrial complex, and the group businesses included cement, paper, chemicals, asbestos, spun pipes, and vegetable oil manufacturing, along with sugar. The original factory complex was renamed Dalmianagar.

The foundation of this business empire had owed to protective tariffs on sugar. But it diversified quickly in the 1940s using an unconventional method: takeovers. In the 1940s, Ramkrishna Dalmia, the group's head (1893–1978), made several attempts, some successful and some not, to acquire controlling stakes in British firms based in Calcutta, Kanpur, and Bombay. The mode of acquisition in cases like these usually involved doing secret deals with stock market brokers, and using one firm's cash reserves to acquire other firms. Companies acquired by the group included the New Central Jute Mill, Punjab National Bank, Bennett Coleman (publishers of the largest English daily, Times of India), Bharat Insurance, and in part, British India Corporation. Some of these takeovers made him a controversial figure.

Other Groups

In southern India, protectionism was a less important driver to industrial diversification. The locally rooted engineering industry set South India on a different course from northern India.

For example, R. and V. Seshasayee were Tamil Brahmins from Tiruchirappalli who ran an engineering repair shop during World War I. After the war, R. Seshasayee went to the United States of America to take training in electrical engineering, while his brother-in-law, V. Seshasayee managed the firm. In the 1920s, the firm executed several large contracts for the electrification of public complexes, and started an electric supply company. Although dependent on expatriate engineers and imported equipment, the firm 'Indianised' its technology to some extent. Between 1941 and 1947, the Seshasayees (R. Seshasayee was killed in 1936 in a plane accident) diversified into chemicals and fertilisers by first taking over Mettur Chemical and Industrial Corporation, and then starting The Fertilisers and Chemicals Travancore Ltd. The Madras and the Travancore-Cochin governments actively helped and participated in these businesses. Governments held the most shares in these firms. The factories also depended crucially on foreign engineers and technical collaboration.[17]

Another famous engineer-entrepreneur was Laxmanrao Kirloskar (1869–1956). He studied mechanics in the J. J. School of Arts in Bombay,

---

[17] Dwijendra Tripathi, 'House of Seshasayees', IIM Ahmedabad Case Studies No IIMA/ECO0145, 1970.

taught in the same school, before leaving in 1890 to set up a small metal products shop in his home town Belgaum. The shop opened a foundry and made agricultural tools, especially iron plough. Through product improvement, he established a secure business in the plough. Eventually, the business moved from Belgaum to a factory set up in land given him by a princely state (Aundh). World War I had an initially disruptive effect, but in the end a beneficial one. After the war, the company went public, and expanded the products. During the Great Depression, when farmers stopped buying as many agricultural tools, the firm diversified into oil engines, electric motors, machine tools, furniture, and automobile chassis. In the 1940s, Kirloskar was invited by the Mysore state to start a branch of the firm there. After 1947, Kirloskar was well positioned to grow in an environment that valued a home-grown engineering enterprise. The leadership then came from Laxmanrao's son, Shantanu Kirloskar, an MIT-trained engineer.[18]

In chemicals and pharmaceuticals, only a few companies were started by the Indians, but these found the 1930s a more congenial time than before. In 1905, T. K. Gajjar, a chemist from Baroda who had established a technical college there, and one of his students Koti Bhaskar, jointly set up a chemical factory in Baroda, called Alembic, to manufacture spirits for industrial use. The spirit was manufactured using a flower locally grown. The demand for the product was strong, but the company faced competition from imports and established producers. It had problems raising capacity, and on one occasion had to run the unit to the breaking point to stay in the competition. Although spirit was, to the two pioneers, a stepping stone to diversification into chemicals and pharmaceuticals, that step did not materialise quickly for want of capital. The company's fortunes changed somewhat after the 1919 constitutional reforms. Indian members in the new legislature could influence government stores' purchasing decisions in the firm's favour. The company grew steadily thereafter, and soon after independence diversified into the production of antibiotics.[19]

Only a few of the other chemical firms deserve a mention. In 1919, Ratansi Dharamsi Morarji (1889–1959) established a phosphatic fertiliser company in Bombay named after himself, which grew to become one of India's largest and most profitable chemical companies. In 1901, the chemist P. C. Ray set up the Bengal Chemiscal and Pharmaceutical Works in Calcutta. During World War II, production of serums and vaccines in India expanded, but the industry was still very small. Most drugs were imported.

[18] Makrand J. Mehta and Dwijendra Tripathi, 'The Kirloskar Brothers Limited', IIM Ahmedabad Case Studies No IIMA/ECO0080, 1968.
[19] Dwijendra Tripathi and Makrand J. Mehta, 'The Alembic Chemical Works Company Limited', IIM Ahmedabad Case Studies No IIMA/ECO0146, 1970.

Many biographical accounts of Indian business in the interwar years tend to focus on the politically active figures, those close to the Congress, and participants in the discussions on the future shape of economic policy (see next). Such accounts cannot do justice to the scope of Indian enterprise in the early twentieth century, which was shaped by hard-fought protective tariffs and the opportunity to join public and political life no doubt, but also by mobility within the British Empire, the chance to integrate trade, finance, and manufacturing, and growing engagement with scientific and engineering education (see Figs. 6.4–6.6). A random selection of individuals who made use of these drivers bring up many names who remain unknown in standard textbooks in business history. The power of two of these drivers – mobility and finance – was limited after 1947, whereas the power of politics and science expanded in both India and Pakistan.

British Multinational Companies

As we have seen in Chapter 4, in the 1930s several selling agents and trading firms operated in India to market imported products. Some British engineering firms, which had entered India in the interwar period as a marketing office, started manufacturing on the side.

In the 1920s, a series of amalgamations of British tinplate manufacturers and traders, box-making firms, and printers, led to the emergence of the Metal Box Company, registered in that name in 1930. While manufacturing tin boxes for packaging commodities was an established industry, it was populated by small partnership firms. Metal Box changed the model, was big enough to experiment and innovate (it pioneered beer cans), and became multinational. During World War II, the demand for canned food exploded, and Metal Box was a major gainer from the boom. Calcutta was one of its main centres of operation at the time of Indian independence.

Two other groups had significant foreign participation, but were not foreign firms. British individuals started Britannia Biscuit in Calcutta in 1892. Five years later, two brothers named Gupta bought it. In 1918, the owners inducted one C. H. Holmes as partner, and registered the new company as Britannia Biscuit Company. In 1924, the factory was sold to Peek, Frean, one of the largest biscuit companies in Britain, which, along with Huntley and Palmers, were a subsidiary of Associated Biscuit Manufacturers. The second example of an Indo-European firm was the engineering and construction company Martin Burn, and Indian Standard Wagon, founded in 1918 to manufacture railway wagons, carriages, and railway equipment. These two companies had common parent in a partnership between a Bengali individual and a British engineer (see Chapter 5).

Another company like Metal Box would dominate the Calcutta landscape in the 1960s, and like it, had its origin in the 1920s. The Indian branch of the

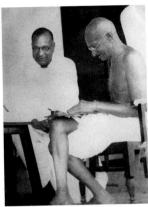

Fig. 6.4 Three businessmen of the interwar years with active public life
Left: Jamnalal Bajaj, Marwari merchant from Rajasthan, and the founder of a major
industrial group; seen here with M.K. Gandhi, with whose political and social activities
Bajaj was closely associated (see text). Middle: Ambalal Sarabhai, leading cotton mill
owner of Ahmedabad, an associate of Gandhi, known for socially progressive views
(see text). Right: Purshottamdas Thakurdas, cotton merchant in early life, later a
member of the Round Table Conference, a director of the Reserve Bank of India, and
holders of other offices.
Source: Alamy Stock Photo for Bajaj and Gandhi, and Thomas Peters, *Famous
Business Houses and Who's Who in India and Pakistan*, Bombay: Modern Press and
Publicity, 1949 (author's collection). Source for Figs. 6.4 and 6.5 is Peters

Midlands metallurgy firm Guest Keen Nettlefolds (or GKN) was the product of
an amalgamation of three enterprises, that of the eighteenth-century Welsh
ironmaster John Guest, the late-nineteenth century London ironworks of
Arthur Keen, and the Birmingham firm Nettlefold. One Henry William part-
nered with GKN to start Guest, Keen and William (or GKW) in Calcutta in the
1920s. The Manchester engineering firm Mather and Platt started an Indian
subsidiary in 1913, with a plant manufacturing electrical pumps in Calcutta.
These firms gained by reinventing themselves as multinational manufacturing
firms. For them it was a change of role from a manufacturer in England to a
trader in India to a manufacturer in India, as the Indian market for their
products had grown big enough to enable economies of scale.

Corporate Banking

In the port cities, banks emerged regularly and died often, because of over-
dependence on a few trades. A parallel tradition of banking functioned in the
princely states. Indigenous bankers took part in revenue farming and war

Fig. 6.5 Three multinational entrepreneurs of the interwar years
Left: Mohamed Haji Hashim Rangoonwalla, head of a Halai Memon textile and dye merchant firm in Rangoon. Halai Memons originated from Hala in Sindh, and were concentrated in Dhoraji in Kathiawar at the time of independence. Several prominent Memon firms left India and Burma for Pakistan, including Mohammed Aly Rangoonwala, the leading manufacturer of edible oils in Pakistan in the 1960s. Middle: Nanjibhai Kalidas Mehta (1889-1969), entrepreneur from the mercantile Lohana caste of Gujarat, who established an extensive business interest in British East Africa, including sugar, sisal, plantation, and textile industries in Kenya and Uganda. Right: Framroz Adenwala, representative of the famous Parsi trading and shipping firm of Aden (and East Africa), Cowasji Dinshaw.

finance in the eighteenth century, in short, their fortunes came to depend on those of the princely rulers. Bankers also helped the treasury in a variety of ways in normal times. The surviving Indian-origin banks in both British India and the states usually had similar origins as the failed ones, but managed their assets conservatively.

The Bank of Baroda and the Punjab National Bank were two such surviving firms. Baroda was a princely state that depended a lot on banking firms. Interestingly, the Bank of Baroda (established 1908) did not emerge from the locally based private banking enterprise, but from the state's attempt to reduce dependence on private enterprise. It was established mainly as a banker for the state, though part-financed by the merchants of the town, including Vithaldas Thackersey, Lalubhai Samaldas, Ambalal Desai, and Chimanlal Nagindas. The Bank depended heavily on the state's custom. By pursuing a conservative lending policy, it managed to keep risks low. At the same time, being founded by merchants, the Bank could take part in bill discounting within the city easily. After 1947, the Bank faced the prospect of immediate nationalisation, since its business was mainly with the state, and the state had

Fig. 6.6 Three industrialists from non-business backgrounds in the
interwar years
Left: Khwaja Abdul Hamied (1898–1972), an Allahabad University graduate in
chemistry, briefly a teacher at the Aligarh Muslim University, and a researcher in
Berlin University. He set up the Chemical, Industrial and Pharmaceutical
Laboratories Ltd (CIPLA) in 1935. CIPLA is now one of the largest multinational
pharmaceutical companies of India. Middle: Mahadeo Laxman Dahanukar, from an
agricultural family, prominent in construction, sugar industry, and as mediator
between business and politics after 1947. Dahanukar, like Kirloskar (below), sent
his son to study engineering in the USA. Right: Laxmanrao Kirloskar (1869–1956),
a teacher of mechanical drawing in early life, established an engineering industrial
complex in western India (see text for more details).

been included in the Indian Union. However, nationalisation did not happen
immediately. In a move to reinvent its identity, the Bank spread branches
overseas.[20]

The Punjab National Bank started in Lahore in 1895, and moved to Delhi
after independence. Although it is often projected as a nationalist institution,
with which political leaders like Lala Lajpat Rai were associated, Punjab at
the turn of the twentieth century had well-developed banking and moneylending business thanks to its extensive agricultural commodity trade.[21] It
was not unusual that a successful joint-stock bank would emerge in this
region.

In 1929–30, the worldwide capitalist machine spluttered. Until then, Indian
capitalists had rarely challenged the Empire or questioned its usefulness for
their own interests. Their criticisms of the Raj were issue-based. But when

[20] Dwijendra Tripathi and Priti Misra, *Towards a New Frontier: History of the Bank of Baroda,
1908–1983*, New Delhi: Manohar, 1985.
[21] Malcolm Darling, *Punjab Peasant in Prosperity and Debt*, London: Humphrey Milford, 1928.

the nationalist movement became a mass movement in the 1920s and even more so in the 1930s, aspiring industrialists formed an alliance with the leaders of the movement. Together they set out an agenda for the future, when Indians would write their own economic policy. This alliance, however, was not an easy one, for industrialists and politicians disagreed on fundamental issues.

Business and Politics in the 1940s

The depression left many British companies selling jute or tea abroad in temporary shortage of funds. The leading European chambers of commerce formed cartels and tried to limit competition (in jute especially), inevitably attracting Indian entry, and then appealed to the state for help when their efforts failed. The state did not help, but the matter became politicised.[22] In the 1980s, B. R. Tomlinson and others explored business archives available in Britain.[23] The articles and books that appeared out of this enterprise contributed to a reinterpretation of the position of British business in India towards the end of colonial rule. Studies on business-politics connection, again with the endgame of colonialism as the theme of interest, attracted some attention.[24] These works suggest that expatriate industry had become destabilised, but does not definitely suggest that the shock was beyond their capacity to cope with.

If the expatriates were weakened by world economic collapse, Indian industrialists were empowered, a first time by windfall profits earned during World War I, and a second time by tariff protection. As we have seen earlier in the chapter, an alliance of sorts between the Indian National Congress and some business groups emerged late in the interwar period. The industrialists close to the Congress included Kasturbhai Lalbhai (1894–1980) and Ambalal Sarabhai (1890–1967), both heads of textile-based conglomerates in Ahmedabad, Jamnalal Bajaj (1889–1942), trader and industrialist, and Ghanshyam Das Birla. Almost all of them had diversified or expanded their business interests in the 1930s. Birla, as we have seen, had moved into jute

---

[22] Bishnupriya Gupta, 'Why Did Collusion Fail? The Indian Jute Industry in the Interwar Years', *Business History*, 47(4), 2005, 532–52; Samar Ranjan Sen, *Restrictionism during the Great Depression in Indian Tea Jute and Sugar Industries*, Calcutta: Firma KLM, 1997.

[23] B. R. Tomlinson, 'The Political Economy of the Raj: The Decline of Colonialism', *Journal of Economic History*, 42(1), 1982, 133–37; Omkar Goswami, 'Then Came the Marwaris: Some Aspects of the Changes in the Pattern of Industrial Control in Eastern India', *Indian Economic and Social History Review*, 22(2), 1985, 225–49; B. R. Tomlinson, 'British Business in India, 1860–1970', in R. P. T. Davenport-Hines and Geoffrey Jones, eds. *British Business in Asia since 1860*, Cambridge: Cambridge University Press, 2003, 92–116.

[24] Cited in Chapter 7.

manufacturing, while Lalbhai purchased discounted machines from England to start Arvind Mills in 1931.[25] Bajaj was the head of steel and engineering factories in the 1940s.

Whereas these individuals were personally close to Mahātmā Gandhi, other prominent Indian businessmen of that generation, such as members of the Tata group, also had political influence, but they were not close to Gandhi. Gandhi himself, with his accent on rural development rather than large-scale industry, stood at odds with a socialist lobby within the Congress that wanted to encourage modern factory industry.

Businesses often took part in public debates about future economic policy. There is a rich literature on the role of business leaders in influencing these debates on Indian economic policy. In this scholarship, those individuals who donated money to the Congress, or to Gandhi, or were close to its leaders tend to figure prominently. They were the public face of Indian business, and straddled nationalism and capitalism.

But they were not representatives of the business world at large. That world would include numerous trading firms, bankers, and moneylenders, foreign firms, and small firms. All of them keep a shadowy profile in the historical scholarship. The corporate world was deeply divided in this time. Foreign and domestic capitalists did not collaborate in politics, not because all foreigners were imperialists, but because the interest of foreign capital was tied to international trade, which the Congress ideologues were not keen to nurture. Some industrialists joined the political mainstream because they were wary of the trade unions. That issue did not inspire the traders and the bankers. Whereas the Congress had goodwill among traders and bankers, few among the latter took part in the discourse on industrial policy. Historians have not explored that diversity of views in great depth.

Subject to that limitation, contributors to this literature agree on the point that a broad alliance between publicly engaged business leaders and political leaders developed around 1940. They do not agree on why it developed and what it meant. One author sees the alliance as a shared platform opposing British hegemony in politics and business.[26] Another author shows that business was either wary of or indifferent to the Congress and its policies until 1937, when the Congress-led provincial governments started introducing pro-labour legislation and policies.[27] Alarmed by the tendency, capitalists took a more active part in politics. The

---

[25] He also played a major role in the development of education in Ahmedabad, and donated land for the Indian Institute of Management.

[26] Mukherjee, *Imperialism, Nationalism*.

[27] Claude Markovits, 'Indian Business and the Congress Provincial Governments 1937–39', *Modern Asian Studies*, 15(3), 1981, 487–526.

relationship between business and Congress was also fraught because the former did not like Jawaharlal Nehru, the socialist face of the party and an admirer of Soviet Union, and backed the softer, if not pro-capitalistic face represented by Gandhi and Vallabhbhai Patel, partly from genuine admiration, and partly to keep Nehru under check. In short, the relationship was a complex one.

When the National Planning Committee of the Congress started to discuss the future shape of economic policy, a cross-section of business leaders did take part in it. In around 1938, in statements and speeches, Congress leadership projected a vision for Indian development defined by an accent on industrialisation, and a devaluation of trading. The Bombay Plan, drafted by business leaders of the city, and published in 1944, agreed on prioritising industrialisation. The Bombay Plan left an uncertain and possibly a small legacy on actual policymaking, but it was still significant as a symbol of capitalists' assent to the idea of socialist planning. Where Bombay's capitalists and Congress intellectuals may have differed was in the future role of the state in the development process.[28]

We can exaggerate these divisions, and lose sight of an important area of agreement. There was substantial agreement on protectionism as the means to achieve industrialisation. The capitalists close to Congress leadership had little or no contact with international trade, and did not think restraints on foreign trade could have any cost for them. There was also agreement in principle on retraining foreign investment.

The End of Discriminating Protection

At the turn of the 1940s, the Indian Tariff Board was not too active. The voices heard on tariff policy were those of Congress politicians and nationalist economists. And this voice wanted an indiscriminate and unconditional tariff protection as an industrial promotion policy. In their interpretation, Indian industry had meekly accepted the little protection it received, as much as the concessions that Imperial Preference offered to British industry, 'following the policy of half a loaf is better than none'.[29] The full loaf must 'serve the true national interests of the country'.[30] Industry-specific duties had created an unnecessarily complex system, which needed to be simplified if tariffs were to act as 'an effective instrument of a properly worked out national economic policy'.[31] The

---

[28] Medha Kudaisya, '"The Promise of Partnership": Indian Business, the State, and the Bombay Plan of 1944', *Business History Review*, 88(1), 2014, 97–131.
[29] AICC, *Indian Tariff Policy*, 29.   [30] Ibid., 34.   [31] Ibid., 32.

implication was that India needed generalised protection unburdened by efficiency conditions.

During World War II, the discussion took a turn from protection against trade to protection against foreign capital and labour. In the All India Manufacturers' Conference of 1941, representing mainly small-scale industrial interests of Bombay, the president brought in a motion in favour of investment regulation. India's industrialisation, the motion explained, was for the exclusive benefit of 'the sons of the soil' and therefore must regulate 'non-nationals', not only from owning industry but also from participating in management. Neither consumer welfare nor labour productivity were arguments mentioned in the 100-page document charting out a policy framework for industrialisation.[32]

Economists joined the attack on conditional protection, and on foreign capital. The 1929 Arthur Balfour Committee report on British industry and trade had pointed out structural inefficiency in British industry. The Indian economists used the report to turn the efficiency debate on its head. 'To expect India to subsidise this [British] inefficiency', B. N. Adarkar wrote in the best-known contemporary book on tariffs, 'and that too at the expense of her own industrial development is so selfish a procedure that only political power can make it feasible'.[33] The argument did not explain why Indian industry needed protection from the rest of the world, but projected efficiency as an imperial ploy, one which, like the countervailing excise duties on cotton textiles from an earlier time, delayed 'the rapid development of the Indian industry by reserving the Indian market to the British producers'.[34]

Eminent economists and public intellectuals made the case for rejecting discriminating protection. Mokshagundam Visvesvaraya, the former Prime Minister of Mysore, blamed the weak protection policy for India's underdevelopment in a plan published in 1944.[35] In a series of radio speeches delivered in 1938, V. K. R. V. Rao, the Cambridge-educated economist soon to play a large role in Indian economic administration, called for 'unqualified' protection, that is, for the tariff wall to be raised as high as needed for Indian concerns to survive, and somewhat paradoxically, raised the fear that 'behind the tariff wall, giant foreign concerns are erecting their factories, and threatening to wipe out the financially and technically less equipped Indian concerns'.[36] Shriman Narayan Agarwal, a prominent Congress politician and intellectual, later a member of the Planning Commission, and the author of a book on Gandhi's

---

[32] All India Manufacturers' Conference, *Proceedings of the First Session*, Bombay: publisher not stated, 1941, 49.
[33] B. N. Adarkar, *The Indian Fiscal Policy*, Allahabad: Kitabistan, 1941, 530.   [34] Ibid., 76.
[35] M. Visvesvaraya, *Reconstruction in Post-War India: A Plan of Development All Round*, Bombay: All India Manufacturers Association, 1944, 30.
[36] V. K. R. V. Rao, *What Is Wrong with Indian Economic Life?*, Bombay: Vora, 1938, 76.

economic principles, declared that 'the doctrine of free trade is now dead as dodo', before endorsing unqualified tariff protection for Indian industry, while at the same time advocating protection for small industry from large-scale industry.[37] Left-leaning economists saw the efficiency issue as an apology for capitalism.[38]

With eminent economists using the language of xenophobia as freely as Rao did, publicists hardened attitudes towards foreign capital. Foreign firms should be forced to train Indians rather than hire managers and skilled workers from abroad.[39] Foreign firms should also be forced by law to register in Indian share markets and mandatorily sell 50 per cent shares to Indians. The origin of that idea (which was in fact implemented after 1947) was a 1906 speech by Vithaldas Thackersey, a Bombay-based textile mill owner.

Although full independence was almost a *fait accompli* towards the end of the War, the Partition of India into two nation states, India and Pakistan in 1947 caught all sections of business unprepared. The abrupt way the partition was announced, implemented, and designed left everyone a loser. Several foreign trading firms (for example Ralli, see Chapter 4) saw their assets divided up between two countries. Land producing raw material for jute and cotton textiles fell in one territory, whereas the mills processing the material in another. At the same time, there began a process of migration of merchants.

The Partition and Its Aftermath

At the time of independence, Karachi and Lahore were both large and populous business towns. Most of the businesses there were owned by Hindus (including Sindhi), Parsis, and Sikhs. Most of them left Pakistan for India in 1947. Khatri businesses left western Punjab, as did the factories and trading firms of Punjab, like Shri Ram. Their counterparts who left India for Pakistan were without exception trading firms, with interest in tea, textile, leather, coastal shipping, and financial services. They were mobile and had bases in the port cities of Asia. Some had their main offices in Calcutta. They were cosmopolitan as well as Muslim in their public profile.

Some of the most prominent firms of Pakistan in the 1960s had been invited into the country by the leadership on generous terms such as land grant, and

---

[37] Shriman Narayan Agarwal, *The Gandhian Plan of Economic Development for India*, Bombay: Padma Publications, 1944, 97.

[38] P. A. Wadia and K. T. Merchant, *The Bombay Plan: A Criticism*, Bombay: Popular Book Depot, 1944.

[39] Ibid., 150.

were subsequently helped with bank loans and import licences. All major communities of Muslim merchants responded to the open invitation from the other side to some extent. Members of the Halai Memon community of Gujarat, a trading group, migrated to Karachi and took over the textile trade (see also Fig. 6.5). Other migrant merchants included the Ismaili Khojas from Bombay and East Africa, the Khojas who followed the Ithnā Ashari sect of Shiism – to which the first ruler of Pakistan Muhammad Ali Jinnah's family had converted from Hinduism – and the Dawoodi Bohras of western India. Chiniotis, a small group from Punjab (Chiniot) who had migrated to Calcutta and traded in leather, returned to their homelands, and played a role in the textile industry. Among Pakistan's leading business families in the 1960s, the Monnoo and Crescent groups were Chiniotis, Adamjee and Kassim Dada were Gujarati Memon firms, the Saigols were Punjabis based in Calcutta, Ahmed Dawood was from Kathiawar, and the textile house Bawany originated in a Gujarati trading firm. The trading firms eventually diversified into textile production and financial services. The Gujarati Ismaili Mohammed Ali Habib founded Pakistan's largest private bank, Habib Bank, and was encouraged by Jinnah to shift base from Gujarat to Karachi. Saigols headed the United Bank from 1959.

These people, whose homes were in Bombay, Gujarat, or Calcutta, influenced the economic policy of Pakistan after 1947, but the nature of their influence was very different from that in India. Whereas the mainly Hindu business groups close to the Congress had begun to diversify into manufacturing, the Muslim groups that had some say in the movement for Pakistan or which migrated to the new country were almost without exception merchants. This distinction shaped policy. In Pakistan, business and politics held a benign outlook on trade, and did not try to regulate it too much except during a socialist interlude in the 1970s. The extremist form of protectionism that took hold in India was missing in Pakistan. In independent India, by contrast, trade was relegated to a low position and repressed by a range of instruments. The loss of many trading firms to Pakistan, therefore, did not worry Indian leaders. They wanted trade to be weak anyway.

Conclusion

Via a new equation between business and politics, the thinking on Indian economic policy came to rest, ever more firmly, on the idea of protectionist industrialisation. The business lobby in India that had a say in the matter of policy did not always agree completely with the politicians, but there was a substantial shared ground between them. They endorsed a Congress narrative that free trade and foreign capital had damaged India and discriminating protection was an imperialist trick. The business lobby in Pakistan was made up of traders who did not read the economic history of the Empire with such a dark lens, in fact, did not read history at all to justify the relatively open policy that came into being.

India was different. The government of independent India decided that trade was undesirable, and moneylending was evil. The socialists among the Indian politicians wanted a Soviet-style industrialisation. Metals, machines, and chemicals were to be the favoured fields. The technology had to be bought from western markets. Trade, textiles, and foreign firms – the three pillars of the colonial modernisation – would recede in priority in the future strategy of industrialisation. Thirty years on, the port cities had more bankrupt businesses than healthy ones. Agricultural trade was greatly constricted when not banned. Land and sea trades disconnected. Most dangerous of all, export capacity was impaired when import needs had arisen, making serious balance of payments crisis a way of life.

The strategy left many losers. And yet, from the ashes of this disaster, there did arise indigenous business conglomerates with interests in metals, machinery, and chemicals. This process and its consequences will form the subject matter of Chapter 7.

7   State and Industrialisation: 1950–1980

Protectionism was limited and conditional in the interwar period. The emphasis on industrialisation did not devalue the role of trade. National policy after 1947 changed the balance. It prioritised industrialisation, prioritised the production of machinery and chemicals in India, and devalued traditional activities like textiles and trade. State regulation of markets had increased in extent during World War II, and at the end of the war, the measures stayed on and acquired a developmental meaning. Breaking with the past, the regime increased the role of the state and reduced the role of the world economy as the driver of economic development.

Protectionist industrialisation delivered unprecedented opportunity to established domestic groups to diversify in the priority areas, and away from the older foundations of capitalist enterprise, trade, and textiles. Government efforts sharply raised industrial investment, and rewarded entrepreneurship with the permission to buy technology abroad through collaborations. This process favoured the already established conglomerates, who started production of machinery, chemicals, cement, and metals. It also nurtured many offbeat enterprises, and encouraged little known business groups to become conglomerates.

But protectionist industrialisation came with two types of cost. First, the closed economy hurt business formerly integrated with the world economy. Thus, the corporate textile industry went bankrupt, trade and banking were part-nationalised, part-regulated, and part-outlawed, and restrictions were imposed on cross-border capital and labour movements damaging the managing agency companies. In the process, some of the traditional sources of investment funds, like profits from foreign trade, played a reduced role in the new regime. Second, the regime compromised macroeconomic stability. Whereas earlier India exported agricultural commodities and bought machines and services with the proceeds, now traditional exports were restrained to conserve investment funds, even when the decision to go for heavy industry needed more imports than before. With the repression of trade, textiles, and global firms, the capacity to export and earn exchange had been impaired. Banks were under pressure to lend to new clients of uncertain capacity, such as peasants, and when they did not

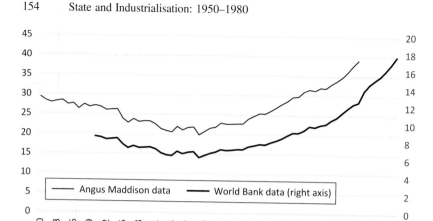

Fig. 7.1 The Great Nehruvian Divergence (Indian per capita income, constant price, percentage of world)

Sources: World Bank, World Development Indicators, http://data.worldbank.org/data-catalog/world-development-indicators; Groningen Growth and Development Centre Database, www.ggdc.net/maddison/oriindex.htm (both accessed 1 August 2017)

comply easily, were nationalised. In this way, the economy's capacity to pay for investment was impaired. Repeated shocks from the world economy (1967, 1973, 1979, and 1991) underscored this obvious fact.

A business history account of the time must recognise that there were gainers in the new regime, and there were losers too. In conventional economic and business history of India, the losses tend to be glossed over. The standard narrative is that a new dawn of capitalism emerged after the dark age of colonial repression. In fact, these years saw India fall behind the world average growth (Fig. 7.1), which should suggest that the losses were significant. Who gained and who lost, and why, during these years? The present chapter is an exploration into this question.

It is useful to start with two themes that help us understand the origin and meaning of these changes, how business shaped policy, and how policy shaped business.

How Business Shaped Policy

Indian big business contributed money and leadership to the movement that hastened an end of colonial rule. And yet, instead of rewarding them with unrestrained capitalism, post-independent India reserved large fields of investment for the state and regulated private enterprise. There was a paradox here.

The experience of liberal reforms between 1980 and 2015 makes it an even bigger puzzle. Economic and business growth was slow in the 1950s and the 1960s compared with these recent times. The huge outburst of private enterprise that followed the economic reforms of the 1990s makes the earlier regulation difficult to understand. What did the politicians think they were doing when they made a choice that hindsight shows to be an obviously bad choice?

A broadly right-wing answer to the question would be: the appeal of socialist ideology. India, the argument would go, had always been capitalistic and entrepreneurial, but in the 1950s and the 1960s, politicians, goaded by socialist ideology, repressed the capitalist. The first Prime Minister Jawaharlal Nehru's years (1947–64) were a triumph of socialism, a regime where capitalists were shackled and repressed. The idea brings in sharp relief how very different post-reform India was. It was a triumph of capitalism, by contrast with Nehru's India.

An influential commentator on Indian development says: ' ... the Fabian socialist policies of Prime Minister Jawaharlal Nehru and his imperious daughter, Prime Minister Indira Gandhi, ... oversaw India's darkest economic decades'.[1] Another writer calls the liberalisation, 'escape from the benevolent zookeepers'.[2] In the spirit of the rightist view, Stanley Kochanek in some of his writings suggests that the corporates did grow weak after 1950.[3] But he has a different interpretation for it. He shows how divided in scale, capability, and interest private enterprise always was. After independence in 1947, big business was dominated by the public sector and bureaucratic intervention. Exporting businesses were small firms that did not have lobbying power. Trading firms were dwarf family units that would not have much in common with industrial companies. Multinational companies preferred to keep a low profile. The regime, thus, made collective action by industrial capitalists more difficult than before.

A broadly left-wing position disputes the thesis that socialist politicians repressed capitalists in these years. Soviet analysis of India in these times, as well as the French Marxist Charles Bettelheim, stressed the monopoly power of big business.[4] An Indian Marxist called the regime 'tycoon capitalism'.[5] Another author suggests that the Indian capitalists had sufficient influence on the policies to resist attempts by the state to discipline them.[6] The average

---

[1] Gurcharan Das, 'The India Model', *Foreign Affairs*, 85(4), 2006, 2–16.
[2] Swaminathan S. A. Aiyer, *Escape from the Benevolent Zookeepers*, Mumbai: Times Group Books, 2008.
[3] Stanley A. Kochanek, 'The Transformation of Interest Politics in India', *Pacific Affairs*, 68(4), 1995–96, 529–50.
[4] A. I. Levkovsky, *Capitalism in India*, Delhi: People's Publishing House, 1972; Charles Bettelheim, *India Independent*, New York, NY: Monthly Review, 1968
[5] Asim Chaudhuri, 'Conglomerate Big Business Groups in India: Some Traits of Tycoon Capitalism', *Social Scientist*, 8(7), 1980, 38–51.
[6] Vivek Chibber, *Locked in Place: State-building and Late Industrialization in India*, Princeton, NJ: Princeton University Press, 2004.

article on business published in the 1970s in the highly influential centre-left magazine, the *Economic and Political Weekly*, reflected a similar worldview about business and politics, that capitalists had more power than they deserved.

Others read the policy regime differently, though staying within the broadly left-wing view that Nehru's India was neither socialist nor an easy time to understand. Nasir Tyabji suggests that, not socialist sympathies, but anxieties about exploitative trade and finance reinforced by corporate scandals, led to regulation.[7] Another contribution shows that in the 1940s and the 1950s, political opinion and business opinion about the desired mix of socialism and capitalism differed. No matter the officially stated policy, on pragmatic grounds, political opinion needed to move away from a hard-socialist stance from the late 1950s, give away ground to private enterprise, and renegotiate the ideological position with representatives of business.[8] Much new work has appeared alongside this literature, which, when not joining the debate directly, focuses on the mid-twentieth-century business-state interaction.[9]

I find both these positions unpersuasive. Those who believe that India was a haven of capitalism, and that the mid-twentieth-century socialism held capitalism back, should be reminded that the cost of capital had always been very high in India, from well before the modern times (Chapter 1). There is an obvious problem with the thesis that the state repressed capital in the 1950s and the 1960s. The problem is that capitalists gained massively from protection in these years. Some of India's best-known consumer brands to emerge since the 1950s, from the Ambassador car to the Godrej typewriter, to the Bajaj scooter or the Usha sewing machine, might not have survived at all but for the unbounded generosity of the state, which did everything in its powers to drive out foreign competition for these products.

Those who believe that the mid-twentieth century was capitalistic after all, need to answer why that capitalism was a sickly type. They should be reminded that India did fall behind the world during these years of socialism (Fig. 7.1). There were substantial losers in the new regime, and their losses have not been accounted for. Both accounts tend to be pre-occupied with the so-called 'big' business, and neglect most firms that did not command such

---

[7] Nasir Tyabji, *Forging Capitalism in Nehru's India: Neocolonialism and the State, c. 1940–1970*, New Delhi: Oxford University Press, 2015.

[8] Kamal Aron Mitra Chenoy, *The Rise of Big Business in India*, Delhi: Aakar, 2015.

[9] Medha M. Kudasiya, *The Life and Times of G. D. Birla*, New Delhi: Oxford University Press, 2006; Manali Chakrabarti, 'Why Did Indian Big Business Pursue a Policy of Economic Nationalism in the Interwar Years? A New Window to an Old Debate', *Modern Asian Studies*, 43(4), 2009, 979–1038; Manali Chakrabarti and Biswajit Chatterjee, 'Business Conduct in Late Colonial India: European Business in Kanpur', *Economic and Political Weekly*, 41(10), 2006, 904–11.

political influence as big business did, and which traded, banked, ran small firms, and ran the exporting managing agencies. Many among these, I argue in this chapter, paid a price for the Nehruvian experiment. Socialism did not hurt them as badly as the closure of the economy to free movement of goods, capital, labour, and technology. It was the constriction of the role of the world economy that made Indian capitalism weaker than it could be.

This leads us to the question of what was done and why that mattered to business.

How Policy Shaped Business

The new regime is sometimes called import-substituting industrialisation or ISI, since the average level of tariffs on manufactured goods was raised. During much of the late twentieth century, many countries in the developing world pursued ISI. In India, however, ISI was much more than protectionism. In India, it was ISI with at least three added elements.

First, there was a deliberate turning away from the traditional foundations of industrialisation, textiles, and trade. Between 1950 and 1980, the share of the cotton mills in domestic cloth production fell from 80 per cent to 40 per cent. The share continued to fall to just 7 per cent in 1995. This was the intention behind the Textile Policy of 1950, which wanted to protect craft textiles from mill competition. The consequence of the policy was quite an unexpected one: growth of power looms (Box 7.1). Consistently overvalued exchange hurt the textile mills in the export market. The state tried to appropriate the trading function to a certain extent (Box 7.2), but its role was limited in this regard.

Secondly, in 1956, the state defined clear priorities about what kind of industry it wanted to sponsor, these being the capital and intermediate goods industries. Certain fields of industrial investment the government reserved for itself, such as steel, oil, fertilisers, telecommunications, and heavy engineering. The reservation would mean that the companies that were established to produce these goods were much more than mere publicly owned firms, they were also monopolies or near-monopolies. The major fields of industrial investment by the state were steel, oil, and equipment. Steel and equipment is discussed in Box 7.3. Other fields where the government took over private firms included finance (banks were nationalised in 1969) and aviation (Fig. 7.2).[10]

---

[10] Commercial aviation in India began with a small service Jehangir Ratanji Dadabhoy Tata had started in 1932 to carry mail between Karachi and Bombay, and evolved into the Tata Airlines in the 1940s. The airline was nationalised in 1953. Between then and 1994, government carriers monopolised commercial aviation.

Box 7.1 **Small-scale industry, 1950–80**

At the time of independence, 90 per cent of industrial employment was in small firms. In 1991, 70 per cent of industrial employment in India was still in units not registered as factories. In 1950, small-scale industries were composed mainly of the traditional handicrafts.

Chapter 5 suggests that there were enduring links between the craft heritage and modern business. Nowhere was this link clearer than in the power-loom factory of western and southern India. In a sense, these factories were an outcome of the natural progression of a handloom business (Chapter 5). The growth of power-loom factories also reflected accumulating advantages of the small towns where they were located. These advantages were: lower rent and wages; a flexible labour market; local repair industry; coordination and cooperation among community members; and accumulation of capital 'below', among artisans and among a Green Revolution farming elite. Apart from these strengths, the Textile Policy (1950–85) helped them by restraining capacity expansion in the cotton mills. Power looms were illegal (because they supposedly hurt handlooms), but local politicians did not enforce the law for they were a useful business, and many power looms were set up by handloom weavers themselves. While power looms could produce basic cloth cheaply, they were poor in marketing, and did not use high-capability equipment to deliver good quality. They did not have the capital to do any of this.

In 1977, a new government inspired by Gandhian ideology strengthened support for small firms. By the end of the 1980s, virtually '[a]ny item that can be produced by small manufacturers is banned from production by any other means'. (Guhathakurta, see next). In the 1980s, the number of products reserved for small firms exceeded 800. The small firms did have a comparative advantage, the same ones the power looms had. But like the power looms, small firms making consumer products had a huge disadvantage in marketing, advertisement, quality control, and brand creation.

Readings: Tirthankar Roy, 'Development or Distortion? The Powerlooms in India, 1950–97', *Economic and Political Weekly*, 33(16), 1998, 897–911; Supriya Roy Chowdhury, 'Political Economy of India's Textile Industry: The Case of Maharashtra, 1984–89', *Pacific Affairs*, 68(2), 1995, 231–50; S. Guhathakurta, 'Economic Independence through Protection? Emerging Contradictions in India's Small-scale Policies Sector', *World Development*, 21(12), 1993, 2039–54; S. P. Kashyap, 'Growth of Small-sized Enterprises in India: Its Nature and Content', *World Development*, 16(6), 1988, 667–81; J. C. Sandesara, 'Small-Scale Industrialisation: The Indian Experience', *Economic and Political Weekly*, 23(13), 1988, 640–54.

The third feature was licensing, to conserve both capital and foreign exchange. Outside the public sector, private investment was allowed but investment and foreign exchange demands were regulated by licences. Both traditional industry and heavy industry needed to buy technology

Box 7.2 **The state as trader**

As a measure to reduce private trade, in 1956, a public company called State Trading Corporation was established. Its mission was to 'canalise' imports, assist small firms with exports, and implicitly, interfere in domestic trade where there was suspicion of excessive profits being made. In 1970, an estimated four per cent of foreign trade was managed by the Corporation, the percentage was higher in India's trade with the communist countries, in which trade, the Corporation acted as a major intermediary. The Corporation was intermittently assigned the duty to import food, fertiliser, steel, milk products, and coal, and export the odd product, including human hair used in wigs.

The Corporation was a catastrophic failure. Because it might need to act as an enemy of the capitalist, from the start its board was filled with bureaucrats who did not understand trade. No member from the merchant community was admitted into the organisation. Its mission being broad and undefined, ministries made contradictory demands upon its services. Although the expectation was that state trading would mitigate shortages, the reality was that it worsened shortages through inexperience and bureaucratic interference. For example, the Corporation was involved in the marketing of cement, and baby food. These were articles in which acute and persistent shortages developed in the 1970s. One of the mandates of the Corporation, to promote export abroad, was badly served because it had no expertise in the matter. The Corporation still made money, in ways that were quite bizarre. Foreign diplomats stationed in New Delhi could import cars through the Corporation, which cars would be sold second-hand to Indians. The business was a highly profitable one for all concerned. The diplomats got the cars they wanted, the state earned tariffs of 200–300 per cent, and given the famously dull design and inefficiency of Indian cars, second-hand cars sold at a premium on the original price, the benefits of which the Corporation pocketed.

Private trade's own view of state trading and the Corporation was understandably scathing. But trade was apprehensive too, because politicians in the Parliament frequently demanded to expand the Corporation's reach and eliminate more areas from private trade. That this did not happen was probably a testimony to the Corporation's incompetence than political wisdom.

Note: I have drawn on G. R. Kulkarni, 'The State Trading Corporation of India (A)', Indian Institute of Management Ahmedabad, Case Study IIMA/BP0033(A), 1970. Interpretations are mine.

from abroad; the former to modernise themselves and the latter to start operations in India. Now technology could come in under licensed technical collaboration with foreign firms, and these licences were restricted to heavy industry mainly. Restraints were imposed also on hiring abroad,

Box 7.3 **The state as industrialist**

From the 1950s, the government decided to set up steel factories, while not curbing expansion in the private sector. The policy succeeded to the extent that by 1964, half of domestic production came from the public sector (the combined enterprise was called Steel Authority of India Limited), and this proportion was projected to be 75 per cent by the early 1970s. New investment depended on foreign aid and technical collaboration. Among other large public companies, the Indian Telephone Industries (ITI) was formed in 1948 to make telecommunication equipment; in 1953, the Hindustan Machine Tools started, which later diversified into tractors and watches; the Heavy Engineering Corporation (1958) was to make steel plant machines; manufacture of machines and components for the power utilities was done by Bharat Heavy Electricals Ltd. or BHEL (1964); in 1964, Bharat Earth Movers Limited started making railway coaches and mining equipment. Railway equipment was mostly made by the railways, which were already nationalised. The last major field of government investment was petrochemicals, which began operation in the late 1960s, as an extension of the government-owned oil refineries.

BHEL and ITI are good case studies. BHEL was set up to supplement an already existing plant started in 1956. Its three manufacturing units were in Hardwar, Tiruchirapalli, and Hyderabad. In 1974, the two firms merged to form the largest engineering firm of India. In 1976, it acquired two ailing engineering firms set up by the government in the last days of the Mysore kingdom, in a badly planned and hasty attempt to speed up industrialisation in the state. In 1990, the company employed 75,000 persons. BHEL maintained a good record on quality of work, thanks partly to its privileged position in obtaining technical collaboration licences. But its profits depended on the conditions of its major clients in the state sector, especially the state electricity boards. In the 1970s, bankruptcy in the electricity boards put BHEL in trouble. BHEL had meanwhile grown into a flabby organisation with large overheads, and poor inventory management. As a first step towards reform, the central government refused to provide budgetary support (1980). The move from a soft to a hard budget changed the game for BHEL.

Dilip Subramanian's study of ITI shows that a soft budget constraint caused this monopoly to underperform, underinvest, fail to innovate, and run into financial difficulties. But this was not the whole story. Like BHEL, inside this company, there was a substantial managerial-technocrat cadre that tried to gain decisional autonomy and pushed for a profit-oriented performance. After the economic reforms, in a subset of state-owned enterprises, the latter pull won, whereas others declined rapidly. ITI's traditional business was captured by new private manufacturers, but BHEL reinvented itself as a professionally managed company.

Readings: Dilip Subramanian, *Telecommunications Industry in India: State, Business and Labour in a Global Economy*, New Delhi: Social Science Press, 2010.

Fig. 7.2 An Indian postage stamp ('the factory worker 1954') celebrating industrialisation
© Ivan Vdovin/Alamy Stock Photo

private borrowing abroad, and repatriation of profits of foreign subsidiaries and joint ventures in India.[11]

Some of these ingredients have been discussed in the large literature on postcolonial India. The restraints imposed upon private trade and finance have gone largely unnoticed in that literature.

Repression of Trade and Finance

Chapter 6 outlined the transition from discriminatory protection to a 'sons of the soil' type of protection. After independence, the Tariff Commission considered the case for protection, a job the Tariff Board had done in the interwar years, on a case-by-case basis in response to applications from industry. Protective tariffs were given to fewer industries after 1947, and the number declined steadily. In several cases, industries were officially 'deprotected'. This was not a move towards more openness. The need for case-by-case or discriminating protection was becoming obsolete because of indiscriminate revenue tariffs set at high levels. Further, direct import controls that were tightened from

---

[11] An excellent study of the prehistory of import controls in India is Ashok V. Desai, 'Evolution of Import Control', *Economic and Political Weekly*, 5(29–31), 1970, 1271–7. Desai shows that the control system was established in response to wartime trade regulations, and stayed on to serve a different purpose, in the process becoming increasingly complex and opaque.

1958, had made the import of consumer goods in the private account practically impossible by 1966. Tariffs were raised, progressively and sharply, after 1947. Just before the economic reforms of 1992, unweighted average tariff rate in India, at over 100 per cent, was likely the highest among large countries in the developing world. Tariff protection by then had been reinforced by non-tariff barriers. Tariffs were not significantly lower for machines, materials, and intermediate goods, so that costs of inputs passed on to the price of the final good. Import licence added another layer of protection.

In the export-oriented industries like jute and tea, trade repression involved different instruments. The exchange rate was state-managed and overvalued. Overvalued exchange was bad for commercial exports. The contribution of tea to total exports fell from over 20 per cent in 1947 to nearer 10 per cent at the end of the 1960s.[12] Exportable goods like tea and jute paid a large export tax in the mid-1960s.[13] Exchange control also meant restriction on imports of machinery. Deprived of access to either foreign technology or foreign markets, the tea industry turned to the home market (which did not consume much higher-grade tea), reduced investment, neglected stocks, and relaxed on quality. The export-production ratio declined from 70 per cent in 1950 to 27 per cent in 1991. Jute packaging faced international competition from polypropylene from the 1960s.[14] But well before this competition became serious, the one hundred odd jute textile mills of Calcutta were going bankrupt, because of change of leadership and lack of access to capital, technology, and managers.

Within India, commodity trade came under significant restrictions. The restrictions began as temporary measures during World War II. The Defence of India Rules announced during the War prohibited trade in food grain except with a licence issued by the provincial government. After the War ended, continued shortages in some articles led to a more comprehensive legislation called the Essential Commodities Act 1955, which declared many commodities besides food as 'essential' and reserved the right of the government, whether central or provincial, to issue licences and fix prices.

These regulations stayed on, and were used recklessly by local agencies. The new economic ideology frowned upon trading as a rule. From the beginning, Congress politicians announced that the new regime would not

---

[12] I. S. Gulati, 'Competitiveness of India's Tea Exports', *Economic and Political Weekly*, 3(7), 1968, 325–32.

[13] Gary Pursell, 'Trade Policies in India', in Dominick Salvatore, ed., *National Trade Policies*, Amsterdam: North Holland, 1992, 423–58.

[14] Synthetic substitute prices were approximately two-thirds that of comparable jute goods in the international market in the late 1960s. The ratio did not change very much, in fact marginally converged in the 1980s. The Government of India protected domestic consumption of jute. On relative price trends, Goutam K. Sarkar, 'The Fading Fabric-II: Jute Manufacturing Sector', *Economic and Political Weekly*, 21(50), 1986, 2188–97.

encourage private trade. The government introduced bans on export of agricultural goods, on future markets, on private trade, and on the sale of agricultural goods except in approved sites. In short, agricultural trade was throttled by restrictions. Coastal trade was not fully nationalised, but protected for Indian-origin firms. Intervention in trade also included setting up a public sector trading firm, and regulation on prices. The trading firm in question, while taking business away from private trade, did not add to the state's own capacity to do commercial business. Box 7.2 explores this history.

The Industries (Development and Regulation) Act, 1951, Section 18G, empowered the central and provincial governments to take over, reserve for itself, and regulate trade in manufactured goods. Using these laws, governments would enact 'control orders' to regulate specific trades. The Imports and Exports (Control) Act, 1947, did the same thing in the field of foreign trade. A comprehensive list of orders does not seem to appear anywhere except in the annual trade policy documents of the ministry of commerce. Since these orders were often challenged in the court, browsing court judgments gives us an idea of at least the most disputatious ones. The list is frighteningly long. Table 7.1 lists the control orders that I could find references to in legal sources. Almost certainly, this is a subset of the orders that were passed.

The government's price control policy in cotton, cement, steel – practically any essential intermediate good – was to serve two aims at once: make the good cheap for the consumers while ensuring a reasonable profit to the producers. The strategy was to set a floor and a ceiling price, and revise the band from time to time. Repeatedly, the ceiling price did not serve any purpose other than encourage a black market in times of shortage. And the floor price left the producer dissatisfied and unwilling to invest. Intervention in trade, in short, discouraged investment and turned trade into a field for intense lobbying.

A few examples will help illustrate the operation of the orders. The Cement Control Order 1956 reserved the distribution and sale of cement for the State Trading Corporation. The Corporation fixed prices of cement, keeping it low for the consumer and barely profitable for the producer. By 1980, there was an acute shortage. The bureaucratic process of operation of the cement control order 'resulted in the fall of the fresh investments in the cement industry', a Supreme Court judgment claimed.[15] Government pricing policy calculated cost plus a mark-up that varied by grade of cement, but the cost did not fully account for the rising price of energy, frequent electricity shortages, and very high trade cost (cement freight cost 30 per cent of the final price in 1974).

---

[15] Supreme Court of India Shree Digvijay Cement Co. Ltd. & . . . v Union Of India & Another on 17 December, 2002 [Appeal (civil) 46 of 1993].

Table 7.1 *Price control orders, 1943–84*

Umbrella laws under which control orders were passed	Central government	State governments
Essential Commodities Act 1955 Industries (Development and Regulation) Act, 1951 Imports and Exports (Control) Act, 1947	Imports (Control) Order, 1955. Ethyl alcohol (Price Control) Order Newsprint Control Order 1962 Drugs (Price Control) Order, 1979 Sugar and Sugar Products Control Order 1946 Sugarcane Control Order, 1955 Cement Control order, 1967 Cotton Textiles (Control) Order, 1948 Colliery Control Order, 1945 Fertiliser (Control) Order, 1957 Non-Ferrous Metal Control Order, 1958 Export Control Order 1968 Levy Sugar Supply (Control) Order, 1972 Iron and Steel Control Order, 1956 Pulses, Edible Oils Storage Control) Order,1977 Edible Oils (Storage Control) Order, 1977 Aluminium Control Order, 1970 Scrap Control Order, 1943 Iron and Steel (Control) Order, 1956 Cotton Cloth and Yarn (Control) Order, 1945 Jute Price Control Order Indian Cotton (Control) Order, 194 Paper (Control) Order, 1979	Assam Food Grains (Licensing and Control) Order, 1961 Wheat (Uttar Pradesh) Price Control Order, 1959 Madhya Pradesh Foodstuffs (Distribution) Control Order 1960 Rice (Andhra Pradesh) Price Control order 1963 Haryana Rice Bran (Distribution and Price) Control Order, 1981 Kerala Kerosene Control Order, 1965 Orissa Foodgrains Control Order, 1951 Rajasthan Wheat (Export Control) order, 1981 Bengal Silk Control Order, 1943 Bengal Rice Mills Control Order, 1943 Uttar Pradesh Coal Control Order, 1953 UP Milk and Milk Products Control Order, 1977 Karnataka Rice Procurement (Levy) Order, 1984

Source: See text.

Perversely, the response to shortage was more regulation on trade. Noting that the ceiling price often failed, the Cotton Corporation of India started buying and selling cotton in bigger quantities. The Maharashtra counterpart monopolised cotton trade. In 1974, the Paper (Control of

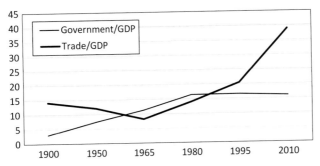

Fig. 7.3 Foreign trade and government expenditure in GDP (in per cent) for
India, 1900–2010

Productions) Order was passed, in response to shortages of paper, forcing
the producers to conform to a fixed proportion between white printing
paper, cream laid papers, and other varieties. After these regulations,
shortage of paper became acute.

The impact of the trade repression can be measured to some extent. With
foreign trade, the trade-GDP index is easily measurable, and shows a
significant dip in the 1950s, 1960s, and the 1970s (Fig. 7.3). The ratio of
foreign trade in national income fell to a third of what it was (7 in
1970 compared with 20 in 1920). It is difficult to reconstruct the relative
scale of domestic trade. The Indian National Accounts does not report trade
data in sufficient detail. The figures are usually clubbed together with
hotels; and show only retail trade. A great deal of the wholesale commodity
trade took place under the direction of the government and para-statal
agencies, for which no separate breakdown from general administrative
income is available. The National Sample Surveys report a different set of
numbers from the National Accounts. I have collated together the numbers
that are available and created a graph (Fig. 7.4). It is patchy, but tells a
consistent story: the importance of domestic trade *in the private sector*
experienced a relative decline in the 1950s, 1960s, and possibly the
1970s. There was no absolute decline, for growth rates of real GDP arising
from trade remained positive throughout. The growth rate was small, and
stayed marginally above the average GDP growth rate in these decades,
speeding up only from the 1990s. Rather than a depression, this is a
condition of *repressed* trade when compared with periods before or after.
The dip in the proportion of GDP was greater than the dip in the proportion
of workers, which suggests that units which had higher labour productivity
(that is, corporate firms) declined relatively more. Tax records tell a similar
story. In the 1920s, half of India's highest income taxpayers described

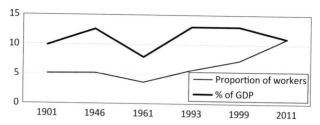

Fig. 7.4 Status of domestic trade in the Indian Economy (numbers are percentages)
Sources: S. Sivasubramonian, *National Income of India in the Twentieth Century*, New Delhi: Oxford University Press, 2000; J. Krishnamurty, 'Occupational Structure', in Dharma Kumar, ed., *The Cambridge Economic History of India*, Vol. 2, Cambridge: Cambridge University Press, 1983; India, *Economic Survey 2014–15*, Delhi: Government Press, 2015, Vol. 2. EPW Research Foundation, 'National Accounts Statistics of India - 1: Macro-Aggregates', *Economic and Political Weekly*, 30(46), 1995, 2955–64; K. Sundaram, 'Employment and Poverty in India in the Nineteen Nineties', Working Paper of CDE Delhi School of Economics, 2002

themselves as traders.[16] In the 2000s, trading firms occupied 9–10 per cent of the private corporate sector.[17]

A similar story unfolded in private finance. Private moneylending did not become either obsolete or illegal but became far less visible than it was before 1947. Marwari moneylending firms in the interior towns disappeared from banking studies and surveys after 1950. The 1920s Banking Enquiry Committee and contemporary sources reported clusters of banking houses in Mathura, Benares, Ahmedabad, Patna, Jubbulpore, or Jaunpur (see also Chapter 4). They became obscure too. The repression of agricultural trade damaged the bankers and moneylenders who had earlier run the machine of grain trade and rural credit.

Corporate banking remained private and had a healthy growth between 1947 and the mid-1960s. The largest of the banks were owned by big industrial conglomerates like Tata (Central Bank), Birla (United Commercial Bank), Dalmia (Bharat Bank), and Thapar (Oriental Bank of Commerce). Between 1966 and 1969, the ruling party Congress followed a policy called 'social control' of banks, in response to public criticism that the banks preferred to lend to big businesses at the expense of small ones and the socially weaker sections. It is not clear what social control meant in terms of practical

[16] V. K. R. V. Rao, 'National Income of India', *The Annals of the American Academy of Political and Social Science*, 233, 1944, 99–105.
[17] R. Nagaraj, 'Size and Structure of India's Private Corporate Sector: Implications for the New GDP Series', *Economic and Political Weekly*, 50(45), 2015, 41–7.

regulation during these years. It did help to show the Congress, and its leader Indira Gandhi, as a force rising above the corrupt world of big business. As a logical corollary, Gandhi announced full bank nationalisation in 1969, except the small number of foreign banks. Only one foreign bank, Allahabad Bank, was nationalised by mistake. Eventually, social control took on a more concrete shape with the policy of 'priority sector' lending; that is, the corporate banks were forced to lend to farmers and small business.

By contrast with minerals, metals, 'essential goods', and agricultural goods, where the government acted as if the ideal would be to abolish private trade if possible, in manufactured consumer goods, private trade was not touched, except for numerous price controls. However, with large capital losing interest in consumer goods, the marketing system lacked imagination, was undercapitalised, and lacked consumer focus (Box 7.4).

Such was the fate of traditional activities like textiles and trade. Foreign capital presents a more ambiguous history.

Foreign Capital

A few Indian business groups had an extraordinary influence on policymaking in post-independence India. They did not have influence over all aspects of policy, and even failed to anticipate some aspects of it, such as public-sector dominance. Different accounts of this relationship exist, and they stress either the degree of control or the lack of it. Chapter 6 surveys these views (see also the previous section). These accounts overlook and oversimplify the case of foreign capital.

Businesses with political clout displayed undisguised xenophobia. Sections of Indian business wanted foreign capital out, even sequestration. A journalist for the *New York Times*, Herbert Matthews, visited Calcutta in 1942, and in January next year published an article in the newspaper on the challenges faced by British capitalists in soon-to-be-independent India.[18] He spoke to prominent Indian business leaders, including Braj Mohan Birla, Badridas Goenka, and Jagdish Chandra Mahindra, heads of chambers of commerce, directors of Bird and Co. and Mackinnon Mackenzie, editor of the newspaper *Capital*, and government officials. Matthews believed that Indian capitalism had become a battlefield, and predicted that the battle would intensify after independence. He found the British directors 'greatly worried' about 'the fact that big Indian firms like the Birla Brothers ... finance the All India Congress ... the Congress will have a debt to pay to them ... and that the payment will result in the

---

[18] Herbert L. Matthews, 'India Challenges British Finance', *Current History (pre-1986)*, 3, 1943, 496–8.

Box 7.4 **Private trade**

Unlike agricultural goods and minerals, private trading remained intact in manufactured goods, subject to numerous controls. What systems did private traders follow?

Cotton textiles were sold wholesale and retail in Bombay's Moolji Jetha market. Cloth was picked up by wholesalers and sent to regional shops. Garment manufacturers also picked up a certain part of the output. In 1965, there were 1,000 units manufacturing garments. The garment industry served urban retail shops, and produced mainly men's apparel such as shirts. The mills sometimes tried to establish their own brand by either manufacturing garments, or set up their own shops. DCM did this during and after World War II. The motivation to do so was strong, because the government's textile policy otherwise denied the mills the chance to grow and diversify.

In export goods, marketing systems differed. In jute, Calcutta's Marwari houses had their own trading firms that contracted for orders abroad and shipped goods. The fact that some of them owned the mills made for an integration between the trading and production functions, but compromised innovations in marketing. At least, the producing mills never advertised or sought buyers and markets abroad, and the trading firms worked in unimaginative ways. In tea, marketing relied on auction houses of Calcutta and London. Partnership between producing firms and multinational trading-auction firms was of vital importance.

In everyday consumer goods like oils, soaps, and packaged food, the wholesaler ruled. Manufacturers owned warehouses or depots, where finished goods were stored. Sometimes, the manufacturers sent goods to freight forwarders and clearing agents, who owned the warehouses. The latter is a common system today. A main or sole selling agent arranged to collect goods from these depots to send these to subagents in different regions. Neighbourhood shops collected the goods from the latter. Credit sales occurred only between the operators who dealt directly with each other. The system was bottom-up, in that wholesalers judged the market and sent feedback. The manufacturer's own sales team performed a monitoring function rather than dealing with consumers directly. No doubt many industries thought about setting up retail stores, but that option was expensive. Given that most products sold less on the merit of quality and more on the merit of price, cost-saving was a paramount factor. A late 1970s government move to reserve many consumer goods for the small-scale producer may have further discouraged investment in direct marketing.

On all of these benchmarks, 1980–2015 saw a revolutionary change take shape in marketing (Chapter 8). It became top-down, under control of the manufacturers' sales teams, more reliant on direct communication between manufacturer and consumer, more advertising-based, more retail-centred, and more quality-conscious.

Readings: C. N. S. Nambudiri, 'A Note on the Readymade Garment Industry in India', IIM Ahmedabad Case Studies, IIMA/BP0038TES, 1966. B. C. Dalal, 'Merchants India Limited', Indian Institute of Management Ahmedabad Case Material, IIMA/MAR0025, 1965. I have benefited from conversations with Hemant Bangur on the history of jute trading in Calcutta.

elimination of British business interests'. His interviews with the Indian industrialists confirmed these prospects. 'Mr. Birla wants to use India's sterling credits . . . to acquire the British holdings'.

The government of India did not want that and opted for a formal equality between foreign and indigenous capitalists. The formal equality had little meaning, however. Unlike the Indian-origin industrial capitalists, foreign investors were not invited to discuss and negotiate policy with the politicians. Nehru and his cabinet offered them policy packages in a take-it-or-leave-it spirit. The package adopted helped some foreign firms and hurt others.

In 1950, there were two types of foreign firms in India: those selling goods to Indians (multinational companies or MNCs), and those selling goods in the export market (British-owned companies, run by managing agencies). Foreign investment proposals in the former class were encouraged. The regime welcomed foreign capital in engineering, chemicals, and metals. But these measures were irrelevant for the managing agencies, whose comparative advantage was in selling Indian goods in London and colonial markets. The relevant issues for the latter were continued prospect of hiring abroad, borrowing abroad, buying machines from, and forming trading partnership abroad. These avenues were practically closed off.

The policy adopted around 1956 forced these companies to register in India and dilute equity holdings, which exposed them to predatory take-overs. Regulation also closed off foreign capital markets, and forced the firms to 'Indianise' management. These provisions hit the managing agencies. Their export orientation required them to maintain connections with markets, partners, and agents based in Britain. From the late 1950s, the Indian state made it difficult to maintain such connections. The Finance Act of 1955 reformed the tax system, which sharply raised the tax burden on expatriates. A range of expenses the expatriate managers had come to depend on as part of their hiring practices now became taxable. The effects of this tax system, wrote Owain Jenkins, 'was to get rid of the British element in business. No one ever said so'.[19] The Chambers of Commerce voiced the same anxieties. 'By and large, since Indian independence, the previously established British mercantile community have been fighting a rear-guard action against an encroaching Government, rising labour costs,

---

[19] Owain Jenkins, *Merchant Prince: Memories of India 1929–1958*, Salisbury: Michael Russell, 1987, 218. Jenkins was head of Balmer Lawrie and the Associated Chamber of Commerce and Industries for several years after independence in 1947. He was described as an 'old school East India merchant' in an obituary in *The Telegraph*. He cited the example of George Farmer, the head of Jokai Tea. When Farmer developed cancer, and had to be flown back to London for an operation, the air ticket was taxed at 70 per cent, and when the company paid him for the fee, the reimbursement was taxed.

and diminishing personal returns. Where they have not been doing this, they have been disinvesting'.[20]

Overall, foreign capital declined. The statistics are quite clear on this. Foreign direct investment as a proportion of capital stock was nearer 10 per cent before World War II, dropped sharply to 2 per cent after independence, remained depressed, and regained the interwar level around 2002 or 2003.[21] Despite having money, foreign companies were insignificant as investors in the 1950s and the 1960s. 'Domiciled foreign houses', which included the British managing agencies of Calcutta, accounted for only 1 per cent of approved (licensed) investment between 1958 and 1966, and multinational company investment amounted to 7 per cent.[22]

This discussion on policy provides a framework to distinguish the gainers from the losers in the new regime. Let us start with the positive side of the story.

Big Business: 1958–1981

At the time of independence, there were 127 large companies in India. This set can be divided into three subsets. Fifty-eight of these companies were foreign-owned, including the Indo-British managing agency firms and the multinational corporations. The British managing agencies included Andrew Yule, Bird and Heilgers, and McLeod.[23] Some of these conglomerates had their main interest in tea plantations, and some of the tea companies operated in Ceylon (Sri Lanka) and East Pakistan (Bangladesh) as well as India. The managing agencies were ordinarily registered in India. However, some of the companies under their management were registered in Britain. The MNC had a parent abroad, and the Indian subsidiary was incorporated under the Indian Companies Act as a distinct legal entity. Most of the MNCs were also British in origin, engaged in chemicals, cosmetics, pharmaceuticals, and mainly engineering. The third set was formed of the Indian business groups and families. The textile, trading, and financial companies were mainly owned by Indian families.

---

[20] Stephen Garvin, A *Survey for British Industrial Firms*, London: Federation of British Industries, 1956, 35.

[21] Michael Twomey, *A Century of Foreign Investment in the Third World*, Abingdon: Routledge, 2000, 118, for the earlier estimates.

[22] R. K. Hazari, *Industrial Planning and Licensing Policy: Final Report*, New Delhi: Planning Commission (Government of India), 1967, 5.

[23] For a full list of companies under some of the largest groups in 1951 and 1958, see R. K. Hazari, *The Structure of the Corporate Private Sector*, Bombay: Asia Publishing House, 1966.

Table 7.2 *Top 20 business groups, 1958 and 1981*

Top 20 managing agents in 1958 by asset	Top 20 business groups (or companies) by asset in 1981
1	Tata	Tata
2	Birla	Birla
3	Martin Burn	Mafatlal
4	Dalmia Sahu Jain	Singhania
5	Bird Heilger	Thapar
6	Andrew Yule	ACC
7	Bangur	ICI
8	Thapar	Sarabhai
9	J. K. Singhania	Bangur
10	Shri Ram	Kirloskar
11	Shapoorji	Reliance
12	Khatau	Shri Ram
13	Walchand	Ashok Leyland
14	Mafatlal	Hindustan Lever
15	Kasturbhai	Modi
16	Seshasayee	Scindia
17	Ramakrishna	Iyengar
18	Indra Singh	Mahindra and Mahindra
19	Mahindra and Mahindra	Larsen and Toubro
20	Kirloskar	Bajaj

Source: R. K. Hazari, 'The Managing Agency System. A Case for Its Abolition', *Economic Weekly*, 1964, 315–22; J. Dennis Rajakumar and John S. Henley, 'Growth and Persistence of Large Business Groups in India', *Journal of Comparative International Management*, 10(1), 2007, 3–22.

Chapter 6 described conglomerate formation among Indian business groups. After independence, there was considerable reshuffling among these big groups. Some fell off the leading position, others entered the list of big groups. These changes in ranking reflect several dynamics. A big one is diversification into priority areas where licences were distributed easily. The changing fortunes of the British managing agencies was another. Nationalisation in some cases hurt a few groups. In some cases, the internal situation of the families changed. Tables 7.2–7.4 sum up the overall picture.

Of the groups listed in the column for 1958 (Table 7.2), several were discussed in Chapters 5 and 6 (Tata, Birla, Andrew Yule, Bird, Martin Burn, Shri Ram, Seshasayee, Walchand Hirachand, and Kirloskar). Among the other groups, Bangur and Dalmia Sahu Jain dramatically expanded their assets through takeover of British companies. Shapoorji Pallonji was a nineteenth-century construction company, which acquired the assets of financial firm F. E. Dinshaw in 1936. Sardar Indra Singh started his career as a contractor in Jamshedpur around 1920. In 1936, Indra Singh and his sons jointly owned

Table 7.3 *Analysis of group trajectories, 1958–81*

Type of group by relative position	Group
Groups that dropped off the list	Martin Burn, Bird Heilger, Andrew Yule, Khatau, Shapoorji, Walchand, Kasturbhai, Seshasayee, Ramakrishna, Indra Singh, Kirloskar
Groups that dropped down the list	Bangur
Groups that moved up and into the list	Scindia, Larsen and Toubro, Ashok Leyland, Bajaj, Hindustan Lever, Mafatlal, Mahindra and Mahindra, Singhania, Thapar, Iyengar, ACC, Modi

Table 7.4 *Public companies, number, and share capital, 1951*

Industry group	Companies	Share capital (Rs in million)	Percentage of capital
Cotton Textiles	53	241	11
Jute Textiles	33	125	6
Engineering	45	205	9
Plantations	43	26	1
Mining	55	92	4
Cement	13	201	9
Finance, Trade, Transport	253	459	21
Total	705	2,221	100

Source: Hazari, 'The Managing Agency System'.

Indian Steel and Wire Products Limited of Jamshedpur, a manufacturing and trading entity, with Indra Singh and Sons the managing agents. Velagapudi Ramakrishna was a civil service officer who built a sugar manufacturing company during World War II in coastal Andhra. Khatau, J. K. Singhania, Mafatlal, and Kasturbhai Lalbhai were groups with core interest in cotton mills, at least until then. The Kanpur-based J. K. Singhania had also acquired British interests around the time of independence. Thapar was established as an industrial group by Karam Chand Thapar, a merchant from Calcutta. In 1940s, the group's main businesses were textiles (JCT Mills, 1946) and paper (Ballarpur Industries, 1945). The founders of Mahindra and Mahindra were traders in British steel during World War II. Originally started as Mahindra and Muhammad in 1945 in Ludhiana, Punjab, and renamed in 1948, the company moved into commercial vehicle manufactures soon after the War. As this profile would suggest, several of these groups made profits during the war, which were used either to acquire assets of existing companies or to diversify and expand.

Table 7.3 suggests those who took the diversification route successfully, and those who could not. Thapar diversified into banking (taking over the Oriental Bank of Commerce, originally established in Lahore in 1943), chemicals, leather, pesticides, glass, and construction. Mafatlal, again a cotton mill group, diversified into chemicals, starting with Indian Dyestuffs in 1954. In the 1950s and the 1960s, Mahindra and Mahindra entered technical collaboration agreements with several international companies to produce commercial vehicles, automobile components, machine tools, and a range of equipment and machinery. Scindia Steamships, Ashok Leyland, Bajaj, Mahindra and Mahindra, T. V. S. Iyengar, as well as Tata Engineering and Locomotive Company (TELCO) (Tata), and Hindustan Motors (Birla) all developed around transport equipment, which needed large capital and were offered special privileges by the state (see next). T. V. S. Iyengar (1877–1955) was a bus operator in Madras. After his death, his sons diversified into automotive components manufacture (Sundaram Clayton). Cement was in heavy demand. Between 1947 and 1990, production of cement grew from about 4 metric tonnes to 50 tonnes. A small set of domestic firms, the biggest among them being the consortium Associated Cement Company, led this growth. The emerging player in cement was the Birla conglomerate. In 1981, Modi and Reliance were new entries. Modi was in tyres, and Reliance in synthetic textiles (Chapter 8). Of the Tata and Birla group companies, steel, cement, synthetic fibres, chemicals, and general engineering all did well during these thirty years.

Among those groups that dropped off the list in 1981, the Indra Singh story remains obscure. It appears that the group had acquired coal mines in the princely states in central India and traded in coal and related products in the 1960s.[24] It is probable that the group was a casualty of coal nationalisation (1971–2). Seshasayee and Kirloskar diversified on a limited scale, probably because neither group hailed from traditional business families and did not have access to much finance in-house. Khatau Makanji of Bombay and Kasturbhai Lalbhai of Ahmedabad did not decline in absolute scale, and diversified into several fields, but cotton textiles remained their core business. Khatau's textile mill did relatively well. As the whole cotton mill industry went down in fortune, the next generation of the Khatau family separated, one branch associated with the mill, and another with dyes and chemicals, cables, and shipping. The fall of Martin Burn, Bird Heilgers, and Andrew Yule illustrates the combined effects of hostile policy, managerial failure, and loss of assets to takeovers (see next). The Ramakrishna group continued to grow in

---

[24] Sirdar Bahadur Indra Singh vs Commissioner of Income-Tax, on 18 September 1942 (1943 11 ITR 16 Patna).

sugar, but diversified little after 1950. Dalmia Sahu Jain suffered a slow decline in the 1970s, thanks in part to mismanagement and partly due to government regulation over its core businesses, sugar and cement (see next). One group dropped down the list, Bangur. Their prominence as a corporate group was due to acquisitions of British companies. The group continued to invest and move into new fields, but on a low key.

This broad outline frames the rise and fall of big corporates. Big corporate groups did not make up all of the business world, and what is left out is not captured in any available data on firms. Subject to that limitation, this backdrop can be used to revisit the fortunes of some of the individual successes and failures. Let us start with the Indian groups.

Indian Capital: 1950–1980

Government reports investigating concentration in industry in the 1960s suggested that the top twenty indigenous business groups experienced two types of change since independence. First, they diversified away from textiles, sugar, and trade, to new fields like cement, banking, machines for traditional industry, construction, and real estate. They ended up adding to the group businesses. Secondly, these diversified groups used the process of application for licences to pre-empt investment by others, rather like pre-emptive domain-name registration now. The Birlas were known for doing this most successfully, and were found to hold, around 1970, close to 60 unimplemented licences. In fairness to the Birlas, already in 1948 they were so diversified a conglomerate, and had so many decision-making points, that it would be normal for them to collectively submit more applications than others. Still, the Birlas' political influence in New Delhi, it was said, was used on occasions to keep rivals out of the field.[25]

The Birla group, as mentioned before, included jute, cotton, machinery, automobiles, and chemicals at the time of independence. After independence, the group expanded further in aluminium (Hindustan Aluminium), cement, rayon (Century Enka), fertilisers, and chemicals (Zuari Agro). The government nationalised the insurance and mining companies in the 1960s. One of the major companies, Gwalior Rayon, was the country's first producer of rayon yarn, and with a captive textile factory, it could both supply yarn to others and convert it itself into cloth. In short, as an integrated synthetic fibre producer it was in a strong position. Using its profits and reputation in the market, the company (later renamed Grasim) diversified into cement.

---

[25] A 1980s example of this was the rival Modi group's application to produce Viscose Staple Fibre, which waited eight years, alleged because of Aditya Birla's intervention.

During this phase of almost furious growth, the family divided up. In the 1940s, when the next generation – that is, the grandsons of Baldeodas – was old enough to share management, an informal division had started working. The main figures were Brajmohan Birla's son Ganga Prasad, Rameshwar Das Birla's son Madhav Prasad, and Ghanshyam Das Birla's sons Basant Kumar and Krishna Kumar. Madhav Prasad was a close associate of Ghanshyam Das. Several rounds of reshuffle took place thereafter, the major ones under the oversight of Ghanshyam Das in 1983, the year of his death. Of the major companies in the group, Ganga Prasad's branch controlled Hindustan Motors and Orient Paper; Madhav Prasad's Birla Jute; Basant Kumar's controlled tea, textiles, cement, aluminium, and recently mobile telephony; and Krishna Kumar's branch controlled Texmaco, sugar, newspaper. Another constituent was headed by Ashok Birla, Rameshwar Das's grandson by his second son Gajanan Birla. This branch included Zenith Steel and other minor interests. Several Birla groups also had significant overseas interest. The biggest and most diversified branch by far was Basant Kumar Birla's, now known by his son's name as the Aditya Birla Group (1943–95). The other branches suffered attrition after a period of growth in the 1970s and 1980s. Hindustan Motors closed in 2014 and sold the factory to Peugeot in 2017, which promises to bring out a cheap car in a few years. And Madhav Prasad's legacy was caught up in a bitter dispute (1999–) between a successor chosen by Madhav Prasad's wife and members of the Birla clan.

After India's independence, Shri Ram's DCM diversified into chemicals. Bengal Potteries gained from the growing demand for insulators by power generation firms, and Jay Engineering successfully established the Usha brand of household sewing machine. Usha eventually ousted Singers and Puff, which had ruled the market in the interwar period. Usha fans were also a roaring success. These successes were made not only by entrepreneurial acumen, but also by the generous tariff protection the Government of India gifted Shri Ram, the founder. Sewing machines had a 45 per cent nominal tariff and an effective rate of protection of 274 per cent, and fans 55 per cent nominal tariff and 329 per cent effective rate, in 1962.[26] Like the crudely designed Ambassador car, the fan and the sewing machine ran out of time in the 1990s.[27]

From shipping, Walchand Hirachand diversified into engineering (Walchandnagar Industries near Pune), construction (Hindustan Construction), sugar (Ravalgaon), and automobiles (Premier Automobiles). Walchand Hirachand had set up Indian Hume Pipe in 1926. For a considerable time after

---

[26] Jagdish N. Bhagwati and Padma Desai, *India: Planning for Industrialization*, London: Oxford University Press, 1970. See table on effective rate of protection factors in tariffs on components and quantitative controls (Table 7.3).

[27] The Usha brand has survived in the sewing machine market, thanks to diversification and a range of marketing tie-ups with international producers, for example, the Japanese company Janome.

independence, the company was the single largest manufacturer s of pressure pipes in India. The group's other ventures, aeronautics and shipyards were nationalised during World War II or soon after. After Hirachand's death in 1953, the family of the cotton mill owner of Bombay and Sholapur and one of Hirachand's associates in Scindia, Narottam Morarjee (1877–1929) took control of Scindia Steamship. Hirachand's brothers, Lalchand Hirachand and Vinod Doshi managed the other companies. The engineering arm was controlled by the progeny of Lalchand Hirachand, and the automobiles by that of Vinod Doshi. Despite the loss of two major investments to the government, Nehru's India was good to the group. Shipping and automobiles were protected by the government. Premier automobiles grew to be a major player. Hindustan Constructions performed large job works for the government, including the construction of a major dam in south India.

Between 1948 and 1950, the Ramkrishna Dalmia group's assets were divided between Dalmia himself, his brother, Jaidayal, and son-in-law S. P. Jain. Rohtas Industries, the original complex, went to Jain, and had an undistinguished history during the next thirty years. Its core businesses – paper, sugar, cement – were heavily price-controlled by the government. Obtaining import licences for essential materials was difficult. And whether because of this obstacle or sheer bad management, the company did not modernise. Bihar was notorious for its unreliable electricity system, and Rohtas Industries was a heavy defaulter on its electricity dues. Rohtas workers struck work often. In 1968, the sugar mill closed. A report prepared in the mid-1970s stated that the company was lobbying hard and unsuccessfully with the government to free sugar prices, and that it found Dalmianagar an unsustainable site to carry on business.[28] Between 1979 and 1984, major labour disputes occurred. In 1984, the other units closed as well, rendering 12,000 workers unemployed. The railway line closed to commercial traffic at the same time. The units never reopened, Dalmianagar turned into a ghost town, and Rohtas Industries into a gigantic symbol of mismanagement and bad regulation.[29] The Dalmia branch of the group continued in the traditional businesses. Jai Dayal Dalmia's son Vishnu Hari and grandson Sanjay Dalmia made a series of acquisitions from 1979, starting with Golden Tobacco (from Narsee family), and including Shree Meenakshi Mills, Bharat Explosives, and Premier Paper Mills. The core businesses were in Tamil Nadu and Andhra Pradesh (cement) and Uttar Pradesh (sugar).

The Seshasayee group were indigenous and based in utilities, metals, engineering, and chemicals. They were an exception and of symbolic value to independent India's desire to forge ahead in heavy engineering with

---

[28] S. K. Bhattacharya, 'Rohtas Industries Limited', IIM Ahmedabad Case Studies, IIMA/ F&A0113, 1976.
[29] The region has re-emerged slightly from the bad reputation it fell into, thanks to international interest in the Rohtasgarh Fort.

domestic entrepreneurship. Diversification into aluminium, electrical insulators, and electric meters followed the same pattern as in the past, with the difference that more Indian engineers than before were trained abroad as part of the agreements. Among the set of emerging conglomerates discussed in Chapter 6, Godrej remained a conservative family-controlled and family-managed business group and did not diversify widely. After independence, the Godrej group invested in typewriters and refrigerators, both fields heavily protected. Its older interests, storage and soap, also did well. Godrej as a group made some investments in Southeast Asia, like the Aditya Birla group.

In some of the priority industries, ministers and business leaders collaborated closely to decide entry and production line. Automobiles is a good example of this collaboration. The legacy of the interwar proximity between politics and business was that, on an informal-personal level, several corporate leaders remained friends of politicians in New Delhi and received encouragement and favours; the most common form of favour was the permission to enter a technological collaboration. In the automobile industry, the government decided to retain the existing main companies, and allowed these to enter technical collaboration with foreign partners. Four of the companies were car-makers. The Birla group company Hindustan Motors of Calcutta (1941) produced cars with designs from Morris, Premier Automobiles of Bombay produced cars with designs from Chrysler, Standard Motors of Madras produced cars with designs from the parent firm of Coventry, Standard Triumph, and Mahindra and Mahindra manufactured Jeeps under an agreement with Willys. In the commercial vehicle area, TELCO made engines collaborating with Mercedes-Benz. And Ashok Leyland of Madras made trucks and buses. Another Madras firm, Simpsons, was taken over by an Indian in 1945 (the Amalgamations group, see next) and produced tractors. Finally, Royal Enfield was licensed to produce motorcycles in the 1950s.

In these cases, key figures in the government took personal interest in the enterprise. A famous example was Raghunandan Saran. He had a car assembly plant earlier. With Nehru's encouragement, Saran and the British Leyland Motors jointly started Ashok Leyland in 1954. Before the negotiations ended, Saran died in an air crash. With government oversight and Leyland management, the firm continued. Bajaj, a two-wheeler trader, set up a two-wheeler production plant in 1959, which diversified into three-wheelers in the 1960s. These major investments were undertaken by Kamalnayan Bajaj (1915–72), son of Jamnalal Bajaj, and transformed the Bajaj group into a modern manufacturing conglomerate.[30]

---

[30] I am grateful to Gita Piramal for sharing her excellent biography of Kamalnayan Bajaj, *Kamalnayan Bajaj: Architect of the Bajaj Group*, Mumbai: Kamalnayan Bajaj Charitable Trust, 2015, available in soft copy.

Steel was another field where the government needed to engage with the private sector, if only to divide the boundaries between them. Steel was reserved for the government. India's largest private industrial firm Tata Steel was spared nationalisation, but all new capacity in steel came up in the public sector (on the public sector, only a brief reference is adequate, see Box 7.3). Tata Steel not only survived but grew into an enormous organisation between 1947 and 1980. The protected market for steel allowed it to stay profitable, go easy on innovations, and to exist as a symbol of 'self-reliance'. The organisation, which employed a workforce of 80,000 people in conditions of relative comfort and peaceful industrial relations, prided itself on its welfarism. The price for this happy existence was that by 1981, Tata Steel had become outdated in marketing, technology, and management style.

Such, in broad outline, was the diverse experience of the older groups. New opportunities and the offer of licences in priority areas encouraged new entry. With or without protection, some of these new entrants were highly entrepreneurial, took unusual risks and made good, whereas others were more opportunistic than entrepreneurial.

The New Industrialists

Calcutta's Marwaris

One set among the new or rising groups rose almost entirely thanks to opportunistic takeover of British assets. In Calcutta's industrial scene, the new regime allowed a dramatic transformation of Marwaris from traders to industrialists. Marwaris as a group showed no inclination or tendency to become industrial until 1947. Birla's jute textile mill in Calcutta was an exception. In Ahmedabad, several cotton textile mills were Marwari-owned. A Kanpur mill owned by Baijnath Juggilal, a textile mill part-owned by Anandilal Poddar in Bombay, two cotton mills acquired in Bombay by Ramnivas Ruia and Chaturbhuj Piramal, the acquisition of the Jewish group Elias Sassoon's textile interest by a Marwari trader, and a few sugar mills in North India would exhaust the list. These firms were exceptional in the industrial landscape of India, and even more exceptional in the context of the Marwari world, dominated by banking, share-broking, and trade.

In 1965, by contrast, four of the ten largest business groups of India were Marwari-owned and based in Calcutta. The Marwaris by then owned most industrial companies in Calcutta. The move of the Calcutta Marwari capitalist towards modern industry, thus, reached a completely new and unforeseen level only after 1947, thanks in part to their access to liquid wealth that could be used to raid and buy British companies, and in part to lax regulation protecting shareholders of the companies.

For example, the Bajoria-Jalan group emerged as the jute magnates of Calcutta, practically overnight. Surajmull Jalan and Nagarmull Bajoria were related by marriage. Both were traders of Calcutta in the 1930s, and owned extensive real estate. In the 1940s, the combined group appears to have moved into jute manufacturing on a small scale. Family-owned managing agency Howrah Trading managed Naskarpara Jute Mill near Calcutta. Around 1952–53, Surajmull Nagarmull front companies bought up jute companies under the control of McLeod and Co. McLeod at the time managed and owned ten jute mills, sixteen tea companies, as well as light railways. Other affiliated companies included Marshall, an engineering firm making tea machinery, and a smaller managing agency J. F. Low. The circumstances of the takeover are not available. It appears that in 1952, C. L. Kanoria (related by marriage to Bajoria) and one J. R. Walker ran McLeod, when both were investigated for tax fraud. During the investigation, Surajmull Nagarmull took control of the firm, through an arrangement with Kanoria. An investigative book published in 1972 alleged, citing purported balance sheets of 1965 (the author held shares in some of the group companies), that four group companies used their cash advances made up of bank loans and McLeod worker provident fund provisions to buy up shares in Davenport, a smaller managing agency interested in tea, the Kanpur-based European firm British India Corporation, two jute companies, Britannia Engineering Company, and a group firm, Hanuman Sugar mill.[31] In turn, Davenport purchased debentures floated by Kanoria Industries, owned by C. L. Bajoria's sister's family, and an affiliated company invested a large sum of money in a cotton mill that went into liquidation.

In 1944, the Dalmia-Jain Group acquired a British sugar company in north Bihar (Pursa) that was practically abandoned during World War II. This was the beginning of a spate of takeovers that included the New Central Jute Mills, Albion Jute, and Lothian Jute, all Andrew Yule concerns. The managing agency Begg Dunlop was taken over in July 1947 through stock market raids, and in 1948–49 was wound up, possibly merged with the related agency, Begg Sutherland. In 1947, Dalmia acquired controlling stake in Bennett, Coleman Ltd, the company that owned the *Times of India*, India's leading English language newspaper, using cash reserves of an insurance business. Kettlewell Bullen was taken over by Magneeram Bangur and Co. in 1952. Kettlewell Bullen had managing agency contracts in Fort Gloster Jute Manufacturing,

---

[31] N. C. Roy, *Mystery of the Bajoria-Jalan House*, Calcutta: Alpha Publishing, 1972. The book takes inspiration from another similarly titled book which deals with allegations of business-politicians alliance, but has nothing to do with acquisitions. Debajyoti Barman, *Mystery of Birla House*, Calcutta: Jugabani Sahitya Chakra, 1950.

Bowreach Cotton Mills, Fort William Jute, Dunbar Mills, Mothola Co., and Joonktollee Co., the last two being tea companies. The attempt to take control over Fort Gloster Jute led to a rivalry between Bangur and another contender, Lakshmipat Singhania.

The facts of some of the other shock acquisitions in the 1950s are merely suggestive. These involved smaller managing agencies whose business were built around one or two factories. One of these cases occurred in 1950–51, when one Kedia family of Calcutta acquired control of Anderson Wright, which had a medium-sized jute mill under its ownership and management. Not a lot is known about Khardah Jute between then and 1983, when it was nationalised in a bankrupt state. The firm George Henderson managed Bally and Baranagar Jute Mills. Giridharilal Mehta sold the controlling stake of Bally Jute in the same year to Jardine Skinner, which merged with George Henderson to form a new company. It appears that Mehta was already in control of Jardine Skinner. Later history of the factory remains unclear.

Another Calcutta adventurer Haridas Mundhra was an unknown entity when he started acquisitions.[32] The manner of these acquisitions remains shadowy, except that most of these were done between 1947 and 1956. In 1956, the major group companies included a pharmaceutical company Smith Stanistreet, the structural engineering firm, Richardson and Cruddas, and the shipping firm Turner Morrison. The firms went bankrupt in a short time. Richardson and Cruddas was nationalised. The British India Corporation of Kanpur, where Mundhra and Dalmia Jain shared control, collapsed in the late-1950s. Turner Morrison was the managing agent of Alcock Ashdown of Bombay, manufacturing and repairing heavy structural, transmission line towers, marine diesel engines, ships, and boats. Eight years after the take-over, Alcock Ashdown stopped production completely under suspicion of mismanagement and fraud. The subsequent history of Turner Morrison is marked by a sordid fight between two Indian claimants for control, Mundhra and one Nirmal Hoon, to the detriment of the company. One of the last targets of Mundhra was Jessop and Co, a structural engineering firm of Calcutta (Chapter 4). Mundhra apparently used the funds of Jessop to buy shares of British India Corporation, where he had previously bought his way into directorship. Mundhra then had Jessop sell these shares to one Sohanlal and Company, which was allegedly a front company working for him.[33] In May 1958, the Government of India took over the management of Jessop and Co. Ltd. In 1963, the Government purchased shares of Jessop & Co.

---

[32] A good discussion of the Mundhra episode can be found in G. Balachandran, *The Reserve Bank of India, 1951–1967*, Mumbai: Reserve Bank of India and New Delhi: Oxford University Press, 1998.

[33] Rameshwar Daga vs The State of West Bengal, 5 May 1964.

Ltd. to obtain a controlling interest, the controlling stake was then vested with two share broker agencies.

In the history of Calcutta's jute industry in the last twenty years, surviving companies made profits only occasionally. The Bajoria group until recently owned a substantial part of the jute interests. But among the rest, there were a great deal of churning, sale, and resale, which placed medium-sized family firms in control of the industry. The names that crop up in this connection include, Sarda (Hooghly Jute, acquired from Bajoria), Kedia (Khardah Jute, originally Anderson Wright), Lohia (Bally Jute, originally Jardine Henderson), S. K. Agarwal (Kamarhatty Jute, originally Jardine Henderson), B. C. Jain (Kanknarra Jute, originally Jardine Henderson), Hemraj Poddar (acquired Gourepur Co. and Ganges Jute in the 1970s), Podar and Oswal (Thomas Duff), Giridharilal Mehta (Thomas Duff, Jardine Skinner or George Henderson or Jardine Henderson), Jajodia (Assam Co.), and Wadhwa (Champdanny Jute, originally James Finlay). Several other names will appear in the discussion of the major European firms below.

From the turmoil, a few strong Marwari conglomerates emerged. B. M. Khaitan, which took over the world's largest tea company Williamson Magor (McLeod Russell), was one of them (see next). Most tea companies were listed in London and escaped stock market predators of India. In some of these cases, the transfer of control occurred in a negotiated way in the form of piecemeal sale of gardens. Important examples of negotiated transfer were Williamson Magor and its affiliates to Khaitan, Kannan Devan plantations in South India sold by James Finlay to the Tata group, Duncan to the Goenka group, and Harrisons and Crosfield to the R. P. Goenka group (see above). Several smaller companies in South India were acquired by individuals of limited means and no previous experience in tea growing.

In the 1950s, when the Goenka group was united under a patriarch, it acquired the tea firm Duncan from the British owners. After the group split between three brothers, the more successful branch, R. P. Goenka or RPG, had control over two large post-independence acquisitions, CESC or Calcutta Electricity Supply Corporation, a utility company, and CEAT, a tyre maker. Other smaller companies acquired included Spencers, Harrisons Malayalam, Asian Cables, Murphy India, Remington Rand, and ICIM, a small firm manufacturing mainframes. The head of the group, Rama Prasad Goenka (1930–2013), was credited for having left the management of these companies to professionals rather than filling top positions with family members and fellow Marwaris, which was otherwise a common practice in Calcutta. A second and less successful Goenka set, Gauri Prasad Goenka or GPG, was led by Star Paper Mills, Duncans Agro, and Duncans Tea. Other group companies included chemicals, cement, engineering, and several finance companies. Most were acquired rather than established by the group.

Among other notable Marwari enterprises that survived and grew bigger, mention should be made of L. N. Jhunjhunwala. A jute trader of Calcutta, Jhunjhunwala started trading in iron goods, and the manufacture of small parts for the railways, in the 1950s. A textile unit, Rajasthan Spinning, started in the 1950s, and expanded into synthetic fabrics in 1970. In 1973, the group set up a joint venture with a German firm to produce graphite. In the 1990s, it diversified into sponge iron.

Outside the takeover set, many examples of unusual enterprise and risk-taking can be found, especially in engineering, chemicals, and metals, priority areas for the state, as the next section will show.

Engineering, Chemicals, Metals

South India maintained a distinct profile from the other regions, with a lead in engineering and in middle-class entrepreneurship. Seshasayee has been mentioned already. There were a few other examples.

In 1928, the politician T. T. Krishnamachari (1899–1974) founded the TTK group. In the 1950s, TTK manufactured one of the two branded pressure cookers, Prestige. The other market leader brand, Hawkins, was started in 1959 by H. D. Vasudeva with technical collaboration from a British firm. TTK stayed a relatively small and closely held family firm until recently. However, it diversified in a few consumer products, including condoms and lingerie, which secured the company both brand image and steady market, at least until the 1990s when competition in these products increased.

The Murugappa Chettiar family set up TI Cycles in 1949 in collaboration with Hercules Cycles of Britain. The company manufactured assembled bicycles in its plant, marketed imported cycles, and later started domestic production of cycle parts as well. As the trade regime tightened from the 1950s, TI Cycles had a field day in the protected domestic market, and did good business making generic or 'standard' models. However, consumers showed steadily less interest in the standard segment, and the company diversified into 'specials', that is, cycles for niche markets from the 1970s. The diversification made it somewhat better prepared for the liberalised trade regime of the 1990s.

A lot of British business changed hands in South India too. Finlay was mentioned. Another notable example was the Madras coachmakers and later auto component firm Simpson, which was acquired in 1941 through a deal that Sivasailam Anantharamakrishnan (1905–64), a director at the time of the transfer, struck with the British owners. The details of the deal are unknown. The new owner's association with the company dated back to 1930. In 1961, the coffee planting company Stanes sold its interest to Anantharamakrishnan.

The holding company that he owned was called Amalgamations, which became the name of the group. After the acquisition, Simpson made diesel engines for automobiles. In 1960, it started a tractor manufacturing firm Tractor and Farm Equipment Co. or TAFE. In Anantharamakrishnan's lifetime, another British car agency, Addison was taken over, and changed its business into a machine tool manufacturing firm.

Import substitution in pharmaceuticals encouraged a spate of new entry. To conserve foreign exchange, the government of India discouraged the import of formulations. That policy, together with a patent law (1970) that recognised process but not product innovation, made it possible for some Indian drug firms to first establish as a bulk drug importer, then obtain the recipe from connections abroad for best-selling products in western markets, and reengineer it for the Indian market with the help of the government-owned Indian Institute of Chemical Technology (Hyderabad). More simply, they read the patent descriptions and copied them. Bhai Mohan Singh's company Ranbaxy was one of the Indian drug companies to benefit spectacularly from this arrangement. In Ranbaxy's case, it led to the development of Calmpose, a best-selling sedative based on Roche's Diazepalm. Another beneficiary of this collaboration was Wockhardt. In 1959, a Bombay merchant Fakhruddin Khorakiwala acquired a chemical factory in the city, and with this base, expanded into bulk drugs, infant food, and a range of parenterals. This was Wockhardt, which now also owns a hospital chain.

After engineering and chemicals, automobiles and automobile accessories were high in priority. If in automobiles, the favoured companies were mainly domestic ones (see above), in tyres, foreign multinationals ruled, but Indian-origin investment was allowed to develop. In the 1950s and 1960s, transport operations by the government, aviation, and defence services were growing. The commercial transportation served by the two large truck makers, TELCO and Ashok Leyland, was also doing well. In short, the 1950s and the 1960s promised a booming market for tyre makers. These then consisted of the four MNCs, Dunlop, Goodyear, CEAT, and Firestone. Two new entrants after independence were Madras Rubber Factory (renamed MRF in 1980) and J. K. Tyres. J. K. Tyres was a J. K. Singhania group company, and was backed up by the group's own financial resources and technical collaboration with an American tyre company. Madras Rubber had a more unusual beginning.

In 1946, Mammen Mappillai set up a balloon-making shed in Madras, which four years later, installed machines to make tread rubber, and moved on to produce tyres. In 1961, Madras Rubber Factory became a public company, and had technical collaboration and shareholding by the US firm Mansfield Tire and Rubber Co. With a large domestic supply of natural rubber, the venture could consider India as the base for export of Mansfield brand to non-American markets. In the mid-1970s, Modi Continental Tyres entered the market with a superior product. But the tyre market was slowing down then. Mansfield wound down its operations in 1980–81. For MRF, defence orders were important for survival, whereas truck and tractor tyre markets were becoming more competitive. MRF, therefore, entered the 1980s as a medium-sized firm with a low profile.

Mappillai was a case of entrepreneurship. There were a few others in engineering. In 1961, Nilkanthrao Kalyani started a forging shop near Pune, Bharat Forge, to produce automotive parts and other goods. Kalyani Steel started in 1973 near Pune with second-hand machines mainly as a supplier of intermediates to Bharat Forge. Forging was not a new business, but the quality and range of the work established Bharat Forge as a market leader. After India's automobile industry opened to foreign investment, several leading producers of cars and two-wheelers located near Pune to take advantage of the ancillary industry that had grown there.

The Delhi-based Eicher was also unusual in some respects. A trading agency for German Eicher tractors, Eicher Goodearth started manufacturing tractors in 1959. The company made strides during the Green Revolution, and was confident enough to take over the management of the ailing German counterpart (then owned by Massey-Ferguson) in 1984. This expensive plan surprised contemporaries and was not carried through. The company, however, made a successful move to manufacture light commercial vehicles with collaboration from Mitsubishi.

In consumer durables, a notable entry was the Punjab firm Hero Cycles. Four brothers, Brijmohan Lal, Dayanand, Satyanand, and Om Prakash Munjal, shifted base from Pakistan first to Amritsar and then to Ludhiana after Partition. They traded in bicycle parts. During the wartime regulations, a small-scale industry making metal products had grown in Ludhiana town. In 1951, Brijmohan Lal took a licence to manufacture bicycles under the brand name Hero. The company became a great success, thanks to good marketing and service, technical collaboration with German partners, and a high productivity level that Munjal attributed to the work ethic of the component makers in Ludhiana. Of course, a protected market helped too.

Shipping was another field where new investment needed to be made, and the government made significant concessions to induce that. A textile merchant (Maneklal Mulji) and a banker (Ardeshir Bhiwandiwalla) joined forces to buy a vessel in 1948 and embark on coastal shipping, with a few trans-oceanic services added later. The protected market and competent management helped the company grow into one of the biggest lines on the Indian coast, the Great Eastern Shipping, despite attempts by the company's rivals to end its career. Its emergence in the 1980s as possibly the largest private shipping companies in India was owed, according to company insiders, to careful management of finance, which meant avoidance of high-cost debt.

The multinationals selling in the Indian market gained from tariff protection, expanded operations, moved from trade to industry, and attracted new entry. If they were engaged in the priority areas like engineering and chemicals, the government wanted them to stay. Overall, they were not the main investors in post-independence India, as we have seen, but not under pressure either.

Foreign Capital (1950–1973): The Gainers

Let us start with the engineering firms first. The German engineering firm Siemens had a trading agency in India from 1903. It survived setbacks during the world wars, and soon after independence, started manufacturing switch-gears and switchboards in Bombay. The India unit had steady technological tie-up with the German parent, and was welcomed by the government because it operated in a priority area. In the 1960s and the 1970s, many power plants in India were set up, and these were equipped by Siemens. The electric power generation and transmission equipment company, English Electric, started operations in India before independence. Its new form, General Electric or GEC, was another electrical engineering company that benefited from technological support of the parent. A nineteenth-century engineer called Andrew Best had established Best and Co. in Madras, which eventually became the managing agent and a shareholder of Crompton Engineering, the branch of the London firm Crompton and Co., manufacturers of electricity generating and lighting systems. In 1975, the two firms merged to form Best and Crompton. About then, Best produced lifts, pumps, and motors, and Crompton did considerable contractual work in Asia in electrification.

The Swedish group Wallenbergs had extensive interests in India, including Asea, Alfa Laval, and Wimco. Alfa Laval specialised in agricultural engineering and machines for the food processing industry. It had set up a trading unit in India in 1937, and moved into manufacturing with a factory near Pune, in 1961. The company specialised in heat exchangers for the dairy industry. Relying on the Swedish parent for technical expertise, the company became successful in the field of project implementation in the food industry. A subsidiary of the Dutch multinational, Philips had started as trader in India in 1930. In 1956, when Philips (India) Ltd. was registered, the company was a leading firm in manufacturing electrical goods, especially lighting systems. Later it diversified in consumer electronics like transistor radio, now using a brand name that was globally valued. The firm maintained its leadership, because the Philips brand in India gained in reputation from the technological advances made by the parent firm.

Two Calcutta companies, GKW and Metal Box, were the largest among the set of Midlands firms that had entered India in the interwar period to sell metals and tools in the Indian market, and turned industrial around independence. The Indian subsidiary of Metal Box plc was started in 1933 in the company's traditional business, containers of various types (Chapter 6). In the 1960s, Metal Box of Calcutta was one of the largest box-makers, and users of tinplate, in the world. Guest, Keen, and William or GKW in Calcutta was established in the 1920s, with a British parent, and enjoyed substantial autonomy of operation. It manufactured nuts and bolts, fasteners, and railway material. Both firms stayed profitable in the 1950s and the 1960s, and started facing problems thereafter. Both tried to change the product set then, apparently without much help from the parents, either because the parents did not believe in a culture to interfere, or they had given up on India when government policy turned hostile to foreign capital in 1973 (see next). In 1974, Metal Box started a joint venture with a French firm to manufacture bearings, which turned out to be a failure. From the late 1970s, the firm ran into trouble with labour. Eventually, these problems proved to be costly for the company, and the bearing unit was sold to the Tatas in 1983–84. Another diversification with a German firm for offset printing was started in the mid-1970s, but apparently did not contribute much to the company's finances. These two stories of decline are described more fully in the next chapter.

An offbeat case of a technically foreign firm that did not really have a foreign parent was Larsen and Toubro. The company was founded by two Danish engineers, Henning Holck-Larsen and Søren Toubro, during World War II. For several years after independence, L and T made machines for steel, cement, and paper plants, but gradually began to diversify into electrical equipment, especially switchgears, and construction contracts. Meanwhile, a major shift occurred in top management. The shareholding of Holck-Larsen and Toubro was always moderate, and until 1969, the company was managed by the agent Mangaldas Desai and Sons. In 1970, managing agency was abolished, and the management vested in the board, in which Desai was a member. The relationship of the founders and the agent/director was not particularly cordial, but the difference did not seem to affect the growth of the firm.[34]

Electrification of the cities and the growth of telephone system increased the demand for cables. New factories established during this time also added to the demand for cables. The first domestic manufacturer of cables was the Indian Cable Company (c. 1920), a British firm managed by Gillanders Arbuthnot of Calcutta. Gillanders then owned India's largest copper mine. In 1955–56, Indian Cable took over the assets of British Insulated Callender's Cables Co or BICC, which had an

---

[34] Labdhi Bhandari, G. R. Kulkarni, and P. S. Thomas, 'Larsen and Toubro Group: A Case Study in Corporate Growth', IIM Ahmedabad Case Studies No IIMA/BP0172, 1982.

extensive trading network in India then.[35] Indian Cable's factory was in Jamshedpur. Indian Cable had a somewhat turbulent history until independence, but between 1953 and 1965 it undertook major expansion programmes. The company's fortunes changed in the 1960s. India's copper production was not nearly enough, and new capacity grew only in the government sector, first the National Mineral Development Corporation (1958), and later Hindustan Copper Ltd. (1967). Copper trade, therefore, was closely regulated, practically monopolised, by the state. In the 1960s, there was an 'end of the liberalised import licensing policy for all practical purposes. This was largely due to the fact, that the country has little foreign credits available'.[36] When the foreign exchange situation improved in the 1980s, import of finished cable was liberalised, and the company was in trouble again. In the 1980s, the British owners divested their stake, and the company was then acquired by a Calcutta businessman, Kashinath Tapuriah. Under Tapuriah's management the company went bankrupt.[37]

Let us now consider some of the chemical firms. Along with the German trading firm Volkart, the Greek house Ralli was a major commodity exporter in India before the Great Depression. It closed the India operations in 1929, to re-enter the country after independence as a manufacturer and trader of agro-chemicals, fertilisers, tractors, jute, and electrical equipment. For some time it had an interest in trading Indian handicraft products on the side. Rallis, for example, had shareholding in a company called Oriental Carpets. The company had a turbulent decade in the 1950s. In 1962 a shared management and ownership made things more stable. Tata was now a partner in the enterprise. Thereafter, it consolidated its business in fertilisers and pesticides, and diversified into pharmaceuticals. The German chemical company Badische Anilin & Soda-Fabrik AG or BASF's association with India had begun around the turn of the twentieth century through export of some of its products, including dyes and tanning agents, which were in demand in India. Shortly after independence, BASF established a manufacturing base in India, by taking over an existing trading agency.

One of the four constituent companies of the speciality chemicals manufacturer Imperial Chemical Industries or ICI, Brunner Mond, opened a trading office in India in 1911, and converted into a manufacturing firm in the 1950s with its main plant located near Calcutta. Thereafter, India became an important field of expansion for ICI. It set up four companies related to its core interest, industrial chemicals. These were Indian Explosives, Alkali and Chemicals Corporation,

---

[35] The Management of Indian Cable Co., Ltd., Calcutta v. Respondent: Its Workmen, Supreme Court of India, 1962.

[36] 'The Indian Cable Company Limited', *Economic and Political Weekly*, 4(35), 1969, 1429–30.

[37] In 1999, in an unusual move, the shareholders of the company removed Tapuriah from management. Tapuriah's name was later embroiled in a high-profile money laundering investigation in the early 2010s. The company closed in 1999, and was re-floated under different ownership recently.

Chemicals and Fibres of India, and Crescent Dyes and Chemicals. There were also foreign firms in paints and solvents. In 1947, British Paints acquired Hadfields (India), a company in Calcutta established in 1923, which sold ready-mixed paints and varnish. The factory became a fully fledged manufacturing unit and a subsidiary of the multinational from then on. Around 1969, British Paints, then owned by the Celanese Corporation, USA, sold the Indian subsidiary to Berger, Jenson Nicholson Limited, UK. The company acquired the name Berger Paints a few years later. The British paints firm Goodlass Wall started manufacturing in India from a trading base acquired in 1920. In the 1970s, a Tata group company gained control of the firm.

The spate of multinational entry in pharmaceutical industry was quite complex. For most multinationals, there were gains to be made by jumping the tariff wall and producing goods in India for Indian markets. That advantage was especially strong in medicines, as buyers of medicines valued global brands and the technology and research that lay behind these. The government discouraged the import of formulations. The global drug companies could still import the bulk drugs and make branded medicines in India. The US firm Pfizer entered India in 1950. Foster, a trading firm, renamed itself Glaxo Laboratories in 1950. The Swiss firm Ciba restructured its Indian trading arm in 1948 (after merger with Sandoz, the company became known as Novartis in 1995). Abbott, the owner of the Boots brand, started trading in the 1940s, and manufacture shortly after independence. The German drug firm Hoechst Fedco Pharma Pvt. Ltd. (renamed Aventis, and again renamed Sanofi in 2012) started manufacture in India in 1956. Merck started operations in India in 1967. Horlicks, the maker of a popular health drink, set up manufacturing in India in 1960.

Interestingly, the largest MNC in India did not manufacture anything that fitted state priority in 1950. Lever Brothers (India) was established in 1933 to produce soaps and detergents. Hindustan Vanaspati Manufacturing Company had been established some years earlier to manufacture hydrogenated vegetable oil. Both were subsidiaries of the Anglo-Dutch parent Unilever. A separate trading company marketed toilet preparations. In 1956, these companies were merged to form Hindustan Lever Limited or HLL. Between 1956 and 1973, HLL expanded in dairy products and animal feed, and continued to produce vanaspati, but its core businesses remained soaps and detergents. HLL owned three top brands in these fields, namely, Lifebuoy soap, Surf detergent, and Dalda vanaspati. Not a producer of goods favoured by the new regime, HLL still survived and prospered, thanks to good marketing and advertisements. In the 1970s, HLL acquired Brooke Bond, a tea trading firm that owned plantations in Assam, and an Indian cosmetic brand Pond's. With the group company Lipton, and marketing help from Unilever UK, Hindustan Lever emerged as a major packaged tea exporter in the 1980s. The group later diversified into chemicals (processed raw material for detergents), edible oil, and readymade garments.

Among other consumer industries, mention must be made of Bata, a Czech firm that migrated to Switzerland and produced shoes. Bata came to India in 1931, like many other companies, as a trading agency, and turned into a producer in 1936. In an industry dominated by small firms of little brand value, Bata established a solid monopoly in the quality-conscious, advertisement-sensitive, in other words, the middle class segment of the market. It developed direct retail of shoes to a degree no other consumer good company did in these years. Its success showed why big firms needed to exist at all in consumer goods. Building consumer focus, advertising, and marketing needed big money that small producers could not afford.

The Swiss milk products multinational Nestlé set up an Indian subsidiary in 1959. India's big domestic production of coffee and milk, and its demography with a growing proportion of children in the population, would mean a strong consumer interest in baby food and milk products. Nestlé, therefore, could sell its international brands successfully. Cadbury India began in 1948 as a firm repacking imported chocolates, and within a few years, started manufacturing chocolates in India. In the heavily protected food processing industry, there was no significant competition in the chocolate market for Cadbury until the 1980s.

An interesting example of an Indo-European firm that acquired a foreign parent was Britannia Biscuits, discussed in the last chapter. For the parent company Peek, Frean, the Calcutta acquisition of Britannia Biscuits was their first step abroad. The 1960s was a period of growth for the company, as it started production in Madras and Delhi, and shifted head office to Bombay. Like Cadbury or Nestlé, Britannia gained from the parent's knowledge of technology and marketing. Finally, again in the consumer goods segment, ITC, the Indian branch of the British American Tobacco (BAT), deserves a mention. The origin of the company was in trading agency in India, and conversion to manufacture came later. BAT had a controlling stake in Imperial Tobacco Company (which became ITC) and the Vazir Sultan Tobacco Company.

Before independence, mineral oil was mainly imported. Burma Shell and a company called the Western India Oil Distributing Co. were the big companies in the trade. The Assam Oil Co., a subsidiary of Burmah Oil Co., produced oil that met 7 per cent of Indian consumption in 1940, but there had been no refinery in India then. In 1948, the Industrial Policy Resolution declared that the state would lead future mineral oil exploration and refining. The 1956 industrial policy resolution reserved this field exclusively for the state. In between, oil exploration and refining were in the hands of foreign firms. After 1956, the companies were either nationalised or a joint venture with the state was forced on them. In 1959, the Oil and Natural Gas Commission put the public sector in charge of future explorations. The Oil India Ltd formed of a joint venture between Burmah Oil and the government.

In refinery, foreign firms were allowed to exist, but the public sector expanded capacity from the early 1960s (Gauhati in 1962, Barauni in 1964,

Cochin in 1966, Koyali in 1965, Madras in 1960; Haldia followed in the next decade). The foreign firms lived under threat of nationalisation, and pressured the US government to negotiate with India a friendlier oil policy. The negotiations did not change anything, and in the mid-1970s, the remaining foreign capital in the business, mainly ESSO and Caltex, were arm-twisted into a sale of stake to the government.

Few MNCs produced services, but some did. Calcutta was the capital of the creative advertising industry in the 1960s and the 1970s. Leading firms, such as Hindustan Thompson Associates, McCann, and Ogilvy and Mather, were MNCs and operated from this city. These companies, and the local firm Clarion, developed a kind of folk expertise in writing effective captions for consumer brands. The industry itself was small then, and had limited expertise beyond writing captions, but it did well until the television age made that artisanal expertise obsolete.

Whereas the MNCs operating in machines, metals, and chemicals had a smooth ride, the Indo-British managing agencies had a rougher one.

Foreign Capital (1950–1973): The Losers

The acrimonious process through which India gained independence had left some British corporate groups nervous about prospects in the new country.[38] They were willing to sell their stake or part of it. The companies managed by the agency firms were mainly owned by the public, which made them easy targets of takeover by Indian raiders. Government rules forcing them to register in India increased the risk. Not all companies were transferred to Indian ownership, but several were. Where ownership did not pass on, management sometimes did, and in a detrimental way. Government directive on compulsory divestment up to 26 per cent of the shareholding induced some firms to recruit Indian partners in a hurry, with the result that the transfer of managerial decision-making went to individuals who were not ready for that role, and not competent to perform it.

There were three stages in the transfer of control of these companies. The first stage occurred between 1947 and 1965 (see Marwaris in Calcutta above). Stock market raids and panic sales were behind the transfer of individual companies, and even whole conglomerates like McLeod and Octavius Steel (to Surajmull Nagarmull), Kettelewell Bullen (to Mugneeram Bangur), British India Corporation (to Haridas Mundhra), Begg Dunlop/Begg Sutherland (to Dalmia-Jain), and Jardine Skinner/George Henderson/Jardine Henderson (to Giridharilal Mehta). The jute

---

[38] This section draws on Tirthankar Roy, 'Transfer of Economic Power in Corporate Calcutta 1950–1970', *Business History Review*, 91(1), 2017, 3–29.

and engineering conglomerates Bird-Heilgers, Thomas Duff, and Andrew Yule lost key companies to raiders. With a few exceptions, these first-generation transfers turned the companies bankrupt. Allegations of asset stripping were rife, and in some cases proven. Managerial style changed, and professionalism was compromised, as the new owners installed relations and family members in key managerial positions. In some of these cases, the former owners and managers gave over control voluntarily, if in a rushed and unplanned manner. In other cases, the takeovers were hostile ones. The brunt of this downfall was borne by industries located in and near Calcutta city.

The second stage of the transfer can be dated in 1965–75, when a few surviving conglomerates failed and were nationalised. Three of the largest British conglomerates, James Finlay, Andrew Yule, and Bird Heilgers, had a downfall in the 1970s. They were divided up, lost assets, sold in bits, and nationalised in a bankrupt state. In 1970–71 Swan Mills Ltd., Finlay Mills Ltd., and Gold Mohur Mills Ltd., which belonged to Finlay, were under sale to Mathuradas Mulji and family. In 1983, the government-run National Textile Corporation took over the management of these companies. In 1983, Tata Tea Co. purchased the south Indian tea estates from James Finlay. These were resold in 2005 to an employee-run company. In 2004, the company's assets in Chittagong formed the core of a company called James Finlay (Bangladesh). This was not part of the James Finlay group. Finlay's Champdany Jute was owned by one Wadhwa group, and nationalised in 1974. A cluster of jute mills belonging to Andrew Yule (Cheviot, Budge Budge) was transferred in 1967 to the Kanoria group. New Central Jute Mill was an early target of takeover by Sahu Jain. Andrew Yule also managed Hastings Jute Mill, established in 1876 by Adam Birkmeyer. Hastings Jute was acquired by Bangur Brothers in 1946, became bankrupt, and was sold to the Kajaria group (Murlidhar Ratanlal Exports) in Calcutta. Bird Heilgers had extensive coal interests that were nationalised in 1971–72. In 1970, the group firm Auckland Jute was acquired by Harakh Chand Kankaria. In 1980, the remaining mineral companies and Kinnison Jute Mill were nationalised. Northbrook Jute Company, of Heilgers, owned by Ganeriwal until 2005, was sold to Choraria. Heilger's Dalhousie Jute is now with a group called Modi, and Naihati Jute with J. K. Bhagat. At the time of its downfall, Bird Heilgers was run by individuals who had moved up the management ladder quickly thanks to 'Indianisation', who had little experience to lead a turnaround, and probably had no serious interest either.

A third stage, and a more negotiated one, occurred in the tea plantation companies from the 1970s (see above). With Khaitan and Goenka's acquisition of tea interests, a large part of the tea industry transferred into Indian hands. But exceptions remained. A few small British companies continued, because they were permitted to (see the discussion on Foreign Exchange Regulation Act (FERA), next). Goodricke was one these. Charles Goodricke and Alex Lawrie, co-founder of Balmer Lawrie, an engineering company in Calcutta with

Table 7.5 *Assets of Indo-British companies as share of top 25 business groups (in per cent), 1939–97*

Year	1939	1969	1997
Indo-British group companies	47	14 (27)	0 (2)
Indo-British group companies of Calcutta	37	14 (27)	0 (2)
Firms of Calcutta in top 25 firms of India	39 (including Birla)	30–33 (depending on allocation of Birla assets)	9
Names of groups	Martin Burn, Bird, Andrew Yule, Inchcape, Sassoon, Begg, Jardine, Wallace, Duncan, Finlay, Killick, Kilburn, Brady, Steel, McLeod	*Martin Burn, Bird Heilgers*, Macneill Barry, Andrew Yule (Surajmal-Nagarmal/ McLeod, *Bangur/ Kettlewell Bullen*, Mehta/ Jardine Henderson, Goenka/Duncan and Octavius Steel, Killick/ Ruia)	(Williamson Magor/ Khaitan)

Notes: In brackets, including Indian owned groups whose asset mainly consisted of the assets of formerly Indo-British firms. Italicised indicates enlisted as 'monopoly' in 1965–6 Monopolies Enquiry Committee. In 1964, the list of ten 'monopoly houses' according to the Monopolies Inquiry Commission 1965–66 included Tata, Birla, Martin Burn, Thapar, Bangur, Sahu Jain, Shriram, Bird Heilgers, J. K. Singhania, and Sarabhai. The Birla group, which possibly gained the most from the industrial licensing system introduced in post-1947 India, was still together in 1969, though expanding mainly outside Calcutta between 1939 and 1969, and had trifurcated in 1997. 1969 figure treats the group as Calcutta-based. In 1997, the Calcutta branch was small in relation to the rest of the group and general corporate ranking. Raw data taken from Tarun Khanna and Krishna G. Palepu, 'The Evolution of Concentrated Ownership in India: Broad Patterns and a History of the Indian Software Industry', in Randall K. Morck, ed., *A History of Corporate Governance around the World: Family Business Groups to Professional Managers*, Chicago: University of Chicago Press, 2005, 283–324.

marginal interest in tea, created the company. It later acquired the trading interests of Duncan. The tea trading arm exists as the MNC, Camelia Plc.

Since the transfer process involved a large-scale attrition of capital, it was damaging not only to the companies and their shareholders, but to the economy of an entire region. The transfer process changed the complexion of the premier business city of India in 1950. Once a hub of global business in Asia, Calcutta de-globalised and de-industrialised after 1947, and failed to play any worthwhile role in the re-emergent Asian trade, as it had done a century before (see Table 7.5). Between 1950 and 1970, Singapore and Hong Kong attracted a great deal of the mobile international capital in trade and services working in the region. At the same time, some of the Indo-British firms left Calcutta to invest money elsewhere. The expansion of the tea industry in East Africa, for example, was helped by firms contracting their Calcutta operations.

Protectionist industrialisation, in short, produced positive and negative outcomes. The losses suffered by textiles, trade, or a section of foreign firms were damaging no doubt, but not the reason why the strategy became politically unsustainable. That reason was the propensity of the new economic regime to fall into balance of payment crises, as we see in the next section.

The Unravelling of the Regime

From the late 1960s, an industrial stagnation set in. Accumulation of regulations depressed industrial investment. Restraints on cotton mills had given rise to bankruptcy among these old companies. When industrial recession deepened in the traditional areas, especially textiles, the government stepped in to protect jobs by nationalising some of these companies. Cotton mills formed the largest cluster among nationalised industrial firms. The National Textile Corporation (NTC) started with the mission to manage 16 bankrupt mills in 1968. Four years later, it was managing 103. In 1974 by a Parliamentary act these units were nationalised. After this, there began a relentless drain of taxpayers' money to protect the jobs of nearly 100,000 employees in factories that had fallen behind in technology, marketing, even the motivation to get well. Several bankrupt engineering and jute companies also came into government hands through nationalisation around this time.[39]

A section of the leftist intelligentsia blamed 'monopoly capital' and foreign intervention, including multinational companies, for the unfolding industrial stagnation. The movement was especially strong in Calcutta, where a large cluster of foreign firms was still based (Fig. 7.5). The leftist message had popular appeal. Indira Gandhi, who headed a new government in Delhi in 1967 and was wary of the growing influence of business lobbies, went after big business with hardly any public criticism of the policy. A tighter licensing policy was introduced in 1970. Firms and business houses in possession of assets amounting to more than a stipulated level had to register themselves with the newly created Monopolies and Restrictive Trade Practices Commission (MRTP Commission), and seek approval for expansion or diversification. Non-registration invited penalty. The concerned department spent a lot of time enforcing registration.

---

[39] Jessops and Bridge and Roof, two ailing British construction companies, were examples of engineering firms.

Fig. 7.5 Communist Party demonstration in 1966
Women, including factory workers affiliated to the communist parties, demonstrating
against US intervention in Vietnam, 25 July 1966, Calcutta.
© Keystone Pictures USA/Alamy Stock Photo

The anti-monopoly measures did not reduce concentration. The share of the top twenty business houses in total assets increased in the 1970s. The finding shows that the power to discipline big business was used with discretion. Permission could be traded for financial or political consideration. Businesses learnt to play by the rules of the game, and continued to expand with some window-dressing. As a former head of the monopolies commission explained in 1982, when the commission's powers had already been curbed, 'the political and bureaucratic authorities wield very large powers ... These discretionary powers are the cause of the largest business in Delhi and in the state capitals, viz, lobbying by various industrial, trading and other economic interests'. The monopolistic character of the industrial system was artificially created by investment licensing itself.

But regulation and restraint on capital was not the real reason the system became unsustainable. The real reason was the rising risk of macroeconomic collapse. The Indian version of import-substituting industrialisation was a gamble with foreign exchange in that, while it raised import-commitments, it compromised export-capacity at the same time. The pressure built up and broke out in 1956, in 1967, and in 1973 in the wake of the first oil shock. The build-up of pressure can be seen in Fig. 7.6. These episodes raised questions on the wisdom of repressing trade and foreign capital, but did not lead to a liberalisation. In fact, on every occasion, restrictions were tightened.

On the third of these occasions, in 1973, one of the responses of the government was to pass a new law, known as FERA, which forced the parents of foreign firms to become minority shareholders. The purpose of the radical

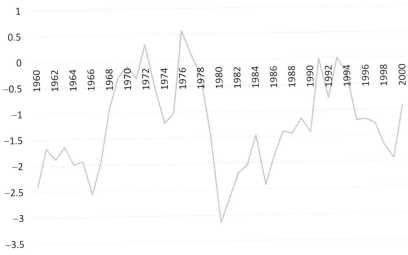

Fig. 7.6 External balance of goods and services, India 1960–2000 (per cent of GDP)
Source: World Bank, World Development Indicators

measure was to reduce outflow of money as much as possible, while scoring a point with the radical left movement at the same time.

The FERA Era: 1973–1980

FERA was approved by the Parliament in 1973 and was in force from 1 January 1974. It replaced an Act of the same name passed in 1947. The new Act shared with its predecessor three general aims, to regulate the entry and operation of foreign firms, to regulate the employment of 'nationals of foreign states' in India (Section 30 of the new Act), and to monitor and reduce outward remittance of foreign exchange. Unlike the more benign 1947 predecessor, the 1973 FERA made it mandatory on all firms to register in India, and required them to reduce the proportion of shares held by non-Indians to no more than 40 per cent.

The new FERA was not as draconian as it may sound or as it was portrayed in media later. Companies that needed to divest shares to achieve the 40 per cent foreign-owned shareholding limit were given some time to do so. The time, it turned out, was negotiable. Companies could escape the provision altogether if they could make a case that they operated in (a) 'core' areas (such as utilities, essential chemicals and industries deemed to be of national importance), (b) mainly exportable products, or (c) worked with 'sophisticated technology'. The negotiations that followed often settled on technology, irrespective of the product line. These negotiations bought the largest firms – about 50 of the 881 foreign firms subject to FERA were large firms – further time to avoid divestment, and in the case of Hindustan Lever, some authority to influence the negotiation process. A still partially foreign-owned industry, tea, was left alone because it was a big export-earner.

The problem, however, began in 1977, when the room to negotiate was taken away, and compliance with FERA was ensured by more 'rigorous enforcement' than in the first four years of its existence. A new government formed by the Janata Party, influenced by a mix of Gandhian and socialist ideology, came to power in 1977. The Law Minister in the new government declared that 'big foreign companies' could not be 'allowed to exploit the country' any longer.[40] George Fernandes, a trade unionist with a reputation for bullying capitalists, was appointed the Minister of Industries. The Janata Party remained in power for about two years. During this period, Fernandes personally ordered Coca Cola and IBM to leave the country, and called up Hindustan Lever and Western India Match Co to ask them to stop producing such low priority goods as soaps and matches. In two years, the government fell, and Fernandes, to the relief of many, was out of the job. But in these two years, a shakeout had been initiated.

FERA enforcement was not just a political idea. Almost certainly, it had the support of small and medium businesses of Indian origin, and especially those who financed the Janata Party. In 1973, 'Indian houses based in Calcutta' were again 'imagining themselves as the natural choice' as successors in an episode of forced divestment by foreign companies.[41] There were reports of 'hectic behind the scenes activity' to induce foreign firms to induct Indians as majority shareholders. Whether these groups also lobbied for FERA before it came into being we cannot say, but FERA was compatible with their interest. Indeed, some companies did change hands, but the process was managed better than in the 1950s.

Severe as it was, FERA elicited quite a diverse response. Several firms selling in the Indian market expanded shareholding, diluted foreign shareholding, and used the proceeds to make new investment commitments. In the process, the Indian subsidiary gained more operational autonomy whereas the new commitments forced the company to move somewhat further away from its core areas of operation. This increasing distance was probably good for the Indian branch where the product line was not high technology (as in

[40] Sudip Chaudhuri, 'FERA: Appearance and Reality', *Economic and Political Weekly*, 14(16), 1979, 733–44.

[41] Anon., 'FERA: Disappointment for Indian Big Business', *Economic and Political Weekly*, 12 (30), 1977, 1160–1.

ITC and BAT's cases), but it may have adversely affected the transfer of technology from the parent to the subsidiary in other cases (GKW and Metal Box are examples). Another set went into hibernation after FERA. Some changed hands. And finally, of course, there was the special case of tea. The rest of the section considers examples illustrating this diversity.

Hindustan Lever is a good example to study, being possibly the largest MNC subject to the regulation.[42] The company chose not to dilute stake to 40 per cent and Indianize, but remain a 51 per cent owned subsidiary of Unilever. FERA allowed that option to foreign companies on condition they exported a large part of their production or were engaged in 'high technology' fields. HLL negotiated with the government that they would subsequently export 10 per cent of their production and diversify in high technology fields. Between 1973 and 1982, the share of soaps and detergents – the two core businesses – in HLL sales fell from 70 to 63 per cent. The export obligations were met by trading shoes, clothing, and seafood. The promise to diversify into high technology fields was met by vertical integration into sodium tripolyphosphate (STPP), and linear alkyl benzenes (LAB), components of detergents. HLL remained a potential target of punitive action because its core products were consumer goods, and it was not obvious that the successes of its main brands owed to innovation.

In 1982, HLL divested from its food products, transferring these to Lipton, a subsidiary company and a non-FERA one. Analysts of Hindustan Lever Ltd. saw its strategy to hive off some of its traditional activity in food processing to subsidiaries as 'direct contravention of FERA with the government turning a blind eye to its activities', which allowed the firm to carry out 'foreign exchange drain' year after year.[43] The company, however, had to pay a price for losing sight of its core business, soaps. It had to give away a lot of ground to its main Indian rival, Godrej. In the 1980s, a small firm called Nirma emerged as a significant threat in its main market, detergents, prompting HLL to change its marketing and advertising system. Later accounts of restructuring in HLL suggest that investments had slowed during the 1980s, to pick up pace only after the liberalisation in the 1990s.

An example of FERA-induced autonomy was ITC. After the reinforcement of FERA in 1977, BAT diluted its stake from ITC, holding 39 per cent in 1979. Under the leadership of A. N. Haksar, an employee of ITC, a group of Indian professionals who had risen from the ranks, took over business strategy matters.

---

[42] The discussion in this section draws on Michael Aldous and Tirthankar Roy, 'Reassessing FERA: Examining British Firms' Strategic Response to "Indianization"', *Business History*, forthcoming.

[43] Ajay Kumar Rath, 'Local and Global Operations of Multinational Corporations: Unilever in India', *Social Scientist*, 10(10), 1982, 30–43. I have also drawn on I. M. Pandey, 'Hindustan Lever Limited', IIM Ahmedabad Case Studies No IIMA/F&A0405, 1985.

FERA pushed the company, like others, to diversify into new fields with high export content. Anti-smoking campaigns worldwide made some diversification a wise idea. ITC moved into marine foods and garments, both ending in failure. However, its hotels division Welcomgroup did well with a collaboration with Sheraton and inflow of money from abroad. Other existing businesses, paper, paperboard, printing, packaging, and of course, cigarettes, did well too. Towards the end of the 1980s, ITC had reinvented itself. The company reduced its workforce, and hired mainly at managerial levels, risking a labour dispute in 1987. Ironically, consistent profitability of tobacco helped the company to move away from tobacco. Middle-class Indians smoked more and better quality cigarettes than before. ITC earned enough cash to create investment funds, which it used to expand into processed food, information technology, finance, and matches. After FERA, from time to time there were rumours that BAT was ready to leave India. Although this did not happen, the BAT involvement in management was reduced and attempts to regain control failed.

After the FERA came into existence (1973), political attitude was often openly hostile to the foreign influence in Larsen and Toubro. In 1977, the company ceased to have any international participation in management at all and became fully Indian. Pushed by the reinforced FERA in 1977, Alfa Laval issued rights shares to its Indian shareholders, and the parent firm diluted its direct holdings to a minority stake. This company also gained more autonomy in the process.

In a cluster of examples, dilution accompanied diversification that strengthened the firm. In 1980, the Swedish parent of Swedish Match Co. diversified into moulding machines, and hydraulic presses. Nestlé managed the FERA dilution of holdings well, and entered the 1980s in a strong position to take advantage of a new consumer market in packaged and processed food. Under FERA, the Indian subsidiary diluted its shareholding, but did not think of leaving the country. FERA did not diminish the importance of GEC in India either.

In several other cases, however, the Indian subsidiary went into a sleepy state after FERA. Siemens faced pressures but did not succumb during the second coming of FERA in 1977. One of its key strengths was a partnership with the largest public-sector engineering firm, BHEL, which came in politically handy.[44] The FERA imposed an obstacle to a restructuring in Philips. In 1979, the parent company became a minority shareholder and Philips India was renamed Peico. Britannia Biscuits was another example of a firm that did not change its operations very much because there was at the same time a transfer of control of the parent firm. Britannia started raising Indian shareholding after FERA. By 1982, the foreign majority shareholder owned about a third of the company's stock. In that year, Associated Biscuit was sold to the

---

[44] Anon, 'Siemens: Power Play', *Business India*, 13 March 1992b, 49–54.

American company Nabisco, paving the way for a struggle that will be described in the next chapter. Existing on a low key, BASF suffered a setback like other foreign firms during the 1977 FERA onslaught. It did not leave India, but did not grow its operations there very much either in the next decade.

A strange case in this set is that of ICI. During FERA period, ICI escaped with 50 per cent shareholding because it operated in priority fields. It never faced a serious takeover threat since the government of India held nine per cent shares, because ICI manufactured explosives. The government also had the option to buy out the company in case of a sale. It is a curiosity, therefore, that the company made few investments in the 1980s. The parents, it was said, had lost interest in India. Inside India, ICI companies had grown inefficient. They employed too many people, and shedding employment led to labour trouble. The experience of Metal Box and GKW also fall into a similar category, that is, they stayed inactive for much too long. But the FERA connection is not clear in these cases.

In the paints industry, there was change of ownership. The paint industry in India began with a manufacturing unit set up in 1902 near Calcutta. It was managed by the British shipping firm Turner Morrison until 1963. The company, known as Shalimar Paints, continued as a subsidiary of the International Paint Co., UK, in turn a subsidiary of Courtaulds Ltd. In 1978, in the aftermath of FERA, the holding company reduced its stake, and sold shares to the Indian financial institutions. In 1989, O. P. Jindal Group and the Hong Kong-based S. S. Jhunjhnuwala group acquired the company. FERA likewise pushed the foreign owner to reduce shareholding in Berger Paints. Vijay Mallya's United Breweries group acquired the controlling stake. In 1991, UB's stake was bought by Kuldip Singh and Gurbachan Singh Dhingra, who now own Berger Paints India Ltd. In tyres, FERA had pushed CEAT Italy into a deal with Rama Prasad Goenka. CEAT retained a small shareholding, but effectively sold the Indian company in 1982.

Finally, export-oriented firms, such as the tea companies, restructured ownership without a plan to expand shareholding. Tea companies, as mentioned, were generally left alone, but they re-adjusted strategy anyhow.

If FERA hurt foreign firms, outbreak of strikes damaged the already beleaguered traditional industries.

The Problem of Labour

For industries under pressure, such as cotton, jute, and metals and machinery, moving money elsewhere and cutting jobs were not an option. The prospect that the employers might want to take these roads disturbed industrial relations. The 1970s and the early 1980s witnessed a spate of violent strikes in the older industries, especially, cotton textiles, jute textiles, and engineering. In January 1982, the Bombay cotton mill workers went on a strike that officially lasted 18 months, and involved more than 200,000 workers.[45] There is little doubt that these strikes impaired the capacity of these industries to weather a crisis originally brought on by failure of policy and failure of law. If they were not in the interests of the workers, why did they happen?

The dynamics differed somewhat between the cotton industry in Bombay and the jute industry in Calcutta. In Calcutta between 1969 and 1977, a spate of industry-wide strikes took place, affecting nearly a quarter of a million workers.[46] Although in 1969–70, two prolonged strikes had the support of all trade unions, the 1974–75 strike was a result of inter-union rivalry. The main unions involved in the one-upmanship game were the three affiliated to four leftist political parties, CITU (Centre of Indian Trade Unions), UTUC (United Trade Union Congress), AITUC (all India Trade Union Congress), and Hind Mazdoor Sabha, and the Indian National Congress' INTUC (Indian National Trade Union Congress). In 1974, for example, an agreement reached with INTUC and HMS was rejected by the other unions, leading to a huge strike. INTUC, affiliated to the ruling party in West Bengal state, complained that they were forced by the others to join the strike. They tried, with the mill managers, to keep the gates of some of the mills open, a move that led to violent opposition from the leftist unions. Despite these incidents, the strike failed, and opposition dissipated around February 1975.

The account of the 1974–75 strike reveals two things. First, rivalry and competition for control between politically affiliated trade unions were behind them on most occasions, in that, an agreement reached with one union was usually rejected by others, leading to repeated breakdown of negotiations. Because the government was a party in the negotiations, the leftists had the incentive to try to ensure failure of the negotiations. Second, two of the demands by the leftist unions – nationalisation of the jute industry, and absorption of temporary or casual workers – were broader political demands that the mill owners were unwilling or unable to fulfil. With the industry already caught up in a falling market, industrial disputes with a political aim could only make things substantially worse, which it did. Not only did the jute industry suffer, but also the economy of eastern India. The railway system, for example, was 'immobile' for weeks because wagons reserved for jute did not move.[47]

[45] H. Van Wersch, *Bombay Textile Strike 1982–83*, Bombay: Oxford University Press, 1992.
[46] Pramod Verma, S. Mookherjee, D. S. Kamat, 'Strikes in Jute Industry (B)', IIM Ahmedabad Case Studies No IIMA/P&IR0069(B), 1978.
[47] Ibid.

Box 7.5 **Business organisation**

With a few exceptions like Larsen and Toubro, companies owned by Indians were managed by family members. In the folklore of Calcutta, Indian companies made sure that a trusted member oversaw the finance department, who reported to the head directly, maintained two parallel sets of accounts, and did not need to take auditors too seriously. Unsavoury practices of this sort were reported also with the MNCs, but the MNCs were in the main professionally managed. The major scandal that they were involved in was transfer pricing, or the allegation that imports were over-invoiced to enable them to access more foreign exchange than allowed by the government. Tax evasion and over-invoicing was a game everybody played, but with the MNCs some of these transactions were intra-firm and therefore less visible.

The Calcutta takeovers episode highlighted some of the key weaknesses of corporate law. Company law did not intervene in managing agency as much as it needed to, and the broad outlines of an agency contract tended to be governed by the generic Contract Act. The upshot was that the capture of one agency firm effectively transferred control of an entire cluster of firms in one sweep, and the shareholders of these other firms could do little to stop this. In 1970, the managing agency system was abolished. Until its abolition in 1970, the managing agency continued to be used to maintain control of family managers as well as professional managers over individual companies. Control over many companies within a conglomerate was also maintained by means of an investment trust company, which was privately and fully owned by a family. The trust invested in some group companies, which then invested in other group companies, and so on.

Whereas banks supplied working capital, and most large groups owned banks until their nationalisation in 1969, investment finance was raised from internal resources as well as the stock market. The stock market route was used cautiously and sparingly during the thirty years in question. Indian family firms suffered from the anxiety that any expansion of shareholding could amount to losing control, and preferred to borrow or channel retained earnings into investment. The stock market raids suffered by the Indo-British firms of Calcutta may have made all companies, including the MNCs, wary about dilution of shareholding. In any case, the reliance on debt than equity made investment costlier than it should be, and limited investment capacity. The anxiety was alleviated somewhat by the government financial institutions empowered to buy company shares. This role was fully in play in the 1980s (Chapter 8).

In Bombay's textile industry, Datta Samant, a trade unionist working outside the main politically affiliated unions, led the strike, making a demand on the employers and preparing to back it with endurance. The unstated but expected reward behind the gamble was full nationalisation, which was a credible promise in 1980 (see also Chapter 8). Organised unions in Bombay were political actors, and preferred negotiations to strikes. Samant's strategy had succeeded on a few occasions, but the cotton mills proved to be the wrong industry to try it. The strike gave many employers the welcome opportunity to clear off unsold stocks and leave the industry.

The historiography of trade union activism focuses on the workers and their patrons in politics. There is a story about how employers dealt with these events, and sometimes used them for short-term gains. Since labour law and bankruptcy law made closing a factory a difficult action, strikes came in handy (see also Box 7.5 on corporate law).

Conclusion

The economic policy adopted after 1950 had a positive effect on private investment. New enterprises formed, there was a major expansion in machinery, metals, and chemical industries, conglomerates formed or emerged, which surely allowed for some economies of scale in the use of managerial resources. Between 1965 and 1980, however, private investment remained depressed, so that, as the government found it difficult to sustain investment effort, total investment in the economy was depressed too.

The investment drought ended around 1980. Thereafter, private investment recovered and started leading economic growth. The end of this regime came unannounced. Regulations on foreign exchange markets and usage relaxed, quietly. Why they did remains an unsolved mystery. Even though Morarji Desai, Prime Minister in 1977–79, and Rajiv Gandhi, Prime Minister 1984–91, were not socialists, little in the public debates of that time suggests any softening of the ideology that had enabled the statist-xenophobic ISI to last so long. Elsewhere, I have offered an explanation.[48] From the late 1970s, South Asian mass migration to the Persian Gulf states greatly increased the flow of inward remittance, thereby easing the balance of payments. It was as if a persistent pain was eased for the first time in the history of independent India. And this allowed the politicians to take a chance.

No matter the reason, a chance they did take.

---

[48] Tirthankar Roy, *The Economy of South Asia: From 1950 to the Present*, Basingstoke: Palgrave Macmillan, June 2017.

8   Revival: 1980–2000

The government introduced certain freedoms in the 1980s. There was not yet a publicly announced reform; the only thing that may explain this was that labour export from India had improved the balance of payments (see Fig. 7.4), the economy was regaining the capacity to import machines again, and this is exactly what was allowed, if on a selective basis. The easing off began with a decision to let the currency float, and depreciate. The government was forced to devalue after the oil crisis; once it was done, it was easy to repeat. During Rajiv Gandhi's Prime Ministership (1985–91), the Textile Policy, which had prevented cotton mills from modernising, was reformed (1985), and investment limits on the so-called 'monopoly houses' were relaxed. Price control on some goods including cement was removed, more goods were shifted from import licence list to tariff list, and FERA enforcement relaxed again. Portfolio investment by non-resident Indians was permitted around 1980, and almost immediately, led to a messy takeover case involving UK's Caparo, and India's DCM and Escorts.

These were disjointed steps, and did not add up to much. Politics was torn between reform, or less state intervention than before, and equity, or more state intervention than before. Too many regulatory roadblocks remained for this to be called a liberalisation. Tariff rates were still high. Bankruptcy, labour militancy, and corporate governance crises took extreme forms in traditional businesses. Industrywide strikes in engineering, cotton textiles, and jute caused disruption to the economies of whole regions (Chapter 7). Several business families split up, and some became obscure after doing so.

Still, there were signs of revival in private investment (see also Fig. 8.1). Behind the revival, there were six processes at work. First, the silent softening of the exchange rate encouraged export of garments and leather goods. Although the main beneficiary of the change were small firms, many larger companies set up subsidiaries to take advantage of the export boom. Second, the slight relaxation of import policy encouraged modernisation and investment in new areas. Third, applications to start joint ventures between Indian and foreign partners were reviewed liberally, so that more foreign investment and foreign technology came in even when import licence and foreign investment policy restrictions remained in place. Fourth, the Green Revolution stimulated consumption and encouraged fresh investment in farm equipment and chemical fertilisers. Fifth, government-owned financial institutions bought shares of private companies, which the banks did not do. In the 1980s, these institutions expanded their holdings of shares, in one estimate, from 24 to 78 per cent of the deficit in requirements.[1] This development stimulated the stock market, where capital mobilised by listed companies increased from around $80–120 million in the 1980s. The emergence of these institutions alleviated the anxiety of family firms about raising money from the stock market, provided the owners were in the good books of the politicians. If not, then institutional shareholding could pave the way for a takeover, and several bids were made in the 1980s by potential raiders to use that route.

The sixth process related to diversification in consumer goods. The consumers were short-changed by the government's accent on capital goods during 1950–80. Cloth manufacturing had not modernised, except for limited use of rayon in women's clothing. Food processing, telephones, mass media, bicycles, fans, automobiles, office machines – everywhere, primitive quality, crude design, and poor performance standards had ruled for thirty years. This was about to change. Joint ventures, easier import of equipment, and television advertising were to change it. Maruti car, Hero Honda motorcycles, Videocon television and washing machine, Pepsi's drinks, HCL computers, and Reliance's polyester fabric were the star products of the 1980s. PCs and Modi Xerox redefined office space. These goods embodied not only foreign technology, also a different marketing strategy from before, one that required reaching out to the consumer directly through advertisements rather than through distributors and wholesalers. 'Marketing ... became the buzzword' of the 1980s.[2]

Early in the 1990s the government initiated a formal reform process, starting with a drastic reduction in tariffs across the board. Industrial licensing was abolished overnight. Foreign investment rules were relaxed, but not drastically. The reform consolidated the corporate revival that had begun in the 1980s, but did not add significant new elements to it. The legacy of forty years of statism and xenophobia persisted in the survival of numerous minor regulations, and lack of reforms in major areas like banking.[3] In the 2000s, by contrast, the growth of service production

[1] R. Nagaraj, 'India's Capital Market Growth: Trends, Explanations and Evidence', *Economic and Political Weekly*, 31(35–37), 1996, 2553–63.

[2] 'Change', *Business World*, 27 March 1991a, 70–4.

[3] One of the best books on this legacy is Ashok V. Desai, *My Economic Affairs*, New Delhi: Wiley Eastern, 1993. 'Xenophobia' is Desai's usage, 230.

changed the direction of private investment substantially (Chapter 9). This chapter will discuss the beginning and consolidation of the corporate revival in the 1980s and the 1990s.

How were businesses affected by these moves? The good news was that the limited reforms permitted long-delayed technological modernisation of some industrial firms. The bad news was that, the ability to embark on such a project depended on three conditions that were difficult to meet. First, during the protectionist era, all large factories had appointed more people than they needed, taking pride in their record in employment generation, a national goal. Now, modernisation, which entailed shedding a lot of jobs, made a confrontation with labour highly likely. Second, raising money from the market made takeover threats more likely. And third, for foreign firms, the FERA had hit some companies just too hard for them to recover.

Retreat of Public Investment

From the 1980s, the government started to reduce its rate of investment (Fig. 8.1). The government did not announce that this was the best way to go. But the strains of sustaining the old strategy of industrialisation were obvious enough. A major problem was meeting the losses made by public sector units, and revival of bankrupt private companies that the government had nationalised. It was a losing battle, at least in the 1980s.

For example, at the end of the 1980s, the National Textile Corporation made colossal losses every year, which were paid for by the budget and the banks. Revival packages failed repeatedly as the government 'lacked political will to cut work force'. Plans to convert some of the mills into workers' cooperatives were rejected by the workers as they feared that when they tried to sell their goods, 'traders will exploit them'.[4] The workers blocked closure of completely nonviable factories. The workers in their turn blamed the 'contractor-administration-politician nexus' and 'heavy duty corruption'.[5] In 1992, the central government practically refused to pay for the losses, and a voluntary retirement scheme was pushed through. Things had gone so bad that resistance to the scheme was more muted than before. However, a full implementation of the scheme did not occur until the 2000s. And even when it did,

---

[4] 'In Tatters', *Business India*, 31 August 1992, 66–8.
[5] Ajoy Ashirwad Mahaprashasta, 'How the Once Flourishing Kanpur Textile Mills Decayed', *The Wire*, 16 April 2016, https://thewire.in/29734/faulty-govt-policies-corruption-and-exploitation-of-labour-how-the-once-flourishing-kanpur-textile-mills-decayed/ (accessed 14 April 2017).

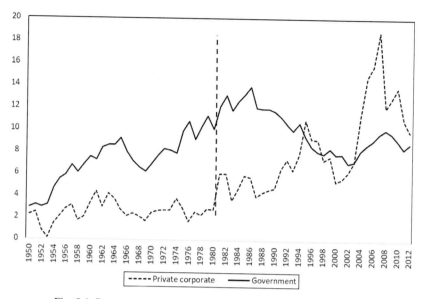

Fig. 8.1 Government and private investment (per cent of GDP)

implementation was sporadic. In theory, the cotton mills were still in operation, so that legally their assets could not be sold. And yet, there was no money available to run them. The workers who opted for the scheme complained of being short-changed, and those who did not opt for the scheme were left unemployed or had to change jobs.

In Calcutta, several Indo-British firms were nationalised in the 1970s in a bankrupt condition. The largest of the British managing agency conglomerates, Andrew Yule, was one example. Jute was in distress in the 1980s, and Andrew Yule withdrew from the industry. Explaining business strategy after nationalisation, a director said (1992), 'we decided to withdraw from jute' before the industry collapsed. In fact, the company had little choice in the matter. By the time it was nationalised, in 1977–78, it had lost its once cash-rich segments, including some tea, and most jute, to predators. Its engineering division, however, was diversified, and along with electrical equipment, had started making belting and mining equipment in 1976–77. Engineering received fresh investment after government takeover, but it was still a struggle to keep it profitable. A joint venture with a German collaborator helped more in the process than public ownership. Andrew Yule was also helped by its remaining tea business. Tea exports revived in the 1990s, and rather like ITC, this traditional arm helped the other divisions to get their act together. Possession of tea made the firm different from other government companies. One of the

Yule brand of packaged tea, Mim, is now visible in many hotels and retail channels in Calcutta city.

Burn and Co. was nationalised in 1976 and amalgamated with Indian Standard Wagon Company, the new government company being renamed Burn Standard Company Ltd. Due to consistent losses, the company was referred to the Board for Industrial and Financial Reconstruction (BIFR) in 1994, the government body in charge of financing bankrupt companies. A rehabilitation package approved in 1999 was declared failed in 2001. A further revival plan was approved in 2010 and in the same year, the company was transferred from Ministry of Heavy Industry to the Ministry of Railways. The move made little practical difference.

A different sort of challenge awaited the government in its steel business. Modernisation of steel was a problem because of the large scale of financing that was needed and the comparatively large workforce that needed to be reduced. The steel industry consisted of a core set of government plants, Tata, and one large firm that had been nationalised, Indian Iron and Steel Co or IISCO. IISCO was burdened with outdated machines, and in need of big subsidies to work at all. The Steel Authority of India Limited wanted to get rid of IISCO, and made some moves in the early 1990s. The response was surprisingly good, in fact suspiciously good. Allegations were made that the bidders had their eyes on the real estate and the captive iron mines that IISCO possessed.[6]

State was still a big trader in the 1980s (see Box 7.2), but not in the 1990s. With tariff reforms, 'decanalisation' of minerals and metals from mandatory procurement via the government, and removal of price controls, private trading in the areas formerly reserved for the government revived. The government companies in charge of trading like the State Trading Corporation and the Metals and Minerals Trading Corporation started losing money, the rationale to carry on, and faced an exodus of executives between 1991 and 1993.

The experience of foreign companies in the post-1980 era was quite mixed, depending on how badly FERA had hit them.

Multinational Companies

Chapter 7 showed that the FERA stimulated the share market and public shareholding. Forced issues of fresh equity was sometimes tied with diversification into fields that the firms could claim to be either high-technology or export-oriented. In short, FERA had some unintended good effects. In any

---

[6] Surajeet Das Gupta, 'Stoking a Controversy', *Business World*, 24 February 1993, 58–9.

case, it universally shook up business strategy. After FERA was made into a paper tiger in the late 1980s, some of the parents returned to India with more money and modernisation plans. In other cases, they did not.

The Aftermath of FERA

Towards the end of the 1990s, several multinational companies (MNCs) had regained control over the companies where they had been forced to reduce shareholdings after 1973. However, to make their return profitable, they needed to invest in new enterprises. This was so because some MNCs had grown lazy during the protectionist years, and entered the 1980s ill-prepared for competition. As the parent firms took a renewed interest in India, they started to grow and diversify.

There were several cases of re-bounce as FERA hold loosened. In 1991, BASF AG was still 'waiting for the day when rules and regulations in this country will get a bit more relaxed'.[7] Between then and 1998, the company expanded shareholding, started new subsidiaries in India, diversified into agrochemicals and plastic intermediaries, and set up new plants near Bombay and in Mangalore. Proctor and Gamble, the American cosmetics and detergent makers, reduced shareholding after FERA, and stopped investing, being 'constrained by the 40 per cent restrictions on its equity holding in P & G India'.[8] Of all its subsidiaries, the Indian one had the smallest holding by the parent. After the reforms, the parent quickly increased stake to 65 per cent, and expanded both production and marketing through joint ventures with Godrej. The Godrej collaboration in the 1990s drew a lot of media attention because both were soap-makers. P & G had better technology, and Godrej had better distribution, and together they hoped to stand up to Hindustan Lever.

For Cadbury, which had a near monopoly in chocolates for many years, Indian competition became keener in the 1980s. Content with a large market share in chocolates, Cadbury had not diversified enough. When it did, into ice creams and biscuits, local ice cream brands offered by Hindustan Lever and others emerged as its rivals. A small firm called Campco and the Amul brand of the Gujarat Milk Marketing Federation took shares of the chocolate market away. In 1990, Nestlé India started making chocolates.

General Electric or GEC did not do well in the 1980s due to an oversized workforce and financial problems. Meanwhile in 1989, the parent of English Electric, GEC, merged with Alstom. The merger lent strength to the

---

[7] 'Inching Ahead', *Business India*, 4 March 1991b, 70–2.
[8] Naazneen Karmali, 'P & G Cleans up its Act', *Business India*, 5–18 December, 1994, 65–8.

restructuring of the Indian subsidiary. The footwear multinational Bata, which had long enjoyed a protected market, also entered the 1990s with an excessively large workforce, high production cost, a limited range, and a huge factory in Calcutta, where trade unions were ready to resist modernisation. Bata survived, and diversified its products, after losing a great deal of its market. The transformers maker Crompton Parkinson sold its Indian subsidiary to the Thapar group, the company being renamed as Crompton Greaves.

Other MNCs were initially small enough to stay flexible. Goodlass Nerolac (see Goodlass Wall in Chapter 7) was a small paint company before 1980. It grew rapidly after a collaboration with Kansai Paints of Japan in the 1980s, which brought its expertise in line with the demand for paints from the part-Japanese Maruti car company. In the 1990s, Kansai took over the company. Alfa Laval had grown little since its start. In the late 1980s, that changed. Its food packaging technology known as Tetra Pak was a great success in the Indian market. The new head of the company Lila Poonawalla led modernisation and managed to keep the growing workforce content at the same time. After the economic reforms began, the company diversified and expanded further. It now has an international presence in environmental engineering. The German engineering company Siemens diversified in the 1980s and 1990s in medical instruments and consumer goods, though these expansions turned out to be expensive, and strained the company's finances.[9]

MNCs that were originally based in Calcutta, and diversified early in northern, western, and southern India were left relatively unscathed by the deindustrialisation and trade union violence of eastern India. In 1978, the parent company of Mather and Platt divested its interests. Mather and Platt India became a subsidiary of the German company Wilo AG. Its main manufacturing centres became Pune and Kolhapur in western India. It still had a plant in Calcutta, on which no information was available in the company's website. Among other companies with a significant presence in Calcutta, ICI was bought up in 2008 by Akzo Nobel, and its Indian subsidiaries merged to form Akzo Nobel India. By then, the manufacturing capacity had shifted out of Calcutta.

Another originally Calcutta firm, Britannia Biscuits, had an eventful history because its parent company, Nabisco, experienced a now-famous meltdown in the late 1980s. A private equity firm acquired Nabisco and sold it in parts to different food companies. In 1989, Singapore-based J. M. Rajan Pillai acquired Associated Biscuits, and with it, the controlling interest in Britannia. Pillai's precarious financial situation forced him to yield Britannia to a joint venture between the Wadia group and the Groupe Danone in 1993. Rajan died in

---

[9] www.businesstoday.in/magazine/special/oldest-mnc-in-india-siemens/story/194630.html

1995 in a Delhi jail, awaiting hearing on an extradition request from Singapore. The joint venture ran into trouble because of clauses that prevented Danone from using its own brand name in India and Britannia brands abroad, and was dissolved in 2007. Despite this acrimonious struggle for control, Britannia survived. It gained from the booming consumer market. Rather like Hindustan Lever, which thrived on a single soap brand, Britannia thrived on a small range of highly popular biscuit brands.

In a few of the cases, the re-bounce came too late or was too weak. Philips, the Dutch electronics firm, had a small-scale presence in India before FERA. Known as Peico after FERA, its brand name was stable enough to see the company through until the mid-1990s. But the FERA seemed to destroy the drive and direction of the company. Even as the market for consumer electronics boomed in the 1990s, all of its consumer electronic products lost market share to new rivals, Japanese and Indian. Meanwhile, the parent had regained control over Philips India, when the only product line left to it was a small share of the lighting market. The company more recently tried to reinvent itself in electrical medical equipment. The FERA affected Indian Aluminium quite badly. The Canadian parent Alcan never gave up on India, but sought merger with Mahindra and Mahindra in 1983. The move fell through. Meanwhile, the aluminium business suffered because of growing electricity shortages. Aluminium smelting consumes a lot of power, and Indian Aluminium had not invested enough money in integrated power plants, unlike its main rival, Birlas' Hindustan Aluminium or Hindalco. When the government set up its own aluminium company, Nalco, licences for modernisation became hard to get. The British office automation company Gestener India suffered during FERA, as the British parent practically removed themselves from management after 1979. Living a dormant existence for the next fifteen years mainly as a trader in office machines, the parent suddenly returned and raised stake in the Indian company from 40 to 51 per cent in 1995. However, competition in the field had by then increased significantly.

During FERA, the parent company of another Calcutta firm ITC, British American Tobacco, distanced itself from management of ITC. When it tried to regain control around 1994 and 1995, the ITC board resisted, disagreed on strategy, leading to a situation the media read as a rift between BAT and ITC. As in many large companies where the owners had diluted their holdings, financial institutions held the key to negotiations between owners and managers.[10] Apparently, the managers won the battle. Already it had diversified out of its core business, cigarettes, and outside Calcutta.

---

[10] Paran Balakrishnan, 'April is not the Cruellest Month', *Business World*, 17 May 1995, 70.

GKW and Metal Box had iconic status in Calcutta's industrial world, since these two companies represented the city's original association with the British engineering industry. In the 1990s, both companies became bankrupt. In both cases, the parent firm seemed to lose interest in India, depriving the Indian firms' access to funds and modernisation opportunities.

GKW produced nuts and bolts, fasteners, and railway material. The relationship between GKN, the parent, and GKW was always an arm's length one, though they did work in similar lines of manufacturing. GKN continued to hold 47 per cent of the GKW shares until as late as 1990, but effectively GKW was an independent company under Indian management. Throughout the 1970s and the 1980s, as GKN was reinvented, there was a divergence between the two firms. GKW remained committed to a product line that was not state of the art, and faced tough competition from small firms, which the government of India preferred to nurture. Its factory in Howrah (near Calcutta) faced labour trouble. Finance dried up and debt became harder to bear. Traditional clients in the automotive industry preferred to manufacture parts in house to suit new designs. Even as GKN moved away from traditional products towards innovation in automotive engineering, military vehicles, aerospace, and industrial services, GKW suffered a fall. GKW still owned substantial valuable real estate, and sold some of it to reduce workforce, but these measures did not make it competitive. In 1994, GKN divested its stake to a trading company and that ended GKW's career.

As for Metal Box, in 1979, the two large foreign shareholders of the company – Metal Box Overseas, and Continental Can Co. Inc. – divested partially from the Indian firm. Metal Box Overseas continued to remain a major shareholder, but the company was effectively an Indian company, now named Metal Box India Ltd. A bad investment in bearings had weakened the finances of the company. In 1982–83, it embarked on delayed modernisation of its core business, box-making. From 1984 onwards, however, an almost unending sequence of labour disputes pushed the company towards bankruptcy. In 1987, the company was in court seeking to wind up, and was prevented from doing so by a countersuit filed by some of its employees. Metal Box Overseas negotiated a partnership with two other Calcutta groups, Brij Mohan Khaitan's Williamson Magor, and the government company Balmer Lawrie, which had a canning unit in Saudi Arabia. But both deals failed. 'The revival hinged on the labour agreement', Deepak Khaitan explained, 'and that started floundering'.[11]

Around 1989, the company was referred to the BIFR. Metal Box and its creditors, government-owned financial institutions, were now in the same predicament in which several other Calcutta firms found themselves in the

---

[11] Palakunnathu G. Mathai, 'Cutting Links', *India Today*, 15 May 1988. See also Sujoy Gupta, 'Metal Box: Saving Grace', *Business World*, 13–28 February 1991, 80–1.

1980s. Its core business was beyond repair because of managerial inertia and trade union resistance, it was heavily indebted, and yet it owned valuable real estate that could in principle fund a modernisation project. Conflicting views of the prospects of the company were voiced. Metal Box Plc expressed hopes of a recovery but was apparently unwilling to stake any money. BIFR was so frustrated as to deny the company an audience. In the 2000s, press reports on the company became less and less frequent, except for occasional news about attempts to sell real estate. Its manufacturing units were closed.

The experience of the MNCs that were already operating in India, therefore, was quite diverse. The FERA regenerated some firms, and weakened others. After FERA was practically immobilised around 1990, some parents returned, others stayed away. An inevitable consequence of delayed modernisation and attempts to reduce workforce was that labour disputes there were everywhere. Settling such disputes seemed particularly difficult in Calcutta, with the result that most MNCs of the city either invested elsewhere or did not return to manage the subsidiary.

In the 1980s, liberal joint venture rules led to new entry, mainly in consumer goods, almost always bringing in new technology and consumer brands. Indeed, the major form of MNC investment in the 1980s was not expansion of incumbent firms. It was the joint venture.

Joint Ventures

In the 1980s, the policy on joint ventures ushered in 'the rat race of asset building' in new technologies.[12] The government was still hesitant to open up doors to foreigners. The patriotic sentiment that 'India has nurtured an entre-preneurial class at great cost [and] by encouraging foreigners to take control ... this entrepreneurial ability was ... being virtually stifled' left some room for Indian family firms to campaign in the media and with the govern-ment for regulatory protection. For the MNC, it made some sense to have a politically connected partner in India. And yet, it was often painfully obvious that the Indian partner firms 'have very little to offer joint venture projects'. Money, technology, and managerial skills all came from the international firms. 'And with their international distribution networks, they can offer access to world markets'.[13] The international firms often saw the joint venture as a transitional tool, to be given up when India opened doors wider.

---

[12] Shri L. N. Junjhunwala, Bhilwara group, see Shashi Shekhar, 'Bhilwara's Asset Chase', *Business World*, 12–25 September 1990, 36–7.

[13] Palakunnathu G. Mathai, 'The Foreign Onslaught', *Business World*, 13–26 January 1993, 46–51.

Still, joint ventures brought in a great many international consumer brands into India. Probably the most important cluster by provenance was Japanese investment in automobiles. Japanese investment took place both as subsidiaries and in joint ventures, such as those between Maruti and Suzuki, Telco and Hitachi, and Yamaha and Escorts in tractors. In Southeast Asia and China, Japanese foreign investment had already led to growth in export capacity. That effect was modest if not missing in India. Home market was a bigger attraction. In the latter half of the 1980s and the early 1990s, the automobile market saw a spate of Indo-Japanese brands introduced in quick succession. These included Hero Honda, DCM-Toyota, Maruti Suzuki, Kinetic Honda, Kawasaki Bajaj, Eicher Mitsubishi, TVS-Suzuki, and Swaraj Mazda, offering a range of bikes, cars, mopeds, and commercial vehicles. In 1985, tractor-maker Escorts entered motorcycles, in collaboration with Yamaha. While selling these new products, the companies advertised more aggressively than before, and devised new finance schemes, such as customer deposits, that made them a lot of money.

In the initiation of some of the pioneering joint ventures, the Indian partner played a significant role. The Delhi-based bicycle-maker Munjal's entrepreneurship was in evidence in the 1970s, when the company made a pioneering move into mopeds, and made a success of it. And in 1984 came its biggest coup, the Hero Honda joint venture in motorcycles. Like Maruti-Suzuki cars, Hero Honda became an icon of the consumerism of the 1980s. In both cases, the Indians were instrumental in implementing the idea and designing the new enterprise.

MNCs Gain Freedom

Inevitably, when doors did open wider, and direct foreign investment norms were relaxed in the 1992–95 reforms, leading foreign firms, which had been running joint ventures or had entered India via that route, started independent operations. The list includes Bayer, Gillette, Goodyear, Datacraft, EMI, Sprint, Suzuki, Merrill Lynch, Xerox, and Vodafone. International companies so far working in joint ventures demanded their shareholding rise to 51 per cent. The government itself had allowed Suzuki Motors to do this in the case of Maruti Udyog. In 1992–93, Gillette (in a joint venture with Poddar), 3M (a joint venture with Ashok Birla group), Honda (joint venture with Firodia in two wheelers) followed suit, whereas ABB, Unilever, Procter and Gamble, and GEC consolidated their shareholding in Indian operations.

In a few cases, the separation was acrimonious, politically charged, and costly for the foreign partner. One notable example was the Britannia Industries (see above). In another case, NOCIL or National Organic Chemical

Industries, a joint venture between Shell and the textile group Mafatlal, Shell breakaway occurred amidst bitterness over new patented technology. In other cases (the battery-maker Lakhanpal National and Matsushita), an arrangement was reached to hand over managerial control to the foreign partner. Trouble plagued a joint venture between Siemens and Khatau (Cable Corporation of India) over Siemen's expansion plans, and between Piaggio and Singhania in LML, a two-wheeler maker. Interestingly, in computers and information technology services, the pattern was quite different. Partnerships with HCL and HP, and between Tata and IBM (Tata Services) or Tata and Bell Canada (Tata Cellular) survived on a more equal footing and without disputes over shareholding. This was so because the Indian comparative advantage in the software side of the business was already internationally recognised.

As MNCs entered and discovered ailing or weak Indian brands, they went for acquisitions and mergers. One set of mergers happened between foreign firms in possession of global brands and Indian firms, such as, Coca Cola buying up a Bombay-based soft drink manufacturer Parle, or Lever buying up the Indian food brand Kissan. A second set of mergers occurred between Indian firms, desiring to restructure and develop areas of core competence, and their weaker competitors. For example, Shri Ram Fibres or SRF, a tyre chord maker, bought CEAT tyres, and big global cement companies like Lafarge-Holcim bought regional cement companies. As a part of the same process, there were also de-mergers. A diversified group, Tata, shed non-core businesses like soaps and oils.

One legacy of the protected era had been the emergence of Indian consumer brands in soft drinks (Parle's Campa Cola, Rasna), consumer electronics and the so-called white goods like refrigerators and air-conditioners (Videocon, BPL in TV and radio sets), watches (HMT, a government firm), cars (Ambassador of the Birla-owned Hindustan Motors, Fig. 8.2), and machine tools. Few of these survived the 2000s, whereas Korean and Japanese brand names swept the consumer market in cars, white goods, and electronics. The sinking of Indian brands did not sink a company, but sometimes led to a move away from finished goods to component manufacture (Videocon, for example, from TV sets to tubes).

Why Indian brands failed to become global brands during this crucial transition remains an unsolved problem. Was the key failure in advertising, in quality control and R and D, or after-sale service? Was nationalistic branding an unsustainable business idea in a globalised world? Was the Indian consumer so fed up being served bad quality for thirty years, that there was a general turning away from Indian brands when the market opened? We do not know the answer yet.

A tortuous modernisation process had begun among big industrial complexes. A few examples will illustrate this.

Fig. 8.2 The end of the ambassador car, 2017
In 2014, production of this iconic car stopped. Hindustan Motors announced in
2017 that the company had made agreement with the Peugeot Group on a sale of the
Ambassador brand.
© Saikat Paul/Pacific Press/Alamy Live News

Indian Capital: Large-Scale Industry

The difficulties the government faced in modernising its own industries
reappeared in the private sector. The 1980s saw the beginning of the end of
the business group as it had existed in the protected era. Conglomerates
divided up, were partitioned between members of the family, and individual
companies gained an identity that was larger than that of the group. Competition and new entry forced companies to modernise, diversify, form partnerships with foreign firms, and raise capital from the market. Not all groups
moved at the same speed in doing these things, but most had to adapt in some
way or other.[14]

In Calcutta's jute industry, a complex restructuring was underway, big
capital retreated making way for groups of smaller means. In the 1980s,

---

[14] Any generalisation we make about transformation of families should be treated as tentative.
Ashok Desai points out to me that, while industrial licensing prevailed, one knew which family
was moving into which industry. Today the data are not readily available, which does not mean
that the families have faded away.

several jute companies changed hands. Some of the bigger business groups, such as Birla and Bangur, reduced their jute interests. There were a few profitable companies and many in a semi-bankrupt state, which encouraged transfers. In the process, Ghanshyam Sarda, B. P. Agarwal, R. K. Mall, and S. Bagaria emerged as owners of significant jute interests. The most successful businessperson of this set was Arun Bajoria, who expanded his profitable Hooghly Jute Co. through acquisitions of Gondalpara from G. D. Kothari, one unit of Anglo-India from J. P. Goenka, Waverley from C. L. Bajoria group, and Hukumchand from the Birlas.

As we have seen in chapter 7, in the history of Calcutta's jute industry since 1980, surviving companies made profits only occasionally. The Bajoria group until recently owned a substantial part of the jute interests. But among the rest, there were a great deal of sale, and resale, which placed medium-sized family firms in control of the industry.

Individually, many of these people who came to control the jute industry were well qualified for the business. Arun Bajoria's success, for example, was attributed to his knowledge of the production process, as well as qualities as a financial entrepreneur, the fact that he understood the raw jute market well. But overall, the pattern of ownership did not serve the industry well at all. Few of the new owners had deep financial capacity, and there were allegations that some used employees' provident fund in running businesses or buying new ones. There was a general disregard for marketing and innovation. The jute market was propped up partly by government protection and partly Soviet bilateral trade. While these props worked, the industry did not do badly. But there was little endogenous effort to create markets outside the comfort zone.

One significant exception to the norm was Fort Gloster Jute, the flagship of that branch of the Bangur family engaged with jute and tea, rather the Kettlewell Bullen assets. Fort Gloster was a more consistently profitable company than most others, thanks to an early innovation in jute marketing. The company's mainstay was bulk packaging of food articles, as in the other cases, but it broke with dependence on a group trading firm for orders, and started talking to international buyers in different industries directly, and thus succeeded in capturing several niche markets abroad.[15]

Steel-making was beset by the legacy of protection, bloated workforce, and delayed modernisation. Public sector dominance in steel and the licensing of steel production in blast furnace meant that steel was more expensive in India than globally. The government decision to allow expansion of scrap-based

---

[15] Conversation with Hemant Bangur, July 2017.

electric furnace units did help the shortage, but demand was growing too fast. The high cost passed on to major steel-using industries such as forging.

And yet, paradoxically, steel as a business faced a growing market ahead. Good economic growth spurred a construction boom. While demand for steel exploded in the mid-1990s, the liberalisation – removal of licensing in 1991, price control in 1992, end of the freight equalisation scheme from 1992, and finally tariff reforms – revealed that 'Indian steel makers are the least competitive in the world'.[16] The combination encouraged modernisation and new entry.

Tata Steel during the three decades of protectionism had grown into a flabby and backward firm, one that prided itself on its large workforce and paternalism towards the employees, but was out of time technologically. Early experience had shown that a serious modernisation plan would not pass the approval of the state, which itself owned the largest steel-making company in the country, and was doing a poor job of running it. In the 1980s, routinised improvements in work practices, based on suggestions made by engineers, were ignored and left unimplemented. The reckoning came in the late-1980s. For the second time in its life, Tata Steel faced a modernise-or-perish choice. It goes to the credit of the management that the modernisation drive began before the liberal tariff regime was announced. In the 1990s, the company halved its workforce, divested from some subsidiary businesses, closed unprofitable plants, introduced continuous casting methods, overhauled the steel product divisions, and improved business-to-business customer service. Marketing earlier had relied too heavily on authorised distributors, which dependence was somewhat reduced in the process. As the 1990s reforms unfolded, some of the planned projects started operation, and the company managed to deal with the competition.

Smaller and more flexible steel-makers like Essar Group, Ispat Group, and Jindal, meanwhile expanded to meet the new demand. Essar is a case in point. The brothers Shashi and Ravi Ruia – described as 'Tamil speaking Marwaris' by a business magazine – diversified from construction into shipping, steel, and oil exploration in the 1980s. Their father Nandkishore had migrated from Rajasthan to Madras in the 1950s, and started an iron ore trading firm, a stevedoring business, and construction agency. There was interdependence between the three fields, which helped the group to expand into these areas in the 1970s, under the leadership of the brothers. The acquisition of a shipping

---

[16] 'Firing up Tata Steel', *Business World*, 19 April 1995a, 42–5; D. V. R. Seshadri, 'Reinventing Tata Steel (A)', IIM Ahmedabad Case Studies No. IIMA/PROD0267(A), 2004. The freight equalization policy (1952–93) offered compensatory subsidies to factories for different transport costs on minerals. Eastern India produced some of these minerals.

company in 1983 set off a rapid and big growth in shipping. Its prior experience in dockyard construction projects contributed to major strides in construction as well. In the 1990s, Essar Group set up a steel factory in Gujarat. By the end of the decade, the group faced a difficult condition, and had to cut down on shipping capacity. In the mid-1990s, Essar made its third big move, into mobile telephony. After a successful few years, the competition became too tough and a series of mergers took place in the industry. More recently, Vodafone has acquired Essar's telecommunication assets. By contrast with Essar, the Ispat group had a somewhat different profile. Mittals hailed from a Calcutta-based steel trading business. In the 1980s they expanded in the Americas, Europe, Central Asia, Southeast Asia, and the Caribbean, taking over bankrupt steel product units, while setting up large electric arc furnace steel units in India. Others, such as Pune's Kalyani, set up steel manufacturing in a move to achieve vertical integration between forging, its main business, and steel.

The 1980s and the 1990s saw a series of setbacks to the Walchand Hirachand group companies. The engineering arm located in Walchandnagar was involved in a large overseas contract that went wrong. Its partner was a government company. This company and Walchandnagar blamed one another for the disaster. One of the company's clients, the Cement Corporation of India for cement machinery, stopped making investments. At the same time, the militant trade unionist Datta Samant set his eyes upon Walchandnagar, and the company faced a series of debilitating strikes and closures.

After the economic reforms, the Thapar group initiated a reorganisation, which involved selling small businesses such as chemicals, and expand core businesses like paper and glass to international scale and technological standards. Trade reforms exposed the core business (paper) to competition from companies in Indonesia. The expansion required money, raising the money from shares without diluting the family's holding was an expensive option. A financially easier option was to enter joint ventures with foreign partners, such as in glass (Owens) and pesticide (Du Pont), which would inject cash and technology, with the risk that the partner might want control.

In automobiles and tyres, there was a shakeout. All of the original six companies did well until the end of the 1980s. Even as Indo-Japanese joint ventures thrived in motorcycles, foreign investment in the car manufacture remained restricted in the 1980s. The removal of licensing requirements of motor cars came in 1993, though regulation of foreign investment still persisted on the grounds that automobiles were not a 'high priority' for the country.[17]

---

[17] Joint Secretary in the Department of Industrial Development, cited in Anjuli Bhargava, 'In Slow Gear', *Business World*, 5–18 May 1993, 22–3.

A number of Indian companies considered joint ventures, but most car manufacturers were struggling with old-fashioned models and limited urban demand.

Meanwhile, the joint venture between the government-owned Maruti and Suzuki Motors had produced a small car that became a roaring success. The first major casualty of the Maruti-Suzuki phenomenon was Standard Motors, which had long been known to produce one of the least fuel-efficient cars in the world. After 1975, Leyland had withdrawn from the management of Ashok Leyland. Its stake in the company was purchased by the Britain-based Hinduja group. After India opened its doors to foreign investment in automobiles, Premier and Hindustan Motors went bankrupt, though their eventual closure was delayed because taxi contracts in Bombay and Calcutta sustained these two companies for some time. In the late 1990s, government of India and Suzuki Motors started fighting for control over Maruti. Foreign investment norms for automobiles were eased, even as protective tariffs on the import of finished cars and commercial vehicles continued to be high. The combination of new entry and the leadership struggle in Maruti was a rapid fall in the latter's market share. The biggest gainer was Hyundai Motors, who offered a technologically superior small car, the market segment in which Maruti had succeeded dramatically.[18] In the 2000s small cars from other makers flooded the market.

Tractor-making companies and commercial vehicle makers did particularly well because of robust demand from large farmers who had benefited from the Green Revolution. In the 1990s, Eicher Goodearth (renamed Eicher Motors) took over the Royal Enfield motorcycle company. In 2000s, Eicher sold the tractor division to the Tractors and Farm Equipment India Ltd. and diversified (with Volvo) into heavy trucks.

Competition in the tyre market changed in the second half of the 1980s. FERA had pushed the British owners of Dunlop, the market leader, to divest, and in a repeat of the formula, to expose itself to a takeover. From 1986–87, Dunlop's new owner Manohar Chhabria started running the company down, whether through incompetence or deliberate misuse of assets remains a controversial point. FERA had pushed CEAT Italy into a deal with R. P. Goenka. CEAT retained a small shareholding, but effectively sold the Indian company in 1982. Better-managed by the R. P. Goenka clan, CEAT avoided the dire fate of Dunlop. With Goenka's acquisition of another British company, Harrison and Crosfield (renamed Harrisons Malayalam), the group had access to natural rubber for its tyre business.

---

[18] Achyut Telang and Souvik Roy, 'Hyundai's Challenge to Maruti Suzuki in the Dynamic Indian Automobile Sector', *Asian Journal of Management Cases*, 13(1), 2016, 56–66.

While Dunlop and CEAT underwent changes, the Modi family started bickering among themselves, with adverse consequences for the company. Goodyear and Firestone (later Bridgestone) were subjected to FERA, had to divest heavily, but managed the process carefully and survived as multinationals. Goodyear helpfully had a joint venture with a government company. The gainers from this turmoil were MRF and a relatively new entrant, Apollo Tyres. The boom in consumer automobile market since the economic reforms changed the fortunes of all tyre companies. All of them actively sought joint ventures and technical collaboration with world leaders. MRF joined hands with Pirelli and Goodrich, CEAT with the Yokohama Rubber Company, and Goodyear and Bridgestone relied on the association with the parent company.

Indian pharmaceutical companies gained from FERA and the process patent regime, which together froze the MNCs' market share to about a third while encouraging the growth of Indian origin firms (Chapter 7). In 1990, the industry was dominated by several thousand Indian firms, almost all of them individually small-scale and making bulk drugs. In this landscape, a few firms had enlarged scale, thanks to profitable process patents and export success in developing country markets. This set consisted of Ranbaxy Laboratories, Cadila, Lupin Laboratories, Unichem, Gujarat Lyka, Standard Organics, Dr. Reddy's Laboratories, and J. B. Pharmaceuticals.

While corporates and MNCs were busy supplying attractive goods to the Indian middle classes, traditional industry led exports of manufactures. Technology again played a role in the process.

Indian Capital: Small-Scale Industry

When the economic reforms were announced, leather and ready-made garments were already marked as promising fields for corporate investment. These fields had been reserved by the Janata government (1977–79) for small firms. Government policy allowed manufacture and trade by large firms on condition that the firms would export a big share of their production (the share was brought down somewhat, but it was still 50 per cent in 1993).

Apart from established trading and textile firms such as Tata, Mafatlal, Morarjee Mills, Bhilwara, Arvind Mills, and DCM, groups without a prior experience in textiles like ITC, Eicher, and the engineering firm Triveni Engineering, set up joint ventures with European, South Korean, and American marketing firms to sell Indian textiles and clothing abroad. These companies and the tie-ups tried to export garments as well as sell foreign brands or foreign-sounding ones to Indian buyers. For many long-running textile mills, such as Mafatlal, Morarjee, or Bombay Dyeing, selling their goods in India was more economical than breaking into the export market. However, marketing costs in

India were rising because of rise in rents and property price in the big cities. Running a string of retail shops in the big cities was going out of reach of most textile companies. Outside the cities, buyers of textiles still purchased fabrics and had these tailored. Not surprisingly, the home market did not sustain the strategy for very long. By the early 2000s, only a few of these Indian corporate brands had survived whether in India or outside, and the garment business was taken over by small-scale and specialised garment manufacturers (on the traditional textile industry and its offshoots, see Box 8.2.

A similar pattern unfolded in leather. India's extensive leather footwear industry flourished on the back of exports to Soviet Union until the 1980s under bilateral deals, and after the collapse of Indo-Soviet trade deals from 1989, the industry had to seek other markets. Regulatory policy favoured small-scale industry in this business too, but made room for trading firms that promised to export a part of their supplies. Leather companies took advantage of this provision, and diversified out of footwear into apparel, business accessories, and luggage.

The leather trading firms were concentrated near Delhi. The city's Da Milano, started by Surinder Malik, was one of the larger firms to have emerged from the boom in leather exports. The strength of the large firms in the business, such as Da Milano, Cristina, and Tata Exports, was in trade, advertising, and retail. These companies tried to access the export market and the rich Indian shoppers at the same time. Delhi was the hub, and yet ironically, most finished leather came from South India. The leather goods manufacturers wanted leather and the processed leather exporters did not want to give them any, unless there was a surplus.

It was natural to expect that a leather export business would emerge also in South India. When one did, the circumstances were unusual. Dilip Kapoor, from Pondicherry, came across leather making when he was a doctoral student in Princeton University in the 1970s. This experience led him to start a leather goods unit in Pondicherry after his return to India in 1978. The town was close to one of the largest hubs of chrome tanning in India, and Kapoor had ideas about design and finish, so the decision made sense. Like many small manufacturers, he lacked access to fashion goods markets overseas. Over the 1990s, commercial partnerships with dealers in leather goods came as a breakthrough, though the financial control of the company passed on to a multinational in the process. In the 2000s, the company expanded direct retailing through franchise within India, and was something of a pioneer in this movement. Today, Hidesign is a visible and respected brand in the airports and shopping malls of Indian cities, sharing space with Italian brands.[19]

---

[19] Abraham Koshy, 'Hidesign', IIM Ahmedabad Case Studies No. IIMA/MAR0380, 2006.

Fig. 8.3 Diamond polishing factory in Western India
© Dinodia Photos/Alamy Stock Photo

A third profitable field yet was polishing of raw diamonds in western India, mainly in Bombay and Surat. The factories themselves were relatively small in scale and did not function as companies. But the trade, all of it for export, was highly organised and controlled by a Gujarati community called Palanpuri Jains. The Palanpuri diaspora, spread literally all over the world with concentrations in the leading diamond trading cities (Antwerp, New York, Tel Aviv, among others), organised the import of raw gems, and the sale of polished ones (Fig. 8.3).

With a few exceptions, in the fields discussed above better housekeeping and modernisation rather than classic entrepreneurship were the need of the hour. But in several new fields of investment, entrepreneurship was in evidence. These new fields included computers and software, television, synthetic fibre, and aviation.

Computers and Software

Two firms, HCL and DCM Data Products, embarked on the manufacture of computers in the late 1970s. In a sense, the DCM Ltd. was the common parent for both, because while HCL was formed of a team of engineers who had been employees of DCM, DCM Data Products was a division of the same company.

The market for personal computers in India was small until the late 1980s. Still, a policy to promote computerisation of public sector banks and government offices encouraged sales. Components and chassis were still mainly imported, so that the manufacturing stage in India consisted of assembling.

After 1992, tariffs on components were brought down, and industrial licensing was abolished. In the next twelve to fifteen years, these changes led to three developments. First, sales of multinational personal computer brands grew rapidly. These brands shared space with domestic brands. By 2003, the largest selling multinational branded PC in India was Hewlett-Packard. Other top brands included Dell, IBM, Zenith, and Acer. HCL, however, held on thanks to government contracts, and competitive pricing. Secondly, there was huge growth of assembly firms, and increasing acceptability of assembled PC in corporate and government contracts, thanks to good customer service. As the market acquired more price and quality spread through these two changes, the office market and the personal market both gained.[20]

The third process was outsourcing, which in turn increased the demand for computers and hardware in India. In the 1970s, Indian companies like TCS and Infosys were set up to supply software services. Outsourcing, however, was a low-key affair in the early 1970s. This was beginning to change. In the late-1970s, the use of information technology started to move from specialised applications to universal applications in corporate business processes. When North American companies started managing their database and operations using IT, they had to hire consultants and pay them huge fees by the hour. Indian companies were available to offer the same services and got paid by the project. No matter which set of workers did it, the job involved coding or writing programmes. Programmers were the key, and either the Indian software companies could supply them, or placement agencies and Indian-owned mediating firms in USA would arrange to hire them from India. There was big saving to be made in shifting business from local consultants to long-distance coding workers.

Between 1990 and 1995, a change was underway in the outsourcing business. Whereas until 1990, over two-thirds of the jobs were done physically in US sites by Indians, by 2000, over two-thirds of the jobs were done in India. Instead of sending people, India was selling their service. Export of software grew at extraordinary pace (annual growth rates over 50 per cent) between 1995 and 2000, and came to form about a quarter to a third of exports in the first half of the 2000s. From this time, Indian domestic software demand also picked up.[21]

---

[20] Arvind Sahay and Ravi Swaminathan, 'Hewlett Packard India', IIM Ahmedabad Case Studies No. IIMA/MAR0361, 2005.

[21] Subhas Bhatnagar, 'India's Software Industry', in Vandana Chandra, ed., *Technology, Adaptation, and Exports: How Some Developing Countries Got it Right*, Washington DC: The World Bank, 2006, 95–124.

Even though most of the software workers came from private technical schools, many of the leading entrepreneurs were graduates of the government-run Indian Institutes of Technology. In the previous decades, the institutes of technology served two aims; that of producing technical manpower needed by domestic industrial firms, and act as a grooming school for doctoral candidates in American universities. As the outflow of doctorate hopefuls surged, the government railed in public about the 'brain drain' at the cost of the Indian taxpayer. No one knew what should be done about it. Meanwhile, engineers formed a large component of the Indian diaspora in the USA. Some of them invested money in starting firms in the Silicon Valley. Some of the others worked in the existing firms. The Indian workforce pool was familiar to these individuals, and recruits could, in principle, receive training and mentoring from them. A relationship that began in this way matured in the late 2000s as many companies, irrespective of the ethnicity of ownership or management, purchased services and products made by India-based ones.

From the end of the 1990s, the industry association and the government played an active role in sustaining the revolution. The government helped by refraining from regulating the computer hardware imports. Although India's statist industrialisation policy and defence modernisation did promote software production, the effort was of limited commercial value until 1980. As software export in the private sector grew in scale, the government relaxed hardware import and foreign investment norms in this industry. Thus it came about that 'the Indian software industry had been highly open to international trade and multinational investment from the early 1980s'.[22] An Information Technology Act (2000) did not directly help the industry, but by recognising data and similar packages as private property, facilitated the production and exchange of information technology products. The industry association, NASSCOM, played a role as negotiator, advertiser of India, and a node to collect and disseminate information on the industry.

Television

In 1959, a television transmitter was erected in Delhi. A few thousand sets were imported from Eastern Europe in the next decade.[23] The government consulted the Central Electronics and Engineering Institute (Pilani) for

[22] Murali Patibandla, Deepak Kapur, and Bent Petersen, 'Import Substitution with Free Trade: Case of India's Software Industry', *Economic and Political Weekly*, 35(15), 2000, 1263–70.
[23] I have used, in addition to several media reports, K. R. S. Murthy, 'A Note on the Television Industry', IIM Ahmedabad Case Studies No. IIMA/BP0225TEC, 1990.

suggestions on how to develop nationwide transmission. However, shortage of foreign exchange forced these initiatives to remain sporadic and small in scale. In 1969, the first Indian firm, J. K. Electronics, started producing black and white TV sets. With transmission still poor or non-existent, the industry did not seem to be going anywhere. Still, consumer interest in TV did grow. In the 1970s, the companies that would lead the television revolution had been established. These included brands like Weston, Televista, Telerad, EC, Dyanora, and Crown. All were small firms. Industrial licensing favoured small firms. These were assembling TV from imported material, the main item of import being the picture tube. Only one firm (Satish Kaura's Samtel) started making picture tube in India.

In 1982, a new game began, literally. Just before the Asian Games were to be held in New Delhi in 1982, the government opened colour TV licensing and invested heavily in transmission. In the wake of the limited liberalisation of the 1980s, television production policy became much more open than before. Foreign collaborations were easier to obtain. Import of components was allowed without licence, with heavy tariffs. The brands of the black and white era quickly became obscure, and joint ventures with Japanese electronic multinationals were formed. Companies invested in quality, advertised aggressively, went for vertical integration into components, and expanded service and retail networks. Making the television was fast becoming a business for the big as well as a big business. From the late-1980s, television was a major new advertising outlet for consumer goods, and money started flowing in into programmes and the contents. It became the symbol of a retail revolution in the making (see Box 8.1). In the 1990s, the start of the cable television boom would consolidate this revolution.

In the competition that followed, three Indian firms, BPL-India, Onida, and Videocon, did especially well. Videocon was established in 1985. The owners, Dhoot, were traders of sugar and cotton, and dealers for two wheelers, before entry into television manufacture in collaboration with Toshiba. The Mirchandani family of Delhi started Onida in collaboration with JVC of Japan. BPL was the most dramatic success story in this set. T. P. Gopalan Nambiar, a UK-returned engineer, started a small firm (British Physical Laboratories) manufacturing panel meters for defence in 1963 in Kerala. For the next twenty years, it remained a small firm. In 1982, its fortunes changed. BPL manufactured colour TV, which found a booming market, especially after the company formed a collaboration with Sanyo Corporation. From Rs. 190 million in 1983, the turnover of the group rose to Rs. 3 billion in 1988. At the same time, numerous small firms, a few state-owned firms, and one European multinational, Peico (earlier Philips), sank.

There was intense competition for retail space in the cities and towns, as marketing required talking to the potential buyer. Companies vied with each other to get dealers, who could create attractive showrooms. Since television

---

Box 8.1 **The rise of retail**

An executive of Tata Steel explained how in the old days the marketing person in a steel factory was just another officer: 'Today we have to *sell* steel' (*Business World*, 19 April 1995, 42–5, emphasis added). When the company was overhauled in the 1980s, not only technology, but also management structure changed. Management responsibility decentralised to local 'profit centres', which were in charge of both marketing and raw material purchases.

What was true of steel was truer of consumer goods. Consumer industries needed to be consumer oriented, rather than distribution oriented. A dramatic instance of how consumers started to matter was the creation of a detergent brand in the 1980s, Nirma, by Karsanbhai Patel. Using advertising and aggressive pricing, Patel took on Hindustan Lever head on, and established a 60 per cent market share in 1990. Patel's rise had a lot to do with the use of TV advertising. During the Asian Games in New Delhi in 1982, television usage started to expand, and by 1985, television was a common household good. Patel was possibly the first industrialist to make the most effective use of television advertising. The short catchy tune extolling Nirma in all major regional languages became an inseparable part of television viewing. Having lost its market share to an upstart, Hindustan Lever responded with new cheap brands, imaginative campaigns, and a low-cost distribution system, eventually wrestling some of the market back.

This transition in marketing from a wholesaler-dominated system to one based on communication with the consumer greatly encouraged the advertising industry. Briefly, this was good news for the advertising industry in the beleaguered Calcutta city. Calcutta eventually fell behind in the game when advertising became more technology driven and the big clients left the city. The fate of the iconic advertising firm, employee-run Clarion, was symptomatic of the decline.

---

alone would not be a viable basis for an expensive marketing model, the dealers traded in a range of consumer machines and brands. In this way, television aided the sale of consumer durables in general. Imaginative (and expensive) advertisement campaign featuring India's biggest film star made BPL a household brand name in the television market.

The 1990s reforms hit the domestic TV makers hard. The entry of Korean multinationals pushed BPL into the defensive, and it steadily lost buyers and employees. The company tried to reinvent itself as a telecom equipment manufacturer, but did not return to its former position. The other 1980s indigenous brands like Onida and Videocon tell the same story.

Rayon and polyester fibres – another dramatic story of the 1980s – were produced in India from the mid-twentieth century, but these were expensive fibres because of the smaller scale of the firms and the high tariffs on raw materials. This situation changed in the 1980s, with surprising results.

Synthetic Fibres

Import tariffs on the major man-made fibres and raw materials were brought down, step by step, from their peak level of 185 per cent in 1991–2 to 30 per cent in 1997–78. This dealt a blow to man-made fibre manufacturers. Between 1995 and 1999, world prices of polyester staple fibre and filament yarn crashed due to excess supply from East Asia. By 1996, the synthetic fibre industry had too much capacity located in too many units operating at an average scale below the world norm. Most firms in India making these products lost money after 1996. Less vulnerable were firms like Reliance, which commanded more assured long-term contracts. Reliance's expansion itself put further pressure on other polyester producers. Between 1990 and 1996, JCT, Baroda Rayon, J. K. Synthetics, Sanghi Polyester and Garware Nylon, leading man-made fibre manufacturers, came to the doors of the BIFR, without much success.

Baroda Rayon, a medium-scale firm engaged in rayon, nylon, and polyester, is a case in point. By 1997, burdened by unsustainable debts, it tried several revival packages that included failed attempts to sell its plants to larger producers. In 1999, its polyester unit began operation under different management, and the rayon unit shut down. From the end of 1999, the company began defaulting on salaries, leading to a spate of protests and rallies from its 4,500-strong workforce. The textile operations of J. K. Synthetics, a company of the G. H. Singhania group, was another casualty of adverse market conditions. In 1997, faced with massive debt (for some time, the company was the leader among private sector bad debtors to the banks), the company closed eight units in Kota and Jhalawar. The unemployment of 5,000 workers had a traumatic impact on the local economy, and numerous small firms ancillary to these plants also closed. In all these cases of closure, there was little resistance from workers, because the state governments showed little sympathy for them.

The nemesis of the industry, Reliance, deserves a longer account.[24] Dhirubhai Ambani (1932–2002), a school drop-out from Chorwad in Junagadh District of Gujarat, was an employee in the Burmah Shell office in Aden in his early life. He returned to Bombay to join a trading firm in partnership with a cousin. The firm imported polyester filament yarn and exported spices, and maintained connection with Aden. The textile trading ran into difficulties and induced Ambani to end the partnership and consider manufacturing cloth in India.

In 1966, Reliance Textile Industries Private Limited was incorporated. It had a synthetic fabrics factory in Naroda near Ahmedabad. In 1973, Reliance acquired another synthetic fabric plant, and in 1975, became a public

---

[24] S. C. Kuchhal et al., 'Reliance Textile Industries Limited', IIM Ahmedabad Case Studies No. IIMA/F&A0339(A, B, C, and D), 1980.

company. In 1980, Reliance was one of the most modern textile factories in India, and one of the largest. It was then an officially designated 'monopoly' concern, and potentially a target for investigation or denial of licences to expand. Polyester fabrics were rising in demand. Many textile mills purchased the yarn produced by the company, though the major part of the yarn was used in the fabrics division of the company.

Its expansion and backward integration had been achieved by two principal means, both of which were unusual in the backdrop of the moribund textile industry in the 1970s. One of these was innovation in marketing. Instead of depending on wholesalers supplying anonymous consumers, Reliance invested in advertisement and dealt directly with retailers of cloth to establish its fabric brand Vimal. By 1980, the firm had more than 1,000 franchised retail outlets, and the company spent four times more on advertising than its nearest rival Bombay Dyeing. The second strategy was financial. Instead of generating resources from retained profits, which would limit growth, or raising money mainly from banks, which would make investments unsustainably expensive, the firm raised money from the market by means of a variety of hybrids between debt and equity, such as convertible debentures and preference shares. These instruments were expensive too, but less so than bank debt. The method of financing diversified the investor base, which included shareholders, holders of debentures of various types, and holders of cash certificates and deposits. Financiers included a large body of ordinary investors, employees and former employees, and banks and financial institutions. This diversity of instruments and investor bases insulated the company from stock market speculation, and allowed it to spread risks.

Ambani used the money in continuous growth and modernisation. After 1977, Reliance shareholders got such exceptionally good value year after year that the conversion of debentures into equity occurred easily and raising more money by fresh debentures became easier too. This combined strategy – continuous modernisation, innovative financing in a high-cost capital market, and advertising – made Reliance a safe bet for the financial institutions. In turn, its goodwill with the banks enabled the company to raise foreign currency loans via Indian banks, which were used to finance machines purchased abroad. The company's extraordinary growth continued into the 1980s. The Naroda plant replaced its machines, and installed a computerised information system.

In 1983, the company, now renamed Reliance Industries Limited, set up a plant in the Patalganga industrial district near Bombay under technical collaboration of Du Pont. The plant backward integrated into petrochemicals, especially the manufacture of purified terephthalic acid or PTA, a major raw material for polyester yarn. The expansion plan became famous for the efficiency and energy with which the plant was erected, in a record time after obtaining the industrial licence. In the mid-1980s, Reliance produced PTA, used PTA in its textile plant, and sold PTA to other polyester yarn manufacturers, which had tended to switch from dimethyl terephthalate or DMT to the use of PTA in the process. A by-product of this tendency was that Bombay Dyeing, Reliance's main rival, and a leading manufacturer of DMT, faced difficulties.

Throughout the 1970s, but especially in the 1980s, Reliance was a controversial company. It constructed its accounts in such a manner that it legally evaded paying taxes. The textile plant was always dependent on import of expensive raw material in a regulated regime. When it was a fabric manufacturer and importer of polyester yarn, it needed import licence. Licence was more easily obtained upon a commitment to export the goods made with imported material. The company, it was alleged, used its influence in chambers of commerce to obtain import licence and divert the material to the market. Polyester was expensive in India, but the government between 1982 and 1984 was said to have given the company special tariff privileges. Reliance got away with investment plans without seeking all the necessary clearances from the Monopolies and Restrictive Trade Practices Commission, the Industries Ministry, and the Commerce Ministry, it was alleged. Financing ran into rough weather when, in 1994, the government-owned Unit Trust of India suffered heavy losses because a private placement of Reliance shares lost value soon after the deal. Again, it was said, the deal had been managed.[25]

Although he was close to several political figures, Ambani's achievement cannot be explained fully with political favours. In fact, friendships in Delhi had a price attached in the form of rivalry and bad publicity, and Reliance experienced both. There were two other ingredients in the success of the firm, relentless backward integration from textiles to yarn to fibre to petrochemicals to natural gas extraction; and financial innovation. Those who attacked Ambani underestimated the innovations in marketing, financing, and technological modernisation, and the synergy achieved between the three, on which the extraordinary growth of the company was founded. Corporate scandal in the backdrop of an insanely regulated economy can have a different meaning from just any scandal. As Prem Shankar Jha, an economics writer, pointed out, honesty was a relative virtue. Did 'the laws that reliance has violated ever made sense'?[26]

[25] For more details on these controversies, see Hamish McDonald, *Mahabharata in Polyester: The Making of the World's Richest Brothers and Their Feud*, Sydney: University of New South Wales Press, 2010.

[26] 'The Reliance Example', *India Today*, 15 September, 1986. An excellent short biographical sketch of Ambani cites the view that the flouting of rules exposed the irrationality of the rules, and made liberalization inevitable. Sunil Khilnani, *Incarnations: A History of India in 50 Lives*, London: Penguin, 2017, 419–28.

In the 1990s, after India's economic reforms had enabled Indian firms to access foreign capital markets, the last major expansion plan in Dhirubhai Ambani's lifetime took place. Foreign institutional investment was still modest in India. But it was possible to raise shareholding abroad via the bank-mediated route of Global Depository Receipts (GDR). The bank was the depository, which issued receipts to investors carrying an entitlement to share ownership. An Indian company raising equity capital abroad was an unusual event. To Reliance's advantage, its plant was world scale in capacity and technological capability. In 1992, expansion in the petrochemicals plant was expected to be financed by the GDR route. The attempt did not meet expectations, though a convertible bond issue next year was more successful. In 1994, the UTI scandal soured relations between Morgan Stanley, the bank that mediated Reliance's entry in global capital market, and the company. In the second half of the 1990s, the company shifted to Euro and 'Yankee' bonds, a move that was eased by relatively low and steady interest rates.

Aviation

Commercial aviation was reopened to private investment around 1990, while retaining a slew of rules and regulations about where private companies could operate, about the scale and fleet composition of carriers, and about the use of state-owned infrastructure. The regulations were sometimes justified with reference to social welfare objectives. In an uncharitable view, they protected the market for the two government carriers, Air India and Indian Airlines. The government taxed aviation fuel heavily. There were not enough pilots and managers with experience in the business. All that added to the costs of the business.

India's airport infrastructure was primitive and not ready for the growth of consumption traffic that was about to take place. In 2005, of the 94 civil airports managed by the government, 29 were not in use, and 54 did not have runways suitable for large aircrafts. They were mostly World War II runways, too short for modern aircraft, and many were far away from the city. The busiest routes were those between the big cities, especially between Delhi and Bombay. These two airports were not then capable of accommodating a rapidly growing load easily. Private companies needed to spend extra money on repairs. Overall, this was a high-cost business, though one with a growing clientele.

Given these problems, it is a surprise that between 1994 and 1997 seven new airlines were started. The reason for the popularity was that consumers were eager to avoid the government carrier and switched to the private ones with pleasure. In 2000, nearly half the business was carried on by private carriers. But only two of the private entrants had survived by then. As we see in Chapter 9, the industry continued to be held back by regulation and insufficient infrastructure, but the entrepreneurial drive that had been unleashed continued to produce offbeat ventures. The story continues in the next chapter, when a spate of new entry in the 2000s will be discussed.

During the worst years of investment regulation, some Indian business groups had ventured abroad. They set a trend.

Indian Multinationals

Godrej and Aditya Birla had made investments in Southeast Asia during the 1970s. Mafatlal's Indian Dyestuff had set up a joint venture in Thailand. The Sanjay Dalmia group acquired a palm oil plantation and refining company in Malaysia. But these remained unusual examples until the 1990s, when several medium-sized businesses decided to go global. The government enabled automatic clearance of such proposals in 1994, following which a number of Indian companies set up joint ventures abroad. At the end of 1994, 524 government approvals were sought for investment abroad under joint ventures with partner firms.[27] These decisions did not necessarily reflect their strengths as global players. More often in this time, the decisions were a response to regulation in India, and sometimes were opportunistic moves. Privatisation of state-owned companies in host countries, for example, presented unusual chances to those willing to move.

Persistence of regulation in the host country or in India was important in the case of Hero Motors' decision to acquire a plant in Mauritius, where assembly of mopeds from imported parts attracted significantly lesser duty than import of assembled mopeds. Controlled drug prices encouraged Ranbaxy to go to Nigeria. By 1995, Ranbaxy had 'a marketing network straddling three continents and fully-owned subsidiaries in four'.[28] Arvind Mills of the Kasturbhai Lalbhai group went to Russia (then Commonwealth of Independent States) to escape textile export quotas imposed by the Multifibre Arrangement. The brand image of Indian products was so low that some firms found export from India more difficult than production abroad. Like Ranbaxy in Africa, Lupin set up production base in Southeast Asia. The Indonesian-Indian firm Indo Rama Synthetics and Mittals in steel went global to access markets in South America, Africa, Southeast Asia, and West Asia, countries where revived income growth had spurred a boom in construction. Due to abysmal conditions of

---

[27] 'Stepping Out', *Business World*, 3 May 1995, 44–6.   [28] Ibid.

Indian ports, and generally limited domestic expertise in trading, trade costs remained high from India, which mattered to bulk goods such as steel especially.[29] A few of the cases where Indian companies acquired companies abroad were dogged by money laundering scandals, including two in Germany.[30]

Business Organisation

Transformation of Business Groups

The industrialisation drive and the licensing regime had encouraged families with money to diversify in a range of unrelated businesses. The 1980s consumer boom strengthened the tendency. Groups wanted to have a share of television, packaged food, and garments: the rising goods. As the deregulation became more general and competition increased, there was a reverse tendency from the 1990s, to de-merge, divide, and divest. Large and diversified business groups divested businesses unrelated to their core advantage, expanded within the core areas, inducted non-family professional managers, and decentralised management. They did this sometimes with the help of consultant companies in a planned manner. From the media attention that the process drew, the changes in the top ten or fifteen groups had a demonstration effect on others. More than that, the changes meant the deepening of a top-end managerial labour market, and a bigger role for paid consultants in family firms.

For example, around 1992, the R. P. Goenka or RPG group of Calcutta, in common with many Indian business conglomerates that had expanded into unrelated fields, faced the prospect of demergers and disinvestments to shed non-priority or losing ventures, and mergers of related businesses to form stronger companies. The latter process was pursued in part with the help of joint ventures (CEAT with Goodyear, ICIN with Ricoh). From the late 1980s, Escorts diversified into several unrelated fields, including garments, food and telecommunications, but returned to concentrate on tractors in the 2000s. The metallurgical firm Kalyani of Pune diversified into unrelated areas (such as television) in the 1980s, eventually returning to its core field, forging.

In several cases, the process of dividing up assets joined a parallel process, division of assets among family members who wanted to separate.

---

[29] 'Surajeet Das Gupta and Usha Nagarajan, 'Global Gambit', *Business World*, 29 December 1993 to 11 January 1994,
[30] Discussed in 'Stepping Out'.

Transformation of the Family

The concept of the family firm underwent a change, from extended families to individualistic ones, even as the prominence of the family as owner-cum-manager remained intact. What was this a change from? As we have seen (Chapter 5), before independence, in most Indian-owned firms, the owner had a large controlling stake, was physically engaged in day-to-day working, recruited managers from friends and relations, and had firm control on leadership succession. That situation continued for some time after 1947. In fact, the licensing system reinforced it. Under the licensing regime, getting licence was a bigger challenge than running a company. Professional skills were not so crucial. Licence would be more easily obtained on the reputation of the group or the family. A Marwari businessperson tells me that the concerns of the patriarch of a business family was often to settle the sons in unrelated businesses so that they would not compete with each other for the rest of their lives. This social ethic would find the government's licensing system, and takeover of vulnerable British companies, useful tools to keep peace in the family. But the expansion of the groups soon hit demographic and cultural limits. The number of sons a patriarch could possibly have, and how peaceful relations in a large family could be, set limits to the ability of the patriarch to maintain control over the group or on the process of transition.

Inside some of the families, the pressure to divide assets between siblings had grown after the death of the founder. Between 1952 and 2000, almost all of the major business groups split, usually among brothers, and not always in a friendly fashion. In the colonial era, few cases of succession disputes and splits can be found. By contrast, in the first thirty years after independence, Goenka, Mafatlal, Modi, Shri Ram, and Birla, among others, divided up their groups. The Delhi-based DCM group split around 1989–90 among three cousins; textiles and Daurala Sugar went to one; real estates, foundry, data products, automobiles to a second; and Mawana Sugar and fertiliser units to a third. Bombay's textile family Piramal divided up the assets among three brothers in the 1980s. One of the brothers Ajay Piramal, inheritor of the Morarjee Goculdas mill, tried to revive the mill in the 1990s with modest success, and at the same time diversified into pharmaceuticals by purchasing a company. With a large market share in sorbitrates, Nicholas Piramal grew into one of the more profitable pharmaceutical companies of the 1990s. In the 2000s, some of the mill land owned by family was converted into shopping malls.

In Calcutta, Magneerum and his brother Ram Kumar's grandsons quarrelled over division of the estate, which allegedly took a toll on the Bangur group in the 1970s and the 1980s. A barely amicable division was effected in 1988, but dissensions continued long after the division partly because the division was apparently done by verbal agreement. One of the group companies, Carbon Corporation, where the succession rule was not clearly set out saw takeover attempts from within the clan. In South India, there were a series of divisions, less high-profile than those that occurred in northern and western India. The leading business family of the textile town Coimbatore, the Lakshmi group started by G. Kuppuswamy Naidu, divided up among three brothers in the early 1980s. At the time of the split, the group was the largest manufacturers of spinning machinery in India. In India Cements, the descendants of the two founders quarrelled, and the company came to be managed by the nominees of financial institutions, and managed badly. In 1989, T. S. Narayanaswamy's son N. Srinivasan took control, and India Cements gradually revived.[31]

Not all family disputes were over division. Some involved struggle for control over individual companies. A famous struggle for control occurred in Dharamsi Morarji Chemical Co. In the 1970s, the two sons of the founder Ratansi Morarji died, and the son-in-law of Ratansi Morarji's daughter, R. M. Goculdas, was invited to take charge of the company. In the 1980s, as the company ran into trouble, the direct descendants of the founder tried to wrest back control, with Goculdas stoutly resisting the move. Goculdas eventually won the battle.

One group that seemingly survived unscathed by division was Godrej. Godrej managed to stay a tightly family-controlled group, which made its expansion path more tradition-bound and undramatic. If there were succession issues, these were settled quietly behind the scenes. Godrej survived the transition to the liberal regime with fewer problems than most. The wave of consumerism in the 1980s was good news for the group, but made competition in cosmetics and soaps between the two market leaders, Hindustan Lever and Godrej, more intense than ever. More niche products were offered, and marketing and advertisement changed in the process.

Economic liberalisation speeded up the process of family division and increased the risk of disputes over control. Competition made running the companies a bigger challenge than obtaining licences. It also made some firms vulnerable and some succeed, which encouraged a parting of the ways between brothers who managed different companies and experienced different fortunes. Studies find that after the split, businesses tended to increase the stake of the owner or family in the firms they now controlled. Around 80 per cent of India's Fortune-500 companies in 1994 were still family-owned. Whether the

---

[31] The company was in the news in recent years, being the largest sponsor of cricket in the country.

aggregate trend should be called continuity of the family or the end of the family is a question of perspective.

There is evidence to show that family-owned and family-managed firms still remain important on a significant scale worldwide. India is no exception to the rule. The finding points at enduring strength of the stem-and-branch type business group, a group that develops around the family name (stem) and uses it to economise on branch operations.[32] Family control over firms is almost identical with concentrated control of shareholding or ownership.[33]

The family still ruled in the 1990s and beyond. But it ruled differently. The family's role in running companies underwent a change in the recent years. Sustaining a total hold of the family upon both strategy and operation, and between investment and management, was incompatible with the growth of the firm itself. After liberalisation, with few exceptions, Indian firms needed to grow bigger to attain something near the scale of their international rivals or joint venture partners. There were several roads available to them. The first road was joint ventures. Where they took the road of forming joint ventures with a much bigger foreign partner, the partner demanded control, and some-times managed to wrest control from the family. The second road was to grow smaller and remain specialised. Conglomerates were divided up between members of the family. If this strategy gave the owners control on strategy and operation, it inevitably left some branches (brothers) with the challenge to grow big quickly. Many older groups – one example being Mafatlal – failed to do this. In short, joint ventures and division into niche areas did not work for all, not at least from the 1990s.

'So what role does the family play now?' asked a magazine article in 1994 in relation to Essar Steel.[34] The article said that increasingly the 'family' component focused on policy-making and new projects, while the operational side was delegated to professionals. In steel, professionalisation worked par-ticularly well, thanks to the ease with which public sector steel companies, including government project consultancy firms, could be poached on for engineers and managers with substantial experience in the industry.

The revival from the 1980s also entailed major changes in the financing of industry.

---

[32] Tarun Khanna and Krishna Palepu, 'Is Group Affiliation Profitable in Emerging Markets? An Analysis of Diversified Indian Business Groups', *Journal of Finance*, 55(2), 2000, 867–91. See also discussion in Chapter 1.

[33] Rafael La Porta et al. interprets the persistence of concentrated control as an effect of legal regimes that emerged in the non-Western world as a result of European expansion. Concen-tration is a by-product of poor legal protection of minority shareholders, or a particular failure and weakness of colonial law. Rafael La Porta, Florencio Lopez-de-Silanes, and Andrei Shleifer, 'Corporate Ownership around the World', *Journal of Finance*, 54(2), 1999, 471–517.

[34] 'The Ruias go Professional', *Business World*, 28 December 1994, 82–3.

Financing Industry

'Major diversifications and expansions in the eighties – cement, shipping, paper and pulp – were all financed from internal accruals and loans.'[35] This statement, made in relation to one of the largest business conglomerates (B. K. Birla group), would apply with greater force to smaller groups. Indian companies preferred to raise money from institutions in this time, and if they went to the share market at all, preferred fixed-interest instruments that would attract investors and yet avoid takeover threats. The strategy raised the debt-equity ratio above the international standards, and made investments either more expensive or more risky or both than it should be. It discouraged investments, relatively speaking.

The financial institutions changed the rules of the game in the 1980s. A string of financial institutions had been set up between 1955 and 1965, including the Industrial Credit and Investment Corporation (1955, joint venture with the World Bank and domestic companies, and parent of the ICICI Bank today), the Industrial Development Bank of India (1964, parent of IDBI Bank now), and the Industrial Finance Corporation of India (1956). IDBI was initially a subsidiary of the central bank, and nationalised in 1976. IFCI was initially meant to fund government projects, and could finance private investment from 1972. Their involvement in the private corporate sector sharply increased in the 1980s. These semi-government financial institutions bought company shares.

With or without government participation, the resort to equity finance made Indian firms more vulnerable to losing control. A few well-publicised episodes of the 1980s reveals the risk, and the unpredictable role the government institutions could play in struggles for control. Government institutions were critical to the success of takeover bids in Shaw Wallace (Chhabria), CESC (R. P. Goenka), Best and Crompton (Vijay Mallya), and India Cements (N. Srinivasan and N. Sankar), and critical to the failure of the bid in Larsen and Toubro, Gammon India, Escorts, and DCM.

The unsuccessful attempt by the British businessman Swraj Paul to take over DCM and Escorts in 1982 was one of the first such episodes. A Dubai-based trader, Manohar Chhabria raided Shaw Wallace, Mather and Platt, and Dunlop in quick succession in the 1980s. His bid for a fourth company, Gammon India, failed. Without tacit support of the financial institutions which held chunks of shares in these firms, the moves would not usually work. In Shaw Wallace, after a protracted battle with the incumbent management, Chhabria got that support. In Gammon, he did not.

---

[35] N. Radhakrishnan and Durgesh Shah, 'A Fine Finish', *Business India*, 20 February 1989, 68–71.

The post-takeover history of these firms was colourful. Chhabria succeeded in inducing a bunch of top managers to leave their employers and join these companies, and then failed to persuade them to stay on. Within three to four years of the takeover, the companies were in trouble. Insiders attributed the syndrome to Chhabria's 'feudal' style of management.[36] He apparently expected his senior executives to oversee birthdays and marriages in the family. At the very least, he was said to constantly interfere with and overturn executive decisions. By 1994, the companies were experiencing a 'run' on executives. Whether Chhabria could have turned them around is an academic question, for he died in 2002, and the companies were either sold or went bankrupt.

In July and August 1988, Larsen and Toubro shares rose sharply, when first Manu Chhabria and then Dhirubhai Ambani started buying up large quantities of the shares of the firm, while maintaining in public that they did not plan a takeover. Early in the contest, Ambanis went ahead of Chhabria and were invited to join the board. For Reliance, the acquisition would achieve synergy between the engineering firm and petrochemical projects under construction. The transfers involved large-scale transactions between the government-owned financial institutions, in particular, Life Insurance Corporation, a finance company set up by the Bank of Baroda, and Ambani's friend the Unit Trust of India. The media hinted at collusive arrangements between some members of the company's board, the Ambanis, and the institutions. In 1989, a suit was filed in court challenging the takeover by Ambani, and a new centre-left government in Delhi decided to act against the bid. On this occasion, as in several others, the governmental financial companies appeared to the media as tools in the hands of corporate raiders. Hints of corruption and collusion were present. At the very least, the institutions appeared arbitrary in the way they intervened in the boards.

Mahindra and Mahindra was another company in which the family stake was small, and the majority shareholders were the institutions. Since the Swraj Paul episode, the press speculated frequently about imminent takeover moves on the company. In 1990, a series of magazine articles speculated that a Delhi-based businessman whose son had married into the Mahindra family, and 'his NRI friends', had acquired sufficient stake from the market to take control of the company, and that the institutions had 'blessed' the alliance. The company vehemently denied the stories, inducted the successor Anand Mahindra into management of the company, and eventually media interest died down.[37]

---

[36] 'Manu Chhabria's Vanishing Managers', *Business World*, 29 December 1993 – 11 January 1994, 64–6.
[37] N. Radhakrishna, 'An Unseemly Affair', *Business India*, 9–22 July 1990, 71–2.

Box 8.2 **Small-scale industry, 1980–2000**

The Green Revolution of the 1970s created savings among wealthy and middle-class farmers. The hosiery cluster in Ludhiana and Tiruppur, and the power-loom cluster near Erode town in Tamil Nadu, reflect such local capital accumulation process especially well. One well-researched case is that of the Gounders of Tamil Nadu. Originally small peasants, they had an involvement with the handloom industry going back to the interwar period. This link between textiles and farming was more firmly established in the 1980s. In surveys done in the late 1980s, the older generation of Gounder heads of textile firms still straddled agriculture and industry, though the younger generation had committed themselves to industry. A further cluster of successful enterprise came from garments, gems and jewellery, leather, and spinning mills, where local capitalists at large moved in to take advantage of a booming export market since the 1980s. The generic category 'handicrafts' emerged a major export item in the 2000s.

Notwithstanding segments of export success, the general picture within the small-scale sector was very mixed. The growth rate of small firms fell in the 1990s. Product reservation for the small firm harmed the interests of those whom it sought to protect. It discouraged small firms from expanding in a legal way. Down-the-scale biases led to poor technological effort, quality control, marketing, and brand-creation. Small firms were badly served also by corrupt customs office and poor infrastructure of the small towns.

The government of the states nurtured the traditional forms of handloom weaving (see Chapters 3–5 on their history) by encouraging cooperatives and subsidisation. In the face of a steady fall in demand for traditional apparel, these moves were of doubtful effect, though they certainly did sustain a large number of otherwise unviable craft textiles. On the other side, a segment of traditional crafts continued to rely on private marketing to elite consumers, persistence with traditional designs and small innovations, to cater to a wealthy urban market. It is impossible to be accurate on the proportion of these two segments.

Readings: M. H. Bala Subrahmanya, 'Small Industry and Globalisation: Implications, Performance and Prospects', *Economic and Political Weekly*, 2004, 1826–34; Maureen Liebl and Tirthankar Roy, 'Handmade in India: Status Report on Indian Artisans', *Economic and Political Weekly*, 38(51), 2003–4, 5366–73; Tirthankar Roy, 'Handicrafts', in Kaushik Basu, ed., *Oxford Companion to Economics in India*, New Delhi: Oxford University Press, 2007, 241–43.
On Gounder enterprise, see Sharad Chari, *Fraternal Capital: Peasant-Workers, Self-Made Men, and Globalization in Provincial India*, Stanford, CA: Stanford University Press, 2004; Harish Damodaran, *India's New Capitalists. Caste, Business, and Industry in a Modern Nation*, Basingstoke: Palgrave Macmillan, 2008.

In the 1990s, the game changed again. Soon after the reforms began, the financial institutions reinvented themselves as banks, and the cushion of joint ventures was no more available either. Stock markets would play a bigger role than before. Market capitalisation data before 1990 are hard to obtain. In 1990, market capitalisation of listed companies in the Indian stock markets was less than half a per cent of the world. From that level, there was a large but unsteady increase in the share in the next 25 years (Chapter 9).

Conclusion

Towards the end of the period studied in this chapter, India faced a recession. Coalition governments formed with the support of leftist and populist parties revived the prospect of a return of regulation, and slowed the process of reform. The East Asian economic crisis hit India hard, partly because of contagion effect on foreign investment elsewhere, and partly, in the previous decade the two regions had developed closer ties than before.

The recovery came from an unexpected source: Indian software technicians' creditable performance in sorting out the Y2K problem. From the 2000s, corporate investment revived, but now with a substantial interest in the service industries – software, communication, travel and tourism, education, health-care, and construction – as we see in the next chapter.

9   Capital and Globalisation: 2000–2015

In the wake of the economic reforms of 1992, there was a burst of investment and export, and the economy grew at 6–8 per cent per year for the next four years. In 1997, there was a sharp drop. Thereafter, for about six years, overall economic growth in India fluctuated a lot. The Asian economic recession contributed to the 1997 dip, but short-lived governments formed of unstable coalitions, with the communist parties as partners, contributed to the uncertainty. From 2002–3, the political situation stabilised. The prospects for the world economy improved, and Indian growth bounced back.

Some things changed between the years before the erratic growth phase and the years after. 'Globalisation' is a useful expression to summarise the changes, since both foreign trade and foreign investment played a bigger role during the latter years. Globalisation means different things to different people. It is necessary to make its use more precise here. I use 'globalisation' to mean the capacity to buy knowledge from the world. In the late nineteenth century, this capacity was created in India via export of textiles and agricultural commodities. In the middle years of the twentieth century and the Nehruvian pursuit of 'heavy' industry at any cost, the capacity was impaired. The companies making and selling textiles or agricultural goods, and companies with pre-existing contact with traders abroad, were damaged. From the turn of the twenty-first century, the capacity to buy knowledge abroad was regained by selling labour services and labour-intensive manufactures. This in turn enabled corporate firms to procure the know-how needed to make things for Indian buyers.

Business development is a macroeconomic balancing act because the process in India needs capital, knowledge, and some types of skills still in shortage in the country. Openness to trade and factor movements is an absolute necessity for macroeconomic balance. The balance was restored from the 1990s. The restoration was not all scripted by the state. India was lucky too. The huge fall in communication cost, and the maturing of the information technology revolution made services – traditionally not traded very much – more tradable throughout the world. Indian capital joined the movement as a supplier as well as a consumer. As it did, more money than before flowed from abroad into India, much of it going into the services.

Good market conditions prevailed for well over a decade since 2003. The world recession of 2008–09 disturbed the process, but only for a single year. Besides, depending on their exposure to trade and currency fluctuations, companies were affected in different ways during the 2008–09 international economic crisis, and some escaped with little damage.[1] Stable conditions prevailed for a length of time, which was necessary for deeper institutional changes to occur.

If these changes lead us to expect a paradigm shift, the expectation may well be justified. Few companies and few business groups that dominated the post-1950 import-substitution experiment in India figured among the largest companies in the recent years. There was a similarly progressive obscurity of the business group or the conglomerate. Companies followed their own trajectories, based on an identity and customer base quite independent of those of the family or the group name. Tata is a good example of this. Among the dozens of companies that the group owns, the most valuable are automobiles and software, and these are completely unrelated businesses. The reduced power of individuals and increased value of companies and managers made lobbying more institutionalised than before. Political attitude changed. The lobbying process involved, as before, trying to influence party positions during legislation. But the role of lobbying-by-bribery is less visible now than before.

The time is too recent to offer definite conclusions on how deeply business conditions changed, and why some things did not change. We can only identify some dominant and unfinished tendencies, which this chapter will attempt to do.

The Structure of Investment

How different were the fifteen years of the new millennium, from 1950 to 1980, and from 1980 to 2000? Fig. 9.1 shows that gross investment rate was higher than ever before, but there was a substitution of government investment for private corporate investment. The graph has three separate hills, the first one (1955–65) was led by the government with a minor contribution from the corporate sector, the second one (1971/2–1994/5) was driven by the government and a slow recovery of private investment, the third one (2003–07 in Fig. 9.1, the graph picks up after the 2007–08 world depression) was mainly a contribution of private investment.

The government in the period 1950–80 recycled the taxpayers' money or took foreign aid from abroad. In the 1980s, aid proportion (in GDP or net investment) fell, but borrowings increased. Where did the private sector get

---

[1] Avinash Paranjape, 'Economic Slowdown and the Indian Corporate Sector', *Vikalpa*, 34(3), 2009, 53–8.

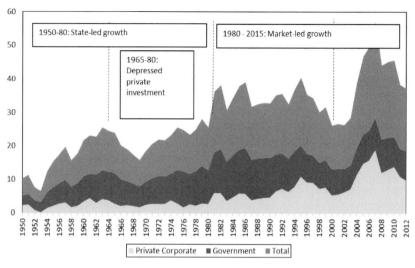

Fig. 9.1 Gross capital formation (per cent of GDP) 1950–2012

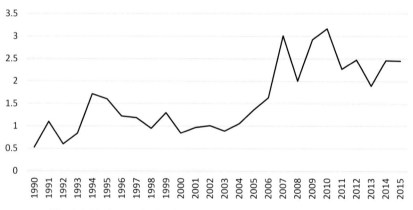

Fig. 9.2 Market capitalisation of Indian companies (per cent of world) 1990–2015

its savings from? It did mainly from its own savings, which increased as a proportion of GDP. In the 1980s, however, the stock market played an increasing role in providing investment finance. As a joint outcome of stock market contribution and economic growth, market capitalisation of listed companies rose (Fig. 9.2). In the 2000s, foreign institutional investment changed the game substantially. Subsequently, market capitalisation trend was not only larger, but also more unsteady than before. Despite the surge

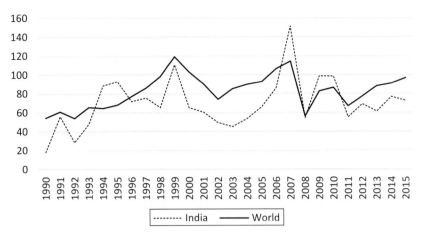

Fig. 9.3 Market capitalisation of listed companies (per cent of GDP)
1990–2015

in investment and the bigger contribution of the stock market, it cannot be said that the private corporate sector had a larger presence in 2015 in the national economy than it had in 2000 (Fig. 9.3). It had a bigger presence no doubt, but the rise was unsteady. With the occasional outflow of foreign money, there were big falls too. In relation to world trend, India's public companies have grown in market capitalisation as a proportion of national income, but again, the difference in the trend is not large. It is probable that there was a wider divergence in the 1970s. Comparative data for that decade are rather patchy.

What were the big companies? And who were the non-corporate business investors in these 15 years?

Big Companies and Small Ones

The list of 20 large business groups or companies in 1980 contained textiles, steel, automobiles, shipping, and cement. A similar list for 1990 still figured old textile groups like Mafatlal, JCT (Thapar), Grasim and Century Textiles (both Birla), Tata Steel, and TELCO. Fertilisers and aluminium would be added items. In a similar list for 2016, Tata Steel, textile, cement, aluminium, and fertiliser dropped out of the list (by market capitalisation, see Table 9.1), even though with a few exceptions the individual companies have seen expansion. Nearly half of the big private companies in the list were companies that started to rise in the 1980s, and were of a comparatively new type. IT firms, pharmaceutical companies, and Reliance are the main examples.

Table 9.1 *Top 25 Companies 2016 (bold means private ownership)*

	Economic Times, based on revenue	Forbes 2000, based on market capitalisation
1	Indian Oil Corporation	**Reliance Industries**
2	**Reliance Industries**	State Bank of India
3	**Tata Motors**	Oil and Natural Gas Corporation
4	State Bank of India	**ICICI Bank**
5	Bharat Petroleum Corporation	**HDFC Bank**
6	Hindustan Petroleum Corporation	**Tata Motors**
7	**Rajesh Exports**	Indian Oil Corporation
8	Oil and Natural Gas Corporation	**Tata Consultancy Services**
9	**Tata Steel**	NTPC
10	**Tata Consultancy Services**	Housing Development Finance Corporation
11	**Bharti Airtel**	**Bharti Airtel**
12	**Larsen & Toubro**	Coal India
13	**ICICI Bank**	**Axis Bank**
14	**Hindalco Industries**	**Larsen & Toubro**
15	Coal India	**Infosys Ltd.**
16	National Thermal Power Corporation (NTPC)	Bharat Petroleum Corporation
17	**Mahindra & Mahindra**	**Wipro**
18	**HDFC Bank**	**ITC**
19	**Vedanta**	Bank of Baroda
20	**Infosys**	Punjab National Bank
21	**Maruti Suzuki India**	**Kotak Mahindra Bank**
22	Punjab National Bank	**Mahindra & Mahindra**
23	Gas Authority of India Ltd	Power Grid of India
24	**Wipro**	**HCL Technologies**
25	Housing Development Finance Corporation	Canara Bank

Source: http://economictimes.indiatimes.com/et500 (accessed 5 May 2017); www.forbes.com/global2000/#/country:India (accessed 5 May 2017).

In 2016, 56 Indian companies figured in the Forbes Global 2000 list. The number is small, measured in market capitalisation the aggregate is smaller still, but the number is growing. In 2007, it was 34. And individually, the ten largest privately owned Indian companies in the list improved their rank. The list, in fact, is dominated by banks and oil companies, with a few exceptions, all government-owned. Among private firms, Reliance, Tata Motors, Larsen & Toubro, and ITC, which figure among the ten largest Indian companies, mainly do business in the Indian market. Reliance Industries is diversified, but its major interest is in energy and petrochemicals. If we exclude the exporting IT companies, the extraordinary growth of the others had owed to the growth of the Indian market in the 1980s, combined with better capability to raise capital abroad.

Two other sets emerged to prominence by exporting knowledge-intensive goods in the 2000s. The IT firms, TCS, Wipro and Infosys, are export-oriented companies developing software and IT-enabled services. And close behind are a cluster of pharmaceutical companies. Pharmaceutical production was helped by the import-substituting state, but the three firms that figure in the Forbes list expanded after that regime had ended.

Except for software and drugs, the large company was not the dominant player in exports in the 2000s. The bulk of the exports originated in firms that are unlikely to figure in a listing of big companies like Forbes 2000. The most global segment in Indian business consisted of smaller sized firms that dominated the IT industry, as well as garment, leather, and gem exports. Small firms did get big. The Bangalore-based jewellery manufacturer and trader, Rajesh Exports, shown in the left-hand column of Table 9.1, is the tip of that particular iceberg of labour-intensive industry and trade. But broadly speaking, it is the small and the non-corporate that defined India's comparative advantage better than did companies like Reliance or Tata Motors.

The presence of small firms in the export industries can be attributed to low wages and labour abundance. But that would be too simplistic an explanation. In fact, the success of the garment industry in South Asia showed that skills, technology, and marketing mattered as much as low wages. The importance of craft skills was a very important inherited resource in India. The major centres of garment production for trade in India were quite different between them, the difference emerged from local capability, culture, and institutions. For example, a pool of skilled craft labour made Calcutta a hub of niche fashion garments. Caste-based recruitment and employment were, until recently, common in the knitwear cluster of Tiruppur in South India. In garment clusters near Delhi, a combination of male migrants and female home workers were more common.[2] These variations suggest that reducing the success of garment export to the low wages of generic labour is not enough. Skills mattered, and organisation mattered because skills needed to be managed. The ability to create value by saving on a variety of transaction cost over a chain of transactions from the small firm to the department store makes for business success in this sphere. The value chain analysts (see next) recognises this point. The people who performed these tasks were trading firms. Innovations in trade and internationalisation of trade joined craft skills to make these exports successful.

Of the exporting clusters, software firms represent a distinct type of comparative advantage. The start of the software industry has been discussed in the previous chapter. The next section discusses some of the differences between the 1990s and the 2000s.

---

[2] Alessandra Mezzadri, 'Backshoring, Local Sweatshop Regimes and CSR in India', *Competition and Change*, 18(4), 2014, 327–44.

Information Technology

The two major processes in the industry – explosive growth of outsourcing and the shift from projects to sale of products – had started in the 1990s and continued in the 2000s. One other factor joined the trend: the growth of domestic demand for IT. The industry polarised in the process. A few large corporate firms specialised in export, and several thousand small firms catered mainly to domestic clients. The large companies included domestic giants, such as, HCL, TCS, Wipro, and Infosys, and the Indian branches of Western companies like IBM, Cognizant, and Accenture. One explanation for this structure is the general and persistent shortage of capital in India. Although the government subsidised the costs of infrastructure of software firms by setting up technology parks, the capital costs of large-scale operation could still be overwhelming. Among other costs, global operation requires investment in branches, subsidiaries, and partner firms abroad. On the other side, entry barriers in the domestic market were small, and with a good communication line, work-sites could be set up anywhere. These conditions favoured the small firm. Scale and global operations enabled access to large contracts. Thus, size reinforced growth.

After 2000, academic research on the IT business flourished. The software export phenomenon seemed to call into question received views about skills, entrepreneurship, and firms. One long-held idea to become unstable was, why multinational companies or MNCs existed at all. In the 1970s and the 1980s, MNC presence in the third world would be explained in relation to technological or brand monopoly, and direct knowledge of the host country milieu. Companies like TCS or Infosys that became international from an Indian base did not fit this description. These 'new-international' or 'born global' firms, of which the software industry worldwide had many examples, required a substantial revision in the concept of the MNC. Rather than technological monopoly, a capability of technology development accounts for their globalisation better.

Another idea that was called into question was the drain of skills or 'brain drain'. Being a people-oriented industry, IT involved systematic migration of individuals, sometimes resettlement. Until 2000, in the academic literature skilled outmigration was seen to cause brain drain. In the IT case, however, brain drain was a misnomer, since migration was part of integrated communications and a means to nurture tacit knowledge. When migrants returned, or communicated with their Indian offices, the quality of work changed. More than draining skills, the process enhanced the creative use of brains.[3]

---

[3] Ashish Arora and Alfonso Gambardella, eds., *From Underdogs to Tigers: The Rise and Growth of the Software Industry in Brazil, China, India, Ireland, and Israel*, Oxford: Oxford University Press, 2005.

Since most software firms were small, young, and successful; analysts of the business often draw lessons on entrepreneurship from this example. One article contrasting the trajectories of the small local and the large global firms distinguishes between low-risk and high value business process outsourcing market where the big players operated and the high-risk but potentially high-value technology development areas of entrepreneurs.[4] This dualism gives a precise meaning to entrepreneurship in the field.

Despite an obvious role for entrepreneurship, who owned the IT companies mattered little; who managed them mattered more. Of course, the managers and the owners in small firms converged. The point rather is that, whereas in the older times, talent at raising money defined entrepreneurship in India, in the IT industry, skills management mattered more to performance than talent at raising money. From the beginning of the software boom, electrical and electronic engineers were running the show. Infosys was set up by a consortium of engineers. The management of TCS and Wipro was left to professionals with similar qualifications. Qualification and experience made much more difference than ownership, financial acumen, and managerial styles. Qualifications mattered not only in giving direction to work in-house, but perhaps more crucially, to building networks with industry associations, potential clients, making recruitments at senior level, and in predicting and preparing for new types of business.

The people who started these firms and managed them did not fit the traditional entrepreneurial stereotype. They did not come from business families. They accumulated wealth by using skills rather than tangible assets. They worked in a world that involved a great deal of interaction, collaboration, and frequent exchange of tacit knowledge, rather than one of competition and secrecy. They tended to be more cosmopolitan than the traditional business family representatives were before liberalisation. Caste and community were not so relevant in forging relationships in this milieu, though caste was still relevant as a predictor of scientific and technological education.

The software entrepreneurs, in other words, saw themselves as members of the 'middle class'. Their story was that of middle-class capitalism in an integrated world. The life story of key entrepreneurs (such as that of the Infosys co-founder Nagavara Ramarao Narayana Murthy) became a symbol of this narrative of a new kind of capitalism in India that had no link with the old capitalism, and was even at odds with it. That story of the making of capitalism is tied to another story, that of a responsible and ethical capitalism that these new entrepreneurs believed they led. The new cosmopolitan capitalism faced challenges, such as in the IT hub Bangalore, where regional politics

---

[4] Sumit K. Majumdar, Davina Vora, and Ashok K. Nag, 'Industry Structure Characteristics and International Entrepreneurship in India's Software Industry', *Journal of Entrepreneurship*, 19(2), 2010, 109–36.

occasionally treated the IT industry as an imposition by outsiders. But it proved robust enough to become a part of the remaking of India as a cosmopolitan business destination.

The software export boom formed part of a larger process of service sector growth, which was fundamentally a global process. India's position in this world market needs a comment.

Growth of Services

The services accounted for more than 60 per cent of global output and 30 per cent of global employment around 2015. These percentages had risen steadily from 1960, but the traded component of the services increased much faster in recent decades. According to World Bank data, trade in services formed 6 per cent of world trade in 1975, and 8 per cent in 1996. In the next twenty years, the percentage increased from 8 to 13. The growth was faster in the exporting country India, and accelerated since 2003.

One interpretation of the late twentieth century surge in service trade would see 'globalisation' and trade in services as two parts of an interdependent process. The logic of 'late' capitalism encouraged multinational firms to outsource a part of their business, and create global chains of production. The MNCs always exploit the people of the host country, the belief goes, now they exploit by partnering with the new compradors like TCS and Infosys. Other scholars emphasise more the agency and capability of local service production, even the 'flowering of a 'new spirit of capitalism' in post-liberalisation India' on the back of middle-class entrepreneurs in the IT industry.[5]

No matter how we interpret the surge in services, information technology applications were a critical element. IT improved the productivity of firms in general, by reducing transaction costs, or by enabling changes in factor input composition. If this explains the universal demand for services, the tradability of IT and IT-enabled services also increased, enhancing supply. Services are traditionally limitedly tradable, because they are embodied in people, and because movements of people are regulated, even discouraged. The fall in communication cost increased portability by making complex ideas transmittable in packages. Information technology made it possible to unbundle services. These changes, sometimes clubbed under the death-of-distance idea, started some time ago. Their potential to revolutionise business was visible more recently.

---

[5] Carol Upadhya, *Reengineering India: Work, Capital and Class in an Offshore Economy*, New Delhi: Oxford University Press, 2016, 5–6, for a discussion of service trade and what it means. Cited text appears on page 59.

An active service trade could not be done by satellite communication alone. In the development and transmission of tacit knowledge, some role for face-to-face interaction between people must remain. Barriers to migration exist at both ends of the service transaction. Political sentiments about immigration in a net service exporter country like India were generally negative. Negotiations to free up the market further, in areas such as legal services, was a politically charged game.

Besides IT, what were the services being traded more than before? Provision of mobile phone technology is one obvious example. Unlike the software case, where the world market boom had started before the liberalisation, so that policy needed to adapt to sustain initial Indian gains, in mobile telephony the world market boom and economic reforms in India coincided in the mid-1990s. The telecommunications industry was a government monopoly until 1995 on a fixed-line system. The abysmal levels of penetration of telephones revealed how badly the system served the users. In 1995, simultaneously mobile services and private enterprise were allowed. The country was divided into zones or 'spectrums' and licences sold. Very quickly, private and state operators entered the business. Initially, the Department of Telecommunications, a government body, resisted the move to invite private investment, and then acceded to it while setting fees and rentals at such high levels that most private firms made losses.[6] The concerned ministry became infamous for corruption scandals. The situation stabilised from the late 1990s. After the establishment of the Telecom Regulatory Authority in 1997, government interference receded. The density of phone services increased 30 times in less than ten years. Between 2000 and 2005, government monopoly in domestic and international long-distance lines ended, and licensing and tariff policies were deliberately aimed at fostering entry and competition.

All studies of market structure agree that the industry was highly competitive, that profit margins were low even without the regulator trying to keep these low, and that natural barriers to entry such as the choice of radio systems did not stop new entry from happening.[7] And yet, the club of big players in the industry remained a small one and even shrank. Six companies – Bharti, Reliance, Vodafone, A.V. Birla group's Idea, Tata Teleservices, and Aircel – accounted for a big part of the market. Outside the club, the mobile telephone story was a story of short lives, falling behind, mergers, and takeovers. To some extent, this is a reflection of the regionalisation of the licensing system,

---

[6] A good survey of the early history is Ashok V. Desai, *India's Telecommunications Industry: History, Analysis, Diagnosis*, New Delhi: Sage Publications, 2006.

[7] Sunil Mani, 'The Mobile Communications Services Industry in India: Has it Led to India Becoming a Manufacturing Hub for Telecommunication Equipment?', *Pacific Affairs*, 85(3), 2012, 511–30; Subhashish Gupta, 'Cellular Mobile in India: Competition and Policy', *Pacific Affairs*, 85(3), 2012, 483–510.

so that only few companies have the capability to offer similar services throughout India. Partly, the market works on volume of transactions at tiny transaction cost.

Education, especially technical and higher education, was another big growth area. Education joined the market in a big way in the 2000s. Private colleges offering technical education degrees in the small towns was a derived form of business development. Engineering education was always a coveted field, but entry into the elite government institutions located in or near big cities was competitive and restricted. This changed in the 1990s, when most states allowed private colleges to be set up. At the same time, demand for engineers rose rapidly thanks to the IT industry growth. Between 2000 and 2014, engineering student enrolment increased from half a million to almost four million, and the share of engineering students in higher education from 3 to 16 per cent. In 2007, 90 per cent of the students in undergraduate programmes in engineering studied in private colleges.[8] Little research has been done on the entrepreneurs who made this revolution.

Transportation, hotels, travel, and tourism services were magnets of new entry in the 2000s. These businesses were for domestic consumption and attracted small firms and many self-employed individuals. Commercial aviation, however, was a different kind of game, because it occurred on a different scale of investment. Chapter 8 showed the early and turbulent history of opening the sector to private enterprise. The trend was maintained, and so was the turbulence. Aviation business experienced a huge change in the 2000s. In 2003, the entry of a new player, Air Deccan, India's first low-cost no-frills service, made headlines in the business newspapers. The company collapsed and then was bought over by Kingfisher Airlines, which too collapsed thanks to the acquisition. The experience of otherwise viable companies going under showed that the attraction of a booming market was a deceptive one. Successful companies needed to maintain a large enough fleet and make enough profits from the lucrative routes to deal with the still inadequate infrastructure. Although a few new airlines (Kingfisher, Air Sahara, Air Deccan) sank, the survivors (Jet Airways, affiliated to the Abu Dhabi based Etihad Airways; and Tata's Indigo Airlines) captured over 80 per cent of the business by 2016. In-between, thoughtless expansion plans in the government carrier Air India weakened a company already deeply unpopular with consumers.[9]

---

[8] Pradeep Kumar Choudhury, 'Growth of Engineering Education in India: Status, Issues and Challenges', *Higher Education for the Future*, 3(1), 2016, 93–107.

[9] Kingshuk Nag, 'How Indian Aviation was Destroyed'. http://blogs.timesofindia.indiatimes .com/The-wonder-that-is-indian-politics/how-indian-aviation-was-destroyed/ (accessed on 26 April 2017).

Trading re-emerged as a field of investment and consolidation. The success of garment exports was based in a large measure on innovative marketing. The concepts of 'commodity chain' and 'value chain' are sometimes used to show how regions of production and processing form complementary parts of a global trade network. Department stores in Western cities were the biggest final buyers of clothing and accessories made in India, but they did not make direct foreign investment in the country that they bought from. Nor was the trade driven by independent intermediaries. Instead, value was created by managing the chain through which cloth moved, and in the process, savings were made on transaction cost.[10] The managers of the chain were predominantly local trading firms.

The one field in which change was slow to come was banking. In the 2000s, the government and the Reserve Bank of India actively encouraged entry of private banks and conversion of the old state-owned financial institutions into banks. The move succeeded to the extent that the share of private banks in total deposits increased from less than 10 to more than 25 per cent between 1997 and 2007. Some of these, like ICICI Bank and Kotak Mahindra Bank, were new private banks. Other were old private banks like the Oriental Bank of Commerce, and a few were foreign banks. The growth occurred mainly in the new banks. At the same time, there were huge changes in technology, retail banking, assets, liabilities, and corporate governance mechanism. But change was slow to come in reforming the still dominant government-owned banks, which continued to be burdened by 'non-performing assets'. The problem varied from bank to bank. The source of bad assets ranged from policy-directed lending to weak borrowers, to politically influenced lending to powerful corporates, to heavy exposure to clusters of bankrupt firms as in Eastern India. At a deeper level, the syndrome reflects the banks' inability to emerge as independent and responsible players in the financial market under state ownership.

All along this spectrum, foreign investment has played a transformative role.

Inward Foreign Investment

After 2003, foreign investment surged in India. Investment came both as institutional investment by foreign funds in Indian companies, and as direct

---

[10] Gary Gereffi, 'The Organisation of Buyer-driven Commodity Chains: How US Retailers shape Overseas Production Networks', in Gary Gereffi and Migues Korzeniewicz, eds., *Commodity Chains and Global Capitalism*, Westport, CT: Praeger, 1994, 95–123; K. V. Ramaswamy and Gary Gereffi, 'India's Apparel Exports: The Challenge of Global Markets', *Developing Economies*, 28(2), 2001, 186–210.

investment by multinational companies. The surge changed the complexion of the business world, popular views about foreign investment, and academic scholarship in important ways. For example, corporate governance returned as a big theme, a reminder of the managing agency discussion from 80 years ago.

One of the changes was a renewed interest in the distinction between closely held and owner-manged family firms and publicly held professionally managed firms. Analysts asked, did foreign institutional investors discriminate between the two? The answer is that they did, they preferred to invest more money in professionally managed firm.[11] What was once only a difference became a divergence between two broad types of firms, one traditional and the other relatively modern. But how sharp was the distinction between these types anyway? In many small or mid-sized IT firms, the owner was also a professional. And IT firms received more institutional investment than any other type.

The issue of investor selection linked to the larger theme of corporate governance. In India, corporate governance norms were formally coded and enforced by the regulator, the Securities and Exchange Board of India (SEBI), from 2000–1. Although most companies complied with the formal norms, the move had more symbolic than substantive effects on management cultures. Scholars who have carried our pioneering research on the subject discuss these issues, which include investor selection, ownership structure, and preferences and policies of institutional investors.[12]

At the same time, greater openness to investment added a market-based pressure on governance. Foreign investors selected the better-governed firms, they also tried to shape or influence governance practices as a matter of strategy. The global influence on corporate management raises the prospect of a homogenisation of practices. One article concludes that the global influence 'point towards a corporate convergence pattern with all the firms moving towards the... largely dispersed share ownership'.[13] The prediction depends on how far foreign investment alone could make the family firms with concentrated ownership unstable. The answer to that question depends on two things on which there is still insufficient evidence. First, are family firms necessarily poorly governed? The theoretical justification and empirical evidence for believing so are not particularly strong. Secondly, how worried are sources of funds, like the institutional investors, about corporate governance? The sad state of Indian banks in 2015–16, which continued to lend to politically

---

[11] Vidya Sukumara Panicker, Sumit Mitra, and Rudra Sensarma, 'Corporate Governance Determinants of FII in Indian IT Firms', *Indian Journal of Corporate Governance*, 9(1), 2016, 1–18.

[12] Jayati Sarkar and Subrata Sarkar, *Corporate Governance in India*, New Delhi: Sage Publication, 2012.

[13] Panciker, Mitra, Sensharma, 'Corporate Governance'.

connected bad debtors, suggests that a much bigger change in institutional culture is needed than just opening doors to foreign investment.

Family versus professional management can still matter, if not to rates of return, to growth of firms. If family firms were not necessarily poorly governed, they might still have bigger problems raising money cheaply. They did tend to be leveraged more, and the debt market was expensive. They had poorer access to foreign funds, as we have seen. They tended to rely more on institutional investors, and played politics more than professionally managed firms needed to do.

Foreign investment changed the game in other ways too. Between the first half of the 1990s and the second half, mergers and acquisitions activity sped up, led by the re-entry and consolidation of multinational companies.[14] Analytical research on mergers and acquisitions asked if we could better predict target firms and measure effects of the moves. This scholarship need not concern us here. But one of its findings is significant. A predictive benchmark is leverage, and it was found that low leveraged firms in India were more likely to be targets of acquisitions. The finding suggests why companies may prefer dealing with the politically connected banks, rather than the market in raising finance.

Along with foreign inward investment, there was a larger-than-before outflow as well.

Outward Foreign Investment

As we have seen in the previous chapter, Indian companies expanded the scale of asset holdings abroad between 1948 and 1982, though a precise division of these assets into private industrial and other types is unavailable. In any case, the scale of the recent increase dwarfs the older outflow. The recent outflow was industrial and reflected a globalisation of Indian corporate capital. How large was the tendency? And what does it mean? Despite the rising scale of overseas investment from India, at least until 2008 when the flow began to drop, the relative scale of Indian investment was not really large enough to be excited about, not nearly so in comparison with the counterpart investment flow from China or South Korea.

It is harder to answer the second question because outflows were still influenced by factors specific to industries and individual firms. In the

---

[14] '[T]ransaction volume increased by 2.5 times from the first phase to the next, and within this MNC involved deals grew 12 fold'. Debarati Basu, Somashree Ghosh Dastidar, and Deepak Chawla, 'Corporate Mergers and Acquisitions in India: Discriminating between Bidders and Targets', *Global Business Review*, 9(2), 2008, 207–18.

software industry, acquisition of foreign branches and partnerships occurred systematically. In a pattern reminiscent of the managing agencies, the leading firms in software established partnership with local firms, or established fully owned companies in countries where the clients were. But these were not the most discussed instances. Overseas collaborations and acquisitions by three automotive firms (Tata, Mahindra, and Bajaj) received much more attention, but what lessons these cases have for overseas investment in general it is not clear.

Nevertheless, the existence and visibility of Indian multinational has spawned a scholarship. It overturns common prediction that foreign investment should flow from capital-rich to capital-scarce regions. In one interpretation, favoured by the leftist economists in India especially, the overseas expansion represents the success of import substitution, when India learnt to industrialise, and the state nurtured some firms to become strong and capable.[15] But as we see from the preceding paragraph, very few private sector firms of the import-substitution era appear in the list. Other scholars refer to special dimensions of state aid. For example, some make use of the 'varieties of capitalism' literature to suggest that globalising firms in India shared certain inherited and distinctly Indian advantages, including help from the state in the form of a special patent regime, for example.[16] Large firms in emerging markets tend to be state-dependent, as another article on Indian MNCs shows, illustrating the point with investment by state-owned financial institutions in large corporates.[17] Public sector banks have indeed opened more services abroad, responding to more relaxed rules about non-resident Indian investment in India. Quantitatively speaking, this is a small outflow since Indian banks are minnows in the global financial market.

None of these explanations suit the global software firms particularly well. Overall, it remains difficult to explain overseas investment as a single process.

Conclusion

Business development in India changed from the 1990s not because it bade goodbye to socialism, but because India reset its transactions with the world economy. In spirit, this was a return to the kind of economic change the region

[15] Deepak Nayyar, 'The Internationalization of Firms from India: Investment, Mergers and Acquisitions', *Oxford Development Studies*, 36(1), 2008, 111–31.

[16] Andreas Nölke and Heather Taylor, 'Indian Multinationals, Comparative Capitalism, and Implications for Global and Host Country Economic Institutions', in Louis Brennan, ed., *The Emergence of Southern Multinationals*, Basingstoke: Palgrave Macmillan, 2011, 317–30.

[17] Lawrence Sáez and Crystal Chang, 'The Political Economy of Global Firms from India and China', *Contemporary Politics*, 15(3), 2009, 265–86.

had seen in the late 1800s, when transactions with the world economy created extraordinary opportunities to borrow abroad, or buy technology and skills from abroad. In practical terms, the goods and services now exchanged differ a great deal from those of the past.

It is easy to go overboard celebrating all this. Years after the liberal reforms began, India scores poorly on several benchmarks that indirectly measure the quality of capitalism. Some parts of the older historic legacy, such as the lingering effect of family management and lax corporate governance may still persist, along with the legacy of the statist and closed regime, like the inefficient government-dominated banking system. It is time to take stock.

10 Conclusion

Why Write a Business History of Modern India?

The mood of the present shapes opinions about the past – perhaps nowhere is this effect stronger than in business history. In the bleak 1970s, western scholars attributed Indian poverty to the weakness of its entrepreneurship.[1] The 'immaturity' of Indian capitalists, Marxist economists held, was an outcome of British colonial rule; though Karl Marx himself believed that, after the despotic Mughals who bullied merchants, the British would set capitalists free.

In the new millennium, resurgence of economic growth led to a different view of history, one that suggested that Indian entrepreneurship was always robust – only politics or external factors held it back. 'The common belief,' writes a team of eminent executives, entrepreneurs, and academics, 'is that India has risen from nowhere a few years ago.' History, the team goes on, proves this belief to be wrong. India was a great place for doing business in the distant past, but fell from grace thanks to 'waves of invasion'.[2] In the same spirit, India's emergence represents, for one author, the persistence of a 'long tradition as buyers and sellers ... Indians are very entrepreneurial'.[3]

But the new mood cannot be trusted either, for India gets very bad scores on the Global Competitiveness Index, and the Ease of Doing Business Index. Key services from retail trade, to healthcare, hotels, print media, tourism, banking and finance, education and films, which together contribute about half of the gross domestic product (GDP), have grown in scale but not much improved in

---

[1] For discussion, see Milton Singer, 'Religion and Social Change in India: The Max Weber Thesis, Phase Three', *Economic Development* and *Cultural Change*, 14(4), 1961, 497–505; Morris David Morris, 'Values as an Obstacle to Economic Growth in South Asia: An Historical Survey', *Journal of Economic History*, 27(4), 1967, 588–607.

[2] L. C. Jain et al., 'Understanding India from a Business Perspective: Opportunities and Challenges for MNCs', *Vikalpa*, 31(3), 2006, 95–119. The authors of the report were L. C. Jain, Rakesh Makhija, Ajay Mookerjee, Venkatesh Mysore, Achal Raghavan, J. Ramachandran, Ashok Rao, Shyamal Roy, Anand Shah, Ravi Viswanathan, Arun Vora, and D. V. R. Seshadri.

[3] N. Kumar, 'Indian Companies as Customers, Competitors and Collaborators', *Indian Journal of Industrial Relations*, 45(1), 2009, 148–59.

the quality that they deliver. India has the world's largest film industry, but its films do not win prizes in international competitions. India has one of the biggest university systems, but only a handful figure among the 500 best universities of the world. An HSBC index comparing the quality of expatriate lifestyle ranks India very low (20–30 among 34 countries) on healthcare, accommodation, utilities, finance, and ease of local travel. India is hardly the haven of capitalism that it is projected to be. If it is not now, perhaps it was not in the past either.

One reason to write a business history, then, is to free the subject from all manners of belief about the present, and restore the primacy of evidence. The immediate advantage of an evidence-based history is that it questions all ideas of an essentially changeless Indianness in the story. A further advantage is that it allows us to develop the type of story Chapter 1 called connected, one that can link different times, Indian history with world history, and changes in the environment with the experience of firms, families, and communities. Such an account can interpret shocks credibly, not only the kind of shock that the citation above calls 'invasion', but also events and episodes like the Great Depression, World Wars, nationalism, and globalisation. The aim of this book was to produce such an account.

But the challenge posed by glib views about history remains. In what ways, if any, does the distant past persist into the present times? Is there anything distinctly *Indian* about Indian business? Taking a cultural line is not a useful method to tackle this question. By cultural line, I mean either the assumption that Indian entrepreneurship was always strong but for the malign influence of invaders, or, after the followers of Karl Marx and Max Weber, that it was always weak but for the benign influence of the modern West. Both these approaches are mythical, not testable, and sadly, both refuse to die whether in academic or in popular history.[4]

A better method is to start from the premise that capitalist choices are necessarily constrained by resource costs, information costs, and political risk, that these conditions are variable, and that a business history should show not only how these obstacles were overcome, or failures occurred in the process, but also if any of these obstacles and the means persisted in the long run. Do we see a persistence of advantage or disadvantage in doing business in this region of the world? We will still be speculative about deep continuity, but the hypotheses advanced should be more testable than ethnic myths about the genius of the Indian capitalist.

---

[4] The question – what is distinctly Indian about Indian business – can be asked for emerging economies as a whole. For example Gareth Austin, Carlos Dávila, and Geoffrey Jones, 'The Alternative Business History: Business in Emerging Markets,' *Business History Review*, 2017, 1–33.

In this book, I offer a thesis in response to this question. These obstacles were indeed formidable in India, in the past, and in the recent times. In the long run, two things helped businesses overcome the obstacles – openness or integration with the world economy, and the state during the mid-twentieth century. Openness helped in different ways. India sold grain and cotton in the 1800s and software and clothing in the 2000s. These are different types of trade, but both acts of sale created the power in private hands to purchase know-how and skills abroad. Openness also enhanced this power by enabling migration and inward foreign investment. The state's role in the mid-twentieth century was to direct investment away from trade and traditional industry into machines, metals, and chemical industries; in this mission it was successful. Its major failure was to imagine that the state could substitute for the world economy. Discouragement to openness led to an unravelling of not only protectionist industrialisation, but industrialisation itself. The more recent times restored the world economy as a driver of change, with a different set of effects on enterprise from before.

There are three elements in this story that suggest enduring links between the past and the present. These are, access to capital, openness, and migration. These three things do not exhaust the possible ways of thinking about continuity (or discontinuity) in the long run. We can bring in to this discussion evolution of firm structures, political economy, or ideology. I restrict the scope of the discussion to these three points to keep it manageable. These are good example of enduring links anyway.

Capital

Capital was always costly and the financial markets always less than ideal in shape in India (Chapter 1). I have elsewhere attributed this to a structural or geographical condition. The condition of high seasonality of demand for money in the tropical monsoon climate pushed up interest rates to extraordinarily high levels in a few months of the year. The attraction of making a quick buck by lending short-term in the busy season was so great that money would rather remain idle in the slack season than be offered to long-term borrowers. Stock markets, banks, and cooperatives eased the situation, only slightly.[5] As far as we can tell, historical data suggest that seasonal variability of the cost of capital was unusually high in India, compared with Western money markets. Long-term investment funds are still difficult to raise in India.

---

[5] 'Monsoon and the Market for Money in Late Colonial India', *Enterprise and Society*, 17(2), 2016, 324–57.

Despite this feature of the money market, institutions emerged to channel more money from agricultural trade to industry. During the first episode of company formation in India (c. 1850–1930), investment funds were obtained by two methods. One of these was the family, community, and internal and cheaper credit markets among friends and relations. Among Indian investors, these had an extremely important role to play in making long-term business investments possible at all. The investors themselves were often recycling profits earned in commodity trade to long-term projects. The so-called community networks reigned in this sphere. The community network did not necessarily help pioneer entrepreneurs, but once an idea had been shown to succeed, network effects could spread its use by others. The importance of own savings implicates the importance of trading profits. Without the profits of Indo-Chinese opium trade, and Indo-British cotton trade, Bombay would not get its factories. The nineteenth century agricultural trade and associated banking businesses centred in the port cities and their satellites. This was one of the factors that made new and modern enterprise geographically concentrated in a few places. Such manners of raising capital imposed limits on what could be done with it, entrepreneurs confined themselves to known field like cotton production, and avoided areas like machinery production, relying on the market for that purpose.

There was another route through which investment money became available: this was equity raised abroad. The managing agency contract enabled some companies to go to the stock market without the fear of takeover. Foreign companies used both the informal and the formal routes.

After 1947, state intervention prioritised protectionist industrialisation and directed investment funds to desired industries. In doing so, somewhat unnecessarily, it also reduced the role of foreign capital and foreign equity in investment, repressed trading, and repressed private banking. As a result, the role of the stock market in investment remained small, and the reign of the family was reinforced. As late as the 1990s, the share of debt and reserves in investment by industrial firms remained substantially higher than equity, a possible way to invest but an expensive way. Before independence there were large banking firms, corporate- and family-owned, as well as extensive moneylending tied to trade. Some of these private actors could potentially lead the emergence of a strong and independent financial system, the prospect of that organic process of financial maturity receded due to state intervention backed up by a superstitious fear of moneylending inherited from British administrators.

At the same time, the nationalised banking system failed to deliver enough support to capitalist enterprise. Indian banks are a distinct species of animal. After the economic reforms, they benefited from new technology, and from the chance to take part in a freer and much enlarged government securities market. But there was little change in institutional culture. Some of them suffer from an identity crisis, unsure whether they should behave like a private enterprise, or as a department of the government. Introducing better systems of corporate governance has been a struggle for the regulators. The best Indian banks are dwarfs by global standards.

The slow development of an independent and capable financial system imparted an element of inertia upon the ongoing transformation. Still, in the last twenty years, investment did ease with the inflow of foreign money. How deep a transformation these processes wrought, it is too early to say. Foreign investment has transformative capacity particularly because it is associated with technology and institutional change, and entails discrimination along governance standards. The scale of the effect is yet unknown.

Knowledge could be purchased, especially in a cosmopolitan milieu that allowed entry of different types of economic actors.

Knowledge and Cosmopolitanism

In trade, Indians were indeed very good for very long. This the European traders on the coasts readily acknowledged in the 1600s. But already, an organisational divergence was in motion. Indian trading and shipping firms relied on their own money to run businesses, European joint-stock companies recycled other people's money. This difference explains a persistent contrast between Indian and European firms. Indian merchants operated on the coasts and the interior, while Europeans took over intercontinental shipping and trade. Patriotic Indian historians believe the Europeans removed the Indians from a position of dominance by unfair means like the navigation acts of the 1600s. The truth is, they did not need to. Although the British state helped the British shippers, the latter also had a comparative advantage in possessing the knowledge of interoceanic navigation, matching ships and guns, and the joint-stock company. The joint-stock company gave them a scale advantage, which mattered to trade in the 1600s and 1700s, when commercial success in the seas required investment in a complex infrastructure consisting of ports, gunships, and walled settlements. With a few exceptions, Indians did not operate on comparable scale.

This divergence was of little consequence for long-term inequality. Once agricultural trade took off from the early 1800s, European and Indian firms specialised in complementary fields and converged on organisational practices to some extent. Another far-reaching divergence was unfolding in the 1800s in the development of machinery. The machines for textile production were invented in Britain. Like the joint-stock company, this technological lead as such explains little of the emerging world inequality. Economic historians based in the West make a big deal out of the British Industrial Revolution as an explanation for world economic inequality. It was no such thing. Anyone could buy these machines anywhere. The whole world traded in textile machinery as actively as it traded in textiles in the nineteenth century. Indian merchants of the port cities were a part of the machinery trade, thanks to their strong position in cotton markets.

Mechanised production or industrialisation was a new game for a wholly different reason. It cost a great deal more money to play the game, and *money was scarcer in India*. The process that Simon Kuznets called modern economic growth, one driven by productivity rather than resource accumulation, was far more capital-intensive than trade, and not within easy reach of Indian merchants and bankers. Only those families joined the process who could raise significantly larger sums of money than before.

For several reasons, the process was confined to the port cities and their satellites. One of these, the role of trading profits in new investment, has already been mentioned here. Another reason was, the port cities were more cosmopolitan spaces than the business towns in the interior of the country. They fostered unorthodox partnerships, associational activity, and investment in education. And all that facilitated knowledge of foreign institutions and technology in India, and of Indian resources and capability among foreigners. Their exposure made the port cities develop as settlements of migrant technicians and artisans. The textile factories depended on such migrants.

In short, thanks to open borders to people, the port cities and their satellites in the nineteenth century became sites for a unique encounter between European know-how and India's capitalism. Indian firms and organisations routinely hired foreigners bringing in skills unavailable in the country. Cities like Bombay and Calcutta industrialised despite high cost of capital, absence of government policy to help industry, and shortage of skilled labour, thanks to resourceful merchants, migration of skilled workers, and foreign capital inflow. This was the sphere where the joint-stock company, limited liability, managing agency, and new technology had a significantly better chance of being adopted. I call this process globalisation (Chapter 9). We can also call it cosmopolitanism.

The British Empire that ruled India between 1858 and 1947 did not play a direct role in either making modern enterprise grow in India or obstructing such growth. But it did provide a giant integrated market place, kept capital and labour markets open, and provided basic institutional support such as codification of commercial law. It fostered cosmopolitanism. The Raj denied Indians political choice. It was, however, keen to promote economic choice and protect a system of free markets in goods, capital, and labour. Colonialism was bad politics. But openness was good economics. By bringing in know-how and capital from Britain into India, the open economy enabled huge growth in trade and an offbeat industrialisation in the nineteenth century.

From the early 1900s, the Indian nationalists rejected colonialism and lack of representation in politics, an admirable and courageous thing to do in that time. In the process, they dismissed the open economy as well, which was a regrettable thing to do. Indian nationalists made a lot of people believe that colonial rule was bad *because* the open economy had made India poor. There was an unfortunate muddle between market liberalism and political liberty, for which post-1947 India paid a price.

Influenced by that ideology, post-independence India weakened cosmopolitanism between 1950 and 1980. In the mid-twentieth century, the country shut itself to trade, migration, and foreign investment, and repressed exporting businesses like textiles and tea. Economic growth fell behind the world average. Since 1980, reformists tried to rebuild the cosmopolitan environment, bit by bit, in the next twenty years. Since then, Indian growth caught up with and surpassed world average growth. Joint inflow of capital and knowledge played a major role in that success.

The return to openness, however, has been piecemeal. For example, India formally opened its doors to some services, but stayed protectionist about its service industries. Unlike in the colonial times, India attracted few skilled immigrants. In-migration speeded up of late, but involved semi-skilled workers from other South Asian countries.[6] Key services catering to the domestic consumers employed poorly equipped and poorly trained workers, and were behind world standards in the quality that they delivered. There was little discussion in the media on India's poor record in quality and professionalism. The print media itself was (and still is) protected, and lacked maturity and professionalism. India-watchers believed that a bolder opening was unlikely in some of these protected areas, because political sentiment against it was too strong. A media debate in 2012 about allowing foreign firms in multi-brand retail showed how fierce nationalistic sentiment could be when it came to embracing openness.[7]

In one aspect, India always enjoyed a comparative advantage: people. It is in the abundance of labour, migration of labour, and the opportunities mobile labour creates for the domestic economy, that another line can be drawn between the past and the present.

People

How does 'labour' matter to business history? It matters because remittance can act as an investment fund, or add to the capacity to purchase know-how

---

[6] Binod Khadria and Perveen Kumar, "Immigrants and Immigration in India A Fresh Approach," *Economic and Political Weekly*, 2015, 65–71.
[7] Sonal S. Pandya, 'Why foreign investment still polarizes India', *Washington Post* blogs, 2014. www.washingtonpost.com/blogs/monkey-cage/wp/2014/09/30/why-foreign-investment-still-polarizes-india/

and goods from the world market, and because migration could enhance human capital. Low wages of skilled labour like those engaged in the crafts or even technical services are good news when there is growing market for such skills and services. Over centuries, this factor has worked wonders for India.

India exported a large quantity of cotton textiles in the eighteenth century, thanks to accumulated craft skills. The recent export success of the garment industry (or leather, or gems) reconfirms the importance of craft skills. This is revealed more sharply when we look at export clusters like Calcutta, where many other forms of organised business did not fare well in the last forty years, but garment exporters did well because they did types of work that only local labour could supply. Bengali skilled artisans can be found in many Indian cities working in specialist tasks in small industries. These stories hundreds of years apart bear a similarity.

There is another way in which labour abundance matters to business history: Indians' propensity to migrate. In the nineteenth century, India supplied several million migrant workers to plantation societies in the New World. Some of these flows forged enduring cultural, demographic, and economic links between littoral societies in South and Southeast Asia, as Sunil Amrith has shown in a series of works on the Bay of Bengal.[8]

Radical historians often contend that the migration process involved coercion and repression. This is true. And yet, such order of migration could not but destabilise the traditional servile and coercive labour relations from which some of the millions of migrants had emerged. Hundreds of thousand people went to work for wages inside the country, in factories, plantations, and new areas of commercial agriculture. The elastic supply kept wages depressed even as more people were hired into wage-work, thus giving the employers a windfall gain. The workers' skill levels did not always match the skills in demand, so that European migrants initially filled the higher positions in the factories and plantations. But as the industries progressed, the skill gap closed. Parsi foremen, for example, replaced their British counterparts in Bombay's cotton mills, almost completely in the interwar period. A similarly organic 'Indianisation' can be discerned in the tea plantations as well.

Indian small traders, and branches of banking firms were also exceptionally mobile since the nineteenth century. Gijsbert Oonk and Claude Markovits, among others, have drawn attention to these links with different regions and

---

[8] *Migration and Diaspora in Modern Asia,* Cambridge: Cambridge University Press, 2011; and *Crossing the Bay of Bengal: The Furies of Nature and the Fortunes of Migrants,* Cambridge, MA, Harvard University Press, 2013.

communities as case studies.[9] Although the money flows are not measurable, they sometimes followed certain established channels in which both workers and businesses circulated. Some corporate banks of Indian origin followed these channels too. The mid-twentieth-century nationalist movements stopped or reversed some of these flows, but by then the migration of capital and labour had created a legacy.

Recent research explores the legacy, and reveals deep connections between history and memory of past migrations and the continuing outflows of people from the South Asia region. 'Drawing on recent national survey data and unique census data at the district level,' a recent study finds, 'that for regions covering 20% of the population of India, poor *and* rich, mobility has been persistently high in magnitude and has been male-dominated, remittance based and circular in nature for well over a 100 years.' This stable historical relationship is called migration persistence.[10] A book on Bengali migration, similarly, argues that 'contemporary patterns of migration and resettlement ... can best be understood by grasping the historical connections between places of origin and places of arrival'.[11]

Why does persistent mobility of people matter in a business history? Although most of the people engaged in past and present episodes of migration have generic skills, migration as such has a powerful effect on intergenerational mobility via education, human capital investment, and accumulation of experience. Remittances sent home by international migrants, recent research shows, systematically flowed back to education. Students formed a growing outflow, and students who acquired specific skills abroad tended to make use of them in global labour markets. Remittance creates the capacity to buy technology used in production for the home market.

When this whole process matures, there is always a prospect of a reverse flow of knowledge and money from the diaspora to the country of origin. Today, one can hardly think of an Indian start-up that does not involve the participation of someone educated abroad. This is happening not just in information technology start-ups, where it is most talked about, but in general. How deep or big is this reverse flow? We should know in a few years, when the next edition of this book is prepared.

---

[9] Gijsbert Oonk, *Settled Strangers: Asian Business Elites in East Africa (1800–2000)*, New Delhi: Sage Publications, 2013; Claude Markovits, *The Global World of Indian Merchants, 1750–1947: Traders of Sind from Bukhara to Panama*, Cambridge: Cambridge University Press, 2008.

[10] Chinmay Tumbe, 'Migration Persistence across Twentieth Century India', *Migration and Development*, 1(1), 2012, 87–112.

[11] Claire Alexander, Joya Chatterji, and Annu Jalais, *The Bengal Diaspora: Rethinking Muslim Migration*, Abingdon and New York, NY: Routledge, 2016, 3.

What, then, is the key 'takeaway' from the book? Business history of India in the last three hundred years is not a heroic story about the triumphs of indigenous entrepreneurs and business communities. Nor is it a tragic story of how invasions and colonial repression stopped Indians from doing as much business as they wanted to do. Instead, it is a story about how the world economy and state policy – cosmopolitanism and nationalism – shaped private investment, mainly by making capital and technology less scarce or more. With India's economic reforms since the 1990s, the mix between cosmopolitanism and nationalism has changed for the better, at the same time, raising the tension between these two forces.

References

Adarkar, B. N. (1941), *The Indian Fiscal Policy*, Allahabad: Kitabistan.

Agarwal, S. N. (1944), *The Gandhian Plan of Economic Development for India*, Bombay: Padma Publications.

Ahuja, R. (2004), '"Opening up the Country"? Patterns of Circulation and Politics of Communication in Early Colonial Orissa', *Studies in History*, 20(1), 73–130.

Aiyer, S. S. A. (2008), *Escape from the Benevolent Zookeepers*, Mumbai: Times Group Books.

Aldous, M. (2015), 'Avoiding "Negligence and Profusion": Ownership and Organization in Anglo Indian Trading Firms, 1813–1870', PhD dissertation, London School of Economics and Political Science.

Aldous, M. and T. Roy (forthcoming), 'Reassessing FERA: Examining British Firms' Strategic Response to "Indianization"', *Business History*.

Alexander, C., J. Chatterji, and A. Jalais (2016), *The Bengal Diaspora: Rethinking Muslim Migration*, Abingdon and New York, NY: Routledge.

All India Congress Committee (1935), *Indian Tariff Policy*, Allahabad: AICC.

All India Manufacturers' Conference (1941), *Proceedings of the First Session*, Bombay: publisher not stated.

Allami, A. F. (1891), *Ain I Akbari* (translated by H. S. Jarrett), Calcutta: Baptist Mission Press.

Amatori, F. and A. Colli (2011), *Business History: Complexities and Comparisons*, Abingdon and New York, NY: Routledge.

Amrith, S. (2011), *Migration and Diaspora in Modern Asia*, Cambridge: Cambridge University Press.

(2013), *Crossing the Bay of Bengal: The Furies of Nature and the Fortunes of Migrants*, Cambridge, MA.: Harvard University Press.

Amsden, A. H. (1991), 'Diffusion of Development: The Late-Industrializing Model and Greater East Asia', *American Economic Review*, 81(2), 82–6.

Anon. (1960), *A Century of Progress (Greaves Cotton & Company)*, Bombay: Greaves Cotton.

Anon. (1963), *Andrew Yule & Co., Ltd, 1863–1963*, Edinburgh: privately printed.

(1967), *Indian Leather Trades and Industries Year-Book*, Madras: Indian Leather Association.

(1969), 'The Indian Cable Company Limited', *Economic and Political Weekly*, 4 (35), 1429–30.

(1977), 'FERA: Disappointment for Indian Big Business', *Economic and Political Weekly*, 12(30), 1160–1.

(1986), 'The Reliance Example', *India Today*, 15 September, 99–100.

(1991a), 'Change', *Business World*, 27 March, 70–4.

(1991b), 'Inching Ahead', *Business India*, 4 March, 70–2.

(1992a), 'In Tatters', *Business India*, 31 August, 66–8.

(1992b), 'Siemens: Power Play', *Business India*, 13 March, 49–54.

(1994), 'The Ruias Go Professional', *Business World*, 28 December, 82–3.

(1995a), 'Firing up Tata Steel', *Business World*, 19 April, 42–5.

(1995b), 'Stepping Out', *Business World*, 3 May, 44–6.

Antrobus, H. A. (1947), *A History of the Jorehaut Tea Company*, London: Tea and Rubber Mail.

Arasaratnam, S. (1980), 'Weavers, Merchants and Company: The Handloom Industry in Southeastern India 1750–1790', *Indian Economic and Social History Review*, 17(3), 257–81.

Arnold, D. (2011), 'Global Goods and Local Usages: The Small World of the Indian Sewing Machine, 1875–1952', *Journal of Global History*, 6(3), 407–29.

Arora, A. and A. Gambardella, eds. (2005), *From Underdogs to Tigers: The Rise and Growth of the Software Industry in Brazil, China, India, Ireland, and Israel*, Oxford: Oxford University Press.

Arrighi, G. (1994), *The Long Twentieth Century*, London and New York, NY: Verso.

Austin, G, C. Dávila, and G. Jones (2017), 'The Alternative Business History: Business in Emerging Markets,' *Business History Review*, 91(3), 1–33.

Bagchi, A. K. (1972), *Private Investment in India 1900–1939*, Cambridge: Cambridge University Press.

(1985), 'Transition from Indian to British Indian Systems of Money and Banking 1800–1850', *Modern Asian Studies*, 19(3), 501–19.

(1997), *The Evolution of the State Bank of India, Vol. 2, The Era of the Presidency Banks 1876–1920*, New Delhi: State Bank of India and Sage Publications.

Balachandran, G. (1988), *The Reserve Bank of India, 1951–1967*, Mumbai: Reserve Bank of India and New Delhi: Oxford University Press.

Balachandran, G., ed. (1999), *India and the World Economy 1850–1950*, Delhi: Oxford University Press.

Balakrishnan, P. (1995), 'April Is Not the Cruellest Month', *Business World*, 17 May, 70.

Bala Subrahmanya, M. H. (2004), 'Small Industry and Globalisation: Implications, Performance and Prospects, *Economic and Political Weekly*, 1826–34;

Barclay, M. J. and C. G. Holderness (1989), 'Private Benefits from Control of Public Corporations', *Journal of Financial Economics*, 25(2), 371–95.

Barker, B. (1961), *Investment in India*, Bombay: Bombay Chamber of Commerce and Industry.

Barman, D. (1950), *Mystery of Birla House*, Calcutta: Jugabani Sahitya Chakra.

Basu, C. (1988), *Challenge and Change: The ITC Story: 1910–1985*, Calcutta: Orient Longman.

Basu, D., S. Ghosh Dastidar, and D. Chawla (2008), 'Corporate Mergers and Acquisitions in India: Discriminating between Bidders and Targets', *Global Business Review*, 9(2), 207–218.

Bayly, C. A. (1990), *Indian Society and the Making of the British Empire*, Cambridge: Cambridge University Press.

Bengal (1930), *Bengal Provincial Banking Enquiry Committee 1929–30*, Vol. 1 (Vols. 1–3), Calcutta: Bengal Government Press.

Benjamin, N. (1978), 'The Trade of the Central Provinces of India (1861–1880)', *Indian Economic and Social History Review*, 15(4), 505–14.

Benjamin, N. and P. N. Rath. (no date), *Modern Indian Business History: A Bibliographic Survey*, Pune: Gokhale Institute of Politics and Economics.

Bettelheim, C. (1968), *India Independent*, New York, NY: Monthly Review Press.

Bhagwati, J. and P. Desai (1970), *India: Planning for Industrialization*, London: Oxford University Press.

Bhandari, L., G. R. Kulkarni, and P. S. Thomas (1982), 'Larsen and Toubro Group: A Case Study in Corporate Growth', IIM Ahmedabad Case Studies, No. IIMA/BP0172. Available at: cases.iima.ac.in/ (accessed 30 January 2017).

Bhargava, A. (1993), 'In Slow Gear', *Business World*, 5–18 May, 22–3.

Bhatnagar, S. (2006), 'India's Software Industry'. In V. Chandra, ed., *Technology, Adaptation, and Exports: How Some Developing Countries Got It Right*, Washington D.C.: The World Bank, 95–124.

Bhattacharya, J. (1896), *Hindu Castes and Sects*, Calcutta: Thacker Spink.

Bhattacharya, S. K. (1976), 'Rohtas Industries Limited', IIM Ahmedabad Case Studies, No. IIMA/F&A0113. Available at: cases.iima.ac.in/ (accessed 30 January 2017).

Bhukya, B. (2007), '"Delinquent Subjects": Dacoity and the Creation of a Surveillance Society in Hyderabad State', *Indian Economic and Social History Review*, 44(2), 179–212.

(2010), *Subjugated Nomads: The Lambadas under the Rule of the Nizams*, Hyderaba: Orient Blackswan.

Bihar and Orissa (1930), *Report of the Bihar and Orissa Provincial Banking Enquiry Committee, 1929–30*, Vol. 1, Patna: Government Press.

BKS (1950), 'The European Steel Industry: Production Trends and the World Market', *The World Today*, 6, 265–74.

Bogart, D. and L. Chaudhary (2015), 'Railways in Colonial India: An Economic Achievement?' in L. Chaudhary, B. Gupta, T. Roy, and A. V. Swamy, eds., *A New Economic History of Colonial India*, Abingdon and New York, NY: Routledge, 140–60.

Bombay (1924), *Report of the Bombay Stock Exchange Enquiry Committee*, Bombay: Government Press.

Brennig, J. (1986), 'Textile Producers and Production in Late Seventeenth Century Coromandel', *Indian Economic and Social History Review*, 23(4), 333–55.

Briggs, J. (1819), 'Account of the Origin, History, and Manners of the Race of Men called Bunjaras', *Transactions of the Literary Society of Bombay*, Vol. I, London: John Murray, 1819, 170–97.

Brimmer, A. F. (1955), 'The Setting of Entrepreneurship in India', *Quarterly Journal of Economics*, 69(4), 553–76.

Broadberry, S., J. Custodis, and B. Gupta (2015), 'India and the Great Divergence: An Anglo-Indian Comparison of GDP per Capita, 1600–1871', *Explorations in Economic History*, 56(1), 58–75.

Brogan, C. (1951), *James Finlay and Co. Ltd: Manufacturers and East India merchants, 1750–1950*, Glasgow: Jackson.

Brown, C. and M. Thornton (2013), 'How Entrepreneurship Theory Created Economics', *Quarterly Journal of Austrian Economics*, 16(4), 401–19.

Brown, H. (1957), *Parry's of Madras: A Story of British Enterprise in India*, Madras: privately printed.

Buchanan, D. H. (1934), *The Development of Capitalistic Enterprise in India*, New York, NY: Macmillan.

Cain, P. (1999), 'British Free Trade, 1850–1914: Economics and Policy', ReFresh (Economic History Society). www.ehs.org.uk/dotAsset/11cabff5-3f6a-4d69-bba0-1086d69be6c7.pdf (accessed 1 August 2017).

Carlos, A. M. and S. Nicholas (1988), '"Giants of an Earlier Capitalism": The Chartered Trading Companies as Modern Multinationals', *Business History Review*, 62(3), 398–419.

Carter, L. (2002), *Chronicles of British Business in Asia 1850–1960: A Bibliography of Printed Company Histories with Short Accounts of the Concerns*, Delhi: Manohar.

Chakrabarti, M. (2009), 'Why Did Indian Big Business Pursue a Policy of Economic Nationalism in the Interwar Years? A New Window to an Old Debate', *Modern Asian Studies*, 43(4), 979–1038.

Chakrabarti, M. and B. Chatterjee (2006), 'Business Conduct in Late Colonial India: European Business in Kanpur', *Economic and Political Weekly*, 41(10), 904–11.

Chakrabarti, S. (2004), 'The English East India Company and the Indigenous Sloop Merchants of Bengal: Akrur Dutta and His Family, 1757–1857', *Studies in History*, 20(1), 131–57.

Chandavarkar, R. (1985), 'Industrialization in India before 1947: Conventional Approaches and Alternative Perspectives', *Modern Asian Studies*, 19(3), 623–68.

(1994), *The Origins of Industrial Capitalism in India*, Cambridge: Cambridge University Press.

Chandra, B. (1966), *The Rise and Growth of Economic Nationalism in India: Economic Policies of Indian National Leadership, 1880–1905*, Delhi: People's Publishing House.

Chandra, B., A. Mukherjee, and M. Mukherjee (2008), *India Since Independence*, New Delhi: Penguin.

Chari, S. (2004), *Fraternal Capital: Peasant-workers, Self-made Men, and Globalization in Provincial India*, Stanford, CA: Stanford University Press.

Chase-Dunn, C. (1998), *Global Formation*, Lanham, MD: Rowman and Littlefield.

Chatterji, B. (1992), Trade, Tariffs *and* Empire: Lancashire and British Policy in India 1919–1939, Cambridge: Cambridge University Press

Chaudhuri, A. (1980), 'Conglomerate Big Business Groups in India: Some Traits of Tycoon Capitalism', *Social Scientist*, 8(7), 38–51.

Chaudhuri, K. N. (1985), *Trade and Civilisation in the Indian Ocean: An Economic History from the Rise of Islam to 1750*, Cambridge: Cambridge University Press.

Chaudhury, S. (1979), 'FERA: Appearance and Reality', *Economic and Political Weekly*, 14(16), 733–44.

Chaudhury, S. (1995), *From Prosperity to Decline: Eighteenth Century Bengal*, New Delhi: Manohar.

Chaudhury, S. and M. Morineau, eds. (1999), *Merchants, Companies and Trade: Europe and Asia in the Early Modern Era*, Cambridge: Cambridge University Press.

Chibber, V. (2004), *Locked in Place: State-building and Late Industrialization in India*, Princeton, NJ: Princeton University Press.

Chinoy, K. A. M. (2015), *The Rise of Big Business in India*, Delhi: Aakar.

Choudhury, P. K. (2016), 'Growth of Engineering Education in India: Status, Issues and Challenges', *Higher Education for the Future*, 3(1), 93–107.

Clark, G. (1987), 'Why Isn't the Whole World Developed? Lessons from the Cotton Mills', *Journal of Economic History*, 47(2), 141–73.

Clark, G. and R. C. Feenstra (2001), 'Technology in the Great Divergence'. In M. Bordo, A. M. Taylor, and J. G. Williamson, eds., *Globalisation in Historical Perspective*, Chicago, IL and London: University of Chicago Press.

Colebrooke, H. T. (1804), *Remarks on the Husbandry and Internal Commerce of Bengal*, London: Calcutta.

Damodaran, H. (2008), *India's New Capitalists: Caste, Business, and Industry in a Modern Nation*, Basingstoke: Palgrave Macmillan.

Dantwala, M. L. (1937), *Marketing of Raw Cotton in India*, Bombay and New York, NY: Longmans Green, 31–2.

Darling, M. L. (1928), *Punjab Peasant in Prosperity and Debt*, London: Humphrey Milford.

Das Gupta, S. (1993), 'Stoking a Controversy', *Business World*, 24 February, 58–9.

Das Gupta, S. and U. Nagarajan (1993–4), 'Global Gambit', *Business World*, 29 December to 11 January.

Das, G. (2006), 'The India Model', *Foreign Affairs*, 85(4), 2–16.

Dasgupta, A. (1984), 'The Maritime Merchant and Indian History', *South Asia*, 7(1), 27–33.

Dasgupta, A. (2001), *The World of the Indian Ocean Merchant 1500–1800*, New Delhi: Oxford University Press.

Datta, D. and B. Agarwal (2014), 'Corporate Investment Behaviour in India during 1998–2012: Bear, Bull and Liquidity Phase', *Paradigm*, 18(1), 87–102.

Dejung, C. (2011), 'Bridges to the East: European Merchants and Business Practices in India and China'. In Robert Lee, ed., *Commerce and Culture: Nineteenth-Century Business Elites*, Farnham: Ashgate, 93–116.

Desai, A. V. (1968), 'The Origins of Parsi Enterprise', *Indian Economic and Social History Review*, 5(4), 307–18.

(1970), 'Evolution of Import Control', *Economic and Political Weekly*, 5(29–31), 1271–77.

(1993), *My Economic Affairs*, New Delhi: Wiley Eastern.

(2006), *India's Telecommunications Industry: History, Analysis, Diagnosis*, New Delhi: Sage Publications.

Dodwell, H. et al (tr.) (1904–28), *The Diary of Ananda Ranga Pillai*, Vols. 1–8, Madras: Government Press.

Dunn, R., and J. Hardy (1931) *Labor and Textiles: A Study of Cotton and Wool Manufacturing*, New York, NY: International Publishers.

Edwardes, S. M. (1920), *A Memoir of Rao Bahadur Ranchhodlal Chhotalal*, Exeter: William Pollard.

EPW Research Foundation (1995), 'National Accounts Statistics of India – 1: Macro-Aggregates', *Economic and Political Weekly*, 30(46), 2955–64.

Franselow, F. S. (1989), 'Muslim Society in Tamil Nadu (India): An Historical Perspective', *Journal of the Institute of Muslim Minority Affairs*, 10(1), 264–89.

Furber, H. (1940), 'Review of A. Mervyn Davies, *Clive of Plassey: A Biography* ', New York: Charles Scribner's Sons, 1939, *American Historical Review*, 45(3), 635–7.

Gadgil, D. R. (1959), *Origins of the Modern Indian Business Class*, Poona: Gokhale Institute of Politics and Economics, mimeo.

Garvin, S. (1956), *A Survey for British Industrial Firms*, London: Federation of British Industries.

Gereffi, G. (1994), 'The Organisation of Buyer-driven Commodity Chains: How US Retailers shape Overseas Production Networks'. In G. Gereffi and M. Korzeniewicz, eds., *Commodity Chains and Global Capitalism*, Westport, CT: Praeger, 95–123.

Ghemawat, P. and T. Khanna (1998), 'The Nature of Diversified Business Groups: A Research Design and Two Case Studies', *Journal of Industrial Economics*, 46 (1), 35–61.

Ghosh, S. K. (1985), *The Indian Big Bourgeoisie*, Calcutta: Subarnarekha.

Gladstone, J. S. (1910), *History of Gillanders Arbuthnot and Co., and Ogilvy Gillanders and Co.*, London: publisher not known.

Godley, A. (2006), 'Selling the Sewing Machine around the World', *Enterprise and Society*, 7(3) 266–314.

Goswami, C. (2011), *The Call of the Sea: Kachchhi Traders in Muscat and Zanzibar, c. 1800–1880*, Hyderabad: Orient Black Swan.

(2016), *Globalization before Its Time: The Gujarati Merchants from Kachchh*, New Delhi: Penguin.

Goswami, O. (1985), 'Then Came the Marwaris: Some Aspects of the Changes in the Pattern of Industrial Control in Eastern India', *Indian Economic and Social History Review*, 22(2), 225–49.

Granovetter, M. (1983), 'The Strength of Weak Ties: A Network Theory Revisited', *Sociological Theory*, 1, 201–233.

Green, H. (1852), *The Deccan Ryots*, Bombay: Bombay Gazette.

Guha, A. (1970), 'The Comprador Role of Parsi Seths 1750–1850', *Economic and Political Weekly*, 5(48), 1934–5.

(1984), 'More about Parsi Seths – Their Roots, Entrepreneurship and Comprador Role, 1650–1918', *Economic and Political Weekly*, 19(3), 117–32.

Guhathakurta, S. (1993), 'Economic Independence through Protection? Emerging Contradictions in India's Small-scale Policies Sector', *World Development*, 21 (12), 2039–54.

Gulati, I. S. (1968), 'Competitiveness of India's Tea Exports', *Economic and Political Weekly*, 3(7), 325–32.

Gupta, B. (2003), '*Work and Efficiency in Cotton Mills: Did the Indian Entrepreneur Fail?*', University of Warwick Working Paper.

(2005), 'Why did Collusion Fail? The Indian Jute Industry in the Interwar Years', *Business History*, 47(4), 532–52.

(2013), 'Discrimination or Social Networks? Industrial Investment in Colonial India', Competitive Advantage in the Global Economy (CAGE) Working Paper No. 110.

Gupta, S. (1991), 'Metal Box: Saving Grace', *Business World*, 13–28 February, 80–81.

Gupta, S. (2012), 'Cellular Mobile in India: Competition and Policy', *Pacific Affairs*, 85(3), 483–510.

Habib, I. (1964), 'Usury in Medieval India', *Comparative Studies in Society and History*, 6(4), 393–419.

(2003), 'The Eighteenth Century Indian Economic History', in P. J. Marshall, ed., *The Eighteenth Century in Indian History*, Delhi: Oxford University Press, 100–22.

Hardgrove, A. (2001), *Community and Public Culture: The Marwaris in Calcutta, 1897–1997*, New York, NY: Columbia University Press.

Harrison, G. (1964), *Bird & Company of Calcutta, 1864–1964*, London: Anna Art Press.

Hasan, F. (1991), 'Conflict and Cooperation in Anglo-Mughal Trade Relations during the Reign of Aurangzeb', *Journal of the Economic and Social History of the Orient*, 34(4), 351–60.

Hausman, W. J., P. Hertner, and M. Wilkins (2008), *Global Electrification: Multinational Enterprise and International Finance in the History of Light and Power, 1878–2007*, Cambridge: Cambridge University Press.

Haynes, D. E. (2012), *Small Town Capitalism in Western India: Artisans, Merchants, and the Making of the Informal Economy, 1870–1960*, Cambridge: Cambridge University Press.

Hazari, R. K. (1964), 'The Managing Agency System: A Case for Its Abolition', *Economic Weekly*, 315–22.

(1966), *The Structure of the Corporate Private Sector*, Bombay: Asia Publishing House.

(1967), *Industrial Planning and Licensing Policy: Final Report*, New Delhi: Planning Commission.

Hejeebu, S. (2005), 'Contract Enforcement in the English East India Company', *Journal of Economic History*, 65(4), 496–523.

Heston, A. (1983), 'National Income', in D. Kumar, ed., *Cambridge Economic History of India*, Vol. 2, Cambridge: Cambridge University Press, 376–462.

Hodgson, G. H. (1938), *Thomas Parry: Free Merchant, Madras, 1768–1824*, Madras: Higginbothams.

Homer, S. and R. Sylla (2005), *A History of Interest Rates*, New Jersey, NJ: John Wiley, (4th ed.), 125, 139.

Hoselitz, B. F. (1960), *Sociological Aspects of Economic Growth: An Adaptation*, Bombay: Vakils, Feffer, Simon.

Hossain, H. (1988), *The Company Weavers of Bengal: The East India Company and the Organization of Textile Production in Bengal, 1750–1813*, Delhi: Oxford University Press.

Hurd II, J. (1975), 'Railways and the Expansion of Markets in India 1861–1921', *Explorations in Economic History*, 12(4), 263–88.

Hurd, J.M. (1983), 'Railways', in Dharma Kumar, ed., *Cambridge Economic History of India*. Vol. 2, Cambridge: Cambridge University Press, 1757–970.

India (1942), *Fact-Finding Committee (Handlooms and Mills)*, Calcutta: Government Press.

(1894), *Index to the Report of the Commission Appointed to Inquire into the Working of the Deccan Agriculturists Relief Act*, Calcutta: Government Press.

(1896), *Royal Commission on Indian Currency and Finance*, Vol. 4 of 4, London: HMSO.

(1897), *Papers Relating to the Deccan Agriculturists' Relief Act during the Years 1875–94*, Calcutta: Government Press.

(1918), *Minutes of Evidence Taken before the Indian Industrial Commission,
1916–18*, Vol. 3, London: HMSO.

(1920), *Report of the Stores Purchase Committee*, Vol. I (Report), Simla:
Government Press.

(1931), *Royal Commission on Labour in India*, Vol. 2, pt. 2 London: HMSO.

(1940), *Report on the Marketing & Transport of Jute*, New Delhi: Government Press,
1940.

(1942), *Statistical Abstract for British India 1930–31 to 1939–40*, London: HMSO,
652–70, 712.

Indian Central Jute Committee (1940), *Report on the Marketing and Transport of Jute
in India*, Calcutta: Government Press.

Indian Law Commission (1847), *Copies of the Special Reports of the Indian Law
Commissioners*, London: HMSO.

Ingham, G. (2003), 'Schumpeter and Weber on the Institutions of Capitalism: Solving
Swedberg's "Puzzle"', *Journal of Classic Sociology*, 3(3), 297–309.

Ito, S. (1966), 'A Note on the "Business Combine" in India', *The Developing
Economies*, 4(3), 367–80.

Jain, L. C. et al. (2006), 'Understanding India from a Business Perspective:
Opportunities and Challenges for MNCs', *Vikalpa*, 31(3), 95–119.

Jenkins, O. (1987), *Merchant Prince: Memories of India 1929–1958*, Salisbury:
Michael Russell.

Jensen, M. C. and W. H. Meckling (1976), 'Theory of the Firm: Managerial Behavior,
Agency Costs and Ownership Structure', *Journal of Financial Economics*, 3(4),
305–60.

Jones, G. and J. Wale (1998), 'Merchants as Business Groups: British Trading
Companies in Asia before 1945', *Business History Review*, 72(3), 367–408.

Jones, S. (1961), *Merchants of the Raj*, Basingstoke: Macmillan, 1992.

Joshi, A. N. (1939), *Life and Times of Sir Hormusjee C. Dinshaw*, Bombay:
Taraporevala.

Kagotani, N. (2001), 'Up-country Purchase Activities of Indian Raw Cotton by Toyo
Menka's Bombay Branch, 1896–1935'. In S. Sugiyama and L. Grove, eds.,
Commercial Networks in Modern Asia, Richmond: Curzon Press.

Karmali, N. (1994), 'P & G Cleans up Its Act', *Business India*, 5–18 December, 65–8.

Kashyap, S. P. (1988), 'Growth of Small-sized Enterprises in India: Its Nature and
Content, *World Development*, 16(6), 667–681.

Khadria, B. and P. Kumar (2015), 'Immigrants and Immigration in India: A Fresh
Approach', *Economic and Political Weekly*, 65–71.

Khanna, T. and K. Palepu (2000), 'Is Group Affiliation Profitable in Emerging
Markets? An Analysis of Diversified Indian Business Groups', *Journal of
Finance*, 55(2), 867–91.

(2005), 'The Evolution of Concentrated Ownership in India: Broad Patterns
and a History of the Indian Software Industry', in R. K. Morck, ed.,
*A History of Corporate Governance around the World: Family Business
Groups to Professional Managers*, Chicago, IL: University of Chicago Press,
283–324.

Khanna, T. and Y. Yafeh (2007), 'Business Groups in Emerging Markets: Paragons or
Parasites', *Journal of Economic Literature*, 45(2), 331–72.

Khilnani, S. (2017), *Incarnations: A History of India in 50 Lives*, London: Penguin.

Kirzner, I. M. (1976), 'Equilibrium versus Market Process', in Edwin G. Dolan, ed., *The Foundations of Modern Austrian Economics*, Kansas City, MO: Sheed & Ward.

Kiyokawa, Y. (1983), 'Technical Adaptations and Managerial Resources in India: A Study of the Experience of the Cotton Textile Industry from a Comparative Viewpoint', *Developing Economies*, 21(2), 97–133.

Kling, Blair. (1966), 'The Origin of the Managing Agency System in India', *Journal of Asian Studies*, 26(1), 37–47.

(1977), *Partner in Empire: Dwarkanath Tagore and the Age of Enterprise in Eastern India*, Berkeley and Los Angeles, CA: University of California Press.

Kochanek, S. A. (1995–6), 'The Transformation of Interest Politics in India', *Pacific Affairs*, 68(4), 529–50.

Koshy, Abraham (2006), 'Hidesign', IIM Ahmedabad Case Studies No IIMA/MAR0380.

Kranton, R. E. and A. V. Swamy (2008), 'Contracts, Hold-up, and Exports: Textiles and Opium in Colonial India', *American Economic Review*, 98(5), 967–89.

Krishnamurty, J. (1983), 'Occupational Structure', in Dharma Kumar, ed., *The Cambridge Economic History of India*, Vol. 2, Cambridge: Cambridge University Press, 533–50.

Kuchhal, S. C. et al. (1980), 'Reliance Textile Industries Limited', IIM Ahmedabad Case Studies No IIMA/F&A0339(A, B, C, and D).

Kudaisya, M., ed. (2011), *The Oxford India Anthology of Business History*, New Delhi: Oxford University Press.

(2014), '"The Promise of Partnership": Indian Business, the State, and the Bombay Plan of 1944', *Business History Review*, 88(1), 97–131.

(2006), *The Life and Times of G. D. Birla*, New Delhi: Oxford University Press.

Kumar, N. (2009), 'Indian Companies as Customers, Competitors and Collaborators', *Indian Journal of Industrial Relations*, 45(1, 148–59.

La Porta, R., F. Lopez-de-Silanes, and A. Shleifer (1999), 'Corporate Ownership around the World', *Journal of Finance*, 54(2), 471–517.

Lamb, H. (1955), 'The Indian Business Communities and the Evolution of an Industrialist Class', *Pacific Affairs*, 28(2), 101–16.

Landström, H. and F. Lohrke, eds. (2011), *Historical Foundations of Entrepreneurship Research*. Cheltenham: Edward Elgar.

Langley, W. K. M., ed. (1962), *Century in Malabar: The History of Peirce Leslie & Co. Ltd. 1862–1962*, Madras: Madras Advertising Co.

Leonard, K. (1979), 'The "Great Firm" Theory of the Decline of the Mughal Empire', *Comparative Studies in Society and History*, 21(2), 151–67.

Levi, S. C. (1999), 'India, Russia and the Eighteenth-century Transformation of the Central Asian Caravan Trade', *Journal of the Economic and Social History of the Orient*, 42(4), 519–48.

(2002), *The Indian Diaspora in Central Asia and Its Trade, 1550–1900*, Leiden: Brill.

Levine, R. (2005), 'Finance and Growth: Theory and Evidence', in Aghion, P. and S. Durlauf, eds. *Handbook of Economic Growth*, Vol. 1, Amsterdam: Elsevier, 865–934.

Levkovsky, A. I. (1972), *Capitalism in India*, Delhi: People's Publishing House.

Liebl, M. and T. Roy (2003–4), 'Handmade in India: Status Report on Indian Artisans', *Economic and Political Weekly*, 38(51), 5366–73.

Lockwood, D. (2012), *The Indian Bourgeoisie: A Political History of the Indian Capitalist Class in the Early Twentieth Century*, New York, NY: I. B. Tauris.

Macaulay, R. H. (1934), *History of Bombay Burmah Trading Corporation Ltd.*, London: privately printed.

Machado, P. (2010), 'A Regional Market in a Globalised Economy: East Central and South Eastern Africans, Gujarati Merchants and the Indian Textile Industry in the Eighteenth and Nineteenth Centuries'. In Riello, G. and T. Roy, eds., *How India Clothed the World: The World of South Asian Textiles 1500–1850*, Leiden: Brill, 2010, 53–84.

(2014), *Ocean of Trade: South Asian Merchants, Africa and the Indian Ocean, c.1750–1850*, Cambridge: Cambridge University Press.

Madras (1930), *The Madras Provincial Banking Enquiry Committee*, Vols. 1–4, Madras: Government Press, Vol. 3.

Madras Presidency (1937), *Mayor's Court Minutes, 1745–46*, Madras: Government Press.

Mahadevan, R. (1978), 'Pattern of Enterprise of Immigrant Entrepreneurs – A Study of Chettiars in Malaya, 1880–1930', *Economic and Political Weekly*, 13(4–5), 329–58.

Mahaprashasta, A. A. (2016), 'How the Once Flourishing Kanpur Textile Mills Decayed', *The Wire*, 16 April 2016, https://thewire.in/29734/faulty-govt-policies-corruption-and-exploitation-of-labour-how-the-once-flourishing-kanpur-textile-mills-decayed/ (accessed 14 April 2017).

Majumdar, S. K., D. Vora, and A. K. Nag (2010), 'Industry Structure Characteristics and International Entrepreneurship in India's Software Industry', *Journal of Entrepreneurship*, 19(2), 109–36.

Mani, S. (2012), 'The Mobile Communications Services Industry in India: Has It Led to India Becoming a Manufacturing Hub for Telecommunication Equipment?', *Pacific Affairs*, 85(3), 511–30.

Markovits, C. (1981), 'Indian Business and the Congress Provincial Governments 1937–39', *Modern Asian Studies*, 15(3), 487–526.

(1985), *Indian Business and Nationalist Politics: The Indigenous Capitalist Class and the Rise of the Congress Party 1931–39*, Cambridge: Cambridge University Press.

(2003), 'Merchant Circulation in South Asia (Eighteenth to Twentieth Centuries): The Rise of Pan-Indian Merchant Networks'. In C. Markovits, J. Pouchepadass, S. Subrahmanyam, eds, *Society and Circulation: Mobile People and Itinerant Cultures in South Asia 1750–1950*, London: Anthem, 2003.

(2007), 'Structure and Agency in the World of Asian Commerce during the Era of European Colonial Domination c. 1750–1950', *Journal of the Economic and Social History of the Orient*, 502/3, 106–23.

(2008), *The Global World of Indian Merchants, 1750–1947: Traders of Sind from Bukhara to Panama*, Cambridge: Cambridge University Press.

Martin, M. (2012), 'An Economic History of the Hundi 1858–1978', PhD Dissertation of the Department of Economic History, London: London School of Economics and Political Science.

Mathai, P. G. (1988), 'Cutting Links', *India Today*, 15 May.

(1993), 'The Foreign Onslaught', *Business World*, 13–26 January, 46–51.

Matthews, H. L. (1943), 'India Challenges British Finance', *Current History (pre-1986)*, 3, 496–8.

Mazumdar, S. (2012), 'The Indian Corporate Structure and the "Theory" of Emerging Market Business Groups', *History and Sociology of South Asia*, 6(2), 87–109.

McGuire, J. (2004), 'The Rise and Fall of the Oriental Bank in the Nineteenth Century: A Product of the Transformations that Occurred in the World Economy or the Result of its Own Mismanagement', paper presented at the 15th Biennial Conference of the Asian Studies Association of Australia, Canberra.

McDonald, H. (2010), *Mahabharata in Polyester: The Making of the World's Richest Brothers and Their Feud*, Sydney: University of New South Wales Press.

McLane, J. R. (1993), *Land and Local Kingship in Eighteenth-Century Bengal*, Cambridge: Cambridge University Press.

McPherson, K. (1998), *The Indian Ocean: A History of People and the Sea*, Delhi and Oxford: Oxford University Press.

Mehta, M. (1991), *Indian Merchants and Entrepreneurs in Historical Perspective*, New Delhi: Academic Foundation.

Mehta, M. J. and D. Tripathi (1968), 'The Kirloskar Brothers Limited', IIM Ahmedabad Case Studies No. IIMA/ECO0080.

Mezzadri, A. (2014), 'Backshoring, Local Sweatshop Regimes and CSR in India', *Competition and Change*, 18(4), 327–44.

Misra, M. (1999), *Business, Race, and Politics in British India c. 1850–1960*, Oxford and New York, NY: Oxford University Press.

Moosvi, S. (2008), 'The Indian Economic Experience 1600–1900: A Quantitative Study', in Moosvi, *People, Taxation and Trade in Mughal India*, New Delhi: Oxford University Press, 1–34.

Morris, M. D. (1967), 'Values as an Obstacle to Economic Growth in South Asia: An Historical Survey', *Journal of Economic History*, 27(4), 588–607.

(1967), 'Values as an Obstacle to Economic Growth in South Asia: An Historical Survey', *Journal of Economic History*, 27(4), 588–607.

(1979), 'Modern Business Organisation and Labour Administration: Specific Adaptations to Indian Conditions of Risk and Uncertainty, 1850–1947', *Economic and Political Weekly*, 14(40), 1680–7.

(1979), 'South Asian Entrepreneurship and the Rashomon Effect, 1800–1947', *Explorations in Economic History*, 164, 341–61.

(1983), 'The Growth of Large-Scale Industry to 1947', in D. Kumar, ed., *The Cambridge Economic History of India, Volume 2: 1757–1970*, Cambridge: Cambridge University Press, 551–676.

Mukherjee, A. (2002), *Imperialism, Nationalism and the Making of the Indian Capitalist Class, 1920–1947*, New Delhi, Thousand Oaks, CA, and London: Sage Publications.

Mukherjee, R., ed. (2011), *Pelagic Passageways: The Northern Bay of Bengal before Colonialism*, Delhi: Primus Books.

Munro, J. F. (1998), 'From Regional Trade to Global Shipping: Mackinnon Mackenzie & Co. within the Mackinnon Enterprise Network, in G. Jones, ed., *The Multinational Traders*, London and New York, NY: Routledge, 48–65.

(2003), *Maritime Enterprise and Empire: Sir William Mackinnon and His Business Network, 1823–1893*, Woodbridge: Boydell and Brewer.

Murthy, K. R. S. (1990), 'A Note on the Television Industry', IIM Ahmedabad Case Studies No IIMA/BP0225TEC.

Nadri, G. A. (2009), *Eighteenth-Century Gujarat: The Dynamics of Its Political Economy, 1750–1800*, Leiden: Brill.

(2017), *The Political Economy of Indigo in India, 1580–1930: A Global Perspective*, Leiden: Brill.

Nag, K. (2013), 'How Indian Aviation Was Destroyed'. http://blogs.timesofindia.indiatimes.com/The-wonder-that-is-indian-politics/how-indian-aviation-was-destroyed/ (accessed on 26 April 2017).

Nagaraj, R. (1996), 'India's Capital Market Growth: Trends, Explanations and Evidence', *Economic and Political Weekly*, 31(35–37), 2553–63.

(2015), 'Size and Structure of India's Private Corporate Sector: Implications for the New GDP Series', *Economic and Political Weekly*, 50(45), 41–7.

Narayan, S. and D. N. Mukerjea (1993–4), 'Manu Chhabria's Vanishing Managers', *Business World*, 29 December–11 January, 64–6.

Natesan & Co (1930), *Famous Parsis*, Madras: Natesan.

Naoroji, D. (1901), *Poverty and Un-British Rule in India*, London: Swan Sonnenschein.

Nayak, M. (2013), 'Siemens: Built to last', *Business Today*, 26 May (accessed 15 May 2017) www.businesstoday.in/magazine/special/oldest-mnc-in-india-siemens/story/194630.html

Nayyar, D. (2008), 'The Internationalization of Firms from India: Investment, Mergers and Acquisitions', *Oxford Development Studies*, 36(1), 111–131.

Nölke A. and H. Taylor (2011), 'Indian Multinationals, Comparative Capitalism, and Implications for Global and Host Country Economic Institutions, in L. Brennan, ed., *The Emergence of Southern Multinationals*, Basingstoke: Palgrave Macmillan, 317–30.

North, D. and B. Weingast (1989), 'Constitutions and Commitment: The Evolution of Institutions Governing Public Choice in Seventeenth-Century Britain', *Journal of Economic History*, 49(4), 803–32.

Oak, M. and A. V. Swamy (2012), 'Myopia or Strategic Behavior? Indian Regimes and the East India Company in Late Eighteenth Century India', *Explorations in Economic History*, 49(3), 352–66.

Oishi, T. (2004), 'Indo-Japan Cooperative Ventures in Match Manufacturing in India: Muslim Merchant Networks in and beyond the Bengal Bay Region, 1900–1930', *International Journal of Asian Studies*, 1(1), 49–85.

Oonk, G. (2013), *Settled Strangers: Asian Business Elites in East Africa (1800–2000)*, New Delhi: Sage Publications.

(2014), 'The Emergence of Indigenous Industrialists in Calcutta, Bombay and Ahmedabad, 1850–1947', *Business History Review*, 88(1), 43–71.

Otsuka, K., G. Ranis, and G. Saxonhouse (1988), *Comparative Technology-Choice in Development: The Indian and Japanese Cotton Textile Industries*, London: Macmillan.

Palit, C. (2006), 'Bengali Business Enterprise and the BNCCI', in C. Palit and P. K. Bhattacharya, eds., *Business History of India*, Delhi: Kalpaz, 251–8.

Pandey, I. M. (1985), 'Hindustan Lever Limited', IIM Ahmedabad Case Studies No. IIMA/F&A0405.

(1990), 'Bharat Heavy Electricals Limited (BHEL)', IIM Ahmedabad Case Studies No IIMA/F&A0408.

Pandya, S. S. (2014), 'Why foreign investment still polarizes India', Washington Post blogs, 2014 (accessed 18 November 2017). www.washingtonpost.com/blogs/ monkey-cage/wp/2014/09/30/why-foreign-investment-still-polarizes-india/

Panicker, V. S., S. Mitra, R. Sensarma (2016), 'Corporate Governance Determinants of FII in Indian IT Firms', *Indian Journal of Corporate Governance*, 9(1), 1–18.

Paranjape, A. (2009), 'Economic Slowdown and the Indian Corporate Sector', *Vikalpa*, 34(3), 53–8.

Parthasarathi, P. (2001), *The Transition to a Colonial Economy: Weavers, Merchants and Kings in South India, 1720–1800*, Cambridge: Cambridge University Press.

(2011), *Why Europe Grew Rich and Asia Did Not: Global Economic Divergence, 1600–1850*, Cambridge: Cambridge University Press.

Patibandla, M., D. Kapur, and B. Petersen (2000), 'Import Substitution with Free Trade: Case of India's Software Industry', *Economic and Political Weekly*, 35(15), 1263–70.

Pavlov, V. I. (1964), *The Indian Capitalist Class: A Historical Study*, Delhi: People's Publishing House.

Piramal, G. (1998), *Business Legends*, New Delhi: Penguin.

(2015), *Kamalnayan Bajaj: Architect of the Bajaj Group*, Mumbai: Kamalnayan Bajaj Charitable Trust.

Playne, S. (1914–5), *Southern India: Its History, People, Commerce, and Industrial Resources*, London: Foreign and Colonial Compiling and Publishing Co.

(1917), *Bengal and Assam, Behar and Orissa: Their History, People, Commerce, and Industrial Resources*, London: Foreign and Colonial Compiling and Publishing Co.

(1917–20), *The Bombay Presidency, the United Provinces, the Punjab, etc.: Their History, People, Commerce and Natural Resources*, London: Foreign and Colonial Compiling and Pub. Co.

Pointon, A. C. (1964), *The Bombay Burmah Trading Corp. Ltd., 1863–1963*, Southampton: Wallace Brothers.

Prakash, O. (1985), *The Dutch East India Company and the Economy of Bengal, 1630–1720*, Princeton, NJ: Princeton University Press.

(1998), *The New Cambridge History of India; Vol. II.5. European Commercial Enterprise in Pre-colonial India*, Cambridge: Cambridge University Press.

(2004), 'The Indian Maritime Merchant, 1500–1800', *Journal of the Economic and Social History of the Orient*, 47(3), 435–57.

(2007), 'From Negotiation to Coercion: Textile Manufacturing in India in the Eighteenth Century', *Modern Asian Studies*, 41(5), 1331–68.

Pugh, P. (1991), *Williamson Magor Stuck to Tea*, Cambridge: Cambridge Business Publishing.

Punjab (1930), *Report of the Punjab Provincial Banking Enquiry Committee, 1929–30*, Vol. 2, Calcutta: Government Press.

Pursell, G. (1992), 'Trade Policies in India', in D. Salvatore, ed., *National Trade Policies*, Amsterdam: North Holland, 423–58.

Purves, J. (1819), *The East India Merchant; or, a Guide to the Commerce and Manufactures of Bengal and the Upper Provinces*, Calcutta: publisher not known.

Radhakrishnan, N. and D. Shah (1989), 'A Fine Finish', *Business India*, 20 February, 68–71.

Rajakumar, J. D. and J. S. Henley (2007), 'Growth and Persistence of Large Business Groups in India', *Journal of Comparative International Management*, 10(1), 3–22.

Rajan, R. and L. Zingales (1998), 'Financial Dependence and Growth', *American Economic Review*, 88(3), 559–86.

Ramaswamy, K. V. and G. Gereffi (2001), 'India's Apparel Exports: The Challenge of Global mMrkets', *Developing Economies*, 28(2), 186–210.

Rao, V. K. R. V. (1938), *What Is Wrong with Indian Economic Life?*, Bombay: Vora. (1944), 'National Income of India', *The Annals of the American Academy of Political and Social Science*, 233, 99–105.

Raposo, M., D. Smallbone, K. Balaton, and L. Hortoványi, eds. (2011), *Entrepreneurship, Growth, and Economic Development*, Cheltenham: Edward Edgar.

Rath, A. K. (1982), 'Local and Global Operations of Multinational Corporations: Unilever in India', *Social Scientist*, 10(10), 30–43.

Ray, A. (2006), 'Two Indian Brokers of the French East India Company in Eastern India during the first half of the Eighteenth Century'. In C. Palit and P. K. Bhattacharya, ed., *Business History of India*, Delhi: Kalpaz Publications, 2006, 113–36.

Ray, I. (2011), *Bengal Industries and the British Industrial Revolution, 1757–1857*, New York, NY, and Abingdon: Routledge.

(2012), 'Struggling against Dundee: Bengal Jute Industry during the Nineteenth Century', *Indian Economic and Social History Review*, 49(1), 105–46.

Ray, R., ed. (1992), *Entrepreneurship and Industry in India, 1800–1947*, Delhi: Oxford University Press.

Ray, R. K. (1979), *Industrialization in India: Growth and Conflict in the Private Corporate Sector, 1914–1947*, Delhi: Oxford University Press.

Raychaudhuri, T. (1962). *Jan Company in Coromandel 1605–1690*, The Haugue: Martinus Nijhoff.

Reinhart, G. (1926), *Volkart Brothers: In Commemoration of the Seventy-Fifth Anniversary of the Foundation*, Winterthur: G. Binkert

Riello, G. and T. Roy, eds. (2009), *How India Clothed the World: The World of South Asian Textiles 1500–1850*, Leiden: Brill.

Robbins, L. (1970), *The Theory of Economic Development in the History of Economic Thought*, London and Basingstoke: Macmillan.

Roberts, W. and O. T. Faulkner (1921), *A Textbook of Punjab Agriculture*, Lahore: Civil and Military Gazette Press.

Rosen, G. (1960), 'The Structure of Interest Rates in India', *Economic Weekly*, 799–806.

Rostow, W. W. (1959), 'The Stages of Economic Growth', *Economic History Review*, 12(1), 1–16.

Roy Chowdhury, S. (1995), 'Political Economy of India's Textile Industry: The Case of Maharashtra, 1984–89', *Pacific Affairs*, 68(2), 231–50.

Roy, D. (c. 1976), *A Hundred and Twenty-Five Years: The Story of J. Thomas and Company* , Calcutta: publisher not known.

Roy, N. C. (1972), *Mystery of the Bajoria-Jalan House*, Calcutta: Alpha Publishing.

Roy, T. (1993), *Artisans and Industrialization: Indian Weaving in the Twentieth Century*, Delhi: Oxford University Press.

(1998), 'Development or Distortion? The Powerlooms in India, 1950–97', *Economic and Political Weekly*, 33(16), 1998, 897–911.

(1999), *Traditional Industry in the Economy of Colonial India*, Cambridge: Cambridge University Press.

(2005), *Rethinking Economic Change in India: Labour and Livelihood*, Abingdon and New York, NY: Routledge.

(2007), 'Globalization, Factor Prices, and Poverty in Colonial India', *Australian Economic History Review*, 47(1), 73–94.

(2007), 'Handicrafts', in Kaushik Basu, ed., *Oxford Companion to Economics in India*, New Delhi: Oxford University Press, 241–3.

(2007), 'Out of Tradition: Master Artisans and Economic Change in Colonial India', *Journal of Asian Studies*, 66(4), 963–91.

(2008), 'The Role of Labour Institutions in Industrialization: Japan and the Crisis of the Cotton Mills in Interwar Mumbai', *Economic and Political Weekly*, 43(1), 37–45.

(2008), 'Knowledge and Divergence from the Perspective of Early Modern India', *Journal of Global History*, 3(4), 361–87.

(2009), 'Factor Markets and the Narrative of Economic Change in India, 1750–1950', *Continuity and Change*, 24(1), 137–67.

(2010), *Company of Kinsmen: Enterprise and Community in India 1600–1950*, New Delhi: Oxford University Press.

(2011), *East India Company: The World's Most Powerful Corporation*, Delhi: Allen Lane.

(2011), 'Indigo and Law in Colonial India', *Economic History Review*, 64(1), 60–75.

(2012), 'Consumption of Cotton Cloth in India, 1795–1940', *Australian Economic History Review*, 52(1), 61–84.

(2012), *India in the World Economy from Antiquity to the Present*, Cambridge: Cambridge University Press.

(2013), *An Economic History of Early Modern India*, Abingdon and New York, NY: Routledge.

(2016), 'Monsoon and the Market for Money in Late Colonial India', *Enterprise and Society*, 17(2), 324–57.

(2016), 'The British Empire and the Economic Development of India 1858–1947', *Revista de Historia Economica – Journal of Iberian and Latin American Economic History*, 34(2), 209–36.

(2016), 'The Mutiny and the Merchants', *The Historical Journal*, 59(2), 393–416.

(2017), 'The Origins of Import Substituting Industrialization in India', *Economic History of Developing Regions*, 32(1), 71–95.

(2017), *The Economy of South Asia: From 1950 to the Present*, Basingstoke: Palgrave Macmillan.

(2017), 'Transfer of Economic Power in Corporate Calcutta 1950–1970', *Business History Review*, 91(1), 3–29.

Roy, T. and A. V. Swamy (2016), *Law and the Economy in Colonial India*, Chicago, IL: University of Chicago Press.

Rudner, D. (1994), *Caste and Capitalism in Colonial India*, Berkeley and Los Angeles, CA: University of California Press.

Rungta, R. (1970), *The Rise of Business Corporations in India 1851–1900*, Cambridge: Cambridge University Press.

Russell, R. V. (1916), *The Tribes and Castes of the Central Provinces of India*, London: Macmillan.

Rutnagur, S. M. (1927), *Bombay Industries: The Cotton Mills*, Bombay: The Indian Textile Journal Limited.

Sáez L. and C. Chang (2009), 'The Political Economy of Global Firms from India and China, *Contemporary Politics*, 15(3), 265–86.

Sahai, N. P. (2006), *Politics of Patronage and Protest: The State, Society, and Artisans in Early Modern Rajasthan*. Delhi: Oxford University Press.

Sahay, A. and R. Swamithan (2005), 'Hewlett Packard India', IIM Ahmedabad Case Studies No IIMA/MAR0361.

Sandesara, J. C. (1988), 'Small-Scale Industrialisation: The Indian Experience', *Economic and Political Weekly*, 23(13), 640–54.

Sarkar, G. K. (1986), 'The Fading Fabric-II: Jute Manufacturing Sector', *Economic and Political Weekly*, 21(50), 2188–97.

Sarkar, J. and S. Sarkar (2012), *Corporate Governance in India*, New Delhi: Sage Publication.

Sen, S. R. (1997), *Restrictionism during the Great Depression in Indian Tea Jute and Sugar Industries*, Calcutta: Firma KLM.

Seshadri, D. V. R. (2004), 'Reinventing Tata Steel (A)', IIM Ahmedabad Case Studies No IIMA/PROD0267(A).

Seth Anandji Kalyanji Pedhi (in Gujarati), www.anandjikalyanjipedhi.org/ (accessed 5 August 2017).

Sharkey, J. (1996), 'Attitudes of the Japanese Iron and Steel Industry to Indian Pig Iron Imports, 1919–1929', *Japan Review*, 7, 159–84.

Shekhar, S. (1990), '*Bhilwara's Asset Chase*', *Business World*, 12–25 September, 36–7.

Shimizu, H. (2010), 'The Indian Merchants of Kobe and Japan's Trade Expansion into Southeast Asia before the Asian-Pacific War', *Japan Forum*, 17(1), 25–48.

Shleifer, A. and R. W. Vishny (1986), 'Large Shareholders and Corporate Control', *Journal of Political Economy*, 94(3), 461–88.

Siddiqui, A. (1982), 'The Business World of Jamsetjee Jejeebhoy', *Indian Economic and Social History Review*, 19(3–4), 301–24.

Singer, M. (1961), 'Religion and Social Change in India: The Max Weber Thesis, Phase Three', *Economic Development* and *Cultural Change*, 14(4), 1961, 497–505.

Singh, K. and A. Joshi (1968), *Shri Ram: A Biography*, Bombay: Asia Publishing House.

Sinha, H. (1927), *Early European Banking in India*, London: Macmillan.

Sivasubramonian, S. (2000), *National Income of India in the Twentieth Century*, New Delhi: Oxford University Press.

Stephen, S. J. (2006), 'Revealing and Concealing: The Business World of Middlemen and Merchants in the French Commercial Enterprise in Pondicherry (1674–1741)'. In C. Palit and P. K. Bhattacharya, ed., *Business History of India*, Delhi: Kalpaz Publications, 2006, 99–112.

Studer, R. (2015), *The Great Divergence Reconsidered: Europe, India, and the Rise to Global Economic Power*, Cambridge: Cambridge University Press.

Subrahmanyam, S. (1990), *The Political Economy of Commerce: Southern India, 1500–1650*, Cambridge: Cambridge University Press.

(1992), 'The Mughal State – Structure or Process? Reflections on Recent Western Historiography', *Indian Economic Social History Review*, 29(3), 291–321.

Subrahmanyam, S. and C. A. Bayly (1988), 'Portfolio Capitalists and the Political Economy of Early Modern India', *Indian Economic Social History Review*, 25(4), 401–24.

Subramanian, D. (2010), *Telecommunications Industry in India: State, Business and Labour in a Global Economy*, New Delhi: Social Science Press.

Subramanian, L. (1996), *Indigenous Capital and Imperial Expansion: Bombay, Surat and the West Coast*, Delhi and Oxford: Oxford University Press.

(2016), *Three Merchants of Bombay*, Delhi: Penguin.

Sugihara, K. (1990), 'Japan as an Engine of the Asian International Economy, c. 1880–1936', *Japan Forum*, 2(1), 127–45.

Sundaram, K. (2002), 'Employment and Poverty in India in the Nineteen Nineties'. Working Paper of CDE Delhi School of Economics.

Sussman, N. and Y. Yafeh (2006), 'Institutional Reforms, Financial Development and Sovereign Debt: Britain 1690–1790', *Journal of Economic History*, 66(4), 906–35.

Swarnalatha, P. (2001), 'Revolt, Testimony, Petition: Artisanal Protests in Colonial Andhra', *International Review of Social History*, 46(1), 107–29.

Swedberg, R. (2002), 'The Economic Sociology of Capitalism: Weber and Schumpeter', *Journal of Classic Sociology*, 2(3), 227–55.

Symes Scutt, G. P. (1904), *The History of the Bank of Bengal: An Epitome of a Hundred Years of Banking in India*, Calcutta: A. J. Tobias.

Telang, A., and S. Roy (2016), 'Hyundai's Challenge to Maruti Suzuki in the Dynamic Indian Automobile Sector', *Asian Journal of Management Cases*, 13(1), 56–66.

Timberg, T. A. (1973), *The Marwaris*, Delhi: Vikas.

(1973), 'Three Types of the Marwari Firm', *Indian Economic and Social History Review*, 10(1), 3–36.

(1978), *The Marwaris, from Traders to Industrialists*, New Delhi: Vikas, 88.

(2014), *The Marwaris*, Delhi: Penguin.

(1994), 'Three Types of the Marwari Firm', in R. K. Ray, ed., *Entrepreneurship and Industry in India, 1800–1947*, Delhi: Oxford University Press, 127–56.

Tod, J. (1926), *The Annals and Antiquities of Rajasthan*, Vol. 2 of 3, Madras: Higginbotham.

Tomlinson, B. R. (1982), 'The Political Economy of the Raj: The Decline of Colonialism', *Journal of Economic History*, 42(1), 133–7.

(2003), 'British Business in India, 1860–1970', in R. P. T. Davenport-Hines and Geoffrey Jones, eds. *British Business in Asia since 1860*, Cambridge: Cambridge University Press, 92–116.

Tripathi, A. (1979), *Trade and Finance in the Bengal Presidency, 1793–1833*, 2nd ed, Calcutta: Oxford University Press.

(1971), 'Indian Entrepreneurship in Historical Perspective: A Re-Interpretation', *Economic and Political Weekly*, 6(22), M59–M66.

(1981), 'Occupational Mobility and Industrial Entrepreneurship in India: A Historical Analysis', *Developing Economies*, 19(1), 52–68.

(2004), *The Oxford History of Indian Business*, New Delhi: Oxford University Press.

Tripathi, D. (1970), 'House of Seshasayees', IIM Ahmedabad Case Studies No. IIMA/ECO0145.

Tripathi, D. and M. J. Mehta (1970), 'The Alembic Chemical Works Company Limited', IIM Ahmedabad Case Studies No. IIMA/ECO0146.

(1970), 'The Genesis of the Cotton Textile Industry in Ahmedabad', IIMA Case Study No. IIMA/ECO0115, Ahmedabad.

Tripathi, D. and J. Jumani (2013), *The Oxford History of Contemporary Indian Business*, New Delhi: Oxford University Press.

Tripathi, D. and P. Misra (1985), *Towards a New Frontier: History of the Bank of Baroda, 1908–1983*, New Delhi: Manohar.

Tripathi, D. and M. Mehta (1990), *Business Houses in Western India: A Study in Entrepreneurial Response, 1850–1956*, New Delhi: Manohar.

Tumbe, C. (2012), 'Migration Persistence across Twentieth Century India', *Migration and Development*, 1(1), 87–112.

Twomey, M. (2000), *A Century of Foreign Investment in the Third World*, Abingdon: Routledge.

Tyabji, N. (2015), *Forging Capitalism in Nehru's India: Neocolonialism and the State, c. 1940–1970*, New Delhi: Oxford University Press.

United Provinces (1930), *Report of the United Provinces Provincial Banking Enquiry Committee, 1929–30*. Vol. 2, Evidence, Calcutta: Government Press.

Upadhya, C. (2016), *Reengineering India: Work, Capital and Class in an Offshore Economy*, New Delhi: Oxford University Press.

Vakil, C. N. (1922), *Our Fiscal Policy*, Bombay: Taraporevala.

Van Wersch, H. (1992), *Bombay Textile Strike 1982–83*, Bombay: Oxford University Press.

Varady, R. G. (1979), 'North Indian Banjaras: Their Evolution as Transporters', *South Asia*, 2(1), 1–18.

Verma, Pramod, S. Mookherjee, D. S. Kamat (1978), 'Strikes in Jute Industry (B)', IIM Ahmedabad Case Studies No. IIMA/P&IR0069(B).

Verma, T. (1994), *Karkhanas under the Mughals, from Akbar to Aurangzeb: A Study in Economic Development*, Delhi: Pragati.

Visaria, P. and L. (1083), 'Population', in D. Kumar, ed., *Cambridge Economic History of India*, Vol. 2, Cambridge: Cambridge University Press, 463–532.

Visvesvaraya, M. (1944), *Reconstruction in Post-War India: A Plan of Development all round*, Bombay: All India Manufacturers Association.

Wacha, D. E. (1913), *Premchund Roychund: His Early Life and Career*, Bombay: Times of India Press.

Wadia, J. A. (1902), *The Artificial Currency and the Commerce of India*, Bombay: Jamsetjee Nusserwanji Petit Parsi Orphanage.

Wadia, P. A. and K. T. Merchant (1944), *The Bombay Plan: A Criticism*, Bombay: Popular Book Depot.

Wallerstein, I. (1986), 'Incorporation of Indian Subcontinent into Capitalist World-Economy', *Economic and Political Weekly*, 21(4), PE28–PE39.

Weber, M. (2001), *The Protestant Ethic and the Spirit of Capitalism* (Translated by Parsons, T., edited by Giddens, A.), Abingdon and New York, NY: Routledge.

Webster, A. (1993), *The Life and Business of John Palmer of Calcutta, 1767–1836*, London: Longmans.

(2005), 'An Early Global Business in a Colonial Context: The Strategies, Management, and Failure of John Palmer and Company, 1780–1830', *Enterprise & Society*, 6(1), 98–133.

(2009), *The Twilight of the East India Company: The Evolution of Anglo-Asian Commerce and Politics, 1790–1860*, Rochester: Boydell and Brewer.

Westhead, P. and M. Wright (2013), *Entrepreneurship: A Very Short Introduction*, Oxford: Oxford University Press.

Wolcott, S. (1994), 'Perils of Lifetime Employment Systems: Productivity Advance in the Indian and Japanese Textile Industries, 1920–1938', *Journal of Economic History*, 54(2), 307–24.

Wray, W. D. (2005), 'Nodes in the Global Webs of Japanese Shipping', *Business History*, 47(1), 1–22.

Yang, A. A. (1998), *Bazaar India: Markets, Society and the Colonial State in Bihar*, Berkeley, CA: University of California Press.

Yule, H., A. C. Burnell (1903), *Hobson-Jobson: A Glossary of Colloquial Anglo-Indian Words and Phrases, and of Kindred Terms, Etymological, Historical, Geographical and Discursive*, London: Murray.

Index

Abbott, 188
Abdul Gafoor, 116
Abu'l-Fazl, 28
Acland, George, 103
Adamjee, 151
Adarkar, B. N., 149
Aden, 45, 77, 227
Aditya Birla Group, 175
advertising, 86, 168, 189–90, 197, 204, 214,
     221, 225–6, 228
Africa, 19, 23, 29–30, 32, 42, 47, 75, 78, 84,
     109, 123, 151, 193, 231, 264
Agarwal, Shriman Narayan, 149
agency houses, 57–8, 64, 77, 92
agents, 4, 15, 25, 31, 35–8, 43, 47, 49, 55, 75,
     81, 83, 85, 88, 90–1, 93–4, 99, 101, 116,
     122, 142, 168–9, 172, 187
Agra, 24, 26, 29–30, 38, 84
Ahmedabad, 13–14, 26, 87, 90, 95, 98, 110–13,
     119, 124, 130, 133–5, 140–1, 146–7, 159,
     166, 168, 173, 176, 178, 186, 197, 200,
     217, 221, 223–4, 227
Ahmednagar, 96, 118
Ahuja, Ravi, 50
Air Deccan, 250
Air India, 230, 250
Air Sahara, 250
Aircel, 249
Aiyer, Swaminathan S. A., 155
Akzo Nobel, 209
Albert and Victoria Mill, 111
Alcock Ashdown, 180
Aldous, Michael, 124, 197
Alembic, 141
Alexander, 57
Alexander, Claire, 264
Alexandra Mill, 109
Alfa Laval, 185, 198, 209
Alfred Herbert, 86
Alkali and Chemicals Corporation, 187
All India Congress Committee, 129–30, 148
All India Manufacturers' Conference, 149

Allahabad Bank, 167
Amatori, Franco, 3
Ambani, Dhirubhai, 227–9, 237
American Civil War, 65, 110, 114
Amirchand, 25
Amrith, Sunil, 263
Amsden, Alice H., 13
Amul, 208
Anandji Kalyanji Pedhi, 110
Anantharamakrishnan, Sivasailam, 182
Anderson Wright, 105, 180–1, 216
Andhra Pradesh, 164, 176
Andrew Yule, 19, 82, 104, 123, 170–2, 179,
     191–2, 206
Angus Company, 107
Antrobus, H. A., 123
Antwerp, 221
Arabian Sea, 22, 29–32, 34, 41, 43, 47, 60, 87
Arasaratnam, S., 37
Arbuthnot, 84
Arnold, David, 87
Arora, Ashish, 246
Arrighi, Giovanni, 11
Arthur Balfour Committee, 149
artisans, 28–9, 34–5, 37, 40, 51–3, 65, 84, 108,
     117–18, 120, 125, 127, 158, 261, 263
Arvind Mills, 147, 220, 231
Asa Lees and Co, 85
Asea, 185
Ashok Leyland, 171–3, 177, 183, 219
Asian Cables, 181
Asian Games, 1982, 225–6
Asiatic Steam Navigation Co., 107
Assam, 60, 66, 84, 97, 102, 104–5, 107, 123,
     164, 181, 188–9, 216
Assam Company, 60, 104–5, 123
Associated Cement Company, 173
Associated Chamber of Commerce and
     Industries, 169
Australia, 64, 105
Aventis, 188
aviation, 157, 183, 222, 230, 250